AF478881

The struggle for
a social Europe

Manchester University Press

Critical Labour Movement Studies

Series editors
John Callaghan
Steven Fielding
Steve Ludlam

Already published in the series

Jenny Andersson
Between growth and security: Swedish social democracy from a strong society to a third way

John Callaghan, Steven Fielding and Steve Ludlam (eds)
Interpreting the Labour Party: approaches to Labour politics and history

Dianne Hayter
Fightback! Labour's traditional right in the 1970s and 1980s

Jonas Hinnfors
Reinterpreting social democracy: a history of stability in the British Labour Party and Swedish Social Democratic Party

Declan McHugh
Labour in the city: the development of the Labour Party in Manchester, 1918–31

Jeremy Nuttall
Psychological socialism: the Labour Party and qualities of mind and character, 1931 to the present

The struggle for a social Europe

Trade unions and EMU in times of global restructuring

Andreas Bieler

Manchester University Press
Manchester and New York
distributed exclusively in the USA by Palgrave

Published by Manchester University Press
Oxford Road, Manchester M13 9NR, UK
and Room 400, 175 Fifth Avenue, New York, NY 10010, USA
www.manchesteruniversitypress.co.uk

Distributed exclusively in the USA by
Palgrave, 175 Fifth Avenue, New York,
NY 10010, USA

Distributed exclusively in Canada by
UBC Press, University of British Columbia, 2029 West Mall,
Vancouver, BC, Canada V6T 1Z2

British Library Cataloguing-in-Publication Data
A catalogue record for this book is available from the British Library

Library of Congress Cataloging-in-Publication Data applied for

ISBN   0 7190 7252 2 *hardback*
EAN   978 0 7190 7252 9

First published 2006

15 14 13 12 11 10 09 08 07 06   10 9 8 7 6 5 4 3 2 1

Typeset
by Florence Production, Stoodleigh, Devon
Printed in Great Britain
by CPI, Bath

Contents

Series editors' foreword

The start of the twenty-first century is superficially an inauspicious time to study labour movements. Political parties once associated with the working class have seemingly embraced capitalism. The trade unions with which these parties were once linked have suffered near-fatal reverses. The industrial proletariat looks both divided and in rapid decline. The development of multi-level governance, prompted by 'globalisation' has furthermore apparently destroyed the institutional context for advancing the labour 'interest'. Many consequently now look on terms such as the 'working class', 'socialism' and 'the labour movement' as politically and historically redundant.

The purpose of this series is to give a platform to those students of labour movements who challenge, or develop, established ways of thinking and so demonstrate the continued vitality of the subject and the work of those interested in it. For despite appearances, many social democratic parties remain important competitors for national office and proffer distinctive programmes. Unions still impede the free flow of 'market forces'. If workers are a more diverse body and have exchanged blue collars for white, insecurity remains an everyday problem. The new institutional and global context is moreover as much of an opportunity as a threat. Yet, it cannot be doubted that compared with the immediate post-1945 period, at the beginning of the new millennium, what many still refer to as the 'labour movement' is much less influential. Whether this should be considered a time of retreat or reconfiguration is unclear – and a question the series aims to clarify.

The series will not only give a voice to studies of particular national bodies but will also promote comparative works that contrast experiences across time and geography. This entails taking due account of the political, economic and cultural settings in which labour movements have operated. In particular this involves taking the past seriously as a way of understanding the present as well as utilising sympathetic approaches drawn from sociology, economics and elsewhere.

John Callaghan
Steven Fielding
Steve Ludlam

Tables

Acknowledgements

This book is the result of a research project carried out between January 2001 and August 2005. I am indebted to Ian Bartle, William Brown, David Coates, Jörg Michael Dostal, Ingemar Lindberg, Martin Upchurch and especially Cecilia Goria and Adam David Morton for comments on parts of the book as well as encouragement throughout the project. I am also grateful to Dorothee Bohle, Bernd Brandl, Jan Willem Goudriaan, Alex Heron, Christel Lane, Georg Menz, Mica Panic and Ernst Tüchler for their help on one or the other aspect of the book. Jerine Thomas is thanked for his help with the index. The financial assistance of this project by Newnham College, University of Cambridge and the British Academy (SG-33623) is gratefully acknowledged.

I would further like to thank all the interviewees for their time and effort in assisting me with my research. Without their openness, this project could not have been carried out. Finally, I am thankful to the staff at Manchester University Press and Florence Production Ltd as well as the editors of the *Critical Labour Movement Studies Series* John Callaghan, Steven Fielding and Steve Ludlam for their support.

Abbreviations

AEEU	Amalgamated Engineering and Electrical Union (Britain)
AES	Alternative Economic Strategy (Britain)
AK	Chamber of Labour (Austria)
ANG	Agricultural and Food Processing Union (Austria)
ATTAC	Association pour la Taxation des Transactions Financiers pour l'Aide aux Citoyens
BDA	German Employers' Association
BEPG	Broad Economic Policy Guidelines
BWK	Chamber of Commerce (Austria)
Byggnads	Building Workers' Union (Sweden)
CEC	Confédération Européenne des cadres
CEE	Central and Eastern Europe
CEEP	European Centre of Enterprises with Public Participation and of Enterprises of General Economic Interest
CFDT	French Democratic Confederation of Labour
CFDT-Banques	Banking and Financial Institute Federation of the CFDT (France)
CFE-CGC	Confederation of Professional and Managerial Staff (France)
CFTC	French Christian Workers' Confederation
CGT	General Confederation of Labour (France)
CGT-construction	Construction Sector Federation of the CGT (France)
CGT-finance	Financial Sector Federation of the CGT (France)
CGT-metallurgie	Metal Workers' Federation of the CGT (France)
CME	co-ordinated market economy
COBAS	Comitati di Base (Italy)
CPE	Comparative Political Economy
CWU	Communication Workers' Union (Britain)
DAG	German Salaried Employees' Union
DBB	German Civil Servants' Federation
DG	Directorate General
DGB	Confederation of German Trade Unions
DM	Deutschmark
DPG	Postal Workers' Union (Germany)
ECB	European Central Bank
ECEG	European Chemical Employers' Group

EcoFin	Economic and Financial Council of Ministers
ECU	European Currency Unit
EES	European Employment Strategy
EIF	European industry federation
EFBWW	European Federation of Building and Woodworkers
EFFAT	European Federation of Food, Agriculture and Tourism Trade Unions
EMCEF	European Mine, Chemical and Energy Workers' Federation
EMF	European Metalworkers' Federation
EMS	European Monetary System
EMU	Economic and Monetary Union
EP	European Parliament
EPSU	European Federation of Public Service Unions
ERT	European Round Table of Industrialists
ESC	Economic and Social Committee
ESF	European Social Forum
ESP	Economic and Social Partnership (Austria)
ETF	European Transport Workers' Federation
ETUC	European Trade Union Confederation
ETUC-E	European Trade Union Committee for Education
ETUI	European Trade Union Institute
EU	European Union
EUCOB@	European Collective Bargaining Information Network
EWC	European Works Council
FDI	foreign direct investment
FEN	Federation of National Education
FIOM	Italian Federazione Impiegati Operai Metallurgici
FNIC-CGT	Chemical Workers' Federation of the CGT (France)
FO	Force ouvrière (French trade union)
FO de la Communication	Communication Workers' Federation of FO (France)
FPÖ	Austrian Freedom Party
FSU	Unitary Union Federation (France)
G10-Solidaires	Group of 10-L'Union syndicale Solidaires (French trade union)
GATS	General Agreement on Trade in Services
GATT	General Agreement on Tariffs and Trade
GBH	Construction and Wood Workers' Union (Austria)
GdC	Chemical Workers' Union (Austria)
GdE	Railway Workers' Union (Austria)
GdG	Union of Local Government Employees (Austria)
GDP	gross domestic product
GMB	General, Municipal and Boilermakers' Union (Britain)
GMT	Metal and Textile Workers' Union (Austria)
GÖD	Public Services Trade Union (Austria)
GPA	Union of Private Sector Employees (Austria)
GPF	Postal and Telecommunications Workers' Union (Austria)
GPMU	Graphical, Paper and Media Union (Britain)
Handels	Union of Commercial Employees (Sweden)
HBV	Commerce, Banking and Insurance Workers' Union (Germany)

HGPD	Hotel, Catering and Personal Services Workers' Union (Austria)
HTV	Commerce, Transport and Traffic Workers' Union (Austria)
IG BAU	Construction, Agricultural and Environmental Workers' Union (Germany)
IG BCE	Mine, Chemical and Energy Workers' Union (Germany)
IMF	International Monetary Fund
Industrifacket	Industrial Workers' Union (Sweden)
IPE	International Political Economy
IR	International Relations
IV	Federation of Austrian Industry
KFAT	National Union of Knitwear, Footwear and Apparel Trades (Britain)
Kommunal	Municipal Workers' Union (Sweden)
Lärerförbundet	Swedish Teachers' Union
LK	Chamber of Agriculture (Austria)
LME	liberal market economy
LO	Swedish Trade Union Confederation
M&A	mergers and acquisitions
MNC	multinational corporation
MSF	Manufacturing Science Finance (British union)
NGG	Food Processing and Hotel Workers' Union (Germany)
NHS	National Health Service (Britain)
OECD	Organisation for Economic Co-operation and Development
ÖGB	Austrian Confederation of Trade Unions
OMC	Open Method of Co-ordination
ÖTV	Public Services, Transport and Traffic Union (Germany)
ÖVP	Austrian People's Party
Pappers	Paper Workers' Union (Sweden)
PFI	private finance initiatives
QMV	qualified majority voting
R&D	research and development
RMT	National Union of Rail, Maritime and Transport Workers (Britain)
SACO	Swedish Confederation of Professional Associations
SAF	Swedish Employers' Association
SAP	Swedish Social Democratic Party
SEA	Single European Act
SGP	Stability and Growth Pact
SIF	Swedish Union of Clerical and Technical Employees in Industry
SINCOBAS	Sindacato intercategoriale dei comitati di base (Italy)
SKr	Swedish Krona
SKTF	Union of Local Government Officers (Sweden)
SMEs	small- and medium-sized enterprises
SPÖ	Austrian Social Democratic Party
ST	Union of Civil Servants (Sweden)
SUD-PTT	Postal and Telecommunications Workers' Federation – Solidarity, Unity, Democracy (French trade union)
T&G	Transport and General Workers' Union (Britain)
TCC	transnational capitalist class
TCO	Swedish Confederation of Professional Employees

TNC	transnational corporation
Transnet	German Railway Workers' Union
Transportarbetare- förbundet	Transport Workers' Union (Sweden)
TUC	Trade Union Congress (Britain)
TUfE	Trade Unionists for Europe (Britain)
UCATT	Union of Construction, Allied Trades and Technicians (Britain)
UN	United Nations
UNICE	Union of Industrial and Employers' Confederations of Europe
UNI-EGS	European Graphical Sector branch of Union Network International
UNI-Europa	Union Network International-Europa
UNIFI	Financial Sector Union (Britain)
UNISON	Public Sector Union (Britain)
UNSA	National Confederation of Independent Unions (France)
Ver.di	United Services Union (Germany)
WIF	wage-earner investment fund
WTO	World Trade Organisation

Part I

Trade unions, EMU and the transnational restructuring of social relations: theoretical and methodological considerations

1

Trade unions, EMU and neo-liberal restructuring in Europe

Introduction

The implementation of Economic and Monetary Union (EMU) on 1 January 1999 signified one of the most dramatic steps in the history of European integration. Eleven, now twelve, European Union (EU) member countries agreed to give up their own currencies and adopt the Euro. There is a wide range of literature dealing with the processes leading to the original decision on EMU at Maastricht in 1991 (e.g. Dyson, 1994; Dyson and Featherstone, 1999; Sandholtz, 1993), discussing the economic and political feasibility of EMU (e.g. Giordano and Persaud, 1998; Jones, 2002; Tsoukalis, 2000), and investigating the impact of EMU on member states (e.g. van der Bempt, 1993; Jones et al., 1998; Martin, 2000). Surprisingly, however, with a few exceptions (Josselin, 2001; Strange, 1997, 2002a and 2002b; Verdun, 2000), little systematic emphasis has been placed on trade unions and their positions on EMU. The purpose of this book is to overcome this neglect through a detailed investigation and comparison of the trade unions of five EU member states, Austria, Britain, France, Germany and Sweden, and their positions on EMU. Several European-level trade union organisations will also be assessed. Trade unions have received more attention recently within the general process of European integration, especially in relation to the developments within the multi-sector social dialogue, sectoral social dialogue and European Works Councils (EWCs) at the European level (e.g. Compston and Greenwood, 2001; Falkner, 1998). Nevertheless, this has generally been restricted to workplace and social policy related issues. Little attention has been given to trade unions' possibilities to influence the emerging economic-political model at the European level more widely. The goal of this book, by contrast, is not limited to EMU as a case study. Rather, EMU is regarded as a vehicle to assess trade unions' options and possibilities to respond to global structural change and to participate in the formation of the future economic-political system of the EU.

Two related questions drive this study. First, what is the position of trade unions on EMU? Have they accepted it, have they tried to shape it, or do they continue to challenge it? Second, considering the common pressures of EMU,

which levels of policy-making are emphasised by trade unions in the defence of
the interests of their members? In particular, this book investigates whether
unions continue to focus on the national level in their efforts to influence policy-
making or whether they increasingly concentrate on co-operation at the European level. The following two hypotheses will be analysed:

Hypothesis 1: A labour movement's position on EMU depends crucially on
its length and degree of exposure to the competitive pressures of globalisation. Unions, which represent workers in transnational production
sectors, are more likely to support EMU, because they may support their
companies – on which their own well-being depends – which benefit
from a stable monetary environment and institutionalised free trade within
the EU. Moreover, because they realise that they have lost control over
capital at the national level, they are probably prepared to co-operate with
other unions at the European level. National production sector unions, on
the other hand, are likely to oppose EMU, since it undermines national
policy autonomy and, thus, the support, on which their sectors depend.
Relying on the state, they may also be less concerned about European
co-operation.

Hypothesis 2: Those trade unions, which have lost influence within the
national institutional set-up, are more in favour of European co-operation
and the establishment of an industrial relations system as well as social
regulations at the European level to counter global pressures. By contrast,
unions which still enjoy considerable impact on policy-making at the
national level are likely to be less interested in European co-operation.

A related, yet analytically separate empirical concern is the social purpose
informing trade unions' positions. Trade unions are frequently accused of having
been co-opted into neo-liberal restructuring through a system of 'symbolic
Euro-corporatism', which 'ensures that the trade unions can maintain their
credo in a "European social model" while at the same time participating in
and contributing to an integration project that is progressively destroying this
very "model"' (Ryner and Schulten, 2003: 191; see also Taylor and Mathers,
2002a: 44). In this book, it will be argued that even if a union supported EMU
and/or European co-operation, this did not by default imply that the neo-liberal
contents of EMU and European integration more generally (see below) was
also accepted.

The selection of case studies follows two major principles: (1) it covers EMU
members (Austria, France and Germany) as well as outsiders (Britain and
Sweden); (2) it includes countries with a predominantly national production
structure (Austria), with a partly transnationalised production structure (France
and Germany) and with a highly transnationalised production structure (Britain
and Sweden). A large part of the empirical material for this book has been
collected through elite interviews with trade union representatives between
January 2001 and January 2003. Interviews have the advantage of providing an

insight into the internal decision-making process of a union in contrast to policy documents, which only state the outcome of a debate. The validity of information was cross-checked through the information from other interviews as well as the consultation of further primary and secondary printed sources. Through close coverage of newspapers and the material by the European Industrial Relations Observatory (http://www.eiro.eurofound.eu.int/) as well as recent documents published by unions on their web sites, it was ensured that any new developments since conducting the interviews were taken into account. In the next section, the pressures on trade unions resulting from EMU are outlined in more detail. Then, a more general overview of the models of capitalism literature is provided, which is linked to the revival of European integration since the mid-1980s in the subsequent section. A section on the different labour movements under investigation follows, before an overview of the book is presented.

Trade unions and the pressures of EMU

Workers, and by extension trade unions as their representatives, are most under pressure by the implications of EMU for three main reasons. First, due to the fixing of exchange rates and the introduction of the single currency, exchange rates can no longer be used to counter economic differences between regions. At the same time, it is easier to compare the different employment conditions within the EU. Hence,

> [i]f a deterioration in relative (unit) costs cannot be reversed by productivity improvements, unions in affected areas will be pressed to accept nominal wage reductions or low increases as well as cuts in nonwage costs, eroding bargained statutory social benefits. This may happen even without asymmetric shocks, insofar as employers (and governments) seek price advantages, no longer attainable by currency depreciation, through wage and benefit cuts instead. (Martin and Ross, 1999b: 345)

In short, wage restraint could be used by national collective bargainers as an alternative to devaluation, no longer possible within the Euro-zone (Crouch, 2002: 297). As a result, there is a danger that the general deregulation and liberalisation within the Internal Market and EMU will result in a logic of competitive deregulation, leading to an undermining of national employment conditions and social standards (Bieling, 2001: 94; Schulten, 2000: 232). The late 1990s/early 2000s saw the first signs of this type of regime competition. Described by Rhodes (1998) as a shift from social to competitive corporatism, so-called social pacts between capital, labour and the state were established in all EU member states, with the exception of Britain and France (Fajertag and Pochet, 2000). 'Their principle aim is not to guarantee a smooth interaction of macroeconomic policy (as in the Keynesian concept) but to increase the overall national competitiveness' (Bieling and Schulten, 2003: 239). Thus, they generally included the following features: (1) wage restraint with agreement results below productivity increases; (2) flexibilisation of the labour market and reduction of social wage costs; (3) a shift to indirect and lower corporate taxes; and (4) restructuring of the welfare state to ease budgetary pressures on governments within EMU (Bieling and Deppe, 1999: 284; Ryner and Schulten, 2003: 189). The potential danger for trade unions and workers of a downward spiral in wages and working conditions are clear. 'Almost all new social pacts have contained more or less binding wage policy guidelines that either aim to undercut the average wage trend in the most important rival countries or generally seek to lower national labor costs by concluding pay settlements below the growth of productivity' (Bieling and Schulten, 2003: 242). Instead of receiving compensation from the government in exchange for wage moderation, unions could hope for a negotiated adjustment of voluntary wage restraint at best (Hassel, 2003). In sum, trade unions are the clear losers of this new type of corporatism under conditions of EMU.

Second, the pressures on the labour market are further intensified through the neo-liberal macroeconomic policy regime 'that could keep the growth of demand in Euroland as a whole too low to allow a significant reduction of unemployment to occur' (Martin, 2000: 365). Within EMU, monetary policy for the single currency is set by the independent European Central Bank (ECB), which is solely committed to low inflation and price stability. Economic policy is tightly co-ordinated at the European level through the Stability and Growth Pact (SGP), committing members to stay within the neo-liberal convergence criteria and their focus on low budget deficits and national debt levels even after the start of EMU on 1 January 1999. The requirement to adhere to the Broad Economic Policy Guidelines (BEPG) including a general commitment to a balanced budget further emphasises the overriding focus on low inflation (Jones, 2002: 37–40).[1] Demand stimulation and job creation at the national level via lower interest rates and public investment in infrastructure projects has been made almost impossible. Instead, EMU 'impels structural reforms in areas such as privatisation, taxation, social security and – most significantly here – labour markets' (Josselin, 2001: 56). Importantly, as the operation of the SGP is embedded within the BEPG, issued by the Economic and Financial Council of Ministers (EcoFin) for the whole EU, its constraints also apply to non-EMU members such as Britain and Sweden (Hancké, 2003: 7). Institutional analyses raise the additional concern that in the absence of co-ordinated wage bargaining at the European level a system with an independent central bank can only achieve low inflation at the cost of higher unemployment levels (Hall and Franzese, 1998).

Finally, during the post-war decades until the late 1970s, unions used to exert most pressure at the national level. Since then, macroeconomic decisions have been shifted upwards to international agreements, while wages and working conditions have increasingly been decided at the company level. European integration is part of this development. 'The Single Market Program and EMU have enshrined market liberalization, price stability and austerity in international treaties . . . ; this renders unions and welfare states vulnerable regardless of the domestic political support they have' (Ross and Martin, 1999: 15).[2] In sum, it is workers who foot the bill for EMU in the form of a higher level of worker exploitation through lower wages, longer working days and labour market flexibilisation (Bonefeld, 2001: 89; Carchedi, 1997: 95–101).

Within the literature on comparative political economy there has been an increasing discussion about the competition between different national models of capitalism in times of global restructuring. Importantly, here it is argued that we are currently also experiencing a struggle over the future EU model of capitalism (Cox, 1993; van Apeldoorn, 2002: 13). Different models of capitalism provide trade unions with different opportunities. In order to assess trade unions' possibilities to participate in the shaping of the future EU model of capitalism, the next section will first provide a brief overview of the varieties of capitalism literature, before the following section investigates the contents of the revival of European integration since 1985 in order to establish towards which model the EU has been moved.

Varieties of capitalism and the struggle over the future EU model of capitalism

There are a range of different typologies. Albert distinguishes between 'American' and European 'Rhine capitalism' (e.g. Albert, 1992). Due to its large spending on the welfare state, Britain is put in the same group as continental European countries, not in the group with the USA. While insightful, this typology is not suitable for this book, since it overlooks the core differences between a liberal market economy such as Britain and more organised, networked economies such as Sweden. Others, taking these differences into account, speak about a division between liberal market economies (LMEs) on the one hand, including Britain, and co-ordinated market economies (CMEs) such as Sweden and Germany on the other. According to Hall and Soskice, 'in liberal market economies, firms coordinate their activities primarily via hierarchies and competitive market arrangements . . . ; in coordinated market economies, firms depend more heavily on non-market relationships to coordinate their endeavors with other actors and to construct their core competencies' (Hall and Soskice, 2001: 8; see also 27 and 32; and Iversen and Pontusson, 2000). CMEs are sometimes subdivided into keiretsu/chaebol-type co-ordination economies to be found in Japan and South Korea and industry-co-ordinated market economies, themselves further subdivided into 'those with national concertation [e.g. Scandinavian countries] and those with primarily sectoral coordination [e.g. Germany]' (Kitschelt et al., 1999b: 429). Another example would be Rhodes and van Apeldoorn, who call CMEs network-oriented models, subdividing them into Germanic and Latin varieties. The main difference here is that the latter scores worse on the advantages of network-oriented models, i.e. the provision of a 'generally productive environment for firms – with high levels of education and research and development (R&D) support and patient capital' (Rhodes and van Apeldoorn, 1998: 411). Amable, finally, rather than sub-dividing individual models, identifies five different varieties of capitalism including the market-based model, the social-democratic model, the Continental European model, the Mediterranean model and the Asian model (Amable, 2003: 13–16).[3]

In this study, I follow typologies, which distinguish three different ideal-type models of capitalism, i.e. market-led capitalisms also called the Anglo-American model of capitalism, state-led capitalisms and negotiated or consensual social capitalisms (e.g. Coates, 2000: 6–11; Schmidt, 2002: 112–18). In the neo-liberal Anglo-American model, the capitalist social relations of production are organised through competition based on neo-liberal economics, with the state focusing on price stability. Trade unions, considered to be an obstacle to economic growth, are excluded from decision-making. State-led capitalism, characterised by a conservative, nationalist ideology, is based on close networks between the state and business organising the economy, while trade unions are marginalised. In consensual or negotiated models of capitalism, employers, trade unions and the state co-operate closely in the running of the economy. Institutionally, it is the negotiated model of capitalism that gives unions most opportunities to participate in decision-making via bipartite or tripartite institutions, including centralised wage bargaining at the sectoral or multi-sector level. As for the contents of the negotiated model of capitalism, in line with the traditional social democratic ideology the main focus is on full employment, an active labour market policy and a generous welfare state providing social security at the workplace and beyond. It is because of these institutional and contents aspects that the negotiated model is often also referred to as the European social model of capitalism.

I agree with Schmidt that the frequent neglect of state-led capitalism (e.g. Hall and Soskice, 2001) is the result of the incorrect assumption that this model has lost its empirical validity. Especially in France, part of this study, the state continues to exercise leadership, albeit in a more indirect way than in the past, which is why Schmidt speaks now of 'state-enhanced' capitalism (Schmidt, 2002: 110, 117; see Chapter 4). Moreover, a twofold typology that subsumes state-led capitalism and negotiated capitalism within one group overlooks the different role of trade unions in these types. While labour has historically been weak in state-led capitalisms such as France, where the core decisions were taken by the government in co-operation with business as the junior partner, trade unions have had a strong, institutionally organised impact on policy-making in negotiated capitalisms such as Germany (Coates, 1999: 648). There has also been a recent shift in the varieties of capitalisms literature to place companies, considered to be the most important actors in a market economy, at the centre of the analysis (Hall and Soskice, 2001). This is rejected here, partly because the importance of the state and labour is unduly diminished as a result. Partly, however, also because in contrast to the understanding that countries have different models of capitalism historically developed over time, the firm-centred approach 'runs the risk of presenting reality as static, with the two varieties of capitalism as systems maintaining a kind of homeostatic equilibrium as they adjust to external economic pressures' (Schmidt, 2002: 111).

While all three types of capitalism will be relevant in relation to the forms of state in the five case studies under investigation here (see Chapter 4), at the

European level emphasis is placed on the differences between negotiated/ consensual capitalism on the one hand, and the Anglo-American model of capitalism on the other. Repeated attempts by French governments to transfer statist features to the European level including grand strategies, intensive European R&D co-operation and a generally interventionist European industrial policy towards the creation of European champions remained unsuccessful (Kassim, 1997: 171). At the European level, 'missing are policies promoting integrated research, public procurement, and industrial champions, along with a civil service élite to initiate *grands projets* or an aggressively protected market' (Schmidt, 1997: 237). The next section analyses the revival of European integration since the mid-1980s to provide an overview of trade unions' structural environment. Particular emphasis is thereby placed on the assessment of the contents of integration instead of the institutional form, because only the contents allows us to establish in which direction the EU model of capitalism has been moved through this new phase of intensified European integration (Bieler, 2003: 3).

European integration since the mid-1980s

Initially, from 1952 onwards, the EU had two main priorities: first, to make another European war especially between France and Germany impossible; and second, to support the reconstruction of Western Europe. Economically, the main goal was the establishment of a customs union, i.e. the removal of tariff barriers between EU members and the establishment of a common external tariff. This was accomplished by the end of the 1960s. European free trade was successfully combined with the national right to intervene in the economy in order to maintain order and social peace. Thus, the EU was part of the compromise of 'embedded liberalism' at the international level (Ruggie, 1982). This period is also sometimes referred to as 'old regionalism' (Spindler, 2003). After de Gaulle had blocked further integration in 1965/1966, little further European integration occurred until 1985. It was against the background of perceived national failure by EU members to respond individually to worldwide economic recession in the 1970s that European integration was revived in the mid-1980s around the Internal Market programme and moves towards EMU.

The deepening of integration

In 1985, the European Commission published its famous White Paper 'Completing the Internal Market', which proposed 300 (later reduced to 279) measures designed to facilitate progress towards the completion of the Internal Market by 1992 through the abolition of non-tariff barriers. The Single European Act (SEA) of 1987, which institutionalised the Internal Market programme, spelled out the goals of the four freedoms, i.e. the free movement of goods, services, capital and people. While tariff barriers had been abolished by the end of the 1960s in the EU, there had been many non-tariff barriers, which had impeded free trade. This was now to be remedied. The rationale underlying the Internal

Market programme was clearly of a neo-liberal nature (Grahl and Teague, 1989). A bigger market was supposed to lead to tougher competition resulting in higher efficiency, greater profits and eventually through a trickle-down effect in more general wealth and more jobs. National markets should be deregulated and liberalised, national companies were to be privatised. An emerging common competition policy was to secure the market so that it was no longer disturbed through state intervention or ownership, including areas such as telecommunications, public procurement and energy. As outlined above, this neo-liberal direction was reinforced by EMU and the convergence criteria, the ECB and its commitment to price stability as well as the SGP and its goal to ensure that member countries remained within the criteria.

The liberalisation and deregulation of the financial sector was to some extent a part of the EU Internal Market programme in that the latter incorporated the free flow of capital within the EU, including the free circulation of 'securitised' financial instruments not quoted on stock markets (e.g. bonds, long-term commercial credit). Banks and non-bank investment firms were provided with a single passport allowing them to set up business across the EU member states. In short, 'the European Union has moved decisively in the direction of a more transnationalised, marketised, and desegmented financial system based on a single legislative framework' (Underhill, 1997b: 118). Bieling outlines well how the project for an integrated European financial space was started with the Internal Market programme and then further developed via EMU, the Lisbon strategy (see below) and more recently the report by the so-called Lamfalussy group, which consisted of financial economists and had the task to develop suggestions of how to improve the legislative process in relation to the European financial market. This implied a clear shift towards the Anglo-American model of capitalism including (1) a further undermining of democratic self-control; (2) pressure on national corporate governance systems to move away from bank-based systems; and (3) the extension of capitalist discipline towards the sphere of social reproduction (Bieling, 2003). Restructuring was further supported through the increasing transnationalisation of production at the material level. While the annual average of inward foreign direct investment (FDI) flows into the EU between 1989 and 1994 was US$ 76,634 million, inward FDI in 2000 was US$ 617,321 million (UN, 2001: 291). The corresponding figures for outward FDI are US$ 105,194 million as annual average between 1989 and 1994, and US$ 772,949 million in 2000 (UN, 2001: 296). Overall, there were 33,249 parent corporations and 53,753 foreign affiliates located in the EU in 2000 (UN, 2001: 239). The fact that this was combined with 'a steep increase in transatlantic mergers and acquisitions between EU- and US-based corporations, reaching a record of US$ 256.5 billion in 1998' (Balanyá et al., 2000: 9), illustrates that European integration was not counterpoised to globalisation, understood as the transnationalisation of production and finance at the material as well as the shift from Keynesianism to neo-liberal economics at the ideological level (see Chapters 2 and 3). If at all, rather than understanding the revival of European integration as a response to globalisation, Ross argues that the concrete policies of deregulating and liberalising national markets and establishing a monetary system with a focus on price stability actually promoted globalisation (Ross, 1998).

The widening of integration

Since the revival of European integration in the mid-1980s, integration was not only deepened but also widened. Analyses focusing on the form of European integration speculate that these are two contradictory processes (e.g. Nugent, 1992). However, when analysing the underlying rationale, it becomes clear that both sets of processes developed along the same line and represented instances of further neo-liberal restructuring (Bieler, 2003). Traditionally, in addition to their neutral status, Austria and Sweden rejected the EU because they both considered their economic-political system based on traditional social demo-cratic values such as equal opportunity, redistribution, gender equality in the workplace, a generous welfare system and full employment, to be superior to the EU, dominated by Christian Democratic parties and big capital. The paradox here is why did they join the EU in a moment when the EU had moved further towards a neo-liberal Anglo-American model through the Internal Market and plans for EMU? Analysed against the background of global restructuring and severe domestic economic recession in the late 1980s/early 1990s, it becomes clear why the two countries had joined the EU in the mid-1990s. Partly due to structural pressure, especially exemplified in Sweden through the relocation of production units and investment by Swedish transnational corporations (TNCs) to locations in the EU, and partly due to a change in hegemonic ideas away from a Keynesian towards a neo-liberal understanding of the economy, the neo-liberal drive underlying the revival of European integration became suddenly an attractive option. In Austria, it was even argued that EU membership would provide the external pressure from Brussels necessary for restructuring the heavily protected agricultural and food processing sectors of the economy (Bieler, 2000).

In Central and Eastern Europe (CEE), the decision on application to the EU was taken by cadre elites within state institutions, who secured neo-liberal economic restructuring externally. Structural change was not driven by domestic coalitions of social forces, but through the incorporation of international ideas and foreign production methods in tandem with an internalisation of trans-national social forces in the national CEE forms of states (Bieler, 2002: 588–9; Bohle, 2000; Shields, 2003). The promise of EU membership and the imagined related economic gains as well as the notion of a cultural return to Europe allowed these elites to convince their citizens that economic hardship was only a temporary sacrifice for a brighter future. The EU itself also realised that the young CEE democracies were not consolidated enough to accommodate the political risks inherent in the transformation process towards a neo-liberal market economy (Cecchini et al., 2001: 157–9). Hence, the promise of member-ship and future wealth can be regarded as a way of keeping the CEE countries on track with transformation. The promise of membership was made at the 1993 European Council summit in Copenhagen. By making a stable democracy, a functioning market economy, the ability to withstand competition within the EU, and to take on the full *acquis communautaire* including EMU preconditions for membership, the EU firmly locked CEE countries into neo-liberal restructuring (Holman, 2001: 178, 180–1). In short, the rationale behind the deepening and widening of European integration since 1985 followed a neo-liberal understanding. This has moved the EU as a whole towards an Anglo-American model of capitalism, exhibiting, therefore, exactly the same rationale underlying neo-liberal globalisation (see Chapter 2). Rhodes and van Apeldoorn are right when they argue that despite this drive of neo-liberal restructuring at the European level, different national forms of state with specific institutional set-ups continue to exist within the EU (Rhodes and van Apeldoorn, 1998: 408, 418 and 425). As it is argued in Chapter 4, neither globalisation nor European integration led to a convergence of national forms of state around the neo-liberal Anglo-American model of capitalism. Nonetheless, the general push within the EU was towards neo-liberal restructuring and even if there was a continuing divergence of national institutions, this did not exclude the fact that the contents of policies decided in different institutional structures was often similar. Rhodes and van Apeldoorn themselves argue that a re-regulation of welfare states and labour markets may require corporatist institutions in some countries (Rhodes and van Apeldoorn, 1998: 421). Thus, neo-liberal goals may be obtained through corporatist consensus. The contents of national policies may change despite institutional stability (Menz, 2005a: 30, 34). Austria, as discussed in Chapter 4, is an example in this respect.

The EU Social Dimension

It would be wrong to argue that revived European integration has been a purely neo-liberal project. Three developments are worthwhile mentioning. First, the Treaty of Maastricht, in addition to EMU, added also the Social Chapter to the EU. The UK initially had an opt-out clause in this respect, but one of the first actions of the New Labour government in 1997 was to sign up to it. The Social Chapter made it possible that, on the initiation by the Commission, the European-level social partners, i.e. the European Trade Union Confederation (ETUC) on behalf of trade unions, and the Union of Industrial and Employers' Confederations of Europe (UNICE) as well as the European Centre of Enterprises with Public Participation and of Enterprises of General Economic Interest (CEEP) for the employers' associations, as the most important organisations, can directly negotiate work-related issues. Agreements are transferred into binding EU law via directives passed by the Council of Ministers without further discussions. First directives were passed along this road. Collective negotiations on the directive on parental leave were concluded in November 1995 and accepted by the Council in June 1996. The directive on atypical work was agreed upon in June 1997 and confirmed by the Council in July 1997 (Falkner, 1998a: 99–155). A social partner agreement and related directive on fixed-term work followed in 1999. Alternatively, collective negotiations can lead to voluntary agreements as in the case of the 2002 telework agreement, to be implemented by the social partners themselves without government involvement (Eironline, 23 July 2002, http://www.eiro.eurofound.eu.int/2002/07/feature/eu0207204f.html; 14/02/2003). The same was the case in relation to the latest agreement on work-related stress in 2004 (Eironline, 20 October 2004, http://www.eiro.eurofound.eu.int/2004/10/ feature/eu0410206f.html; 27/10/2004). A further innovation by the Treaty of Maastricht in the area of social policy was the introduction of qualified majority voting (QMV) in the Council of Ministers. In June 2001, the Directive on Worker Information and Consultation in national enterprises passed in the first Council reading against British reservations mainly thanks to the possibility of QMV (Eironline, 28 June 2001, http://www.eiro.eurofound.eu.int/2001/06/feature/eu 0106219f.html; 12/11/2001). Second, due to pressure by the new French government of Lionel Jospin at the Amsterdam summit in 1997, an employment chapter was added to the EU and a special job summit convened in Luxembourg later in the same year. As a result, member states have to present an annual national action plan on employment policy taking into account Council guidelines. The Commission has the right to make a non-binding recommendation, should a member state fail to observe these guidelines (Barnard and Deakin, 1999: 356–7). In short, employment was firmly put on the European agenda. Third, the June 1999 Cologne European Council summit established the so-called macro-economic dialogue. It provided for two meetings a year, during which repre-sentatives of the European peak-level organisations of unions and employers meet the members of EcoFin and the Council for Employment, Social Policy, Health and Consumer Affairs, the Commission and the ECB to exchange views on macroeconomic policy in the EU (Koll, 2005: 175–87). This provides trade unions with a direct contact to the ECB and the possibility to voice their concerns about the lack of a common economic policy with the goal of creating employment.

Overall, however, while these developments are not insignificant, they should not be overestimated either. The fact that there is an EU social policy is not significant in itself. The real question is in relation to the actual contents of a common social policy. The collectively negotiated directives constitute only framework agreements with an emphasis on minimum standards (Falkner, 1998a: 152). Moreover, the employment guidelines by the European Council must be compatible with the BEPG and EMU in the first place. EMU, however, has locked 'member states into a path of economic development based on economic convergence around tight budgetary controls and the maintenance of price stability. Labour flexibility, in the sense of "structural reforms", is the corollary of this process' (Barnard and Deakin, 1999: 363). Employment policies within the individual EU members consequently focus on supply-side measures such as improved vocational training (Mathers and Taylor, 2005: 23–4). The possibility of active employment programmes, be it at the national or European level in the form of, for example, European-wide infrastructure projects, has been removed from the political agenda. The question of how more employ-ment can be created without more demand is left unanswered. The European Council summit in Lisbon 2000 moved beyond the Amsterdam employment chapter by adopting the so-called Lisbon strategy with the goal to transform the

EU into the most competitive and dynamic knowledge-based economy in the world by 2010. Part of this strategy was for the first time the goal of full employment, mentioned under Point I.6 of the Presidency Conclusions (European Council 2000, http://ue.eu.int/en/Info/eurocouncil/index.htm; 19/02/2003). Nevertheless, a focus on price stability is still the dominating goal in the monetary, economic and social policy-mix. More employment is mainly to be created via restructuring through the deregulation and liberalisation of goods and services as well as capital and labour markets (AK, 2001: 83). Hence, the full employment policy as envisaged by the Lisbon strategy is in full accordance with neo-liberal restructuring. The macroeconomic dialogue is not likely to change this either. 'Not only was the priority of stability-oriented objectives confirmed and fixed in the conclusions of the European Council, but the independence of the actors concerned and their policy autonomy were also strictly observed. Truly new was therefore only the inclusion of trade unions and employers in the European discussion forum, and the attention to wage policy' (Tidow, 2003: 94). Overall, due to the strong symbolic impact of social regulation, social policy has been used to increase the legitimacy of the EU (Bieling, 2001: 104). Considering its actual contents, however, the European Social Dimension to date has not been devised as a protection against market forces, nor has it been developed into a true component of a future European negotiated model of capitalism within the EU. Rather, 'EU social policy interventions have grown up as part of the process of market-building itself' (Leibfried and Pierson, 2000: 289).[4]

This predominance of neo-liberalism does not imply, however, that change is impossible. Political orders are always open to contestation and need to be constantly re-confirmed and re-created (Schulten, 2000: 224). It is in this struggle that possibilities for alternatives to neo-liberalism may emerge. Trade unions' potential role in these alternatives is the core theme of this book. Hence, when analysing trade unions' position on EMU and European co-operation, attention is also directed towards the social purpose underlying trade unions' strategies. It is asked whether they have accepted neo-liberalism or whether they continue to challenge neo-liberal restructuring and the related move towards an Anglo-American model of capitalism be it at the national and/or European level. The analysis of the social purpose is clearly related to positions on EMU and European co-operation, but yet it is a separate analytical issue. In other words, there are a whole range of reasons for why trade unions may support EMU, and a union position in favour of EMU and European co-operation does not automatically imply a pro neo-liberal policy stance. The next section provides an overview of the five labour movements under investigation in this study, before the concluding section of this chapter outlines the structure of the book.

The labour movement in the five countries and at the European level

The Trade Union Congress (TUC) is the only confederation in Britain and 80 per cent of all union members belonged to TUC affiliates in the 1990s. Its position vis-à-vis affiliated unions is rather weak, partly also because some of the affiliated unions are general unions, which organise workers across several industrial sectors. In response to increasing difficulties in recruiting new members and an onslaught on union rights by the Conservative governments in the 1980s and 1990s (see Chapter 4), British unions opted for the creation of large unions via mergers. 'Major union mergers created a general public sector union (UNISON), a general technical union (MSF), a joint engineering and electricians' union (AEEU), a joint transportation union (RMT), a combined communications union (CWU), and a combined print union (GPMU)' (Howell, 1999: 51–2). In March 2001, the members of Manufacturing Science Finance (MSF) and AEEU further decided with overwhelming majority in a postal ballot in favour of a merger of their two unions, resulting in the new union AMICUS (Interview No. 13; London, 26/03/2001). Two further mergers, first with the Financial Sector Union (UNIFI), organising about 150,000 members in banks, and then the printing union, the Graphical, Paper and Media Union (GPMU) in 2004, made AMICUS the biggest British union, representing workers in over twenty industries, from manufacturing and the National Health Service (NHS) to the clergy (AMICUS, 17 August 2004; http://www.amicustheunion.org/main. asp?page=760; 28/02/2005). Because the AEEU, MSF, UNIFI and GPMU were still different unions during the period analysed in this study, they will be treated as separate actors. This also because the AEEU, for example, organised mainly members in transnational manufacturing, while MSF organised workers in manufacturing as well as the public services, thereby representing different labour fractions. As outlined in Hypothesis 1, transnational sector unions are expected to have a different position on EMU and European co-operation than national sector unions. General unions such as the Transport and General Workers' Union (T&G) and the General, Municipal and Boilermakers' Union (GMB) include both a strong manufacturing sector and a significant amount of workers in the public sector. They compete with sectoral unions such as the Communication Workers' Union (CWU) and UNISON for new members and influence. AMICUS is now the biggest TUC affiliate with about 1.5 million members, followed by UNISON with ca. 1.3 million members, the T&G with around 820,000 members and the GMB with about 600,000 members (TUC, http://www. tuc.org.uk/tuc/unions_main.cfm; 28/02/2005). Union density, measured on the basis of potential membership of those in employment, reached a high of 55.8 per cent in 1979, but fell back over the 1980s and 1990s to 32.1 per cent in 1995 (Edwards et al., 1998: 26). Union density stabilised in 2003 just above 29 per cent (TUC, 30 July 2004, http://www.tuc.org.uk/the_tuc/tuc-8365-f0.cfm; 05/10/2004).

In Germany, trade union reorganisation after World War Two transcended the pre-war ideological divisions. Blue- and white-collar workers but also civil servants were united in one trade union according to industrial sector (Jacobi et al., 1998: 200). The Confederation of German Trade Unions (Deutscher Gewerkschaftsbund; DGB) is mainly responsible for policy implementation, while collective bargaining is conducted by sectoral unions. Since the early 1990s, the number of industrial unions affiliated to the DGB has declined from sixteen to eight. 'In 1996 the union of construction workers amalgamated with the union of agricultural workers (now IG Bauen-Agrar-Umwelt; IG BAU); in 1997 the mining and leather industry unions joined the IG Chemie (now IG Bergbau, Chemie, Energie; IG BCE); and in 1998–1999 IG Metall [absorbed] the two unions of employees in textiles and clothing and in wood and plastics' (Jacobi et al., 1998: 202). Most recently, at a special merger congress on 18 March 2001, the Postal Workers' Union (Deutsche Postgewerkschaft; DPG), the Commerce, Banking and Insurance Workers' Union (Handel, Banken, Versicherungen; HBV), the Media Workers' Union (IG Medien) and the Public Services, Transport and Traffic Union (Öffentliche Dienste, Transport und Verkehr; ÖTV) formed the United Services Union (Ver.di). Importantly, this merger also included the German Salaried Employees' Union (Deutsche Angestellten-Gewerkschaft; DAG), which had originally remained outside the DGB (Ver.di, http://www.verdi.de/0x0ac80f2b_0x0003c3f9; 28/02/2005). As in the case of Britain, because EMU had already been discussed while the individual unions were still independent, they are treated here as individual actors, partly also because they represented different fractions of the labour force. The merger made Ver.di with about 3 million members the largest DGB affiliate. The metal workers' union IG Metall is the second largest union with ca. 2.8 million followed by the IG BCE with around 870,000 members. The German Civil Servants' Federation (Deutscher Beamtenbund; DBB) is a further significant confederation. It represents fewer white-collar employees than the DGB, but it is especially well represented within the civil servants group (Beamte) in the public sector. Union density in Germany had generally been around 30 per cent (Jacobi et al., 1998: 202). After an initial increase following German re-unification in the early 1990s, the DGB, however, lost 28.4 per cent of its members between 1993 and 2003 (Eironline, 21 May 2004, http://www.eiro.eurofound.eu.int/2004/03/update/tn0403105u.html; 30/08/2005).

As a result of exclusion from policy-making and ideological splits, the French labour movement represents a complex picture. It 'has traditionally been marked by trade-union pluralism and fragmentation, inter-union rivalry, low union density, and a paucity of financial and organizational resources' (Goetschy, 1998: 360). Five trade union confederations enjoy a representative status and are entitled to conclude collective agreements. The General Confederation of Labour (Confédération générale du travail; CGT) enjoyed close ties with the French Communist Party during the post-war decades. Its emphasis used to be on confrontation, not collective bargaining. The continuing decline of the Communist Party, however, made a change in the CGT's strategy necessary, including a distancing from the party itself since the early 1990s (Daley, 1999: 188). The French Democratic Confederation of Labour (Confédération française démocratique du travail; CFDT) was closely aligned with the French Socialist Party until the second half of the 1980s. Since then, it has strongly favoured collective bargaining with employers and close co-operation with governments, whether they were from the centre-right or centre-left (Daley, 1999: 188).

The General Confederation of Labour – Force ouvrière (Confédération générale du travail – Force ouvrière; FO) is politically independent and strongly anti-communist. 'Despite its internal fragmentation, FO has played a major role in collective bargaining, which it sees as the main element of union action, and has secured significant benefits for its members' (Goetschy, 1998: 363). The French Christian Workers' Confederation (Confédération française des travailleurs chrétiens; CFTC) is one of the smaller unions with a representative status. It emerged from a Christian tradition in the early twentieth century and now focuses on the development of collective bargaining (Goetschy, 1998: 364). Finally, the Confederation of Professional and Managerial Staff (Confédération française de l'encadrement-Confédération générale des cadres; CFE-CGC) mainly organises cadres and managers in companies and has a strong focus on collective bargaining at enterprise level.

The trade union landscape in France became even more complex from the late 1980s onwards, when new moderate as well as radical unions emerged. After the split of the Federation of National Education (Fédération de l'éducation; FEN) in 1992, the independent federation Unitary Union Federation (Fédération Syndicale Unitaire; FSU) emerged as the strongest teachers' union. The FEN in turn participated in the establishment of the National Confederation of Independent Unions (L'Union Nationale des Syndicats Autonomes; UNSA) as an alternative confederation for reformist unions and renamed itself UNSA-Education (Eironline, 28 January 2001, http://www.eiro.eurofound.eu.int/2001/01/inbrief/fr0101118n.html; 05/09/2002; Olive 2002: 19–38). Dissatisfied with the accommodationist position of mainstream unions vis-à-vis neo-liberal restructuring, new, radical action trade unions also emerged. Importantly, the Postal and Telecommunications Workers' Federation of Solidarity, Unity, Democracy (Solidaires, Unitaires et Démocratique; SUD-PTT), which organises workers in the postal services and telecommunications industry, emerged in 1988 after a split from the CFDT (Damesin and Denis, 2005: 18). It had been unhappy about the latter's reluctance to organise strikes in the postal services and hospitals. While the CFDT focuses on negotiations with employers, SUD-PTT conducts a much more confrontational strategy. Since 1989, SUD unions have been founded in the railway, health and education sectors as well as in various companies such as Michelin and Renault (Interview No. 63; Paris, 16/12/2002). The associated formation of the confederation Group of 10-L'Union syndicale Solidaires (G10-Solidaires) goes back to 1981, when ten autonomous unions formed an alliance for the first time. It was only after the entry of SUD-PTT, first as an observer in 1989, then as a full member in 1992, that G10-Solidaires became the focal point for radical, progressive unions (G10-Solidaires, 2002: 9–14). The confederation nowadays unites thirty-two independent unions including the SUD unions (Interview No. 65; Paris, 16/12/2002; Damesin and Denis, 2005: 30). French unions are in general organised into industrial federations. Compared to other European countries, the unionisation degree in France is the lowest. Once around 20 per cent in the mid-1970s, union density dropped below 9 per cent in 1995 (Daley, 1999: 172).[5] The strength of

French trade unions, however, should not be underestimated despite their fragmentation and low membership levels. Being left outside the *dirigiste* policy-making framework, organising strikes and demonstrations was often the only possibility to influence decision-making. And this is something where French trade unions, despite the low membership numbers, have been very successful. Many restructuring programmes had to be shelved in the face of resistance organised by trade unions.

The picture of the Austrian labour movement is much less complex. The Austrian Confederation of Trade Unions (Österreichischer Gewerkschaftsbund; ÖGB) is clearly the dominant actor. It is currently divided into thirteen individual trade unions according to different industrial sectors. They enjoy, however, no legal personality and little independent power (Heinisch, 2000: 73). It is the ÖGB that decides about personnel, finance and general union policies.[6] The only slightly exceptional case is the Public Services Trade Union (Gewerkschaft Öffentlicher Dienst; GÖD). While it is affiliated to the ÖGB, the Christian union fraction dominates this union with about 55 per cent of the vote, while the socialist fraction, dominant in all other affiliated unions and the ÖGB overall, comes only second with 29 per cent. As a result, the GÖD is affiliated with the Christian European and international union federations and thus not the ETUC at the European level (Interview No. 34; telephone interview, 14/05/2002). It will be interesting to see whether this slightly different ideological background had an impact on this public sector union's positions on EMU and European-level co-operation. For the purpose of this study, all thirteen unions affiliated to the ÖGB have been treated as independent actors organising workers in different industrial sectors. Finally, the Chamber of Labour (Arbeiterkammer; AK) needs to be mentioned as a labour institution parallel to, not in competition with, the ÖGB. While the latter is mainly responsible for collective bargaining, the former functions as the Austrian labour movement's think tank with the task of developing economic, social and monetary policy proposals (Interview No. 26; Wien, 19/03/2002; Menz, 2005a: 37). 'For a long time [the ÖGB] represented more than 60 percent of blue and white collar workers' (Tálos 1996: 105). In recent years, however, similar to other unions elsewhere in Europe the ÖGB lost a significant number of its members and the unionisation degree fell below 50 per cent (Eironline, 21 May 2004, http://www.eiro.eurofound.eu.int/2004/03/update/tn0403105u.html; 30/08/2005).

By contrast, the degree of unionisation in Sweden could be maintained to a large extent and is still around 80 per cent. In contrast to Austria, Britain and Germany, however, there is no single trade union confederation. The Swedish Trade Union Confederation (Landsorganisationen; LO) organises blue-collar workers and lower non-manuals. Its membership has fallen over recent years to clearly under 2 million members, but it remains the largest trade union with 1,892,000 members in 2003. The Swedish Confederation of Salaried Employees (Tjänstemännens Centralorganisation; TCO) with 1,275,975 white-collar workers as members and the Swedish Confederation of Professional Associations (Svenska Akademikers Centralorganisation; SACO), which organises 556,000 professionals with a university degree, enjoy a strong and independent position (Eironline, 10 May 2004, http://www.eiro.eurofound.eu.int/2004/05/inbrief/se0405102n. html; 17/09/2004). All three confederations consist of a whole range of affiliated unions, organised according to the industrial principle in the case of the LO and TCO, and the craft principle in the case of SACO. Similar to Germany and in contrast to Austria, these affiliated unions enjoy a considerable degree of decision-making and bargaining autonomy vis-à-vis their confederation. The organisational structure of the Swedish trade union movement has generally been remarkably stable with very few discussions about possible mergers until recently.[7]

At the European level, the main union is the ETUC, which has as its members seventy-six national confederations from thirty-four European countries. Importantly, there are also eleven European industry federations (EIFs), which are sectoral trade union organisations at the European level (ETUC, http://www.etuc.org/r/13; 30/03/2005). These European-level union structures have been significantly developed parallel to the revival of European integration since 1985 (Dølvik, 2000). Chapter 8 is dedicated to European trade unions with a special emphasis on whether these union organisations are simply secretariats with the task to organise international co-operation of their national members, or whether they have developed into supranational actors in their own right. This chapter will analyse transnational sector unions such as the European Metalworkers' Federation (EMF) and the European Mine, Chemical and Energy Workers' Federation (EMCEF) as well as national sector unions such as the European Trade Union Committee for Education (ETUC-E) and the European Federation of Public Service Unions (EPSU).

Overview of the book

It is argued in this book that unions' positions on EMU and European-wide co-operation have to be analysed against the background of globalisation. After all, 'monetary union is most accurately seen here as reinforcing certain tendencies already induced by globalisation and sectoral change. All economies have already found that the globalisation of financial markets in particular has intensified competition and produced difficulty in using exchange-rate manipulation as an economic policy tool' (Crouch, 2002: 304). Chapter 2 will, therefore, first assess in what way labour can be conceptualised as an international actor in times of globalisation. As the conceptualisation of labour depends very much on how different approaches conceptualise globalisation, this chapter will also include the definitional development of the latter. More specifically, in accordance with O'Brien (2000a: 554), it will be argued that in order to understand structural change and the historical specificity of capitalism, within which trade unions' struggles occur, it is essential to place the 'social relations flowing from production at the centre of the study of international relations'. Hence, the focus will be on a neo-Gramscian, historical materialist perspective concentrating on social forces as engendered by the production process as the core collective actors. Nevertheless, social forces are not only engendered and shaped by the social relations of production, but they also operate within and through different forms of state, i.e. different institutional set-ups at the national as well as European level. Chapter 2, will, therefore, also include a conceptualisation of the structural impact of institutions on social forces. Following the development of the neo-Gramscian perspective in Chapter 2, Chapter 3 has the task to identify the core social forces in the individual case studies through an analysis of the impact of globalisation on the Austrian, British, French, German and Swedish social relations of production. After a general discussion of the restructuring processes related to globalisation, this will, first, be done through an overview of the historical emergence of capitalism in these countries. Second, the degree of the transnationalisation of a country's production structure is based on an assessment of FDI levels. In addition to general levels of outward and inward FDI and stocks of FDI, the following indicators are used to provide a better estimate of the actual relative importance of FDI levels: (1) outward and inward FDI flows as a percentage of gross domestic fixed capital formation; (2) outward and inward FDI stocks as a percentage of gross domestic product (GDP); as well as (3) outward FDI as percentage of exports of goods and non-factor services. Chapter 4 provides the second part of the study's empirical background with an analysis of the impact of global and European restructuring of the social relations of production on the Austrian, British, French, German and Swedish forms of state. This investigation allows the outline of the country-specific institutional set-up within and through which social forces, identified in Chapter 3, operate. Specific emphasis will be placed on the changing role of trade unions within the restructured national institutional set-ups.

Chapter 5 is the opening of the empirical analysis. It investigates the positions of the confederations in the five case studies on EMU and European co-operation. This does not relate directly to the first hypothesis, since confederations include both transnational and national forces of labour, but it provides a good first marker of the empirical situation in the countries under investigation. Confederations' positions are also important because their affiliated sectoral unions have frequently either aligned with, or contrasted their positions to, the peak associations. Because there are several trade union confederations in France and Sweden, more space is dedicated to these two countries in Chapter 5. In accordance with the first hypothesis, Chapter 6 concentrates on the transnational sector unions in the five case studies and their positions on EMU and European co-operation, while Chapter 7 focuses on national production sector unions. This analytical division is also preferable over a country-by-country presentation of empirical material, since it guarantees an equal emphasis on the commonalities across borders as much as the differences. A country-by-country presentation, in contrast, often simply asserts the obvious fact of national diversity and overlooks the international dimension (Haworth and Hughes, 2002: 67–8). Chapter 8 concludes the empirical part of the book through an analysis of European trade union organisations and their positions on EMU and European co-operation. The first part of this chapter concentrates on the European form of state in order to identify trade unions' possibilities to influence policy-making at the European level. Related to the second hypothesis of this book, the degree of engagement at the European level will also depend on a comparison of the possibilities of influence at the regional level in comparison with the national institutional set-up. The second part investigates various EIFs' positions on EMU, before the third part asks to what extent they have developed from international organisations, which co-ordinate the activities of their national affiliates, to independent, supranational actors at the European level. The conclusion of this chapter analyses the ETUC and its role at the European level. It looks at the wider activities and the way the ETUC tries to stem neo-liberal restructuring including the organisation of inter-union European level co-ordination of national collective bargaining and co-operation with other social movements.

Chapter 9 sums up the core results of the book in relation to trade unions' positions on EMU and European co-operation, including also a country-by-country summary at this stage. Throughout the book, the rationale of trade unions' activities is assessed. In other words, it is evaluated whether they have accepted neo-liberal restructuring and the move towards the Anglo-American model of capitalism within the EU or whether they continue to question this and struggle in favour of a negotiated, social model of capitalism at the European level. This issue is re-emphasised in Chapter 9, including also a discussion of the related possibilities of resistance against neo-liberal restructuring. It takes up the discussion of Chapter 8 and provides a brief outlook on the possibilities of co-operation between trade unions and other social movements within the European Social Forum (ESF). The latter has emerged as the main forum in Europe for organising resistance against neo-liberal globalisation in Europe. It took place first in Florence in November 2002, in Paris in November 2003 and then in London in October 2004. Trade unions' participation in the forum is of primary significance in that it shows their determination in resisting neo-liberal restructuring as well as their capabilities and willingness to restructure themselves internally in order to pursue this new strategy successfully. Overall, it will be concluded that the future of the European model of capitalism is wide open and trade unions are in a good position to shape the outcome of this struggle towards a socially embedded model of capitalism and possibly beyond.

Notes

1 France's and Germany's recent breaking of the Pact demonstrates the power of big countries in the EU, but cannot be interpreted as a fundamental break with low inflation policy at this stage. Both countries continue to aim at meeting the criteria at least in the medium-term.

2 Unlike the analysis presented here, Hancké argues that the existing system of monetary policy and SGP would resemble more a 'soft Keynesian framework' in that expansionary fiscal policies, which do not threaten the low inflation policy, are not punished (Hancké, 2003: 8). As proof, he cites the criticism of Ireland by the Economic and Financial Council of Ministers in 2001, demanding a higher budget surplus to curb inflation, and the non-punishment of Germany in 2002, when German budget deficit

levels approached 3 per cent. While the Irish situation, although not in breach of the SGP, endangered the overall goal of low inflation and was, therefore, sanctioned, Germany's possible breaking of the Pact was overlooked, since it was not a danger for the price stability policy. While interesting, here it is argued that the different treatment of the two countries has more to do with their different size and importance for the EU, than a Keynesian rationale of the SGP and EMU.

3 For an overview of the wider literature around the varieties of capitalism debate, see Coates (2005).

4 For a more optimistic assessment of the Social Dimension and its potential especially with regard to EU employment policy, see Strange (2002b: 358–60).

5 Membership numbers for the individual French unions are difficult to obtain. A recent survey of trade union membership in twenty-three EU members points out that self-reported data is only available for the CFDT and CGT. The CFDT is the larger union of the two, increasing its membership from 617,000 in 1993 to 889,000 in 2003. The CGT registered an increase in members from 639,000 members in 1993, at this time still bigger than the CFDT, to 668,000 in 1998, but no data is available for 2003 (Eironline, 21 May 2004, http://www.eiro.eurofound.eu.int/2004/03/update/tn0403105u.html; 10/09/2004). An additional indicator to compare individual trade unions' strength vis-à-vis each other is provided by results of industrial tribunal elections and works council elections. Industrial tribunals in France consist of elected non-professional judges. Half of the judges are employers' representatives, half of them employees' representatives. 'Without publicly admitting it, trade unions recognise that the industrial tribunal elections are a "full-scale" test of their representativeness in the private sector' (Eironline, 7 February 2003, http://www.eiro.eurofound.eu.int/2003/01/feature/fr0301107f.html; 10/09/2004). In the December 2002 industrial tribunal elections, the CGT maintained its leading position with 32.1 per cent before the CFDT with 25.2 per cent, although the latter has more members than the former. Third came FO with 18.3 per cent, followed by the CFTC with 9.7 per cent, the CFE-CGC with 7.0 per cent and a remarkable success by UNSA with 5.0 per cent. G10-Solidaires, which contested the elections for the first time, gained 1.5 per cent. The results of the works council elections in 2001 show the CFDT just ahead of the CGT with 22.8 per cent over 22.6 per cent, followed by FO with 13.1 per cent, the CFE-CGC with 6.1 per cent and the CFTC with 6 per cent. No data is available for UNSA and G10-Solidaires (Eironline, 13 November 2003, http://www.eiro.eurofound.eu.int/2003/11/inbrief/fr0311102n.html; 10/10/2004). At sectoral level, SUD-PTT became the second-largest union in the two companies France Telecom and the Post Office (Damesin and Denis, 2005: 18).

6 There have been some attempts at restructuring within the Austrian labour movement over the recent years. On the one hand, seven of the sectoral trade unions have formed the union alliance *infra*. They retain their own independent existence, but aim at a better co-ordination of their negotiation strategies in order to obtain a stronger position vis-à-vis employers and government. Efficiency gains in the provision of services for members are also cited as a reason for the alliance (infra, http://www.oegb-infra.at; 07/12/2004). On the other hand, five unions around the Metal and Textile Workers' Union (Gewerkschaft Metall-Textil; GMT) and the Union of Private Sector Employees (Gewerkschaft der Privatangestellten; GPA) have moved towards forming a new, larger trade union. This would allow a better co-ordination of strategies and bargaining policies across sectors and, thus, give the unions a stronger position vis-à-vis government and employers. The merger has, however, been put in

doubt recently. Partly because the Chemical Workers' Union (Gewerkschaft der Chemiearbeiter; GdC) withdrew from the process because it felt that its position had been neglected, and partly because the ÖGB had proven itself capable of organising successfully industrial action, thereby removing one of the reasons for forming the new union in the first place (Eironline, 8 June 2004, http://www.eiro.eurofound. eu.int/2004/06/inbrief/at0406201n.html; 24/08/2004).

7   On 1 January 2002, the Agricultural Workers' Union joined the Municipal Workers' Union (Kommunal) (Eironline, 13 March 2002, http://www.eiro.eurofound.eu.int/ 2002/03/inbrief/se0203101n.html; 17/06/2002). In August and September 2004, the LO-affiliates the Swedish Metal Workers' Union and the Industrial Workers' Union (Industrifacket) discussed a possible merger for the beginning of 2006 (Eironline, 4 October 2004, http://www.eiro.eurofound.eu.int/2004/10/inbrief/se0410101n.html; 14/02/2005). As for the white-collar unions, in December 2000 the Social Insurance Employees' and Insurance Agents' Union (Försäkringsanställdas förbund; FF), affiliated to LO, announced its application to the TCO for membership (Eironline, 28 December 2000, http://www.eiro.eurofound.eu.int/2000/12/feature/se0012178f. html; 17/06/2002). A merger of four white-collar unions affiliated to the TCO collapsed, however, in December 2001 (Eironline, 18 January 2002, http://www.eiro. eurofound.eu.int/2002/01/inbrief/se0201111n.html; 17/06/2002). As in the case of other countries, the individual unions will be treated as separate actors, if they were still independent, when EMU was discussed.

2

Transnational restructuring and the conceptualisation of labour as an international actor

Introduction

Labour has been largely neglected in International Relations/International Political Economy (IR/IPE) (O'Brien, 2000b: 89–92). The end of the Cold War, however, implied the disappearance of the major ideological conflict that had split labour movements into social democratic and communist unions. It, therefore, opened up new space for trade unions at the international level (Cumbers, 2004: 830). Globalisation has also been likely to further trade unions' international role. Partly because it puts labour movements under pressure at the national level and, thereby, pushes them to think more about possible co-operation and activities at the international level. As it will be argued in Chapters 5 to 8, intensified co-operation at the European level was justified by some unions through a reference to the loss of control over transnational capital at the national level. Partly also because the transnational organisation of production across borders itself provides new opportunities for trade union internationalism (O'Brien, 2000a: 536–9).[1] Hence, it is argued that IR/IPE should develop a stronger focus on labour. By contrast, Comparative Political Economy (CPE) approaches, which engage less with the international level, have conceptualised the role of trade unions. Overall, this chapter provides the theoretical basis for the empirical analysis of trade unions' positions on EMU and stronger European-level co-operation in that it investigates how the potential role of labour as an international actor can be conceptualised.[2] As this depends very much on how globalisation is defined by a particular approach, the definition of globalisation is also at the centre of the discussion. In the next section, mainstream CPE and IR/IPE theories will be assessed. Neo-realism is rather unimportant for this study due to its state-centrism. As it does, however, have an affinity with CPE approaches, it will be briefly discussed in the next section before liberal IR/IPE theories are assessed. The main part of this chapter is, however, dedicated to the introduction of a neo-Gramscian, historical materialist approach, able to understand transnational class formation in times of globalisation and, thus, comprehend labour as a potential international actor.

Mainstream theories and the international role of labour

Neo-realism and CPE: the centrality of the state and the continuity of national divergence

Neo-realist IR theory regards the international system as anarchic, since there is no overarching authority to impose order. States as the most important actors pursue rational policies of power maximisation and security enhancement to ensure their survival (Waltz, 1979). This state-centrism is reflected in neo-realists' definition of globalisation. Current changes do not affect the whole world, it is argued, and are, thus, not truly global; the conditions across countries are not uniform; countries are less interdependent than often assumed; and multinational corporations (MNCs) are still predominantly based in one country. If at all, it is global finance that comes closest to popular understandings of globalisation. Nevertheless, even here the developments over the last decades are not deemed to be anything new. 'Despite today's ease of communication, financial markets in 1900 were at least as integrated as they are now' (Waltz, 2000: 48). In short, globalisation defined along these lines is nothing more than a drastic increase in cross-border flows of goods, services and capital (Keohane and Milner, 1996). States remain the core international actors and have lost little of their traditional power over the economy and international markets. Neo-realists accept that states are not the only actors, but they are deemed to be clearly the most important ones (Gilpin, 2001: 18). From this perspective, it is evident that labour can at best be understood as operating at the national level, interacting with other domestic actors and the government in response to globalisation. It is this aspect that is picked up by CPE approaches.

Although the link is not openly stated, CPE approaches' affinity with neo-realism is most clearly expressed in the definitions of globalisation and the way the role of states at the international level is conceptualised. Increasing levels of trade and capital mobility are identified as the two core characteristics of globalisation. 'More liberal trade and financial regimes have inspired vast new flows of goods and capital across national borders, including a large increase in foreign direct investment' (Hall and Soskice, 2001: 55; see also Iversen and Pontusson, 2000: 23). In other words, as in the case of neo-realist scholarship, it is increasing cross-border flows that are highlighted. Globalisation is, consequently, simply understood as some kind of external challenge for states (Hall and Soskice, 2001: 56). Different authors refer to globalisation in a different way, when attempting to explain cross-national variations in policy and institutional changes. Iversen and Pontusson, for example, argue that globalisation has hardly any explanatory leverage, since financial market deregulation is a policy choice by states and because it is a rather uniform external pressure on states (Iversen and Pontusson, 2000: 25). They regard globalisation only as one set of pressures for change. Deindustrialisation with the related change towards more employment in the service sector and the rise of new production paradigms thanks to new technologies are regarded as more decisive. What they overlook, however, is how closely deindustrialisation and new production paradigms are linked to the transnationalisation of production. The deindustrialisation in the West is mainly a consequence of the transfer of manufacturing production units to developing countries. Similarly, the very fact that the transnational organisation of production has become possible is due to new technologies, lowering transport costs and making the trading of services possible (Held et al., 1999: 255). In other words, these developments cannot be separated into several independent explanatory variables and globalisation has to be understood as a complex set of processes including these closely related aspects. Kitschelt et al. too understand globalisation as external pressure on states. In contrast to Iversen and Pontusson, however, they focus on how the various different national institutional set-ups mediate these pressures, ensuring a continuation of divergence of national models of capitalism (Kitschelt et al., 1999b: 440–1).

Yet another set of CPE approaches focuses on domestic actors such as trade unions, employers' associations and central banks and their interaction in response to common external pressures, when explaining national divergence. The relation to neo-realist IR theory is the conceptualisation of states as the only actors at the international level by these approaches, concentrating on how domestic actors compete with each other in determining the national position. Thereby, they regard the production sector as an important variable for the explanation of states' behaviour in the global economy (e.g. Frieden, 1991: 438; Gourevitch, 1986: 54–68). The response of trade unions and employers' associations to opening up the economy to international competition and the related lobbying pressure on their government depends very much on the nature of the sector. Unions and employers' associations in export sectors are understood to favour open borders, while unions and employers' associations in domestic production sectors generally prefer closed borders and state protectionism. An early example of this is Katzenstein's (1985) seminal analysis of small states in world markets, where he outlines labour's crucial role in tripartite relations with government and business in adjusting a country's economy to high levels of international competition without causing domestic social unrest. Garrett's analysis of the power by the left and labour on economic policies in times of increasing internationalisation is another example. Here too labour only responds to changes at the international level via increasing or decreasing intervention into the national economy (Garrett, 1996).[3] In other words, the implicit understanding of the international system and, thus, globalisation by CPE approaches is state-centric and, by default, these approaches treat companies and employers' associations, but especially also trade unions as purely domestic-level actors. Even where it is acknowledged that new actors have emerged at the international level in the form of pension funds and TNCs, they are understood as heavily connected to specific countries (Kitschelt et al., 1999b: 446; Schmidt, 2002: 16, 27). Labour would be even less transnationally mobile than capital (Kitschelt et al., 1999b: 449; Schmidt, 2002: 29). Josselin's analysis of the position of British, German and French trade unions on EMU is an example, which is directly relevant for this book. She also treats trade unions as domestic actors, which adjust to external pressures be it EMU, or be it globalisation

(Josselin, 2001: 55). They are not understood as being part of a wider restructuring changing the international state system. They are, therefore, not considered to be potential international actors. Industrial relations literature in general, as a sub-group of comparative politics approaches, neglects the international dimension through its often exclusive focus on different national industrial relations systems and their country-specific features. This is visible in the way research publications are structured. 'Comparative industrial relations texts tend towards country chapters topped and tailed with overviews focusing on similarities and dissimilarities' (Haworth and Hughes, 2002: 67–8).[4]

Nevertheless, as it is argued below, globalisation as a new phenomenon is first and foremost characterised by the transnationalisation of production, not merely by increasing levels of economic interdependence. TNCs clearly differ from export-oriented companies, the production facilities of which are still located at the national level and which, consequently, manoeuvre predominantly in one specific domestic context. Capital and labour related to TNCs are international actors, which potentially operate simultaneously within several different domestic arenas as well as at the international level. It is, thus, clearly necessary to think beyond distinctive national economies. As Watson argues, 'it remains unclear whether such a task is possible with an analytical framework that allows each country to possess its own national variant of capitalism' (Watson, 2003: 228). CPE approaches and here especially the varieties of capitalism literature still assume that industrial capital is immobile across borders. What is, thereby, overlooked are the social relations of production underpinning particular national models of capitalism (Coates, 2000: 176–7). CPE approaches are, therefore, unable to explain why a particular set of institutions was established in the first place as well as to assess change emanating from alterations in the production structure. The next section looks at the liberal approaches to globalisation, before a neo-Gramscian, critical IPE perspective is introduced, emphasising precisely the social relations of production as the starting-point for an investigation of structural change over time.

Liberal IR theory: globalisation and structural change

Liberal IR approaches look at the individual, or to be more precise the aggregation of individuals in interest groups, as the most important actors. The state as a result does not become unimportant, but it is treated as a collective rather than unitary actor. The national interest is then not the result of a state's position in the international system, but the outcome of domestic politics against the background of international pressures. Economic issues have become as important as, if not more important than, military concerns. Structural change is not limited to change in the state structure. Instead it is realised that changes beyond the state system may imply the emergence of new actors. In short, the international system is viewed in a more complex and open-ended way (Zacher and Matthew, 1995). Some liberal approaches argue that globalisation, defined as networks of interdependence over multicontinental distances, is not really a new process. What is new is that these networks become increasingly thick.

'Sheer magnitude, complexity, and speed distinguish contemporary globalization from earlier periods' (Keohane and Nye, 2002: 201). A whole range of liberal approaches, however, do argue that globalisation is a more recent phenomenon, starting from around the early 1970s and the end of the Bretton Woods system of fixed exchange rates. These approaches identify the trans-nationalisation of finance and production as core characteristics of globalisation. The details of, and controversies over, these processes of structural change are dealt with in Chapter 3. Here, only the core features and their assumed consequences are outlined.

As a result of the rise of financial off-shore markets, bypassing national regulations, and the deregulation of financial markets across the world, a fully fledged global financial market has emerged since the early 1970s (Helleiner, 1994; Strange, 1994: 103–18). In the process of national deregulation, finance has become desegmented, marketised and integrated across national borders (Underhill, 1997a: 3). The growth of TNCs, in numbers and size, has driven the transnationalisation of production. They are 'the agents that integrate trade, technology transfer and financial flows for the purpose of [transnational] production in the context of the firms' strategy' (UN, 1991: 83). Their increasing importance is expressed in the rise of FDI. Whether and to what extent this is an appropriate way of measuring the transnationalisation of production will be discussed further in Chapter 3. Here, it suffices to note a drastic increase in FDI flows since the 1980s. FDI outflows rose from US$ 88 billion to US$ 225 billion between 1986 and 1990, which is an annual increase of 26 per cent (UN, 1992: 14) and increased to about US$ 1187 billion in 2000 as peak year (UN, 2004: 372). Overall, there were at least 61,000 parent corporations with more than 900,000 foreign affiliates worldwide in 2003 (UN, 2004: XVII). As a result of these processes of transnational restructuring, 'the nation-state is being supplemented by other actors – private and third sector – in a more complex geography' (Keohane and Nye, 2002: 202). First attempts at conceptualising transnational actors from a liberal perspective were made by Keohane and Nye in the 1970s (Keohane and Nye, 1971 and 1977). Especially, their book *Power and Interdependence* (1977) challenged conventional state-centric assumptions at least in relation to the interaction of developed countries in the West. Their concept of 'complex interdependence' identified multiple channels between states including traditional interstate relations, but also transgovernmental interaction between government institutions across borders as well as transnational relations by non-governmental actors such as TNCs. There would be no hierarchy of issues in 'complex interdependence' with military security not automatically dominating the agenda and the line between domestic and international politics was understood to be blurred (Keohane and Nye, 1977: 24–9).

More recently, liberal perspectives have generally accepted the emergence of new international non-state actors such as TNCs (e.g. Stopford and Strange, 1991) and non-governmental organisations (NGOs) also sometimes referred to as global social movements (e.g. O'Brien et al., 2000). These new actors compete for authority with states in the global political economy (Higgott et al., 2000).

Especially, TNCs are considered to be powerful new international actors deciding who gets what instead of states: (1) TNCs have been more involved in the redistribution of wealth from North to South via FDI than states; (2) TNCs have taken over the role of states to solve interest conflicts between capital and labour in their area; (3) TNCs have escaped high levels of taxation by states; (4) states have retreated from the participation in the ownership and control of the means of production (Strange, 1996: 44–65). Labour from a liberal perspective can be conceptualised as an international actor, next to a range of other actors in a pluralist understanding of policy-making. Smythe's (2000) analysis of the failed Organisation for Economic Co-operation and Development (OECD) negotiations of a Multilateral Agreement on Investment and the struggle against enhanced capital mobility via further deregulation of national financial markets is a good example. Here, the Trade Union Advisory Committee is treated as one interest organisation next to its business counterpart and environmental NGOs such as the World Wide Fund for Nature. Similarly, in Scholte's analysis of the International Monetary Fund's (IMF) interaction with civil society, the labour movement through its various institutional expressions is only one of a whole range of different NGOs, which have lobbied the IMF (Scholte, 2000b). Even O'Brien, who specifically looks at labour and its potential in the resistance to globalisation, only regards it as one of several non-elite groupings (O'Brien, 2000b: 89; see also O'Brien et al., 2000: 67–108, especially 74–7). In short, a pluralist conceptualisation of policy-making is simply transferred from the national to the international level.

While the liberal perspectives of globalisation and the related structural changes are a clear progress in relation to neo-realist and CPE accounts, the fundamental role of labour and trade unions stemming from the capitalist social relations of production, and thus the very nature of the structural changes related to globalisation, is still overlooked. As Coates makes clear, this neglect is mainly the result of an undue focus on capital mobility as the core feature of globalisation. Capital is regarded in a fetishised form as a 'thing' instead of a 'social relationship'. Thereby, it is overlooked that capital can only realise itself on a global scale to the extent that real production processes are created on this scale. 'The enhanced global mobility of capital in the last three decades has social rather than technical roots. Capital is more geographically mobile than it was in the past because it now has more proletariats on which to land' (Coates, 2000: 255). Van Apeldoorn picks up on this neglect of the underlying power structure by liberal approaches and accuses them of being actor-centred, conceptualising 'transnational actors as autonomous entities rather than as embedded in, and indeed constituted by, transnational structures' (van Apeldoorn, 2004: 148). By abstracting interest group interaction from the underlying power structure, however, it is overlooked that there are significant structural power asymmetries, placing especially transnational capital in a privileged position (van Apeldoorn, 2004: 163). Burnham formulates a fundamental criticism of both neo-realist and liberal approaches in IR/IPE, highlighting the conceptual problems leading to these shortcomings identified by Coates and van Apeldoorn.

Most importantly, he criticises mainstream IR/IPE theories for taking 'state' and 'market' in the form of two separate entities as their starting-point of investigation. Hence, '"the state" is fetishised whilst "the market" is dehistoricised and viewed as a technical arena in which the "external" state "intervenes"' (Burnham, 1995: 136). What is, therefore, overlooked is the apparent separation of state and market as an historically specific condition of capitalism. As the social relations of production are organised around private property and wage labour in capitalism, the extraction of surplus labour is not directly politically enforced, because those who do not own the means of production are 'free' to sell their labour (Holloway and Picciotto, 1977: 79; Wood, 1995: 29, 34). Mainstream IR/IPE approaches, however, do not understand the political and economic, the state and market as different forms or expressions of the very same social relations of production. Hence, they find it impossible to consider the internal relationship between the 'state' and 'market', the way, for example, how the former secures the functioning of the latter through the guarantee of private property, the contractual relationship between employer and employee and the process of commodity exchange (Burnham, 1995: 145; Smith, 2002: 262). As a result, 'state' and 'market' are reified and 'state managers confront the implications of economic globalization and footloose transnational capital as an external logic' (Robinson, 2001: 162). This criticism can also be applied to CPE approaches. Understanding the sectoral orientation of unions, for example, as one independent explanatory variable next to other variables such as inter-union competition, union-party relationship and historical attitude on European integration (Josselin, 2001: 56–9) implies an empirical pluralism, which falls into precisely this trap of separating the state from the market and the political from the economic in an ahistoric way. By extension, due to the lack of problematising the internal relationship between state and market, the underlying rationale of activities cannot be assessed by mainstream approaches. For example, Josselin's analysis of unions' positions on EMU remains within the realm of the given and can only examine whether the unions are in favour of European integration in general and EMU in particular (Josselin, 2001: 71). What cannot be analysed is the social purpose underlying unions' actions, indicating what type of EU trade unions aspire to in relation to neo-liberal restructuring, which is at the core of this study. In order to overcome these dichotomies of the economic and the political, the state and market, as well as the national and the global, the next section introduces a neo-Gramscian, historical materialist alternative, which starts an investigation through a focus on the social relations of production.

A historical materialist, neo-Gramscian approach to labour

Neo-Gramscian perspectives are heavily influenced by the work of the Italian Marxist Antonio Gramsci. While one has to appreciate the specific historical circumstances of Gramsci's concepts, these concepts can, nonetheless, be transferred to other historical periods and fruitfully employed in empirical research

(Morton, 2003a). Neo-Gramscian perspectives were introduced by Robert Cox in IPE in two seminal articles in the early 1980s (Cox, 1981 and 1983).[5] At the centre of neo-Gramscian approaches is the notion of hegemony. It appears as an expression of broadly based consent, manifested in the acceptance of ideas and supported by material resources and institutions, which is initially established by social forces occupying a leading role within a state, but is then projected outwards on a world scale. Within a world order a situation of hegemony may prevail 'based on a coherent conjunction or fit between a configuration of material power, the prevalent collective image of world order (including certain norms) and a set of institutions which administer the order with a certain semblance of universality' (Cox 1981: 139). Hegemony is therefore a form of dominance that relies predominantly on consensus rather than coercion.

Hegemony is constituted on three levels of activity within a historical structure: *the social relations of production*, encompassing the totality of social relations in material, institutional and discursive forms that engender particular social forces; *forms of state*, consisting of historically contingent state-civil society complexes; and *world orders*, which not only represent phases of stability and conflict but also permit scope for thinking about how alternative forms of world order might emerge. Within each of the three main levels it is argued that three further elements reciprocally combine to constitute an historical structure: *ideas*, understood as intersubjective meanings as well as collective images of world order; *material capabilities*, referring to accumulated resources; and *institutions*, which are amalgams of the previous two elements and are means of stabilising a particular order (Cox 1981: 135–8). According to Cox (1987: 1–9), patterns of production relations are the starting-point for analysing the operation and mechanisms of hegemony. Importantly, production is understood in a wide sense, covering the production of physical goods as well as related knowledge, social relations and institutions (Cox, 1989: 39). The separation of state and market is avoided through the realisation that both are the expression of the same configuration of social forces. At the same time, this does not imply economic determinism. Neo-Gramscian perspectives as a version of historical materialism do not think in terms of a strictly separated structure and superstructure dichotomy. Rather, 'the productive base itself exists in the shape of social, juridical and political forms – in particular, forms of property and domination' (Wood, 1995: 22).

Hegemony is, however, always contested and needs to be constantly reconfirmed. Thus, hegemony is based on class struggle, driving confirmation and transformation within existing orders at the different levels of activity. As a result of this focus on class struggle, a neo-Gramscian analysis is open-ended. It 'rejects the notion of objective laws of history and focuses upon class struggle [be they intra-class or inter-class] as the heuristic model for the understanding of structural change' (Cox with Sinclair, 1996: 57–8). The essence of class struggle is exploitation and resistance to it. As Ste Croix makes clear, 'bring back exploitation as the hallmark of class, and at once class struggle is in the forefront, as it should be' (Ste Croix, 1981: 57). The analysis of opposed class fractions around exploitation and resistance to it in concrete historical situations implies the potential for alternative forms of development. The patterns or production are referred to as modes of social relations of production, which encapsulate configurations of social forces engaged in the process of production. By discerning different modes of social relations of production it is possible to consider how changing production relations give rise to particular social forces that become the basis of power within and across states and within a specific world order (Cox, 1987: 4). Thus, the investigation of the social relations of production allows neo-Gramscian perspectives to identify social forces or class fractions as the most important collective actors as engendered by the production process.

The next sub-section will analyse the changing social relations of production in times of globalisation, before attention is turned to the special role of ideas in class struggle and how this is played out at the world order level of activity. This is followed by a discussion of the conceptualisation of forms of state in relation to class struggle.

Global restructuring, social forces and class struggle

When defining class from a historical materialist perspective, the Weberian focus on status and social stratification, where the working class is sometimes contrasted with the middle and upper classes (e.g. Collier, 1999: 18), must be avoided (Ste Croix, 1981: 85–91). Instead, by class is meant 'a group of people who share a common relationship to the process of social production and reproduction and are constituted relationally on the basis of social power struggles' (Robinson, 2004: 37). Capitalism in general leads to a division between capital, the owners of the means of production, on the one hand, and labour, those who are 'free' to sell their labour power on the market, on the other. Nevertheless, due to the diversity of the way production is organised, there are rarely two homogeneous classes opposing each other in capitalism. Instead, a whole range of different class fractions can be distinguished. Cox identifies different class fractions though an analysis of the level at which production is organised. Because of the partial transnationalisation of national production and financial systems due to globalisation (see Chapter 3), he argues that 'it becomes increasingly pertinent to think in terms of a global class structure alongside or superimposed upon national class structures' (Cox, 1981: 147; see also Cox, 1993: 259–60). In other words, the transnationalisation of production and finance has engendered new, transnational social forces of capital and labour, which are potentially in conflict with national capital and labour (van Apeldoorn, 2002: 26–34; Robinson, 2004: 49–53; Robinson and Harris, 2000: 12–18). The latter can be further subdivided in nationally oriented social forces, engendered by production processes organised at the national level producing predominantly for domestic consumption, and internationally oriented social forces, stemming from national production, which is geared towards export markets (Bieler, 2000: 9–14). At the European level, it is possible to distinguish between European transnational forces, engendered by production structures organised across borders within Europe, and global forces of capital and labour, stemming from production structures across the world (van Apeldoorn, 2002: 47; Holman, 1992: 15–16).[6] Importantly for this study, Cox does not only identify a split between national and transnational labour fractions. He also points to a likely division between established workers often employed directly by TNCs on the one hand, and less privileged workers on temporary and part-time, hourly paid contracts in the periphery of the labour market on the other (Cox, 1981: 235). This split can be identified when analysing French and Swedish trade union confederations' positions on EMU in Chapter 5. In contrast to other confederations analysed in this study, the Swedish SACO and the French CFE-CGC, which both represent highly educated employees in positions with management responsibilities, were enthusiastic about EMU and the related neo-liberal restructuring and did not pose preconditions for their support. In general, the identification of social forces as engendered by production allows neo-Gramscian perspectives to go beyond simply analysing globalisation as external pressures. They can also focus on the agency behind it and here especially transnational capital and its hegemonic project of neo-liberal economics (see below).

The division between national and transnational forces of capital and labour is, however, only one potential way of identifying different class fractions. Drawing on Marx, van der Pijl outlines the capital fractions approach, considering the different functional forms of capital within the overall process of surplus accumulation. He concludes that due to their different position in the production process, finance capital, consisting of money capital and commercial capital in the sphere of circulation, is likely to have different interests than industrial/productive capital (van der Pijl, 1984: 4–20). For the purpose of this book, focusing on labour and trade unions as its representatives, the relationship between finance and industrial capital is treated as an important structural condition, within which trade unions operate at the national level (see Chapter 4). In relation to the question of unions' positions on EMU and European co-operation, a split of labour fractions along this line is, however, of no explanatory value. As Robinson and Harris make clear in relation to transnational capital, the division between money, commercial and productive capital, forming an interdependent complex, is clearly less relevant than the division between national and transnational capital. After all 'most transnational units of production are simultaneously involved directly or indirectly in financial, productive and commercial capital operations and investment' (Robinson and Harris, 2000: 25; see also Robinson, 2004: 51–3). Sklair's research on the Fortune Global 500 TNCs confirms this conclusion in that many of the TNCs operate across different sectors (Sklair, 2001a: 38–9, 42). 'For the global capitalist system as a whole, these intraclass struggles are less important than what binds the members of the class together globally, namely their common interest in the protection of private property and the rights of private individuals to accumulate it with as little interference as possible' (Sklair, 2001a: 12).

CPE approaches sometimes point to deindustrialisation and the concomitant shift from manufacturing employment to service sector employment and the related split between blue-collar workers and white-collar workers as the more significant fragmentation of the working class (Iversen and Pontusson, 2000: 25; see also Kitschelt et al., 1999b: 445–6). My argument is, however, that this split is secondary to the split between national and transnational labour and, by extension, irrelevant for the issues under investigation in this book. Sweden, one of the few European countries where there exist separate trade unions for blue-collar workers, LO and its affiliates, and white-collar workers, TCO and SACO and their affiliates, is a good example in this respect. It is correct that white-collar worker unions have become increasingly important as far as membership levels are concerned as well as their impact on policy-making vis-à-vis the state and employers. Nevertheless, as it will be demonstrated in Chapter 6, this did not lead to positions on EMU different from those by Swedish blue-collar transnational sector unions. What influenced these unions' positions was the organisation of production across borders in their sectors, not the particular status of workers within transnational production.

Finally, a distinction between labour of the public and private sectors is frequently made, based on the argument that the public sector constitutes an unproductive, but potentially strong labour dimension vis-à-vis government, leading to a potential conflict with private sector unions over the appropriate level of wage increases (e.g. Garrett and Way, 2000). Clearly, the public sector has a specific role within the capitalist economy. Throughout the post-war decades, it has been largely removed from the pressures of market competition aiming at the goal of providing equal services to those in need, regardless of their capacity to pay. Unsurprisingly, it is now the public sector, which is specifically under neo-liberal restructuring pressure. Chapters 8 and 9 will look at trade unions' attempts to counter this threat through co-operation at the European level and closer co-operation with other social movements. However, for the question of unions' positions on EMU and European co-operation, the distinction between public and private sector unions is not helpful. National production sectors, whether they are private or public, service or industry sectors, are likely to differ in their positions on EMU and European co-operation from transnational production sectors, due to their continuing reliance on the state as far as national regulations and financial subsidies are concerned. UNISON, the main British public sector trade union, was as opposed to the restrictive fiscal policy implications of EMU as was the private, but national production sector Union of Construction, Allied Trades and Technicians (UCATT), organising workers in the British construction industry (see Chapter 7).[7] Moreover, once a domestic production sector becomes transnationalised, as for example telecommunications, the position of a trade union in this sector may change. The fact that this traditional national monopoly has been deregulated and privatised is less significant than that privatisation has led to a transnationalisation of production across borders. I will come back to this issue throughout the book when analysing the concrete positions of various trade unions.

The focus on exploitation and resistance makes it possible to extend the notion of class struggle beyond the immediate sphere of production and the workplace. As van der Pijl argues, neo-liberal capitalism is characterised by the fact that capitalist discipline has now also been further extended within the entire process of social reproduction, involving the exploitation of the social and natural substratum. In response to the commodification of social services and the intensified destruction of the biosphere as well as the disruption of traditional life, a whole range of new, progressive but also nationalist rightwing social movements have emerged to defend the environment and sphere of social reproduction (van der Pijl, 1998: 46–8; see also Bakker and Gill, 2003; Cox, 1992: 35; and Rupert, 2000). This has to be analysed as class struggle as much as exploitation and resistance to it in the workplace. Especially in Chapters 8 and 9, I will come back to this wider definition when analysing the increasing co-operation between trade unions and other progressive social movements in the resistance to neo-liberal restructuring.

Importantly, the identification of social forces does not imply that the interests, identity and political strategies are determined by these forces' location in the production process. Production may shape social forces' outlook, but one cannot reduce their behaviour to it. In short, one can only identify the relevant social forces as core actors and may formulate hypotheses for research on the basis of the specific social relations of production (see below). This understanding of production is closely related to Gramsci's own rejection of all kinds of economism, including the idea that communism will come about as a result of an inevitable, automatic historical development (Gramsci, 1971: 168). Moreover, while economic classes exist by themselves through their place in the production structure, class membership does not automatically imply class-consciousness and common class identity and interests (Ste Croix, 1981: 44). Class-consciousness emerges out of particular historical contexts of struggle rather than mechanically deriving from objective determinations that have an automatic place in production relations. People 'identify points of antagonistic interest, they commence to struggle around these issues and in the process of struggling they discover themselves as classes, they come to know this discovery as class-consciousness' (Thompson, 1978: 149; see also Morton, 2006: 66). In other words, a class may exist as a class-in-itself due to the way production is organised, while it has not yet developed a class-consciousness in struggle and, thus, become a class-for-itself. Robinson and Harris, for example, argue that while transnational capital has become a class-in-itself and for-itself, transnational labour so far has only developed into a class-in-itself resulting from transnational production (Robinson and Harris, 2000: 21–3; see also Robinson, 2004: 43). Thus, 'class interest, class position, and material factors are useful, even necessary, starting points in the analysis of any ideological formation. But they are not sufficient – because they are not sufficiently determinate – to account for the actual empirical disposition and movement of ideas in real historical societies' (Hall quoted in Rupert, 2000: 13). Hence, production is determining only in the first instance. How social forces operate in a particular situation has to be established in an empirical investigation. 'The class-based relations of production under capitalism create the possibility of particular kinds of agency, but this potential can only be realised through the political practices of concretely situated social actors' (Rupert, 2000: 14). A neo-Gramscian perspective, thus, implies a dialectical analysis of structure and agency, where there are always several possible courses of class struggle within a given structural framework (Bieler and Morton, 2001b: 16–29). And it is in this practice of class struggle that ideas play an important role. As Gramsci points out, 'it is on the level of ideologies that men become conscious of conflicts in the world of the economy' (Gramsci, 1971: 162).

Class struggle and the material structure of ideas

Social constructivist approaches recognise that ideas in the form of 'intersubjective meanings', which are 'the product of the collective self-interpretations and self-definitions of human communities' (Neufeld, 1995: 77), can become part of the overall structure. According to Adler, for example, 'constructivism is the view that the manner in which the material world shapes and is shaped by human action and interaction depends on dynamic normative and epistemic interpretations of the material world' (Adler, 1997: 322). Nevertheless, as argued elsewhere, the general problem of constructivism is that it cannot address the question of why certain ideas become part of the structure at a particular time and not others, because it overlooks the material structure of ideas, i.e. the interests behind particular discourses (Bieler, 2001: 97).[8] In order to go beyond the limits of constructivism, a reference to Gramsci's definition of 'organic ideas' is helpful. Only those ideas are organic that 'organise human masses, and create the terrain on which men move, acquire consciousness of their position, struggle, etc.' (Gramsci, 1971: 377). Only those ideas are relevant that are in a dialectical relationship with the social relations of production. 'Ideas only become effective if they do, in the end, connect with a particular constellation of social forces' (Hall, 1986: 42). According to Gramsci, therefore, ideologies are produced as a result of class struggle and are thus closely linked to conflicts rooted in the economic structure. For Gramsci, organic intellectuals, emerging from and representing particular fractions of social forces (Gramsci, 1971: 5), play an important role in the class struggle over which ideas become part of the social structure in the form of intersubjective meanings, thereby linking the world of production with the political realm (Vacca, 1982: 37). Organic intellectuals do not simply produce ideas, but they concretise and articulate strategies in complex and often contradictory ways, which is possible because of their class location, i.e. proximity to the most powerful forces in production. It is their task to develop a hegemonic project, which brings 'the interests of the leading class into harmony with those of subordinate classes and incorporates these other interests into an ideology expressed in universal terms' (Cox, 1983: 168). It is, therefore, essential to reveal the social function of organic intellectuals as representatives of class fractions within instances of class struggle (Morton, 2003b: 29–33).

If successful, a hegemonic project leads to the establishment of an historical bloc, which 'is the term applied to the particular configuration of social classes and ideology that gives content to a historical state' (Cox, 1987: 409) and, thus, consists of structure and superstructure. It forms a complex, politically contestable and dynamic ensemble of social relations, which includes economic, political and cultural aspects. The relationship between structure and superstructure is reciprocal. 'Superstructures of ideology and political organisation shape the development of both aspects of production ... [i.e. the social relations and the physical means of production] ... and are shaped by them' (Cox, 1983: 168). In short, an historical bloc indicates the integration of a variety of different class interests that are propagated throughout society 'bringing about not only a unison of economic and political aims, but also intellectual and moral unity ... on a "universal" plane' (Gramsci, 1971: 181–2). This notion of historical bloc consisting of material properties and ideas indicates yet again how ideas, subsumed within the material structure, are an independent but related part of a neo-Gramscian perspective.

It is this type of analysis that allows us to understand why certain ideas pushed by powerful social forces have become part of the overall structure in the form of intersubjective meanings and not others as a result of class struggle. Thereby, the trap of falling into economic determinism, which regards ideas merely as a reflection of material structure, is avoided. Second, this analysis equally bypasses the danger of empirical pluralism, which treats ideas as an explanatory factor completely independent from material social conditions. Clearly, an over-emphasis on ideas implies as much the danger of explanatory determinism as an over-emphasis on material structure. Ideologically, for example, it is sometimes distinguished between 'activist' and 'accommodationist' unions in the German case. While the former are supposed to be fundamentally critical of Germany's political economy and work towards significant social reform, the latter are considered to stress the common interests of capital and labour and work towards a strong social partnership (Markovits and Otto, 1993: 49). It is, however, dangerous to define the ideology of a particular trade union a priori along one of these two lines and then explain its behaviour as a result of it. As Silvia makes clear, 'in practice, this distinction was more often a matter of style than of substance' (Silvia, 1999: 95). Theoretically, it is as deterministic and reductionist as the idea that a particular location in the production process determines a union's strategy. Hyman's (2001) typology of three different national types of unionism each linked to a particular ideology is similarly dangerous. He distinguishes (1) business unionism and its focus on material gains for members through collective bargaining; (2) trade unionism as a vehicle for social integration through improvements in welfare provisions; and (3) radical-oppositional unionism with the goal to advance class interests. By explaining unions' activities through a reference to their particular type of national unionism and, thus ideology, Hyman falls into a deterministic trap and is unable to incorporate the possibility of a change in strategy and ideology despite the historical tradition of a particular labour movement. Of course, the institutional legacy, including norms and values (see below), shapes unions' outlook and strategy. It does not, however, determine them. Hence, the ideology a particular union adopts, the identity it assumes and the way this informs its strategies is a matter of empirical investigation in this study. Whatever the position of a trade union on EMU and European co-operation, this does not determine its position vis-à-vis neo-liberal restructuring. Support on both accounts may high-light an acceptance of neo-liberalism and further European integration along neo-liberal lines. It may also, however, signify a tactical acceptance of the new importance of the European level in decision-making, being used to counter neo-liberal restructuring more effectively.

Returning to globalisation, neo-Gramscians add an ideological dimension to their definition. In addition to the transnationalisation of production and finance, a turn from Keynesian to neo-liberal policies and their focus on dereg-ulation, liberalisation and price stability has been identified behind global restructuring (Cox, 1993: 266–7). Neo-liberal economics first regained credi-bility in the 1970s as the successful political economy critique of Keynesianism, it was implemented during the 1980s especially in the British and US forms of state, before it gained hegemonic status in the 1990s at the world order level of activity (Gamble, 2001; Overbeek, 1999). Hence, 'the mainstream theory of international trade, and the liberal world-view in which it is embedded, consti-tute the governing ideology of the world economy and its central institutions' (Rupert, 2000: 54; see also Robinson, 2001: 184–6; Robinson and Harris, 2000: 41). The fact that neo-liberalism became dominant is, however, not due to some kind of inert qualities. Rather, it was its material structure, the fact that it was pushed by the increasingly structurally powerful class fraction of transnational capital, supported by important forms of state such as the USA and Britain as well as international organisations such as the IMF and World Bank, which pushed it to the fore. Neo-liberalism is further an organic ideology in that it has real material consequences in terms of the organisation of the political economy through market discipline, fiscal austerity, competition, privatisation and monetarism (see Chapter 4). In sum, neo-liberalism is understood as the hegemonic project of an emerging transnational historical bloc with the trans-national capitalist class (TCC) as its leading class fraction (Robinson, 2004: 47–9; Sklair, 2001a: 295), supported by its allies of small sub-contracting and supplying firms, specialised service companies such as accountants and privileged workers (Gill, 1995: 400–1). It is further assisted by the global corporate media, spreading the neo-liberal message, which holds this transnational historical bloc together (Robinson and Harris, 2000: 31).

On the basis of these considerations, the following general hypothesis can be formulated in relation to social forces' position within an integrating global economy along neo-liberal lines: That transnational social forces of capital and labour, the production process of which is organised across national borders, are more likely to be in favour of an open economy than national fractions of capital and labour. While the former depend on the free movement of goods and capital across borders in their business activities, the latter may still rely on state protectionism, which is undermined by an integrating global economy. As outlined in Chapter 1, European integration since 1985 has been part and parcel of globalisation. Hence, on the basis of the general hypothesis, the following hypothesis can be formulated in respect of trade unions' positions on EMU and co-operation at the European level:

> *Hypothesis 1*: A labour movement's position on EMU depends crucially on its length and degree of exposure to the competitive pressures of global-isation. Unions, which represent workers in transnational production sectors, are more likely to support EMU, because they may support their companies – on which their own well-being depends – which benefit from a stable monetary environment and institutionalised free trade within the EU. Moreover, because they realise that they have lost control over capital at the national level, they are probably prepared to co-operate with other unions at the European level. National production sector unions, on the other hand, are likely to oppose EMU, since it undermines national policy autonomy and, thus, the support, on which their sectors depend. Relying on the state, they may also be less concerned about European co-operation.

Importantly, however, whatever the position on EMU and regional co-operation, the issue of what type of European integration unions support has to be analysed separately. It is the notion of open-ended class struggle and the focus on the conflict at the level of ideas, which adds a critical dimension to neo-Gramscian perspectives and allows us to analyse the underlying purpose of European inte-gration as well as actors' strategies (van Apeldoorn, 2002: 11–13, 34–49; Bieler, 2000: 8). As Cox affirms, neo-Gramscian perspectives are a critical theory that 'does not take institutions and social and power relations for granted but calls them into question by concerning itself with their origins and how and whether they might be in the process of changing' (Cox 1981: 129). In this book, the focus is on the rationale of trade unions' activities and positions on EMU and European co-operation. Support for EMU and further European integration does not imply by default that trade unions have accepted neo-liberal economics. The reality of operating within a transnational production structure does not automatically determine these unions' ideological outlook. The empirical analysis of this book, therefore, also includes an investigation of the social purpose of trade unions' activities.

Social forces do not operate in a vacuum, but within a wider structure. The relevant structures of social forces are, first, the production system. It is, however, also the different national as well as European institutional set-ups, within and through which social forces operate. The next section will investigate how the neo-Gramscian perspective can be complemented with an emphasis on institu-tional structures, thereby referring to the second level of activity, forms of state.

Social forces within and through forms of state

The concept of form of state is concerned with the relationship between civil society and the state, and is defined in terms of the apparatus of administra-tion and of the historical bloc or class configuration that defines the *raison d'état* for that form (Cox, 1989: 41). States are, consequently, defined as a social relation that confronts social forces as structures within and through which they operate. Specific state projects within a particular form of state are the result of class struggle. Thus, in a historical materialist understanding, 'the state is the institutionalisation of class relations around a particular configuration of social production' (Robinson, 2001: 163). Transnational production implies that there are transnational class fractions. These do not, however, confront the state as an external actor, but are closely involved in the class struggle over the state project at the national level, and their interests may become internalised within the form of state in this process (Bieler and Morton, 2003: 485–9). The artificial separation between domestic and international spheres is, thereby, overcome, as is the separation between state and market. What is generally lacking, however, is a conceptualisation of the structural impact domestic institutions have on national and transnational social forces.

To overcome this shortcoming, the neo-Gramscian perspective proposed in this book can be extended with a 'strategic-relational' approach to the state, which analyses 'the state as a site of strategic selectivity' (Jessop, 1990: 193).[9] Jessop's strategic-relational approach to forms of state should not be understood as a separate approach, which is combined with a neo-Gramscian perspective. In fact, Jessop's work itself has significantly been influenced by Gramsci as far as understanding the state as a social relation, but also concepts such as hegemony, historical bloc and the role of intellectuals are concerned (Jessop, 2002: 6). Jessop distinguishes between the formal and the substantive aspects of the state. It is the substantive aspects, the social basis of the state and the nature of the hegemonic project, around which the exercise of state power is centred, which demonstrate the common conceptual basis with neo-Gramscian perspectives (Jessop, 1990: 207–14). In relation to the formal aspects of the state, considering the state as a social relation means that it can be analysed as the site, the generator and the product of strategies. With reference to the first point, 'as an institutional ensemble the state constitutes a terrain upon which different political forces attempt to impart a specific strategic direction to the individual or collective activities of its different branches' (Jessop, 1990: 268). Thus, the form of the state is the framework, within which various different strategies are possible. The state in this sense 'can never be considered as neutral. It has a necessary structural selectivity' (Jessop, 1990: 268), favouring certain strategies over others. Importantly, 'the differential impact of the state system on the capacity of different class (-relevant) forces to pursue their interests in different strategies over a given time horizon is not inscribed in the state system as such but in the relation between state structures and the strategies which different forces adopt towards it' (Jessop, 1990: 260). In other words, there is an analytic focus on structure and agency, i.e. strategy, when determining the impact of state institutions on agency. 'Applying this approach involves examining how a given structure may privilege some actors, some identities, some strategies, some spatial and temporal horizons, some actions over others; and the ways if any, in which actors (individual and/or collective) take account of this differential privileging through "strategic-context analysis" when choosing a course of action' (Jessop, 2001: 1223). Institutions select behaviour, but they do not fully determine them. Hence, within a given institutional, structural setting, there are always different possible strategies, from which actors can choose (see also Bieler and Morton, 2001b). Moreover, as an institutional ensemble, the state does not exercise power. 'It has only a set of institutional capacities and liabilities which mediate that power; the power of the state is the power of the forces acting in and through the state' (Jessop, 1990: 269–70; see also 366–7). This leads to the second point.

The state is a generator of strategies in the sense that the political forces in the state, i.e. state managers, can develop strategies to achieve unitary action of the state (Jessop, 1990: 261). Thus, the state must not be theorised in abstraction from state projects. 'To understand the never-ending and ever-renewed process of state formation it is not enough to examine its institutional building blocks. We must also consider the "state projects" which bond these blocks together with the result that the state gains a certain organizational unity and cohesiveness of purpose' (Jessop, 1990: 353; see also 358). When analysing the change in national forms of state, attention has to be paid to institutional changes. Additionally, however, the related social purpose of the state project is equally important. As the example of Austria in Chapter 4 demonstrates, it is possible that forms stay the same, while the social purpose within a particular form changes. Importantly, state power rests on a set of social relations, which goes beyond the narrow state apparatus and capacities and extends into civil society at the national level as well as the international level more generally (Jessop, 2002: 40–1).

Third, 'the structure and modus operandi of the state system can be understood in terms of their production in and through past political strategies and struggles' (Jessop, 1990: 261; see also Jessop, 2001: 1230). Hence, we have to see a given state structure in its historical context and have to acknowledge that this particular structure constrains present actors, on the one hand, which, however, might be able to change this structure via new strategies, on the other (Jessop, 1990: 353). 'Precisely because institutions are never fully constituted, space exists for competing institutional projects and designs' (Jessop, 2001: 1230). In sum, 'the form of the state is the crystallization of past strategies as well as privileging some over other current strategies. As a strategic terrain the state is located within a complex dialectic of structures and strategies' (Jessop, 1990: 269).

The EU, while clearly not a fully fledged state, shows state-like features in its elaborate institutional set-up including a host of different decision-making procedures, offering trade unions new points of contact for attempting to influence policy-making. The structural selectivity of the EU will be dealt with in detail in Chapter 8, when the activities of European-level trade unions are assessed. In Chapter 4, the focus is on the changing forms of state in the five case studies with a particular emphasis on the strategic-relational possibilities of unions at the national level. This leads to the following second hypothesis:

Hypothesis 2: Those trade unions, which have lost influence within the national institutional set-up, are more in favour of European co-operation and the establishment of an industrial relations system as well as social regulations at the European level to counter global pressures. By contrast, unions which still enjoy considerable impact on policy-making at the national level are likely to be less interested in European co-operation.[10]

This implies, of course, that the structural selectivity of a union's national institutional environment needs to be compared with its perceived possibilities within the European institutional set-up.

Conclusion

Due to its focus on the changing social relations of production in times of globalisation, neo-Gramscian approaches are able to comprehend transnational class formation around the emergence of new, transnational social forces. As a result, labour can be operationalised as a potential international actor, initially as a class-in-itself, potentially developing over time into a class-for-itself. Informed by these conceptual considerations, the next two chapters will lay the ground for the empirical analysis of this book. Chapter 3, in line with the neo-Gramscian emphasis on the social relations of production, will analyse to what extent production structures in the five country cases have become transnationalised in order to identify the likely class fractions to be observed. This relates especially to the first hypothesis about a probable split between national and transnational labour over EMU and European co-operation. Chapter 4 will then analyse the transnationalisation of state forms and the way and extent to which the interests of transnational forces have become internalised at the national level, changing the various state projects. This refers back to the second hypothesis about the degree of unions' political influence at the national level having an impact on their decision on whether to co-operate more extensively at the European level or not.

Notes

1 On the new importance of labour at the international level, see also Dunn (2004), Harrod and O'Brien (2002), Munck (2004) as well as Waterman and Wills (2001).
2 Working class/labour is here understood as a collective concept. 'What is at stake is not participation by atomized individual workers, but rather action in which some sense of solidarity or identity and collective purpose must be involved' (Collier, 1999: 15). Such common action is often organisationally expressed. Hence, when analysing collective action by workers, trade unions as the expression of workers' collective agency are an appropriate empirical focus.
3 For another, more recent example, see Menz's analysis of national response strategies to Europeanisation (Menz, 2005a: 21).
4 For examples of this problem, see Ferner and Hyman (1998), Hyman (2001) and Martin and Ross (1999a).

5 Since Robert Cox's path-breaking work in the early 1980s, a whole range of related, yet different neo-Gramscian perspectives have been developed. For an overview, see Bieler and Morton (2004a), Bieler (2005b) as well as the various contributions in Bieler and Morton (2005). The plural of perspectives is important, since it avoids the formation of a school of thought and the related loss of critical theoretical development (Morton, 2001).

6 Picciotto argues that such an approach of focusing on different class fractions is too formalistic and mechanistic, making it difficult to 'grasp the contradictions in the forms of domination' (Picciotto, 1991: 61). The task in this project is, however, to unpack the very processes of class struggle and hegemonic practices revolving around the social relations of production as expressed in trade unions' positions on EMU and European co-operation. Picciotto overlooks that the identification of various class fractions is only the starting-point of an investigation. How these fractions act is a matter of empirical research and not pre-determined by their location in the production process.

7 For an example of incorrectly identifying the split over EMU in the British labour movement as a split between public and private sector unions, see Sisson et al. (1999: 21).

8 Rosamond, for example, argues that the Commission uses patterns of rhetorical practice to expand its policy competencies within the EU (Rosamond, 2002: 162). Why this is done via a neo-liberal offensive, however, instead of an argument in favour of EU social policies and stronger European regulation, able to provide protection against the disruptive aspects of globalisation, cannot be accounted for. It is only when Rosamond refers to the close relationship between the Commission and the European Round Table of Industrialists (ERT), thereby referring to a neo-Gramscian analysis by van Apeldoorn (Rosamond, 2002: 170), that the material interests and power behind the neo-liberal project come to light.

9 Historical institutionalism provides an alternative approach of how to add a focus on the structural impact of institutions on processes of European integration (e.g. Armstrong and Bulmer, 1998). While it contains a useful reference to norms as part of the wider institutional structure, it has not been chosen here, because unlike the strategic-relational approach it (1) is almost exclusively focused on structure, disregarding the issue of agency, and (2) does not include a specific focus on the social relations of production and is, therefore, not directly compatible with a neo-Gramscian perspective.

10 Cumbers, by contrast, argues that those unions that are still strong at the national level, would be more likely to be involved in international strategies thanks to their stronger domestic resources as well as better links to their own government (Cumbers, 2004: 835). My argument is not that unions with a strong domestic position would not engage in international activities. Nevertheless, when focusing on the core union activities such as collective bargaining and lobbying governmental institutions, then a strong position within the domestic institutional set-up is likely to preclude an active engagement in these core areas at the European level.

Part II

Trade unions and the transnational restructuring of European social relations

3
Globalisation and the transnationalisation of the social relations of production

Introduction

In Chapter 2, the transnationalisation of finance and production have been identified as core changes within globalisation. This chapter will, first, look more closely at these restructuring processes and assess the related empirical claims. As it was outlined, neo-Gramscian perspectives concentrate on the social relations of production in order to identify social class forces as the main collective actors as engendered by production. Hence, in a second step this chapter will look more closely at the degree to which the production structures of the five case studies have become transnationalised and whether national and transnational forces of capital and labour can actually be identified in these countries. This will include a historical overview of the emergence of capitalism in Austria, Britain, France, Germany and Sweden, as well as a quantitative assessment of recent transnationalisation processes in these five countries.

Processes of transnational restructuring

The transnationalisation of finance

Since the early 1970s, the transnationalisation of finance has led to the emergence of a fully fledged global financial market. The first component of this process was the rise of financial off-shore markets. 'It was first in evidence in the 1960s when Britain and the United States strongly supported growth of the Euromarket in London' (Helleiner, 1994: 8). While the USA did not control the overseas business of US financial institutions and banks, Britain refused to regulate Dollar trading in London. As a consequence, 'the Eurodollar loan became a new unregulated growth point in the international financial system; and the faster US corporations moved to Europe, the faster their bankers followed to London, and later to other European cities' (Strange, 1994: 106). As non-national money markets, they offered a regulation-free environment for the trading of financial assets and, therefore, facilitated expansion (Gill and Law, 1988: 165,

174–6). Between 1973 and 1984, there was a dramatic rise in the off-shore markets to US$ 1000 billion, having been only US$ 3 billion and US$ 75 billion in 1960 and 1970 respectively (Strange, 1994: 107). The second component of the transnationalisation of finance goes hand in hand with the support of financial off-shore markets. Instead of responding with more regulation, 'the United States from the mid-1970s led the way to more deregulation of money markets and financial operators' (Strange, 1994: 110). Due to competitive pressure, the other two major financial centres responded swiftly. In 1979, the British government abolished overnight its forty-year-old system of capital controls, and Japan followed in the first half of the 1980s (Helleiner, 1994: 149–56). Then, the EU as a whole, New Zealand, Australia and the Scandinavian countries went down the same road (Helleiner, 1994: 156–66). States partly responded to external pressures, but partly also made conscious decisions in favour of deregulation. Some regarded deregulation as a way of competing successfully for FDI (Underhill, 1997a: 6), others contributed actively to the undermining of existing regulations by relying themselves increasingly on global financial markets in order to finance balance of payment deficits and expanding welfare services in the 1970s (Underhill, 1997b: 105). Eventually, due to the deregulation of national financial markets, the differences between them and off-shore markets disappeared and, as a result, an integrated global financial market emerged with the following core characteristics: '(a) the blurring of the line, in terms of ownership structures and market activities, between banking, securities and insurance industries, a process referred to as desegmentation; (b) the liberalisation of traditional cartel arrangements in national sectors through domestic market-oriented reform programmes, understood as marketisation; and (c) the integration of financial markets across traditionally closed national jurisdictions, or transnationalisation' (Underhill, 1997a: 3).

This is also acknowledged by Hirst and Thompson. 'With the progressive harmonization of banking regulations and the abandonment of capital controls this form of integration was effectively established between the advanced countries by 1993' (Hirst and Thompson, 1999: 36). They argue, however, that the period of the Gold Standard and not the current period presented the most interdependent and integrated international economy. Today, the world market, for example, is less integrated in the area of security markets. Additionally, there is a persistent correlation between national savings and investment, and a wide variation between countries in terms of the importance of foreign holdings. They conclude that 'from all these figures what is clear is that there is no obvious convergence of all the advanced countries to a common openness position. By and large the differences between them seem to have been maintained, indicating continued variation in the characteristics and structures of their domestic financial systems' (Hirst and Thompson, 1999: 47). Nevertheless, whether financial markets were more integrated during the Gold Standard period than today is of secondary importance. What is crucial is that there was a clear change in the international monetary system between the first three post-war decades and today. Moreover, while the continuing differences between national financial systems should not be overlooked, it would be incorrect to argue that nothing has changed. National financial markets have increasingly become deregulated, which facilitated the free movement of capital and the related speculative world-wide financial investments. Scholte points to the dramatic increase in the commodification of finance capital. New financial centres have multiplied throughout the world and a drastic proliferation of new types of financial instruments has occurred. 'Global banking, global securities and global derivatives business have hugely increased both the volume and the variety of financial instruments that serve not so much as facilitators of other kinds of production, but as channels of accumulation in their own right' (Scholte, 2000a: 113). As a result, finance has become de-linked from the real economy. 'The annual turnover on world financial markets in the mid 1990s topped US$ 1,000 trillion, while world GDP was still well below US$ 30 trillion' (Scholte, 2000a: 117).

All five case studies of this book have been affected by the transnationalisation of finance. As EU members, the five countries have been subject to the pressures emanating from the creation of an integrated European financial space, briefly referred to in Chapter 1. This does not imply that all five countries have the same financial system – there is a continuing difference as far as the relationship between finance and industrial capital in these countries is concerned – but there have been parallel moves of deregulating national financial markets across the EU from the mid-1980s onwards. In Chapter 4, the exact changes of the five national financial systems will be discussed in detail.

The transnationalisation of production

Scholte identifies the following characteristics of transnational production:

> [I]n so-called 'global factories', different stages of a production process are sited at several (perhaps widely scattered) locations. Thus, in principle, the research centre, design unit, procurement office, fabrication plant, finishing point, assembly line, quality control operations, data processing office, advertising bureau and after-sales service could each be situated in different provinces, countries and regions. Supraterritorial production involves intra-firm trade within a global company as well as, if not more than, international trade between countries. Through so-called 'global sourcing', a producer draws the necessary inputs from anywhere in the global production chain. Supraterritorial production has developed especially in the manufacture of textiles, clothing, motor vehicles, leather goods, sports articles, toys, optical products, consumer electronics, semiconductors, aeroplanes and construction equipment. (Scholte, 2000a: 51–2)

TNCs are at the core of transnational production. When analysing the emergence of a TCC related to TNCs, Sklair (2001a) focuses on the Fortune Global 500 companies, i.e. the 500 biggest TNCs according to the magazine *Fortune*. His analysis makes clear that these large companies regard themselves less and less as national companies with units abroad and 'start to think and act more in terms of "competitive strategies for global marketing"' (Sklair, 2001a: 74). Nevertheless, while the focus on the biggest TNCs is a good way of establishing that something more fundamental has happened in the sphere of production, it does not really give us an idea about the overall importance of transnational production. The rise in FDI is a better indicator of the increasing importance of transnational production because it includes instances of transnational production beyond the biggest TNCs. 'Since FDI, by definition involves the establishment of lasting managerial control, it creates networks of ongoing relationships between parent firms and foreign affiliates and, increasingly, among foreign affiliates' (UN, 1992: 252). Outflows of FDI rose from US$ 88 billion to US$ 225 billion between 1986 and 1990, which is an annual increase of 26 per cent (UN, 1992: 14). There was a downturn in FDI in 1991 and 1992, mainly due to recessions in the biggest economies, but it picked up again from 1993 onwards up to US$ 1187 billion in 2000 as peak year. A new period of recession is reflected in the decline of outflows of FDI three years in a row down to US$ 612 billion in 2003 (UN, 2004: 372). This should not make us overlook, however, the general development of rising FDI as an indicator of the increasing transnationalisation of production. In 2004, first indicators of a recovery of FDI were noted and it is clear that there is no general reversal of the transnationalisation of production (UN, 2004: XVII). If at all, it is the speed of these changes that has slowed down temporarily, but the general direction of how production is increasingly organised across borders remains the same. The significance of FDI demonstrates the close connection between the transnationalisation of production and finance. The deregulation of national currency control systems was a precondition for the free movement of capital, making an increased level of FDI possible.

The increase in FDI on its own, however, does not indicate the overall importance of TNCs in the global economy. One way of doing this is to compare FDI with world exports and world output. Between 1983 and 1989, outflows in FDI increased about three times faster than world exports and roughly four times faster than world output (UN, 1991: 4). 'Between 1985 and 1995 FDI flows expanded at an average rate of 18.4 per cent compared with an annual rate of 11 per cent for global merchandise trade, and 8.5 per cent for world GDP' (Hirst and Thompson, 1999: 69). This is further confirmed by the indicator of the global sales of foreign affiliates in host countries, which is better suited for the comparison with trade flows since it includes the value of output of TNCs' activities in contrast to FDI. Including world exports of commercial services and excluding intra-firm trade, global sales of foreign affiliates were US$ 17,580 billion in comparison to world exports of goods and non-factor services of US$ 9228 billion in 2003 (UN, 2004: 9). Thus, 'global sales of affiliates are considerably more important than exports in delivering goods and services to markets world-wide, which underlines the importance of TNCs in structuring international economic relations' (UN, 1992: 54).

Weiss criticises FDI as a useful indicator of transnationalisation in three ways. First, she argues that most of FDI is destined for non-manufacturing sectors. 'A rising level of FDI in [construction, real-estate markets and financial services] would clearly increase the level of "foreign ownership". But it is hard to see how this has much to do with advancement of the "globalisation of production"'

(Weiss, 1998: 173). This is an important intervention and highlights that FDI levels may overstate the extent of a transnational production structure. In other aspects, however, FDI also understates the extent of transnational production and this may counterweight Weiss' point. TNCs are not only directly important as far as their economic activities are concerned, but also indirectly through their impact on the industries around them in the various host countries. They are not only responsible for the jobs of the people they directly employ, but also for the jobs of those companies that function as their local suppliers. According to Ruigrok and van Tulder, the indirect impact of TNCs on employment is about as large as their responsibility for direct employment (Ruigrok and van Tulder, 1995: 155). Held et al. too argue that FDI understates the degree of transnationalisation of production:

> First, FDI accounts for only approximately 25 per cent of total investment in international production – in the foreign affiliates of multinational corporations – since [TNCs] raise investment capital from a variety of sources to complement their FDI ...; second, as noted, global production and distribution systems do not depend solely on ownership or control but rather may simply involve cross-border production networks between firms. (Held et al., 1999: 237)

Due to new technology, small- and medium-sized enterprises (SMEs) have increasingly been incorporated in transnational production systems as supplier companies to TNCs or started themselves co-operating with other SMEs across borders. Especially cross-border interfirm agreements support the notion of an emerging transnational production system. 'In 1990 there were 1,700 such interfirm agreements, but by 1995 there were some 4,600' (Held et al., 1999: 247). Overall, 'this phenomenal spread since the late 1970s of diverse new economic arrangements, such as outsourcing, subcontracting, transnational intercorporate alliances, licensing agreements, local representation, and so on, parallels the proliferation of FDI, mergers and acquisitions, and underscores another major aspect of the transnational linkage of capitals' (Robinson and Harris, 2000: 38).

Second, Weiss points to the predominance of mergers and acquisitions within manufacturing FDI. 'But mergers and acquisitions (M&A) investment is often of the "arm's-length" variety. This makes it much closer in character to the "portfolio" type of investment (though less short-term in character), and it therefore has little significance for the internationalization of production' (Weiss, 1998: 173). This point seems to be rather overstated. Any acquisition abroad gives TNCs leeway when they have to decide about which production locations to expand and which to cut back and thus increases their structural power vis-à-vis host countries. 'Regardless of whether foreign affiliates are established through new (greenfield) investment or M&As, the upshot is to increase the share of international production activities that comes under the common governance of TNCs' (UN, 1999: 12). Due to increased M&A activities, 'globalizing capitalism has brought substantially increased concentration to many areas of production' (Scholte, 2000a: 129), thereby further increasing capital's structural power. Robinson and Harris (2000: 33) even argue that 'within the last two decades cross-border acquisitions and mergers have become one of the most important ways for firms to expand their activities transnationally'.

Finally, Weiss points to the preponderance of portfolio investment over FDI as part of total long-term transfers (Weiss, 1998: 174). While this is correct as far as the magnitude of flows is concerned – in the 1990s, portfolio capital was three times as large as FDI (Scholte, 2000a: 117) – what is interesting here is that rising FDI has involved the establishment of lasting cross-border production links. It does not really matter that these flows are smaller than portfolio flows. Moreover, high levels of portfolio investment refer to the transnationalisation of finance and are, therefore, as much part of globalisation as rising levels of FDI. These two factors cannot be analytically counterpoised. In sum, FDI levels are a meaningful indicator of the transnationalisation of production, as long as some qualifications are kept in mind.

Hirst and Thompson are further prominent critics of the idea of globalisation. They argue that the international economy was more open in the pre-1914 period than in the period from the 1970s onwards. 'International trade and capital flows . . . were more important relative to GDP levels before the First World War than they probably are today' (Hirst and Thompson, 1999: 32). Hirst and Thompson overlook, however, two crucial points. First, the ratio of exports to GDP is an indicator of the internationalisation of a country's production structure, not of its transnationalisation, since it captures the flow of goods, which are produced by domestic production for the sale abroad. Second, FDI flows are not of a similar nature to trade flows. FDI does not end with the initial transaction. It is an indicator for the establishment of transnational production units, i.e. longer lasting links between economic agents across borders. This is best expressed by the outward stock of FDI. These stocks of productive assets increased by more than 4.5 times from US\$ 1758 billion to US\$ 8197 billion between 1990 and 2003 (UN, 2004: 382; see also Robinson, 2004: 14–16). Thus, despite the temporary decline in outward FDI, indicated above, transnational production as a whole is still increasing, although at a slightly slower rate since 2001. A study of TNCs by the UN concluded in 1992 that 'the growth of cross-national production networks of goods and services of some 35,000 transnational corporations and their more than 150,000 foreign affiliates is beginning to give rise to a [transnational] production system, organized and managed by transnational corporations' (UN, 1992: 5). These figures further increased to 61,582 parent corporations and 926,948 foreign affiliates by 2003 (UN, 2004: 274). In short, 'while analyses of world trade are very important, we need to focus on the production relations that underpin market relations and the social forces that drive production relations in order to identify what is qualitatively new in the current epoch' (Robinson, 2004: 22).

In their rejection of globalisation, Hirst and Thompson further point out that FDI is not globally spread in an equal way, but concentrated within the Triad of North America, Japan and the European Economic Area in respect of both the originators of and destination for FDI. 'Sixty per cent of the flows of FDI over the period 1991–1996 were between just the members of the Triad bloc, which

also accounted for 75 per cent of the total accumulated stock of FDI in 1995'
(Hirst and Thompson, 1999: 70–1). As a result, Ruigrok and van Tulder suggest
speaking about 'Triadisation' rather than globalisation. 'It is worthwhile recalling
that in 1987 the Triad population accounted for only around 15 per cent of the
total world's population' (Ruigrok and van Tulder, 1995: 151). This concentration on the Triad also underlines Weiss' point that 'world trade, production
and investment remain highly concentrated in the wealthy northern countries
of the OECD' (Weiss, 1998: 176). In short, the claim is that the processes
normally referred to as globalisation are in fact only occurring within the wealthy,
mainly Northern countries and there in particular between the three regions of
the Triad. Nevertheless, as Held et al. make clear, 'although there may be a
regional clustering of FDI stocks, there can be no disputing that the data demonstrates significant interregional flows of FDI. In the terms of this study, such
FDI flows are clearly a global phenomenon. The fact that FDI is concentrated
among OECD countries reflects its stratification rather than its regionalization:
that is, it is uneven and organized hierarchically' (Held et al., 1999: 250; see also
270). Thus, while the transnationalisation of production may not be a worldwide phenomenon, but concentrated on the Triad, for the areas of the Triad
including the EU it is reality. In other words, 'regionalization can be seen as a
form of globalization by virtue of the fact that most foreign direct investment
by TNCs is concentrated in the three main regional blocs' (Sklair, 2001b: 67).

Moreover, Hirst and Thompson stress the fact that there are only few 'real'
TNCs without the identification of a home region/country, an internationalised
management and the willingness to invest in the world, wherever the highest
and/or most secure returns are to be expected. Instead, the international economy
is characterised by MNCs, which are still predominantly concentrated on a
home region/country with reference to their assets, sales and profit distribution
(Hirst and Thompson, 1999: 79–84; see also Weiss, 1998: 185). Ruigrok and van
Tulder's identification of two rival globalisation strategies is useful for the definition of TNCs and MNCs. 'Firms adopting a globalisation strategy strive for a
worldwide intra-firm division of labour, whereas firms following a glocalisation
strategy will seek a geographically concentrated inter-firm division of labour'
(Ruigrok and van Tulder, 1995: 9). TNCs, thus, would pursue a globalisation
strategy, while MNCs try to replicate production within a number of regions in
order to avoid the risks of trade blocs. In their assessment of the world's 100
largest non-financial firms, Ruigrok and van Tulder conclude that

> not one is truly 'global', 'footloose' or borderless. There is however a hierarchy in
> the internationalisation of functional areas of management: around forty firms
> generate at least half of their sales abroad; less than twenty maintain at least half
> of their production facilities abroad; with very few exceptions, executive boards and
> management styles remain solidly national in their outlook; with even fewer excep-
> tions, R&D remains firmly under domestic control; and most companies appear to
> think of a globalisation of corporate finances as too uncertain. (Ruigrok and van
> Tulder, 1995: 159)

It is not argued here that the transnationalisation of production has led to a borderless global economy, a level playing field with truly global firms as the prime movers. Nevertheless, in contrast to Hirst and Thompson, it is affirmed that the growth in size and numbers of TNCs with a regional home base, indicated by the concentration of FDI in the Triad, is also part of the globalisation process. Even with production units in only two countries a TNC gains the ability of moving or threatening to move production units between countries and, thereby, some degree of leverage over national regulations. The fact that most of the TNCs still have a home country or region qualifies the amount of structural power they enjoy. It does not, however, question as such the case of the transnationalisation of production. It is simply the degree of trans-nationalisation, which needs to be carefully addressed. Moreover, considering that Hirst and Thompson regard the whole of Germany, the rest of Europe, the Middle East and Africa as the 'home region' for German companies (Hirst and Thompson, 1999: 283), one can see how this insistence on a home region of TNCs incorrectly distracts from the significant degree of transnational produc-tion. In short, globalisation has not affected everybody in the same way and to the same extent. People in the North, in urban centres, being white and male and/or from a propertied and professional background have been more affected than women, ethnic minorities and those who are poor and/or living in the South and rural areas (Scholte, 2000a: 87). This unequal impact does not imply, however, that globalisation is not a real phenomenon for those affected by it. This includes the five countries investigated in this study, since they are a part of Europe, which is one of those geographical areas where globalisation has become a day-to-day reality.

In their rejection of globalisation, Hirst and Thompson, finally, also assess international migration and draw two main conclusions. First, 'there have been phases of massive international migration over many centuries and there seems nothing unprecedented about movements in the post-Second World War period, or those in more recent decades. The second related point is that in many ways the situation between 1815 and 1914 was much more open than it is today' (Hirst and Thompson 1999: 30). Nevertheless, the significant feature of globalisation is not the level of migration, but the creation of new proletariats around the world due to the spread of capitalism. New strata of workers (e.g. women, rural workers and immigrants) have been employed in established capitalism. Additionally, by spreading production processes to developing coun-tries new proletariats were created, doubling the world proletariat to 3 billion people within a generation (Coates, 2000: 256). As argued in Chapter 2, capital is only globally mobile because workers are more widely available for capitalist production nowadays.

This transnational restructuring of social forces has occurred differently in different countries. The impact of globalisation, consequently, has to be analysed from country to country for the purpose of this book. In the following, an attempt is made to assess comparatively the transnationalisation of Austria's, Britain's, France's, Germany's and Sweden's production structures.

The transnationalisation of countries' production structures

So far, it has been established that globalisation, as expressed in the trans-nationalisation of finance and production at the material level and the shift from Keynesianism to neo-liberalism at the ideological level (see Chapter 2), is a real phenomenon and that FDI is an acceptable indicator for the transnationalisation of production. Before addressing the quantitative degree of transnational production in the five case studies, this chapter will provide a brief historical overview of capitalist development in these countries.

The emergence of capitalism in the five case studies

Britain's gradual industrialisation, being the first country to establish capitalist social relations of production from the late seventeenth century onwards, led to the emergence of a strong, independent financial sector, which did not cater for the needs of British industry. While British commercial and financial interests searched for the highest returns across the world, initial industrialisation was mainly financed by record profits due to a booming domestic market further supported by the markets of the empire (Cain and Hopkins, 2002: 62–103, 400–2). At the end of the nineteenth century, however, British manufacturing had fallen behind German and US productivity, but London emerged as a principal financial centre in the international organisation of credit (Germain, 1997: 44–58). Hence, a clear gap developed between financial and industrial capital. Their different location 'in the emerging capitalist system after 1870 gave its financial strata both a set of international orientations and the market power to superimpose them on local industrial capital' (Coates, 2000: 177). Commercial and financial capitalists formed a close alliance with the landed aristocracy and were at the apex of the configuration of social forces in Britain. Industrial capital accepted its subordinated position on the basis of its common interest of controlling the working class (Overbeek, 1990: 45). Britain has always been characterised by the presence of transnational production units. 'Towards the end of the century when growing enterprise scale and more capital-intensive industries called for higher capital investment, finance began to be raised by the sale of equity, and the stock market soon became the most prominent source of outside finance' (Lane, 1995: 30). In manufacturing, major transformations came only about in the 1960s. Then, however, 'merger waves had led to a level of capital concentration which gave Britain the most highly concentrated large-firm sector in the world' (Lane, 1995: 35). In the 1980s and 1990s, consecutive Conservative governments exposed British firms to greater international competition. An emphasis was placed on a strong financial sector and an internationally competitive military-industrial sector, while civilian-based manufacturing was allowed to decline (Coates, 2000: 200). At the same time, Britain was promoted as a location for FDI. 'The notion of Britain offering an EC manufacturing base with an enterprise economy, open markets, and low tax rates is now being extended to other Far Eastern countries' (Grant, 1995: 92). Domestic production, on the other hand, is no longer significant. Overall, one can expect a high degree of transnationalisation and therefore a dominance of transnational forces in tandem with a strong presence of domestic social forces of labour mainly in the public sector.

Germany is an example of late industrialisation. This had a crucial impact on the power balance between finance and industrial capital (Coates, 2000: 176–7). In contrast to Britain, where financial capitalists had an independent international outlook, banks developed in tandem with industry in Germany. Rapid industrialisation in the iron and steel industries required high start-up costs, but there was a lack of accumulated entrepreneurial capital. 'This led to the foundation of a number of private, universal banks, that is, banks which channelled the deposits of small savers towards industrial investment' (Lane, 1995: 31). In order to minimise their risks, these banks acquired extensive industrial expertise, demanded seats on companies' supervisory board and sometimes also acquired large shareholdings in these companies. Industrial capital pursued a strategy of producer economics, concentrating on capital goods at the expense of a consumer industry to make up for lost time in the industrialisation process (Weiss, 1998: 123–4). This dominance of an advanced capital goods sector in combination with a relatively small domestic market implied a strong export orientation of the German economy from early on. After 1945, the German economic-political system had to be restructured. This did not, however, change the close company-bank relationships and the export orientation of the German economy. Corporate liberalism, supported by US intervention, resulted from an adaptation of the earlier concept of control to the growing international competition. 'In the first post-war decade, the old heavy industry lost most of its prominence. The industrial equipment sector on the other hand [engineering, electrical engineering, chemical industry and car industry], was and remained the strongest and most successful branch of West German industry' (van der Wurff, 1993: 169). The underlying class structure with dominant internationally oriented social forces of capital supported by labour in these sectors was also retained, co-existing with nationally oriented social forces mainly from the public sector. Nevertheless, while clearly less transnationalised than the British production structure, German FDI had significantly increased in the 1990s (see below for a detailed analysis of the quantitative changes in FDI). In an analysis of six prominent German TNCs, Hoechst and Bayer in the chemical/ pharmaceutical industries, Volkswagen, Mercedes-Benz and BMW in the automobile industry, and Siemens in electrical/electronic engineering, Lane (2000) confirms this tendency. Hoechst and Bayer were reported to have more employment abroad than in German factories and the automobile companies developed into transnational companies with globally differentiated production networks. Siemens too pursued a more transnationalised strategy in recent years via multiple global co-operations, an increased presence in South East Asia and the adoption of more regional organisational concepts at the expense of the German location. Similar to Hoechst and Bayer, this new global strategy also included the relocation of R&D activity and employment (Lane, 2000: 217). In short, one can expect an increasing amount of transnational social forces engendered by the German production system next to internationally oriented forces stemming from the export sectors and nationally oriented forces resulting mainly from the public sector.

As there had neither been a system of investment banks nor an active stock market, industrialisation in France in the nineteenth century was either financed by family savings (Maclean, 2002: 34) or enterprises in capital-intensive industries joined together and formed financial holding companies. Hence, small, family run companies played an important role, reflecting family over business values. As a late industrialiser without the establishment of mass production, there was a focus on small-scale quality production with an emphasis on luxury goods for the *haute bourgeoisie* and aristocracy. 'The preservation of all but the most inefficient firms through a tacit agreement between efficient and inefficient producers, centring on a regime of high prices, healthy profits, limited production and horizons, was a central feature of the Third Republic' (Maclean, 2002: 36–7). Industrial growth had been a secondary objective. As a result, after World War Two, France was economically backwards with 45 per cent of the active population still working in agriculture (Lipietz, 1991: 23). In a concerted effort led by the state and supported by business as junior partner, later called *dirigisme*, France was rapidly industrialised. First, resources were channelled to those sectors identified for growth. Then, emphasis was placed on 'grand projects'. In the 1970s, the focus was shifted to the creation of national champions, i.e. big export-oriented companies that could cope with the competition on international markets (Gordon and Meunier, 2001: 16; see also Chapter 4). French production was hardly transnationalised until the mid-1980s. In 1986, however, the first wave of large-scale privatisation was enacted. Partly with state support as for example in the case of the French energy provider EdF (Maclean, 2002: 196), partly in their own drive, French companies intensified their transnationalisation in preparation for the completion of the Internal Market from the late 1980s onwards. 'The number of mergers and acquisitions jumped dramatically from 284 in 1986 to 1774 in 1990. In the 1990s, more impressive was the value of the deals, which went from US$ 85 billion in 1991 to US$ 558 billion in 1998, with the average transaction size increasing from US$ 21 million to US$ 104 million' (Schmidt, 2002: 189). Foreign investors have increasingly turned their eyes to French companies. 'The share of foreign investors in the overall capitalisation of French firms at the Paris Bourse has reached 40 per cent, which not only shows a considerable change compared with the situation 15 years ago (10 per cent), but is also considerably higher than in the UK (9 per cent) or the USA (6 per cent)' (Trouille and Uterwedde, 2001: 340–1). The increasing transnationalisation of French production should not make one overlook, however, the continuing importance of small- and medium-sized firms often still family run. As Maclean et al. (2001: 318) make clear,

> the gulf between France's very large companies and those in the next division is striking, in terms of their degree of internationalisation. Indeed, those companies that fall just outside the top 100 often show significantly fewer signs of internationalisation, and are still highly dependent on the domestic market or on

regional markets. This is important, since besides France's 2000 listed companies, it is France's 2,000,000 small- and medium-sized enterprises which remain the backbone of the French economy.

In short, while there are increasing transnational social forces to be expected in France, a major division is likely between internationally oriented social forces and nationally oriented forces.

Austria is another example of late industrialisation. Industrial development from the second half of the nineteenth century onwards was based on the large domestic markets of the Austro-Hungarian empire and comparatively high tariff barriers, not on free trade and export specialisation (Katzenstein, 1985: 187). Financial crises in the 1920s and annexation by Nazi Germany in 1936 ended internationalisation attempts by companies of the much smaller Austrian First Republic early on. This was not reversed after independence in 1955, partly also because most large firms were then either owned or controlled via a majority of votes by the state. Hence,

> Austrian capital consists mostly of numerous small family owned enterprises and large state-owned holding companies. Both these groups have tolerated a heavily regulated political economy, and neither has focused on direct foreign investments. Private business is parochial and uninterested in international diversification. The nationalized firms were discouraged from acquiring assets abroad until the late 1980s. (Kurzer, 1993: 94–5)

In short, Austria's post-war production structure has been predominantly characterised by small-scale industry. In 1992, out of the 2.19 million working population, 55 per cent were employed in small-sized companies with less than 100 employees and 28 per cent in medium-sized companies with less than 1000 employees. This is a relatively high percentage in international terms. In general, these companies contribute only between one- and two-thirds to the overall national employment (Breit and Rössl, 1992: 191). Siegel identified twenty-one Austrian TNCs, but only one of them, Austrian Industries, lived up to international standards in 1990 (Siegel, 1992). It was formed as a state-owned holding company in 1987, when the public industry sector was restructured, but the experiment to create an Austrian TNC of international significance failed in 1992. The company was split up and sold off in parts. The production structures of the twenty-one TNCs were concentrated mainly in Austria, employing only 20 per cent of their workforce abroad (Siegel, 1992: 167). In short, the low number of TNCs and their focus on Austria signals a low degree of transnationalised production. The main line of division is most likely between nationally oriented and internationally oriented forces of labour. Membership in the EU and the privatisation policies since the late 1980s have, however, opened up Austria's protected sectors for FDI acquisitions by foreign TNCs. In addition to the emergence of the Bank Austria group and the Raiffeisengruppe, two new larger Austrian company groups, this has led to an increasing presence of foreign TNCs in Austria (Karazman-Morawetz and Pleschiutschnig, 1997). This is expressed in increasing inward FDI also from 2000 onwards, indicating to some extent that Austria is catching up as far as the transnationalisation of its production structure is concerned (see the quantitative analysis below).

Sweden has fostered an impressive number of large TNCs and important parts of production were transnationalised as early as the turn from the nineteenth to the twentieth century (Andersson et al., 1996: 27–47; Braunerhjelm et al., 1996: 2). 'The most common reason for producing abroad was to exploit unique technical capabilities based on domestic inventions and the redesign of imported technology' (Kurzer, 1993: 120–1). Due to a wave of mergers since the end of the 1960s and a trend towards cross-ownership since the late 1970s, four main ownership groups emerged in a dominant position in the Swedish production structure by the mid-1980s, i.e. the Wallenberg empire, the closely linked Volvo and Skanska spheres, and Industrivarden-Svenska Handelsbank (Olsen, 1991: 117–19). The degree of transnationalisation increased dramatically in the second half of the 1980s, when there was a drastic upturn in outward FDI. While inward FDI had only risen from US$ 396 million in 1985 to US$ 2328 million in 1990, outward FDI increased from US$ 1783 million to US$ 14,136 million during the same period (Luif, 1996: 208). The largest part of this outward FDI went to locations in the EU as a result of the Internal Market initiative (Braunerhjelm and Oxelheim, 1996: 114). This is even more dramatic, if one takes into account that 'in 1989 for the first time ever, Sweden invested more abroad than at home' (Kurzer, 1993: 133). The increasing transnationalisation of Swedish production is also expressed in the change in the Swedish and foreign share of TNCs' employees and production. In 1965, TNCs employed 33.9 per cent of their employees abroad, where they achieved 25.9 per cent of their turnover. By 1990, the situation had drastically changed. Now, 60.6 per cent of the workforce was employed in the production abroad, accounting for 51.4 per cent of the turnover. This increased emphasis on production abroad was especially apparent between 1986 and 1990. The percentage of employees abroad rose by 11.4 per cent, i.e. 42.7 per cent of the overall increase between 1965 and 1990, and the percentage of turnover abroad by 9.1 per cent, i.e. 35.7 per cent of the overall increase between 1965 and 1990 (Braunerhjelm et al., 1996: 10). Initially, foreign production by Swedish TNCs led to increased exports by these companies and, therefore, had no negative effect on the Swedish economy (Swedenborg, 1979: 223). From the mid-1980s onwards, however, increased investment abroad substituted expansion at home and implied the transfer of production units (Andersson et al., 1996: 126). In some instances, this even included the transfer of headquarters. Asea Brown Boveri moved to Zürich/Switzerland and Tetra Pak and IKEA to locations in the EU. In short, a division between transnational and national labour can be expected.

A quantitative analysis of the countries' degree of transnationalised production

This section analyses the degree of transnationalisation in quantitative terms. As has been argued above, FDI is a reliable indicator subject to some qualifications. Importantly, outward and inward FDI have to be taken together, since a production structure is transnationalised due to both foreign TNCs investing in a country and a country's TNCs investing abroad. In Tables 3.1 and 3.2 it can be seen that for all five countries rising levels of inward and outward FDI have been recorded between 1980 and 2003 and 1982 and 2003 respectively. While there were ups and downs due to economic recessions in the individual countries, mirroring also developments at the global level in the early 1990s and the period between 2001 and 2003, the overall tendency is up.

The rates of these increases are staggering. Calculated for the year 2000, the peak year as far as FDI at the global level is concerned (see above), Austria's inward FDI in 2000 was about 34 times as much as the average value for the period 1980 to 1985 and its outward FDI in 2000 was 31 times as much as the average value for the period 1982 to 1987. The respective rates for Britain are 23 and 17, for France 18 and 45, for Germany 286 and 9 and for Sweden 82 and 17. Of course, the high rate of 286 for the increase in Germany's inward FDI is mainly due to an exceptional, out of line year in 2000, while the high rate of 82 for the increase in Sweden's inward FDI is due to an extremely low starting-point in 1980. Nevertheless, the overall conclusion remains the same. From the early 1980s until at least 2000, inward and outward FDI had drastically risen in all countries under investigation, indicating an increasing level of transnationalisation of these countries' production structures.

The comparison of stocks of FDI may, however, provide a better picture, as far as the transnationalisation degree of countries' production structures is concerned, since this takes into account the historical development over time. FDI stock illustrates the current overall situation, while FDI flows indicate tendencies without showing the actual degree of transnationalisation. Again for all five countries in question rising levels of inward and outward stock have been recorded (see Tables 3.3 and 3.4) with similar dramatic rates of increase between 1980 and 2003. As stock of FDI is added up year by year, the fact that the increase in FDI was often smaller from 2001 onwards does not overshadow the overall development of an increasing transnationalisation of production. Hence, the year 2003 can be taken as the point of comparison. As it becomes clear, Britain despite having sometimes lower rates of increasing inward and outward FDI levels has in absolute terms of stock of FDI by far the highest inward and outward stocks, while Austria's levels are significantly smaller in absolute terms than in the other countries. Historically, the transnationalisation of production has played an important role for the British production structure from much earlier on (see above), which implied that the starting-point at the beginning of the 1980s was comparatively high.

Absolute volumes of FDI and stocks of FDI, however, do not necessarily say anything about the importance of these flows for a country's economy. Outward investment and activity in foreign affiliates may, therefore, be compared with domestic investment and activities via the ratio of FDI outflows to gross domestic fixed capital formation to provide a reasonable comparison between countries (Lane, 1998: 471) (see Table 3.5).

Table 3.1 FDI inward flows, 1980–2003 in millions of Dollars

	Austria	Britain	France	Germany	Sweden
1980–1985	259	5163	2343	693	283
1986	284	7309	3256	1060	941
1987	486	14,106	5140	1920	569
1988	436	21,414	8487	870	1514
1989	587	30,553	10,313	10,760	1522
1990	653	32,436	13,183	8950	1972
1991	360	16,158	15,149	7390	5751
1992	947	18,182	21,843	6800	329
1993	1129	15,481	16,439	368	3842
1994	2117	9346	15,580	7134	6350
1995	1904	20,404	23,681	12,026	14,454
1996	4426	25,825	21,960	5636	5070
1997	2384	36,990	23,178	9606	10,910
1998	4533	74,321	30,984	24,593	19,835
1999	2975	87,979	46,545	56,077	60,926
2000	8840	118,764	43,250	198,276	23,242
2001	5919	52,623	50,476	21,138	11,910
2002	952	27,776	48,906	36,014	11,647
2003	6855	14,515	46,981	12,866	3296

Source: UN, 1992: 311 for 1980 to 1987; UN, 1994: 409 for 1988 to 1992; UN, 1999: 477 for 1993 to 1997; and UN, 2004: 367 for 1998 to 2003.

Table 3.2 FDI outward flows, 1982–2003 in millions of Dollars

	Austria	Britain	France	Germany	Sweden
1982–1987	184	13,713	3923	6300	2364
1988	310	37,287	14,496	12,700	7233
1989	867	35,484	19,426	18,310	9694
1990	1701	19,419	34,822	28,600	14,034
1991	1293	15,944	23,932	22,330	6988
1992	1872	16,089	30,993	15,780	1405
1993	1189	26,829	19,732	17,200	1362
1994	1256	34,009	24,381	18,857	6700
1995	1131	44,424	15,760	39,052	11,215
1996	1934	35,114	30,419	50,819	4667
1997	1947	63,630	35,591	40,288	12,639
1998	2745	122,816	48,611	88,823	24,370
1999	3301	201,451	126,856	108,692	21,928
2000	5740	233,371	177,449	56,557	40,662
2001	3137	58,855	86,767	36,855	6380
2002	5252	35,180	49,434	8622	10,683
2003	7083	55,093	57,279	2560	17,375

Source: UN, 1994: 413 for 1982 to 1992; UN, 1999: 483 for 1993 to 1997; and UN, 2004: 372 for 1998 to 2003.

Table 3.3 FDI inward stock, 1980, 1985, 1990, 1995, 2000, 2002 and 2003 in millions of Dollars

	Austria	Britain	France	Germany	Sweden
1980	3163	63,014	25,927	36,630	2852
1985	3762	64,028	36,701	36,926	4333
1990	9884	203,905	86,845	119,618	12,636
1995	17,532	199,772	191,434	192,898	31,089
2000	30,431	438,631	259,775	470,933	93,970
2002	43,508	568,260	386,540	531,738	117,960
2003	60,100	672,015	433,521	544,604	143,230

Source: UN, 2004: 376.

Table 3.4 FDI outward stock, 1980, 1985, 1990, 1995, 2000, 2002 and 2003 in millions of Dollars

	Austria	Britain	France	Germany	Sweden
1980	530	80,434	24,281	43,127	3572
1985	1343	100,313	37,753	59,909	10,768
1990	4273	229,307	110,125	148,456	50,720
1995	11,702	304,865	204,431	258,142	73,143
2000	24,820	897,845	445,091	483,942	123,230
2002	42,485	921,446	586,119	619,939	144,363
2003	59,100	1,128,584	643,398	622,499	189,278

Source: UN 2004: 382.

Table 3.5 Outward FDI flows as a percentage of gross domestic fixed capital formation, 1987–2003

	Austria	Britain	France	Germany	Sweden
1987–1992	3.2	16.1	9.9	5.5	18.0
1993	3.0	19.0	8.5	4.1	5.2
1994	2.9	22.2	10.2	4.2	24.7
1995	2.1	25.9	5.7	7.5	33.3
1996	3.5	19.7	11.3	10.3	12.5
1997	3.9	32.0	15.0	9.5	40.6
1998	5.5	49.1	18.2	19.4	59.7
1999	6.7	80.4	45.7	23.9	50.6
2000	12.5	95.7	67.1	14.0	95.8
2001	7.1	24.5	32.7	9.8	16.7
2002	11.6	13.8	17.7	2.3	26.6
2003	12.4	19.0	17.0	0.6	36.7

Source: UN, 1999: 501 for 1987 to 1997; UN, 2004: 387 for 1998 to 2003.

For comparative reasons, the year 2000 is again taken here as the year of reference, since this was the peak of FDI activity to date. It becomes clear now that Austria's low levels of outward FDI and outward stock of FDI in absolute terms also correspond to a lower level of percentage of gross domestic fixed capital formation of only 12.5 per cent in 2000. Hence, FDI plays a comparatively smaller role for Austrian economic activity. Britain and Sweden, by contrast, show extremely high percentages in 2000 of 95.7 per cent and 95.8 per cent respectively. Their economies are, consequently, strongly affected by FDI, even if this particular year was an exception in this magnitude. France and Germany, although the percentage shows a rising tendency, are clearly somewhere in the middle of the two extreme cases, as far as the importance of FDI for the economy is concerned.[1]

As argued earlier, to assess the transnationalisation of countries' production structures, one has to take together outward and inward FDI. Therefore, it is also necessary to look at the percentage of inward FDI flows to gross fixed capital formation (Table 3.6). A similar picture emerges to the one of the outward FDI flows as a percentage of gross domestic fixed capital formation. The percentage of 19.3 per cent for Austria in 2000 indicates that FDI is comparatively less important for the country's economy, while both Britain and Sweden with 48.7 per cent and 54.7 per cent respectively are strongly influenced by it.[2] France takes again a middle position with 16.4 per cent. For Germany, 2000 was an exceptional year with a ratio of 48.9 per cent. The ratio in 1999 of 12.3 per cent is probably a more realistic expression of its general position in the middle of the two extremes of Austria on the one hand and Britain and Sweden on the other. In general, Hirst and Thompson argue that inward FDI has been relatively unimportant. 'What remains crucial to domestic development strategies are domestic savings, which still remain the main source of financial resources for domestic investment in all advanced and developing economies' (Hirst and

Table 3.6 Inward FDI flows as a percentage of gross domestic fixed capital formation, 1987–2003

	Austria	Britain	France	Germany	Sweden
1987–1992	2.0	13.5	5.3	0.8	5.0
1993	2.9	10.9	7.1	–	14.5
1994	4.8	6.1	6.5	1.6	23.4
1995	3.5	11.9	8.6	2.3	42.9
1996	8.1	14.5	8.2	1.1	13.6
1997	4.8	18.6	9.7	2.3	35.0
1998	9.1	29.7	11.6	5.4	48.6
1999	6.0	35.1	16.8	12.3	140.5
2000	19.3	48.7	16.4	48.9	54.7
2001	13.4	21.9	19.0	5.6	31.1
2002	2.1	10.9	17.6	9.8	29.0
2003	12.0	5.0	13.9	3.0	7.0

Source: UN, 1999: 501 for 1987 to 1997; UN, 2004: 387 for 1998 to 2003.

Thompson, 1999: 86). The data here, by contrast, clearly demonstrate that at least in the case of Britain and Sweden inward FDI is significant for the countries' economic performance in that it forms a substantial part of overall domestic investment.

Moreover, simply to compare the magnitude of outward and inward levels of FDI stock in absolute terms (see Tables 3.3 and 3.4) may distort the comparison of countries' production structures, since the economic size of countries is not taken into account. Clearly, the same levels are less significant for a country with a large GDP than for a country with a small GDP. A way of taking into account the different economic size of countries in the comparison of the transnationalisation of their production structures is to compare the ratio of FDI stock to GDP. Tables 3.7 and 3.8 show inward and outward FDI stocks respectively as a percentage of GDP for the five countries under investigation. When comparing the data for 2000, the tendency of the calculation of FDI flows as a percentage of gross domestic fixed capital formation are confirmed. Austrian inward FDI stocks as a percentage of GDP in 2000 were only 15.9 per cent, outward FDI stocks 13 per cent and, thus, comparatively low. It can be concluded that the Austrian production structure is clearly less transnationalised. By contrast Britain and Sweden show high percentages. Inward FDI stocks were 30.4 per cent of GDP and outward FDI stocks were 62.3 per cent of GDP in

Table 3.7 Inward FDI stocks as a percentage of GDP, 1980, 1985, 1990, 1995, 2000, 2002 and 2003

	Austria	Britain	France	Germany	Sweden
1980	4.0	11.8	3.8	3.9	2.2
1985	5.6	14.1	6.9	5.1	4.2
1990	6.1	20.6	7.1	7.1	5.3
1995	7.4	17.6	12.3	7.8	12.5
2000	15.9	30.4	19.8	25.1	39.2
2002	21.1	36.3	26.9	26.7	48.9
2003	23.7	37.4	24.7	22.6	47.5

Source: UN, 2004: 399.

Table 3.8 Outward FDI stocks as a percentage of GDP, 1980, 1985, 1990, 1995, 2000, 2002 and 2003

	Austria	Britain	France	Germany	Sweden
1980	0.7	15.0	3.6	4.6	2.8
1985	2.0	22.0	7.1	8.4	10.4
1990	2.6	23.2	9.1	8.8	21.3
1995	5.0	26.9	13.1	10.5	29.5
2000	13.0	62.3	33.9	25.8	51.4
2002	20.6	58.9	40.7	31.1	59.9
2003	23.3	62.7	36.7	25.8	62.7

Source: UN, 2004: 399.

the case of Britain in 2000, and 39.2 per cent and 51.4 per cent in the case of Sweden. The production structure of both countries is clearly to a large extent transnationalised. France and Germany are somewhere in the middle. Interestingly, inward and outward FDI flows recovered quickly in the case of Austria after 2000 (see Tables 3.1 and 3.2), as a result of which the level of inward and outward FDI stocks as a percentage of GDP reached levels similar to French and German levels in 2003. This indicates that Austria is catching up as far as the transnationalisation of production is concerned.

While globalisation and the transnationalisation of production are actual phenomena, different areas of the world are differently affected. As indicated above, especially the areas of the Triad including Europe are affected by the globalisation processes. This, however, does not imply that every European country has been affected to the same extent and in the same way. Two principally different ways of how countries are integrated in the global economy can be distinguished. A country that is predominantly integrated into the global economy through exports is a case of internationalisation, while a country with high levels of FDI flows represents a case of transnationalisation. Needless to say every country is likely to be integrated in the global economy through a combination of both internationalisation and transnationalisation. If we accept for a moment FDI as best indicator for a country's transnationalisation, the

Table 3.9 Outward FDI as percentage of exports of goods and non-factor services, 1980–1998

	Austria	Britain	France	Germany	Sweden
1980	0.36	5.43	2.16	2.20	1.69
1981	0.83	6.94	3.46	2.30	2.40
1982	0.56	2.92	2.37	1.55	3.72
1983	0.76	4.39	1.45	1.96	4.41
1984	0.29	6.35	1.76	2.47	4.27
1985	0.28	8.46	1.79	2.62	5.08
1986	0.94	12.07	3.48	3.93	9.07
1987	0.76	18.00	5.03	3.04	9.12
1988	0.65	19.47	7.07	3.43	12.73
1989	1.71	17.63	8.82	4.09	16.83
1990	2.66	7.57	13.44	5.00	21.28
1991	1.95	6.87	9.21	4.93	10.87
1992	2.36	7.05	10.14	3.75	0.61
1993	1.76	10.71	7.18	3.86	2.42
1994	1.71	11.77	8.04	3.82	9.25
1995	1.27	13.64	4.51	6.50	11.84
1996	2.12	9.91	8.48	8.43	4.64
1997	2.28	16.40	9.92	6.92	12.69
1998	2.99	31.94	12.05	14.69	23.90

Source: UNCTAD FDI database; UNCTAD Handbook of Statistics; and IMF Balance of Payments Statistics.[3]

ratio of outward FDI to exports in Table 3.9 may present a good indicator of the balance of integration between internationalisation and transnationalisation.

Very clearly, although there has been an increase in Austria's ratio of outward FDI to exports from 0.36 per cent to 2.99 per cent between 1980 and 1998, the levels are comparatively low, confirming that Austria is mainly linked to the global economy via exports and, therefore, characterised by internationalisation, not transnationalisation. Britain is interesting for two reasons. First, even as early as 1980, Britain already showed a comparatively high ratio of over 5 per cent. Britain's production structure had been transnationalised earlier than the production structures in other countries. After an initial peak just below 20 per cent during the late 1980s, the ratio then climbed to over 30 per cent in 1998, indicating an extremely high level of transnationalisation. Sweden shows a similar development. Prior to the government's announcement about its intention to seek EU membership in October 1990, Swedish capital had started to move production units to the EU in order to benefit from the Internal Market despite Swedish non-membership (Bieler, 2000: 73–4). This is represented in the increasingly high values in the late 1980s culminating in 21.28 per cent in 1990. After lower levels in the following years, partly due to Sweden becoming a member of the EU in 1995, a new record high level was reached in 1998 with 23.90 per cent. In short, Sweden, similarly to Britain, is characterised by a strong degree of transnationalisation. Germany and France, despite the rising levels of outward FDI in both countries, occupy a middle position and thus confirm the conclusions drawn above. Both countries are still very much linked to the global economy via exports and are, thus, strongly internationalised. The transnationalisation of production has really only started in the late 1980s in France and the mid-1990s in Germany. Although the levels are rising, they are still significantly behind Britain and Sweden.

Conclusion

The implications for the identification of social forces in these countries are clear. As outlined in Chapter 2, one can distinguish between transnational and national social forces of capital and labour, with the former being engendered by transnational production and the latter by production organised at the domestic level. The latter group can then be subdivided into internationally oriented social forces, engendered by domestic production, producing goods for the export, and nationally oriented social forces, stemming from domestic production, where goods are predominantly produced for domestic consumption. Countries can generally be expected to have all three different types of social forces and the corresponding production sectors. As discussed in this chapter, in Austria one is most likely to find nationally oriented and internationally oriented social forces of capital and labour, while there are only very few transnational forces. In Britain and Sweden, by contrast, the presence of a strong group of transnational social forces, outweighing even internationally oriented forces can be expected. In Germany and France, the strongest outward-looking section is probably still internationally oriented forces due to the continuing high importance of exports, but significant transnational forces increasingly challenge the dominant position of internationally oriented forces. These social forces, however, do not operate within a vacuum but within and through specific institutional set-ups of different national forms of state. The next chapter looks at the changing forms of state of the five case study countries and the possibilities facing trade unions, as representatives of workers, in their attempt to influence policy-making within each state.

Notes

1　In the case of Germany, the slightly earlier peak of 23.9 per cent in 1999 is the more appropriate figure for comparison.
2　Sweden's percentage of 140.5 in 1999 is clearly out of line with the other data for this country and can be disregarded as a one-off exceptional ratio.
3　I am indebted to Paul Rayment of the UN Economic Commission for Europe for providing these data.

4

Globalisation and the transnationalisation of national forms of state

Introduction

The post-war era can be divided into three different historical periods. The first period was characterised by high rates of economic growth across the Western world and lasted until the early 1970s and the break-up of the Bretton Woods system of relatively fixed exchange rates. According to Ruggie (1982), this period of 'embedded liberalism' successfully combined an international push for increasing liberalisation of trade through a step-by-step reduction of tariff barriers within the General Agreement on Tariffs and Trade (GATT) with the right of governments to intervene into the national economy to obtain social stability through a focus on full employment as main policy goal. The most common forms of state intervention included demand stimulation through budget deficit spending and/or interest rate manipulation, currency devaluations to engender export-led growth, a partial nationalisation of the economy, employment creation via public sector expansion and/or the control and regulation of credit allocation. The exact institutional set-up differed from country to country, but there was a general focus on full employment, expanding welfare provisions and a partial redistribution of wealth. The 1970s, then, were marked by worldwide recession exemplified and exacerbated by two oil price crises in 1973–1974 and 1979–1980. 'Parties, unions, and businesses initially reacted to the economic shocks of the 1970s as if they were cyclical economic downturns. They applied the policy instruments that they had used in the previous era . . . but with greater intensity' (Kitschelt et al., 1999a: 4–5; see also Kitschelt et al., 1999b: 443). Since the 1980s, the third period, it was accepted that the economic problems were of a structural nature. The Fordist accumulation regime based on mass production and mass consumption had run out of steam leading to a declining rate of profit. When companies started increasingly to transnationalise their activities, governments accepted that more radical departures had to be undertaken at the national level. It was also in this situation that European integration was revived around a programme of neo-liberal restructuring (see Chapter 1). In this chapter, through a reference to ideal-type models of capitalism, it will be assessed to what extent these processes of globalisation have had an impact on the national forms of state of the five case studies under investigation. Particular emphasis is placed on the role of trade unions in the changing national institutional set-ups. As outlined in Chapter 2, structural changes related to globalisation have had an impact at the social relations of production as well as form of state level. Chapter 3 dealt with the former, while this chapter concentrates on the latter. Importantly, in line with the neo-Gramscian perspective of this study changes in the structural selectivity of forms of state are closely related to alterations in the underlying class structure in order to avoid a collapse into a purely institutional analysis.

Models of capitalism: continuing divergence of national institutional set-ups?

As outlined in Chapter 1, this analysis refers to three different ideal-type models of capitalism: the market-led, Anglo-American model of capitalism; the state-led model of capitalism; and the negotiated or consensual model of capitalism, also referred to as the social model of capitalism within the European context. They can be defined according to three different sub-areas: (1) the structure of business relations between firms as well as between industrial and finance capital, sometimes also called the system of corporate governance; (2) the role of the state; and (3) the structure of industrial relations and here especially the interaction between employers and trade unions, but also the state (Coates, 2000: 9–10; Schmidt, 2002: 107–8). In the market-led, Anglo-American model of capitalism, the relationship between firms is based on competition and there is a clear separation between industry and finance capital, the former relying on the stock market to raise investment and orienting their strategies according to shareholders' short-term interest in dividend as a result. The state's macro-economic policy mainly focuses on low inflation and price stability, while its industrial policy concentrates on creating competitive markets through deregulation and liberalisation. Industrial relations are characterised by weak involvement of trade unions in economic decision-making at the national and company level. Employee rights at the workplace are limited and the labour market is unregulated to a large extent. Neo-liberal economics is the underlying ideology. In state-led capitalism, there is a strong influence on accumulation decisions by state agencies and banks, which co-operate in close networks. Financial capital is generally supportive of industry on a long-term basis relying on trust. The state is heavily involved in economic management through a close, networked relationship with companies. This may include strategies such as channelling credit to particular industrial sectors, earmarked for expansion. Trade unions are little involved in decision-making, be it at the national or company level. Support by workers in core industries is secured through lifelong employment and generous, company-based welfare provisions. Workers in the periphery of the labour market, however, enjoy only limited rights. The underlying dominant ideology is likely to be conservative-nationalist in content. The negotiated or consensual model of capitalism, finally, is characterised by a close relationship between individual companies secured through cross-share ownership and a dominance of productive capital over finance capital, with the latter supporting the former on a long-term basis. The stock market and shareholder values, consequently, play a much smaller role in companies' investment strategies than in the Anglo-American model of capitalism. The state is heavily involved in economic decision-making. It facilitates the co-operation between capital and labour and actively supports the domestic economy in its macroeconomic, demand-side and industrial policies. In contrast to both the market-led and state-led models of capitalism, trade unions enjoy strong involvement in decision-making at the national level through corporatist arrangements of state-capital-labour institutions as well as at company level in the form of works councils. The underlying ideology is predominantly the traditional social democratic vision of a just and fair society based on the mixed economy and the partial redistribution of wealth.

Within the globalisation literature, Hay (2004) identifies two strands of the convergence hypothesis, arguing that due to globalisation pressures national institutional set-ups would become increasingly similar. First, the so-called hyperglobalists argue that states, in order to attract FDI and to obtain good credit ratings on the global financial markets, would converge around neo-liberal policies of best practice with an emphasis on liberalisation and deregulation of national markets, i.e. the Anglo-American model of capitalism. What they over-look, however, as the varieties of capitalism literature (see Chapter 1) points out, is that there are different national institutional set-ups due to a historic-ally specific development of capitalism, mediating globalisation pressures in different ways. As a result, even if one accepts that there is a convergence of globalisation pressures upon states, this does not necessarily lead to a conver-gence of policies pursued by states to respond to these pressures. Moreover, even if the same policies were pursued, there might not be a convergence in the outcomes of these policies. Finally, convergent outcomes may be the result of different sustaining processes (Hay, 2000: 514–15). The varieties of capitalism literature itself, however, also falls into the trap of a convergence hypothesis, the dual convergence thesis (Hay, 2004: 235–8). Here, it is accepted that national institutions mediate the common globalisation pressures in different ways, but this is expected to lead to two possible optimal solutions: a convergence either around a CME or around an LME (e.g. Hall and Soskice, 2001; Iversen and Pontusson, 2000: 3, 7; Kitschelt et al., 1999b: 444). This literature overlooks that there are several national models that are rather successful in economic terms despite their incoherence in relation to these two optimal models (Hay, 2004: 240; see also Coates, 2005: 18). Hence, instead of thinking in terms of conver-gence around specific models of capitalism, one needs to investigate how concrete national institutional set-ups shape and are shaped by globalisation pressures. Hence, the three identified models of capitalism, rather than expecting them to occur in empirical reality, should be regarded as yardsticks that can be used in order to assess where a particular model is roughly located. They will be applied as an analytical tool to the individual case studies in the reminder of this chapter and are used throughout the book to assess the EU's general direction, but they must not be mistaken for concrete models in order to avoid institutional determinism. As Coates warns, 'the propensity to institutional determinism is likely to be at its greatest in studies which treat the institutional logics mapped out in particular ideal-typical typologies as exhaustive of the actual processes at work in particular national economies' (Coates, 2005: 19). Moreover, as outlined in Chapter 2, when analysing the impact of globalisation on existing models of capitalism, globalisation is not understood as some kind of external pressure. Instead, it is conceptualised as a neo-liberal hegemonic project pushed by a class alliance that is led by transnational capital. When analysing changing state projects, my argument is that one needs to assess in what way and to what extent transnational capital and its interests have become internalised in national forms of state. Emphasis here is placed on an increasing relevance of neo-liberal ideas as well as concrete instances of neo-liberal restructuring in the various state forms as a result of class struggle. Thus, as argued in Chapter 2, the focus is on the material structure of neo-liberalism, i.e. the forces who push it as well as the concrete changes in forms of state inspired by its rationale.

The changing forms of state in Austria, Britain, France, Germany and Sweden

The following analysis will be a country-by-country study, investigating possible changes in the structure of business relations, the role of government, as well as the position and possibilities of trade unions within the industrial relations systems. This is closely related to changes in the underlying class structure.

Britain: towards a market-led, Anglo-American model of capitalism

The post-war British model of capitalism

As outlined in Chapter 3, due to the British empire's dominant international position in the nineteenth century, finance capital developed an international orientation from early on. As a result, capital intensive industries, which required a high level of investment, had to raise money on the stock market. This gap between finance and industrial capital was also prevalent after World War Two. Hence, company strategies were dominated by shareholder values with a focus on high profits in the short-term and there was a chronic lack of investment in manufacturing plant and equipment to increase productivity levels in the long-term (Lane, 1995: 50–1). Especially small- and medium-sized, often regionally based companies did not have access to necessary long-term investment (Rhodes, 2000: 24). While the British industry-finance nexus had always resembled the Anglo-American model of capitalism, the state, on the other hand, pursued a very interventionist strategy in the post-war era. It developed a large public sector as part of an extensive welfare state – see, for example, the establishment of the NHS – and it conducted an active social policy including redistributive transfer payments, and pursued a policy of full employment via a Keynesian demand management policy (Baker, 2000: 362). From 1948 to the late 1950s, there was a considerable amount of wage formation stability within a nationally centralised bargaining system (Brown, 2004: 406–7). Nevertheless, these arrangements did not prove to be stable. Importantly, the formal aspects of welfare policy, consisting of health policy within the NHS, public housing, comprehensive social insurance and universal access to education, could not be linked to informal welfare, including the commitment to full employment, incomes policy and social dialogue, around the notion of a 'social wage'. Unlike the class compromise around a 'solidaristic wage policy' in Sweden (see below), labour could not be included in a comprehensive macroeconomic policy system, in which trade unions agreed on wage moderation in exchange for an expanding welfare state (Rhodes, 2000: 22–3).

A set of tripartite consultative and executive agencies were set up throughout the 1960s and 1970s and large parts of industry were covered by collective bargaining agreements. This was supported by the state through a system of wages councils, which guaranteed minimum earnings. Overall, however, a more permanent corporatist system and organised incomes policy could never be successfully established, because weak national trade unions were unable to enforce agreements on their members. The slow pace of early industrialisation had led to a gradual development of trade unions and an early dominance of craft unions, which resulted in powerful shop stewards at plant level. At sectoral and national level, the labour movement was fragmented (Lane, 1995: 38–9; Overbeek, 1990: 52). General unions competed with specialised unions and several unions organised workers in one workplace. The overall co-ordination by the TUC at the national level was weak and affiliated unions enjoyed a large degree of independence (see Chapter 1). The so-called Social Contract by the Labour government in 1974 was the last attempt to establish an incomes policy. The government promised a repeal of previous Conservative industrial relations laws and more protection against dismissals in exchange for wage stability. The initiative failed, however, similar to previous attempts. 'As industrial wages spiralled out of control in 1975, union leaders failed to deliver restraint: decentralized, plant-level bargaining made local shop stewards pivotal. Basic wage rates escalated to 33.1 percent in spring 1975' (Rhodes, 2000: 35).

In the absence of a successful incomes policy, the British economy experienced constant stop-go cycles. Go-periods of budget deficit spending and general demand expansion to ensure full employment led to rapid wage increases and resulting high levels of inflation. This, in turn, put pressure on the balance of payments and the value of Sterling, which endangered the position of international British finance. In response, a hard currency policy was adopted to combat inflation levels, reducing demand Trade increasing unemployment, before a new expansionary phase was initiated. It would, however, be incorrect to blame solely labour for the failure of an incomes policy. Employers too contributed to a highly fragmented wage bargaining system. It was 'their lack of solidarity that led to the break-up of industry-level bargaining, and their inadequate controls

that encouraged unprecedented workplace bargaining in the 1960s and 1970s'
(Brown, 2004: 404). There had been little pressure towards the formation of
strong, all-encompassing employers' associations, necessary for a centralised
collective bargaining system as the examples of Austria, Germany and Sweden
show (see below). This needs to be related back to the underlying class structure. Big British TNCs had little incentives to co-operate closely with labour at
the national level. Especially transnational finance, which made its profits mainly
from overseas investments, was more concerned about the stability of Sterling
than objectives such as full employment. This led to two, often conflicting policy
objectives. On the one hand, there was a preoccupation with full employment
in response to a strong labour movement and in line with Keynesianism, part
of the post-war overall structure. On the other hand, transnational finance's
concerns about a strong currency were internalised within the British form of
state. It was the latter concerns that led to hard currency policies and the stop-
phases the moment inflation seemed to get out of control. In contrast to France
or Sweden, for example, Britain did not adopt a strategy of devaluation to regain
competitiveness, since this would have undermined the stability of Sterling and,
thus, the interests of transnational finance. The structural power of transnational
finance was clearly felt during the 1960s. 'As revealed by the financial disasters
of 1965–68, the confidence of overseas bankers and speculators had become at
least as important as the state of the real economy. Together speculation and
British capital exports accounted for two-thirds of the total negative foreign
balance of £3.6 billion in 1964–68' (Rhodes, 2000: 30).

This does not imply that unions were weak in the post-war era. A cornerstone of unions' influence on British policy-making was their close link to the
Labour Party (Ludlam et al., 2002: 223–5). This ensured that unions had excellent access to government, when Labour was in power. Moreover, British unions
had experienced a remarkable growth in strength from the mid-1960s to late
1970s as far as membership levels and political influence were concerned (Howell,
1999: 27–8). Nevertheless, this was based on voluntarism and depended on full
employment and state support. Unions did not seek the institutionalisation of
their rights. This made it easy for both the state, then a Conservative government, and the employers to push unions back in the 1980s and 1990s (Brown,
2004: 405–6).

The neo-liberal restructuring of the British form of state
The first turn to neo-liberal policies was carried out by a Labour government
to defend a weakening Sterling even before the agreement with the IMF on a
loan in December 1976 (Ludlam, 1992). The cementation of these policies,
however, occurred under consecutive Conservative governments from 1979
onwards. Against the background of an increasing transnationalisation of British
production (see Chapter 3), the gap between industrial and financial capital was
further deepened. The already transnationalised financial sector was strengthened through the deregulation of the national financial market and the pursuit
of a neo-liberal fiscal and monetary policy focusing on price stability and low

inflation from 1979 onwards. While this constituted a continuation of earlier policies, the Thatcher governments changed the role of the state drastically. New government policies in the 1980s in addition to the liberalisation and deregulation of finance included: (1) an exclusive focus on low inflation instead of full employment; (2) privatisation of nationalised industries; (3) the introduction of market mechanisms into the delivery of public services; and (4) a focus on attracting FDI through tax cuts, a uniform business rate, and the removal of red tape (Baker, 2000: 364; Edwards et al., 1998: 35–8). This internalisation of transnational capital's neo-liberal interests in the British form of state was partly brought about through institutional restructuring. In the national institutional set-up, those institutions linked to the global economy gained a dominant position, expressed in the increasing importance of the Treasury and the Bank of England, while those institutions linked to Keynesian planning such as the National Economic Development Council were abolished. Additionally, those institutions linked to the global economy were internally restructured. Within the Treasury, responsibility for the exchange rate was moved to a domestic monetary team from the overseas finance section, representing the interests of transnational finance (Baker, 2000: 366). The Bank of England was then given independence by a Labour government in 1997 with the sole task to set interest rates to meet a pre-given national inflation target. This is one of the most visible aspects of a more general depoliticisation strategy, in which the government removed decisions from the political decision-making process to a rules-based management by the 'non-political', technocratic Bank of England. It, thereby, altered 'expectations concerning wage claims, in addition to "externalising" responsibility for the imposition of financial discipline' (Burnham, 2001: 134). Internationally, the British form of state was a major actor in pushing towards open markets and stable money around the world through support of the European Internal Market, trade liberalisation including financial services and the IMF's conditionality programmes (Baker, 2000: 365–8). Here too, the support for a rules-based approach in order to entrench neo-liberal economics was visible as, for example, in the British support for the Dispute Settlement Mechanism of the World Trade Organisation (Burnham, 2001: 144).

At the industrial relations level, the labour market was deregulated, making hiring and firing of workers easier and encouraging the use of 'atypical work' contracts. The rights of trade unions, perceived to be obstacles to an efficient economy, were curtailed including: (1) the reduction of union immunities in that unions can now be sued for strike actions organised by officials and committees who do not follow the legal procedures; (2) the introduction of obligatory ballots in respect of industrial action; (3) the introduction of decentralisation of bargaining in some parts of the public sector; (4) a reduction of the powers of wage councils in 1986, before they were abolished altogether in 1993; and (5) the right for employers to choose suitable industrial relations arrangements (Brown et al., 1997: 71–2). Encouraged by government policies, employers too went on an anti-union course. They moved towards the decentralisation of sectoral bargaining to single employer bargaining and they used the strategy of single unionism to create a conflict between competing unions and to gain concessions in exchange for recognition. Some de-recognised unions outright and there was a widespread general hostility to workers representation and participation in decision-making. In 1998, 61 per cent of the public sector workforce, greatly reduced due to privatisation, and only 24 per cent of the private sector workforce were covered by collective wage bargaining be it at the sectoral, company or workplace level. Overall, collective bargaining coverage declined from 80 per cent in 1970 to 40 per cent in 1998 and the related share of sectoral-level agreements declined from 50 per cent to 14 per cent. Especially in the private sector, management has increasingly determined workers' pay (Brown et al., 2003: 199, 204). In short, 'collective bargaining between unions and employers is no longer the dominant system of industrial relations' (Howell, 1999: 30).

While the Labour Party was in opposition, the close party-union ties were relaxed. Unions' share of the party conference vote was reduced to 49 per cent in 1995. The number of seats on party committees was cut back as was the union share of party funding (Ludlam et al., 2002: 228–30). Since Labour's return to power, trade unions have regained better access to government. New Labour also signed up to the EU Social Chapter, introduced a minimum wage and statutory union recognition. Nevertheless, the minimum wage remained below union expectations, the statutory union recognition was watered down and Conservative employment legislation was not repealed. Moreover, social partnership in the form of tripartism was not institutionalised beyond the Low Pay Commission, European social legislation was implemented in a minimalist way and Britain continued to function as an obstacle to a further development of the Social Dimension in the EU (Ludlam and Taylor, 2003: 744; McIlroy, 2000a: 16–26; Waddington, 2003: 337). Privatisation in the public sector continued through New Labour's attempt to attract private investment to the public sector via private finance initiatives (PFI) (McIlroy, 2000b: 9–12). Thus, the New Labour 'approach maintained the essential characteristics of the flexible labour market sought by previous Conservative governments, and it ensured that union recognition and collective bargaining remained marginal in the private sector' (Waddington, 2003: 353). Finally, trade unionists were sidelined in the selection to advisory groups and task forces established by New Labour. 'Only 31 places were occupied by trade unionists, and more than 350 by business people' (McIlroy, 2000b: 5; see also Howell, 1999: 43). This indicates a further avenue of how the interests of transnational capital have become institutionally internalised within the British form of state. In short, unions are still disadvantaged in their influence on policy-making at the British level. The New Labour government has emphasised the lobbying function of unions, but rejects any engagement as part of the labour movement (Waddington, 2003: 353). Overall, in the 1980s and 1990s, Britain experienced a drastic shift from a particular Keynesian form of state towards the Anglo-American model of capitalism (for a graphical illustration, see Coates, 1999: 652). This was not only expressed in different economic policies, but also in the restructuring of the British form of state, internalising the interests of transnational financial capital. New Labour continued these policies and generally embraced neo-liberal economics and the focus on price stability (Howell, 1999: 43–4). Hay and Watson (2003) outline well how New Labour used a particular variety of the globalisation discourse to normalise neo-liberal restructuring in Britain. The harsh economic realities, so the government argued, would leave no alternative to policies of low inflation, the promotion of inward investment through low corporate taxes and a flexible labour market, as well as a residual welfare state. 'So successful was Thatcherism as a "hegemonic" project that its anti-inflation, low tax, and liberal labor market policies have become socially and politically embedded. In making itself elec-table, labour had therefore to embrace the same macro- and microeconomic policy orientation . . .' (Rhodes, 2000: 56).

Germany: consensual capitalism under stress

The post-war German model of capitalism

After World War Two, the German political economy was characterised by the social market economy, which combined market competition with social justice in an export-led growth strategy. 'High costs originating in socially circum-scribed labour markets ruled out price-competitive production throughout the economy and forced firms to seek survival in quality-competitive international markets' (Streeck, 1997: 40–1). The industrial-finance nexus of the German model was based on close relationships between individual banks and firms. 'Every major firm has a house bank, that is one bank with which the firm has a long-standing and close business association, and any given bank may act as a house bank to a number of enterprises' (Lane, 1995: 52). These banks exer-cised control over the firms via seats on their supervisory boards as well as via proxy votes, which banks could cast on behalf of shares, they held in deposit. Relying on a house bank rather than stock markets implied a 'number of advan-tages for firms: it does not dilute ownership; bankers usually accept lower dividend payments than share holders and they do not seek rapid capital gains' (Lane, 1995: 53). Overall, it allowed firms to pursue a long-term strategy and, therefore, gave them more room for necessary restructuring, so important for German companies' focus on quality-competitive products. Additionally, a host of publicly and co-operatively owned smaller regional banks catered for the needs of SMEs (Lane, 1995: 48). An extensive system of cross shareholding among companies further contributed to the establishment of a tightly networked corporate control system.

The German state in this arrangement was sometimes described as an enabling state. Rather than leaving regulation to the market as a laissez-faire state or intervening directly to regulate the market, it assisted voluntary associations in civil society to develop governance functions (Streeck, 1997: 39). The appren-ticeship scheme and collective bargaining were key examples. First, the supply of highly qualified workers was guaranteed by a vocational training system organ-ised in apprenticeships. 'It is described as a "dual" system because on-the-job training is complemented by education in vocational schools' provided by the state (Flecker and Schulten, 1999: 86). Similarly, collective bargaining was solely the responsibility of the representative organisations of capital and labour. However, industrial relations at both the social partner and workplace level were legally regulated (Jacobi et al., 1998: 198–200). Thus, the state ensured that industrial relations were conducted in an ordered way. As for macroeconomic policy, the German state followed the so-called doctrine of ordo-liberalism. It restricted the state to providing a framework of order for the economy, which ensured market competition and was 'protected by the state from the dangers of a concentration of private economic power, liberated from central planning and harnessed to a sense of social responsibility' (Dyson, 1996: 197). The main goal of German governments had always been a policy of low inflation and price stability. Keynesian interventionist policies, based on corporatist negotiations between employers, trade unions and the state in the so-called Konzertierte Aktion were only pursued between 1967 and the late 1970s (Jacobi et al., 1998: 207). The policy of price stability was ensured by the independent Bundesbank legally entrusted with the task of pursuing a policy of low inflation. It was supported by 'tacit tripartism' in the area of incomes policy 'resting more on a mutual understanding between capital and labour than on an explicit bargain between the three most important political actors' (Lane, 1995: 174). Despite a tight low inflation monetary policy, social expenditure was well above the average of other developed countries. In short, economic growth was combined with social protection and a generous welfare system (Weiss, 1998: 150–3). The economic success of the export strategy made the synthesis of monetarism and welfare state possible.

Similar to the German labour movement (see Chapter 1), German employers were also highly organised and extremely loyal to their associations. The German Employers' Association (Bund Deutscher Arbeitgeber; BDA) was mainly responsible for the promotion of employers' interests in the areas of wages, working hours and other workplace conditions. It 'represents German employers in the field of social policy and industrial relations to the government, the public and international organizations' (Jacobi et al., 1998: 205). Collective bargaining was left to its industrial sector member associations. Although voluntary, with more than 70 per cent of all companies in West Germany, the membership level of the BDA was extremely high (Flecker and Schulten, 1999: 84). The most important member association was Gesamtmetall, the Federation of Employers' Associations of the Metalworking Industry, responsible for negotiations with IG Metall. Collective bargaining with employers was a crucial area of influence for German unions. It took place at two levels, the sectoral and the company level. The former was characterised by collective bargaining between sectoral, industrial trade unions and employers' associations, dealing with wages, the specification of the wage-payment system and all other conditions of employment such as working time. 'Sectoral "central or association-level collective agreements" (Flächentarifverträge) are usually negotiated at the regional level [e.g. metalworking, chemicals]. In some sectors (building sector, public sector, banking and insurance) collective bargaining takes place at the national level'

(Hassel and Schulten, 1998: 487–8). A sectoral agreement achieved in one region was in general transferred to the other regions. Negotiations within the metal-working sector operated as pace-setter for other industrial sectors. This was additionally supported by so-called erga omnes decrees by the federal labour minister, who 'declares an existing collective agreement covering a single region and sector to be legally binding on all firms in that sector and jurisdiction for the duration of the agreement including those that are not even members of the relevant employers' association, so long as at least a majority of the employees from that sector and region are already covered under it' (Silvia, 1999: 77–8). About 62 per cent of companies and 83 per cent of the employees were covered by a collective agreement in West Germany in 1995 (Hassel and Schulten, 1998: 488). At the company level, workers were represented by works councils. They were legally guaranteed the right to information, consultation and co-determination on issues such as payment methods and systems, bonus rates, reduced working hours. Beyond the legal regulation of collective bargaining, the state generally consulted trade unions and employers on all major economic and social reforms.

The demise of Modell Deutschland?

In contrast to other Western European countries, the German economic-political system was characterised by continuity during the 1980s and this despite the neo-liberal rhetoric of the Christian Democratic-Liberal Party coalition government in power from 1982 onwards. The labour market was hardly de-regulated and the rights of trade unions remained untouched. The privatisation and deregulation of public enterprises was only half-heartedly adopted (Jacobi et al., 1998: 208–9; Lane, 1995: 185; Zahlnhöfer, 1999: 144–7). In short, the German model with its export-led growth dynamic could be successfully adapted to the changing global economy. This process had already started in the second half of the 1970s under the Social Democratic Chancellor Schmidt, when the Keynesian demand management policy was replaced with a state-run structural policy focusing on infrastructure and technology in order to improve the inter-national competitiveness of Germany's export-oriented sectors (Hassel and Schulten, 1998: 491). The new government simply continued and reinforced this policy from 1982 onwards. According to van der Wurff, 'the continued dominance of the engineering sector in Germany, based on its economic success, contributes to a considerable extent to an explanation of the continuity of West German politics' (van der Wurff, 1993: 182). The model could be successfully adapted, because German production had been hardly transnationalised in the 1980s and was, therefore, still dominated by the underlying constellation of internationally oriented forces of capital that were behind the export-led growth strategy.

Nevertheless, as Chapter 3 has shown, there was a clear increase in outward German FDI in the 1990s. 'In 1996, German FDI was by far the highest in chemicals, followed by, in order of magnitude, road vehicles, electrical engineering and mechanical engineering' (Lane, 1998: 471; see also Lane, 2000). Thus, increasing FDI occurred precisely in those sectors that used to be the bedrock of Germany's export-led growth strategy. In addition to FDI, cross-national co-operations such as strategic alliances and joint ventures increasingly provided an alternative, yet complementary, transnationalisation strategy for firms (Lane, 1998: 472). These changes in the underlying class structure provide one explanation for the problems of the Modell Deutschland in the 1990s. Transnational capital depends much less on the situation within one country, than an internationally oriented company that operates predominantly from within one specific form of state. Additional pressure resulted from the worldwide economic slowdown in the early 1990s combined with the high costs of German re-unification. As a result, unemployment levels climbed to a record high of nearly 5 million in 1998 (Flecker and Schulten, 1999: 105). In this situation, the simple reinforcement of the traditional export strategy, which had been so successful in the adaptation to global changes in the 1980s, seemed to be impossible.

In relation to the industry-finance nexus, increasing pressure has been put on the close relationship between banks and corporations by foreign institutional investors, who criticised the informal system of self-regulation for a lack of transparency and accountability. Moreover, the EU Commission, driving neo-liberal restructuring forward within Europe, has criticised the public banking sector of public savings banks and credit co-operatives for alleged state protectionism (Lütz, 2000: 157–60). Additionally, Lane points out that 'some of the large flagship MNCs, such as Hoechst, Daimler-Chrysler and Siemens, have been or are planning to become quoted on the New York Stock Exchange' (Lane, 2000: 220; see also Lütz, 2000: 162). Several German banks themselves including the Dresdner Bank and the Deutsche Bank transnationalised their operations (Harding, 1999: 82). Finally, 'in December 1999, the Ministry of Finance unexpectedly announced that it would abolish the taxes on capital gains from selling equity stakes, held by one quoted company in another, as of January 2001' (Lütz, 2000: 165). As Lane indicates, this step may initiate the unravelling of Germany's cross-shareholding structure. 'As non-financial firms are the most significant owners of other non-financial firms this would knock out the basis of the current German system of insider control. This will put into question the long investment horizons that patient capital has permitted, as well as undermine the co-operative character of inter-firm and intra-firm relations' (Lane, 2003: 88). The evaluation of these developments differs. On the one hand, it is argued that the close relationship between banks and firms has remained in tact. Especially the small- and medium-sized companies continue to be closely interlinked with banks (Lütz, 2000: 167). There is some evidence of company restructuring along Anglo-Saxon lines in the area of human resource management via learning from practices of their subsidiaries in the UK, but even this occurs in a basically German way (Ferner and Varul, 2000). On the other hand, Lane (2003) notices an increasing focus on the stock market and the rising importance of shareholder values in the internal management of companies including the monitoring of profits with numerical targets and a more transparent organisation. She concludes that the German model is in the process of converging towards the Anglo-American, neo-liberal market-oriented model in the area of corporate governance. This has put pressure on the apprenticeship training system. According to Flecker and Schulten, increasing 'shareholder value' ideology combined with high rates of unemployment has made firms less inclined to invest in training at company level (Flecker and Schulten, 1999: 91).

It is, however, collective bargaining and, thus, trade unions' bargaining strength, which has been under most pressure. Against the background of the recession in 1992–1993 and persistent high unemployment 'unions have made major concessions in wages in exchange for temporary employment guarantees by management; working time has been reduced without fully compensating increases in hourly wages' (Jacobi et al., 1998: 219). Sectoral collective bargaining was undermined in those sectors, which are increasingly characterised by a transnational production structure, which 'lends itself to the emergence of enterprise-bound collective bargaining' (Flecker and Schulten, 1999: 106–7). Moreover, there has been growing pressure towards further flexibilisation of working conditions through regulated decentralisation via opening and hardship clauses, allowing for additional bargaining at the company level (Hassel and Schulten, 1998: 504–5). Additionally, the collective bargaining system itself has been under pressure through non-regulated decentralisation. Many employers especially in the metal sector in East Germany have refused to join their employers' association (Menz, 2005b: 5–6; Silvia, 1999: 103–4; Thelen, 2000) and works councils have accepted illegal company agreements (Flecker and Schulten, 1999: 103; Hassel and Schulten, 1998: 505–7). In order to stem the loss of membership, 'on 31 January 2005, the employers' association for the German metalworking and electrical industry, Gesamtmetall, agreed to admit, with immediate effect, affiliations of establishments that are not bound by sectoral collective agreements' (Eironline, 1 April 2005, http://www.eiro.eurofound.eu.int/2005/03/inbrief/de0503101n.html; 08/07/2005). Trade unions are the clear losers of this pressure on the collective bargaining system, exemplified by the IG Metall's defeat in a strike over the thirty-five-hour week in East German metalworking (Eironline, 23 July 2003, http://www.eiro.eurofound.eu.int/2003/07/feature/de0307204f.html; 04/11/2004).

The changing role of the state has further undermined trade unions' influence. A first attempt to establish a so-called 'Alliance for Jobs' between unions, employers' associations and the state failed in 1996. Only once the Christian Democratic-Liberal government had been replaced by a coalition of the Social Democratic and Green parties in 1998, was the Alliance for Jobs set-up. It was, however, ill-fated almost from the very beginning due to government internal divisions mainly over the Finance Minister Lafontaine's strategy to challenge neo-liberal restructuring: 'Employment was to be promoted without labor market deregulation through a set of demand-pull and substitution effects, driven by the tax reforms. This policy was to be flanked and supported by wage as well as monetary policy, the latter internationally co-ordinated within the EMU framework' (Ryner, 2003: 215). Thus, this strategy relied on a complementary strategy at the European level based on low interest rates and a stronger focus on demand creation as well as tax harmonisation to counter potential capital flight by TNCs. In the end, Lafontaine encountered neo-liberal resistance in Europe as well as Germany and here the group around Chancellor Schröder with its focus on welfare state retrenchment carried the day. Unsurprisingly, against this background the only 'success' of the Alliance for Jobs was a moderate two-year wage settlement (Streeck and Hassel, 2003: 117). The unions, however, received little in return for their acceptance of becoming part of a social pact aiming at increasing national competitiveness through wage moderation. The almost exclusive focus on supply-side economics, be it via the reform of the tax system, of the social security system, the improvement of vocational training or the flexibilisation of labour markets overlooked that rather than a lack of competitiveness, it was the missing internal demand that was the core reason for high unemployment levels (Bispinck and Schulten, 2000: 209–10). When the tripartite Alliance broke apart in 2002, the Schröder government adopted unilateral action on welfare cuts and labour market flexibility through the Hartz Commission, which later led to the Agenda 2010 (Eironline, 31 March 2003, http://www.eiro.eurofound.eu.int/2003/03/feature/de0303105f. html; 04/11/2004; Menz, 2005b: 9; Streeck and Hassel, 2003: 118–19). Most controversial was the suggestion that 'abolishes the second tier of German unemployment assistance and limits eligibility for the more generous upper tier of unemployment benefits to 12 months. Critics point out that the new level of the lower tier in many cases lies below the official poverty line' (Menz, 2005b: 10). Throughout 2004, these cutbacks in welfare provisions led to large-scale protests and demonstrations. Trade unions were closely involved, indicating the end of close union-Social Democrat co-operation. 'On 3 April 2004, around 500,000 people took part in demonstrations called by the DGB trade union confederation' (Eironline, 10 May 2004, http://www.eiro.eurofound.eu.int/2004/05/inbrief/de 0405201n.html; 04/11/2004).[1] The neo-liberal turn was institutionally cemented after the 2002 elections, when Schröder 'dissolved the Ministry of Labour, assigned labour market policy to the jurisdiction of the Ministry of Economic Affairs, and appointed a political heavyweight and proven right-winger, Wolfgang Clement, to the new Superministerium' (Streeck and Hassel, 2003: 120). In sum, neo-liberal restructuring has increasingly been implemented in the German form of state. Trade unions have started to lose their privileged access to the Social Democratic-led government as well as their general participation in tripartite negotiations over social and macroeconomic policy-making. This does not mean that the traditional institutional set-up has been completely unravelled, but, as Menz (2005b) points out, the actual policy output of these institutions has increasingly taken on the characteristics of a neo-liberal state project.

France: from state-led to state-enhanced capitalism

Dirigisme *and the state-led model of capitalism*

At the end of World War Two, France was comparatively underdeveloped, 'expressed in a huge and backward agricultural sector, a traditional industrial structure and a preponderance of firms largely sheltered from, and unsuitable for international trade and economic competition with other advanced countries' (Lane, 1995: 177). In this situation, a planning commission was established with the goal to allocate resources amongst the key industrial sectors in order to facilitate rapid modernisation of the French economy (Hall, 1990: 171). The resulting policy-making regime came to be known as *dirigisme*, in which the government was the senior and business the junior partner in the reconstruction and industrialisation drive. Through an active industrial policy concentrating on the allocation of credit, the French state decided which industrial sectors were destined to develop. The Trésor within the Ministry of Finance was in charge of determining the price of credit and directing its allocation. When medium-term, large-scale planning had become less workable in the 1960s and 1970s, *dirigisme* concentrated on the active creation of so-called national champions, big export-oriented companies (Kresl and Gallais, 2002: 160). In short, Kassim defines *dirigisme* through three characteristics: (1) an economy of administered finance, where the state supervised the allocation of credit; (2) a policy of inflationist expansion including repeated devaluation especially in the 1970s; and (3) the pursuit of grand projects including the creation of national champions through state support (Kassim, 1997: 169). It is this active role of the state in French economic development that made observers associate France with the state-led model of capitalism.

Finance capital, partly owned by the state, partly controlled, was subordinated to industrial capital and mainly responsible for the latter's expansion. The state's control over finance was supported through a complex regulatory framework. As a result, the French banking system had been highly compartmentalised and fragmented with commercial banks, savings banks and financial co-operatives all having their own protected segment of the market and their own specific regulatory system (Coleman, 1997: 276–8). Labour was largely excluded from the process of *dirigiste* policy-making. The little power it enjoyed in industrial relations was more due to the state's intervention than due to its own strength. 'With few members, weak organizations, and competition among themselves, French unions have had to cling to the remaining legal protections for their very survival' (Daley, 1999: 168). Trade unions, for example, gained influence through their participation in state bodies such as the national commissions on vocational training or the improvement of working conditions as well as the Economic and Social Council, advising the government on important policy issues (Goetschy, 1998: 368). State intervention was also visible in collective bargaining. Making up for weak union and employers' confederations, the state pushed both of them towards collective bargaining and frequently set the conditions itself:

> The Ministry of Labor set minimum wages to boost salaries at the low end and push up salary scales. It extended favourable bargaining agreements to larger jurisdictions. It decreed policy on vacations, retirement, and working time. It defended employees threatened with dismissal. It stimulated bargaining by threatening to act unilaterally in the absence of agreement between social partners. (Daley, 1999: 170)

Thus, in contrast to Austria and Sweden (see below), for example, there was no class compromise in France based on collective bargaining by strong trade union confederations and employers' associations. 'The class compromise remained much more brittle and could only be sustained by the frequent substitution of state intervention for autonomous bargaining by the two sides of industry' (Lane, 1995: 123).

Towards a state-enhanced model of capitalism?

As elsewhere in the Western World, the oil price crises and related recessions in the 1970s put the French model of capitalism under pressure. An initial turn-around occurred in 1979, when the European Monetary System (EMS) was established with French participation. The EMS was organised around the exchange rate mechanism with the goal of keeping currencies within an agreed band of +/– 2.25 per cent relative to the European Currency Unit (ECU), an artificial currency unit. In line with these constraints, the French government under Giscard d'Estaing adopted austerity measures in order to counter the overvaluation of the Franc (Cameron, 1995: 126–7). The Mitterand government interrupted this process from 1981 to 1983 through its Keynesian policy programme. It reflated

> the economy by raising the minimum wage, hiring another 100000 public employees, reducing the working week from 40 to 39 hours, devoting large sums to manpower training and early retirement programmes designed to reduce rising unemployment, nationalising 49 firms central to French banking and industry, and expanding annual aid to French industry from 35 billion francs in 1981 to 86 billion francs by 1985. (Hall, 1990: 176–7)

The related higher levels of inflation in comparison with other EMS members and here especially Germany implied, however, that the Franc depreciated further, thereby making French exports non-competitive. The Mitterand government had two options in this situation: either it decided on a large devaluation of the Franc, exit the EMS and put up barriers against rising imports, or it remained within the EMS and bring inflation down to Germany's levels via austerity measures. The government chose the second option, which implied a strong shift away from Keynesian to neo-liberal economic policies.

From 1983 onwards, the financial markets were deregulated. The use of security markets was promoted, they were liberalised and a stronger competition amongst financial service firms encouraged. The banking act in 1983/1984 was intended to support these efforts by overcoming the rigid structure of French finance. 'Wide and ambitious in scope, the new law gathered under one framework deposit banks, merchant banks, savings banks, co-operative, financial holding companies, interbank money-market brokers, finance houses and securities firms' (Coleman, 1997: 283). The restructuring of the financial markets included the liberalisation and promotion of security markets as well as the adoption of a universal bank model, overcoming the market segmentation and inducing competition between the different banks. By the early 1990s, the institutional segmentation had been abolished and a single regulatory system governed the financial markets (Coleman, 1997: 287). As one of the last industrialised countries, France removed all controls of capital movements in 1990 (Kresl and Gallais, 2002: 169). In response, firms have increasingly turned to financial markets to raise capital for investment. 'Market capitalization of the French equity markets as a percentage of GDP went from a low of 5.6 per cent in 1982 to 37.2 per cent in 1993 and up to 111.5 per cent by 1999, while the annual volume of transactions on the French equity markets went from a low of 1.8 per cent in 1982 to 13.7 per cent in 1993 and up to 54.6 per cent by 1999' (Schmidt, 2002: 188). This increasing reliance on transnational capital was one of the ways neo-liberal interests became internalised in the French form of state. Transnational capital's emphasis on neo-liberal restructuring fell on receptive ears among conservative liberal administrative elites within the Trésor and Banque de France. While still slightly more attached to a welfare state and *dirigiste* instincts, they pushed for domestic neo-liberal restructuring (Clift, 2003: 174, 180, 186–7). 'Policy elites keenly felt the disciplinary neoliberal pressures that accompanied increased reliance on foreign capital – the need to control inflation, secure credibility, and offer attractive interest rates and a strong currency' (Clift, 2003: 192). In the process of turning to neo-liberal policies, unemployment was transformed from a main policy priority into an anti-inflationary adjustment tool. Unsurprisingly, while inflation levels were brought down to German levels, unemployment rates increased drastically throughout the 1980s (Cameron, 1995: 149).

The Chirac government of 1986 to 1988 deepened neo-liberal restructuring and initiated the first wave of large-scale privatisations. The various subsequent Socialist-led and Gaullist-led governments continued this policy until today. Interestingly, however, while French governments had started to implement neo-liberal policies, the way this was done often reflected past patterns. In a *dirigiste* manner, the French state ensured that a 'hard core' of French investors retained a core share in privatised companies. In other words, privatisations were state-directed. 'Their dual effect was to reinforce the prerogatives of the State and to bolster the existing establishment, whose members were invited by the Finance Minister to participate in the hard cores of shareholders running newly privatised firms, tightening the ties of loyalty and political friendship which knit together the establishment network' (Maclean, 1997: 219). Further signs of continuity relate to small- and medium-sized companies, which have continued to receive state support (Schmidt, 2002: 198). This needs to be kept in mind especially considering that there is a big gap between large French companies and those outside the top 100, which are much less transnationalised and still dependent on the domestic market (Maclean et al., 2001: 318).

Moreover, financial markets, despite their increasing importance, are still not the main source of financing for corporate investments, some large firms are still controlled by families and there has been a considerable continuity of cross-shareholding (Maclean, 2002: 211; Schmidt, 2002: 192–3). This is fostered by a cultural environment based on education in elite schools supplying leading personnel to both the state and business. 'It is highly unlikely that the French business elite will abandon entirely the system of networks, fostered by the *grandes écoles* and *grand corps*, which has served it so well in the past' (Maclean et al., 2001: 323). Unsurprisingly, only one of the forty top French companies has a foreign President Director General (Maclean et al., 2001: 321).

The continuity of *dirigisme* should not, however, be taken as if there had been no changes to economic policy-making in France. First, there has been a clear increase in foreign ownership of French companies. The hard cores of French investors 'have been breaking down since the mid-1990s as a result of divestment by some hard-core investors and a concomitant rise in foreign investors – which as of 1997 held over a third of shares in French firms compared with no more than a tenth in Germany or the UK' (Schmidt, 2002: 123; see also 192; and Maclean, 2002: 207). Foreign institutional investors have played a major role in this process. They collectively own now 'more than 40 per cent of the share capital of the top 40 French firms' (Maclean, 2002: 41; see also 208). In the late 1980s, French companies themselves increasingly transnationalised their production in view of the impending Internal Market (Schmidt, 2002: 189). The privatisation and concomitant increasing transnationalisation of French production (see Chapter 3) has weakened the government's hold over traditional French companies. This indicates a further way of how the neo-liberal interests of transnational capital have become integrated into the French form of state. Some transnational French companies including foreign members on their board of directors have already developed business strategies different from a French governmental point of view (Maclean, 1997: 226). Schmidt, therefore, speaks about a shift towards market-oriented *dirigisme*, where capital has become the senior partner, government the junior partner. 'Business now leads more, and government directs less' (Schmidt, 1997: 240). Again, one can see how changes in the underlying social relations of production have been factored into a changing form of state.

Further deregulation also took place in the industrial relations system. The Auroux laws of the early 1980s had the intention to strengthen trade unions' negotiation role. The collective bargaining act obliged firms with union branches to negotiate on pay and working hours on an annual basis. The Ministry of Labour was given the authority to impose agreements on individual sectors and employers must abide by the minimum provisions of sectoral agreements, if no union at plant level signed a derogation agreement (Daley, 1999: 175–7). Initially fiercely criticised by employers, they soon realised that company-level bargaining actually made it easier for them to introduce greater levels of flexibility (Goetschy, 1998: 379). Thus, the Auroux laws actually started the process towards the decentralisation of collective bargaining to the company level, overtaking the sectoral level as the most important level of collective bargaining. Works councils were strengthened vis-à-vis unions and provisions were made for company agreements with lower results than sectoral agreements. 'Whereas before the passage of the Auroux laws an agreement at the highest bargaining level prevailed over those at lower levels, now firm-specific agreements can cancel out those concluded at a higher level' (Lane, 1995: 135). Minimum wages are still negotiated at the sectoral level, but 'actual wages are negotiated at company level' (Barrat et al., 2002: 261). In other words, the Auroux laws 'weakened the unions unable to take control of the dialogues and began the process of radical decentralization of wage bargaining that culminated by the end of the decade in the state's abandonment of the entire system of government-organized, centralized wage negotiations' (Schmidt, 2002: 201). With unions losing even further ground at the sectoral level, the labour market has been increasingly flexibilised in France. The thirty-five-hour working week, introduced by two laws in 1998 and 1999, has had a similar effect. Initially intended to increase the rights of employees and reduce unemployment, the thirty-five-hour working week has in fact increased labour market flexibility. 'In exchange for the shorter work week, employers were allowed to negotiate new deals on flexible work time, and often to demand wage restraint as part of the new labor contracts' (Gordon and Meunier, 2001: 36; see also Kresl and Gallais, 2002: 177). Additionally, as these deals were negotiated at company level, the decentralisation of bargaining was further strengthened (Barrat et al., 2002: 265–7).

In sum, it can be concluded that there have been changes to the French model, but various continuities indicate that the French model, although restructured along neo-liberal lines, has not shifted towards a full-blown Anglo-American model of capitalism, nor towards a consensual model. Schmidt, therefore, speaks about a state-enhanced model of capitalism. France, she argues, 'has instituted a more market-oriented capitalism in which the state nevertheless remains much more important than in either market capitalist or managed capitalist systems, even if its interventionism is much more circumscribed and, where it occurs, is more market-oriented' (Schmidt, 2002: 183). The structural selectivity of the French form of state continues to be unfavourable from a union perspective. Trade unions have been and remain weak within this institutional set-up.

Austria: neo-liberal restructuring within corporatist institutions

Austria's post-war economic-political model

Together with Sweden (see below), Austria was generally considered to be one of the main examples of a corporatist country, where interest associations of capital and labour were tightly integrated into the domestic decision-making processes (Bieler, 2000: 27–30). Austrian post-war corporatism, also called Economic and Social Partnership (ESP), was established as a response to the experience of civil war in 1934, repression, defeat in war and foreign occupation (Katzenstein, 1985: 188). The ESP was highly institutionalised in that the four main interest groups the Chamber of Labour (AK), the Chamber of Commerce

(BWK), the Chamber of Agriculture (LK) and the Austrian Confederation of Trade Unions (ÖGB) were co-opted into governmental decision-making through the key institution Parity Commission. The latter had three important sub-committees, i.e. the price sub-committee responsible for the setting of about one-third of all prices, the wages sub-committee controlling the timing and outcome of collective bargaining, and the Economic and Social Advisory Board entrusted with the scientific formulation of proposals for economic policy-making (Marin, 1985: 108–9). The influence on policy-making by the social partners was additionally secured through close links between the social partners and the two main political parties, the Austrian People's Party (ÖVP) and the Austrian Social Democratic Party (SPÖ), which dominated the electoral landscape and government for most of the post-war period until 2000. A system of intensive mutual inter-penetration and multiple activities of functionaries, in which many leading members of the social partners sat in parliament and regularly took up the position of key ministers in government, ensured that social partners were closely involved in decision-making. The AK and ÖGB enjoyed close relations with the SPÖ, while the BWK and LK were tightly integrated in the ÖVP (Tálos, 1996: 108).

The Austrian state was heavily involved in policy-making. The core policy-target of post-war Austrian governments was full employment. Large parts of production and here especially the larger, export-oriented companies, had been nationalised after World War Two to protect them against reparation demands by the occupying powers. The nationalised industry employed 'about one-quarter of the Austrian labour force and [generated] about one-third of net production and almost half of all investment' (Marin, 1985: 121). These publicly owned companies were given subsidies in order to support the government policy of full employment (Kurzer, 1993: 100). Additionally, especially in the 1970s the government practised Keynesian budget deficit spending in times of economic recession. Wage moderation by trade unions was obtained through collective bargaining within the ESP (Lauber, 1996: 127–34). This was complemented by a hard currency policy, established as a legal obligation for the Austrian National Bank after 1945. Following the collapse of the Bretton Woods system of relatively fixed exchange rates in 1971, the hard currency policy was achieved first through linking the Austrian Schilling to a currency basket and then to the German Mark (Dörfel et al., 1993: 116). Overall, Austrian economic policy, shaped in close co-operation between government and social partners, was sometimes referred to as Austro-Keynesianism due to its mixture of supply- and demand-side measures. It 'provided low and stable interest rates for business; promotion of investment via the tax system; a stable currency linked to the German mark; low rates of inflation and unemployment; and a very stable incomes policy with almost no strikes at all' (Lauber, 1996: 132; see also Unger, 1999: 168–73).

The ESP proved to be very stable partly due to the underlying class balance between capital and labour resulting from the particular Austrian production structure. First, Austrian finance capital was dominated by the state, which owned two of the three most important joint-stock commercial banks, the Creditanstalt Bankverein and the Österreichische Länderbank. Moreover, Austrian finance was only moderately integrated into the international financial market. 'Neither commercial banks nor specialized credit institutions were driven by international ambitions' (Kurzer, 1993: 168). They were, therefore, in no position to develop an international accumulation strategy independent from industrial capital. Second, large parts of production had been nationalised (see above) and the overall production structure was dominated by small- and medium-sized companies (see Chapter 3). Finally, at one stage up to 50 per cent of the market including especially the agriculture and food processing industries were sheltered against international competition (Luif, 1994: 26). Almost by default, capital had a rather protectionist outlook depending on the state but also close co-operation with trade unions. The hierarchical and centralised structure of the social partners was a further reason for the stability of Austrian corporatism. The AK, BWK and LK are all based on obligatory membership, only the ÖGB relied on voluntary membership. Similar to the other three social partners, however, it was also highly centralised and hierarchical in its decision-making structure with the confederation clearly dominating the affiliated unions (see Chapter 1).

In sum, Austria was clearly an example for a model close to negotiated capitalism. The relationship between finance and industrial capital was dominated by the state and there was no significant internationally oriented or transnational class fraction of private capital that was in a position to question the domestic co-operation with labour within the corporatist institutions. The state ensured a policy of full employment combined with a hard currency policy. Trade unions enjoyed a strong influence on policy-making through their close relationship with the SPÖ and their involvement in the corporatist institutions of the ESP. Similar to the experience of other Western countries, these arrangements were put under pressure by global restructuring in the 1980s and especially 1990s.

Austrian corporatism under pressure

Against the background of structural change, social partners lost influence on policy-making during the 1990s. EU membership in 1995 pushed the social partners from a decision-making to an advisory role in many areas of economic and social policy-making (Pelinka, 1999: 121–2; Traxler, 1995: 275). On social policy, for example, consensus formation between government and social partnership has been maintained as a principle after EU membership (Eder and Hiller, 1998: 45–51). Now, however, this determines only the official Austrian position in Brussels. The eventual policy outcome at the European level may be very different, even though the social partners gained the right to participate as observers in meetings of the Council of Ministers (Falkner, 1998b: 239). Moreover, the traditional role of the social partners on the governing board of the Austrian National Bank in co-ordination with their responsibility for wage moderation was changed. In order to align the national bank with the EMU requirement of central bank independence the governing board was transformed into a supervisory board without any real competencies (Reischl and Sykora, 1997: 47). A further institutional erosion was reflected in the decline of social partner representatives in parliament from 51 per cent of MPs in 1973, via 56 per cent in 1978, 44 per cent in 1987 and 34 per cent in 1991, to only 19 per cent of MPs in 1995 (Pelinka, 1999: 120–1). Finally, in 1992, when the policy of price-setting had become increasingly impractical due to the increasing integration of the Austrian market into the global economy, the role of the price-sub-committee was changed towards the observation of market tendencies. In relation to the discussions of EU membership, a sub-committee on IR was additionally established (Pelinka, 1999: 123).

Nevertheless, despite these changes it can be argued that the ESP was not dismantled but adjusted to the new requirements. Social partners, it is argued, played an important part as 'modernisation brokers' (Heinisch, 2000: 92). And indeed, Austrian social partners were crucial in the process towards EU membership in 1995. During the discussions on whether to apply for membership or not between 1987 and 1989, the eventual support for EU membership by all four social partners had been crucial to ensure that a majority of the Austrian public endorsed membership in the referendum in 1994 (Bieler, 2000: 58–63, 95–7). Similarly important was the social partners' support for the two austerity budgets in 1995 and 1996, implemented to meet the fiscal requirements of EMU. This helped to make the cut-backs acceptable and avoid widespread opposition amongst the population (Heinisch, 2000: 91; Unger, 1999: 181–2, 186). While the structures of the ESP remained by and large in tact, however, a change of the social purpose of corporatism and, thus, the state project as such took place. A clear shift from a policy of full employment as the most important goal towards neo-liberal restructuring and a focus on price stability and low inflation can be detected. This is sometimes referred to as a shift from demand-side to supply-side corporatism (Traxler, 1995).

Against the background of severe economic difficulties expressed in increasing unemployment, low and even negative growth levels as well as rising inflation, neo-liberal ideas became prominent from the early 1980s onwards, first in the ÖVP but then also in the then governing SPÖ. Franz Vranitzky became the new SPÖ chancellor in 1986 and he and his 'team abandoned [the] policy of relying on the nationalised industries, interventionist industrial policies, and stimulative fiscal deficits to secure full employment' (Schultz, 1992: 189). In a grand coalition with the ÖVP in the following twelve years, a paradigm change took place in governmental economic policy (Tàlos and Fink, 2003: 215): the budget deficit was countered via austerity budgets thereby prioritising a medium-term budget consolidation over demand-led fiscal policies and the nationalised sector was to a large extent privatised including the publicly owned banks. Moreover, tax reforms were carried out in 1989 and 1994 lowering business taxation in order to encourage domestic investment and inward FDI (Bieler, 2000: 39–41; Lauber, 1996: 137–46; Unger, 1999: 173–85). The traditional hard currency policy was now reinforced. When the EU Internal Market programme included the free movement of capital, Austrian decision-makers followed, although Austria

had not yet become an EU member. The gradual liberalisation of Austrian financial markets started in 1986 and 'culminated in the abolition of the last exchange
restrictions in November 1991' (Dörfel et al., 1993: 118). The procedures of
collective wage bargaining, part of the industrial relations system, were also
affected by these changes. Central bargaining co-ordinated by the Parity Commission was replaced with sectoral pace-setting agreements, which increasingly
included opening clauses for further bargaining at plant level (Traxler, 1995:
281; Heinisch, 2000: 89). The shift towards a neo-liberal state project was best
expressed in the move towards EU membership. Acceding to the EU in 1995,
when the EU itself had moved towards an Anglo-American model of capitalism
(see Chapter 1), indicated that neo-liberalism was no longer a major concern.
Overall, Unger (1999) describes this as a shift from Austro-Keynesianism to
Austro-neo-liberalism. The demand-side policies of Austro-Keynesianism have
been abandoned, leaving an exclusive focus on the supply-side policies, including
the hard currency policy. The latter is now secured by the ECB at the European
level, and a continuation of moderate wage increases, plus a new emphasis on
a consolidated budget in Austria. In sum, while there has been no institutional
convergence towards the Anglo-American model of capitalism, neo-liberal
restructuring took place within the existing institutional set-up.

In 2000, when the ÖVP formed a coalition government with the rightwing
Austrian Freedom Party (FPÖ), the institutional set-up of Austrian corporatism
came under pressure, too. In opposition, the FPÖ had criticised vehemently the
social partnership and the related privileging of SPÖ and ÖVP in the distribution of public positions. Now in power, it attempted to put this criticism into
practice. The first sign of change was when the social partners against tradition
were not involved in the formulation of the new government's programme in
February 2000. Then, the government increasingly bypassed the social partners
through direct initiatives in parliament. Expert groups rather than the institutions of the ESP were commissioned to develop new proposals. Moreover,
labour law and labour market competencies were moved from the once powerful
Ministry for Social Affairs and Employment, traditionally dominated by the
trade unions and now re-named Ministry for Social Security and Generations,
to the strengthened and re-named Ministry for Economy and Employment,
sidelining further the social partners of the labour movement. The ÖVP, while
slightly more restrained than the FPÖ, was not opposed to this undermining
of the traditional role of corporatism. When the FPÖ suggested to cut back
the financial contributions to the AK, the ÖVP only criticised the extent,
not the issue as such (Tálos, 2001: 41–2; Tálos and Fink, 2003: 220–4). The
ÖGB did not accept these developments. 'On 29 August 2001, the presidium
of ÖGB unanimously decided to hold a ballot of its 1.44 million members
between 24 September and 25 October 2001, in order to strengthen its political
positions and to legitimise further protest actions against government legislation' (Eironline, 25 September 2001, http://www.eiro.eurofound.eu.int/2001/09/
feature/at0109201f.html; 12/02/2002). More than 800,000 members voted in the
ballot and the ÖGB received overwhelming support for its demands including

the mandate to call a strike, should the government refuse to co-operate (Eironline, 20 November 2001, http://www.eiro.eurofound.eu.int/2001/11/feature/at0111201f.html; 12/02/2002). In an analysis by the ÖGB national committee on 7 March 2002, the then President Verzetnitsch concluded that the government had started to respond to its demands positively and re-started to submit new legislative proposals to the ÖGB for comments thanks to the pressures resulting from the ballot (ÖGB-Bundesvorstand, 2002a; ÖGB-Bundesvorstand, 2002b).

This revival, however, did not last long. In 2003, the ÖVP-FPÖ coalition government returned to a policy of bypassing social partners. It did not only initiate its pension reform without consulting the social partners, but also refused an initiative by the ÖGB and BWK to draft their own proposals in this area (Eironline, 13 May 2004, http://www.eiro.eurofound.eu.int/2004/01/feature/at0401203f.html; 24/08/2004). In response, on 6 May 2003 the ÖGB organised the largest strikes Austria had experienced in the last fifty years, when almost 500,000 workers participated in strike actions (Eironline, 20 May 2003, http://www.eiro.eurofound.eu.int/2003/05/feature/at0305202f.html; 24/08/2004). This was followed by large demonstrations a week later. In general, it can be concluded that the privileged access of social partners to policy-making has been removed in many areas under the new government. Interestingly, it is especially the social partners of the labour movement, which have been sidelined. The BWK and LK still have their traditional access to the ÖVP and those ministries, controlled by the ÖVP (Tálos and Kittel, 2001: 238–9; Tálos and Stromberger, 2004: 169). This does not mean at this stage that the ESP has been completely abandoned. The social partners of the employers themselves continue to demand social partner involvement in decision-making and the trade unions remain open to discussions. There are also some areas of continuing functioning social partnership interaction. Nevertheless, it is clear that the medium- to long-term future of Austrian corporatism is now severely questioned.

In sum, within the transnationalisation of the state, a shift to a neo-liberal state project can be clearly identified in Austria. This transformation took first place within the existing institutions of the ESP, but has now started to break them apart too. My argument is that these changes in the Austrian model of capitalism need to be related to changes in the underlying social relations of production. A driving force in the struggle over the new state project was internationally oriented capital, institutionally expressed by the Federation of Austrian Industry (Industriellenvereinigung; IV), strongly supported by the increasing fraction of transnational capital. Due to the privatisation of the nationalised industry and rising levels of inward FDI, a strong internationally oriented fraction of private capital has emerged over the last twenty years. In this process, the IV has developed from a rather small institution on the margin of policy-making into capital's most important institutional actor (Bieler, 2000: 48–9). In short, 'changes in the economic structure of Austria and greater international penetration catapulted the [IV] into new prominence at the expense of the slightly protectionist and worried voices of small business' (Kurzer, 1993: 238).

The IV's crucial role is most clearly expressed in the fact that it initiated the discussions on EU membership in 1987 and was then the driving force behind the pro-EU movement (Bieler, 2000: 54–7). In this respect, Austrian EU membership is an expression of the internalisation of internationally oriented and transnational capital's interests into the Austrian form of state. Labour, in turn, has lost influence and power. Increasing unemployment levels and the spread of atypical working contracts, which can be linked to a general internationalisation of labour markets and increasing levels of inward and outward FDI in Austria (see Chapter 3), undermined trade unions' capacity to organise workers and made employers less inclined to compromise (Pelinka, 1999: 123; Tálos, 2001: 37; Traxler, 1995: 274). Between 1993 and 2003, ÖGB membership declined by 12.9 per cent (Eironline, 21 May 2004, http://www.eiro.eurofound.eu.int/ 2004/03/update/tn0403105u.html; 10/09/2004).

Sweden: the rise and fall of the Swedish model

The post-war Swedish model

Throughout the post-war era, Sweden was praised for its progressive economic-political model successfully combining international economic competitiveness with generous compensatory mechanisms at the national level to soften the impact of constant structural adjustment. The core feature of the Swedish model at the industrial relations level was multi-sector collective wage bargaining between employers' associations and trade unions according to the so-called Rehn-Meidner model. Based on an equal, solidaristic wage across all industrial sectors, it forced the constant shift of resources, investment and labour from declining to expanding sectors (Ryner, 1994: 400–1). Inefficient companies, unable to pay the centrally agreed wage levels, went bankrupt, but booming companies were allowed super profits for further investment into new production facilities. This resulted in a policy of full employment combined with low inflation. The state supported this agreement through incentives, which made sure that profits would actually be re-invested into the economy (Pontusson, 1995: 27; Ryner, 2002: 89–90), as well as an active labour market policy, including education, job training, information and generous relocation grants for families (Esping-Andersen, 1985: 229–31). Full employment, especially in the 1970s, was further sustained through an expansion of the public sector, absorbing workers, who could not be re-employed in the private sector (Heclo and Madsen, 1987: 165–6), and frequent devaluations to engender export-led growth (Moses, 1995: 418).

In the industry-finance nexus, banks provided long-term loans to industry, with which they maintained close links (Olsen, 1991: 125). This relation was highly regulated by the state. At the outbreak of World War Two, foreign exchange controls and other forms of capital market regulations had been introduced, only to be strengthened during the 1950s. These regulations, including lending ceilings, liquidity ratios, cash ratios, investment ratios, bond issue control and interest rate regulations, were administered by the Riksbank, the Swedish

Central Bank (Jonung, 1986: 109–11; Kurzer, 1993: 176). The Riksbank was directly responsible to the Swedish parliament, and by implication the Swedish Social Democratic Party (SAP), which was in power for most of the post-war era. In fact, 'the Riksbank functioned as an agency affiliated with the Ministry of Finance' (Kurzer, 1993: 175). Together with the pension funds, established in 1960, which gave the SAP some degree of credit steering and investment control capacity, the party's control over the Riksbank and the financial market regulations were a cornerstone of its full employment policy. The control of the financial markets separated the domestic from the international financial markets and provided the necessary economic autonomy for the counter-cyclical Keynesian economic policy (Ryner, 2002: 95–8). In short, the post-war Swedish model was clearly very close to the ideal-type model of negotiated capitalism. Financial capital was subordinated to industrial capital and regulated by the state, trade unions and employers' associations were closely integrated into macroeconomic policy-making in a corporatist system and the state supported this class compromise through an overall focus on a policy of full employment. Trade unions exercised considerable power in the Swedish model due to their close relationship with the governing SAP, the multi-sector collective bargaining as well as their representation on government corporatist institutions.

Economic recession and wildcat strikes endangered the model in the late 1960s (Swenson, 1989: 144–50; Ryner, 2002: 126–44). In response, a joint reform offensive by the ruling SAP and the blue-collar union LO pushed the model into new areas including (1) an active industrial policy by the state; (2) industrial democracy through co-determination in relation to workplace rights; and (3) the plan for workers' control over investment via the so-called wage-earner investment funds (WIFs) initiative (Pontusson, 1995: 28; Wilks, 1996: 96). As a result, in the 1970s, people started to speak about the gradual transformation of Swedish capitalism into socialism. The economic record expressed in unemployment terms was impressive. The 'average rate of open unemployment between 1960 and 1985 was only 2.1 percent' (Olsen, 1996: 7).

The decline of the Swedish model

In 1976, the SAP lost power for the first time in the post-war era. While in opposition, it could not overlook the rising budget deficits and general economic crisis in the late 1970s and early 1980s. In response, it formulated a crisis programme in 1981, which became its guideline for economic policy, when it was back in government in 1982. As a 'third way' between traditional Keynesianism and neo-liberalism, the programme included both traditional policies and departures (Sainsbury, 1993: 56). 'The immediate aim of the "third way" was to reverse the trend of industrial decline through a dramatic increase in net exports, profitability and fixed investments' (Ryner, 1994: 392). A 16 per cent devaluation of the Swedish Krona (SKr) was to ensure export-led growth and the recovery of the Swedish economy. This time, however, the devaluation was the start of a new monetary policy. 'The Big Bang's yield was to be insured with a new commitment to a fixed exchange rate regime' (Moses, 1995: 313).

The SAP's crisis programme of 1981 had spelled out the need for a restrictive fiscal and monetary policy and called for a new hard currency policy with the goal of getting inflation under control. Additionally, the SAP deregulated the financial markets. Amongst others, the liquidity ratio requirements for banks were abolished in 1983 and the ceiling on lending by banks removed in 1985 (Jonung, 1986: 111). In 1986, foreign banks were allowed to open branches in Sweden and, three years later, the SAP government made the final step and abolished foreign exchange controls. The liberalisation of the financial markets gave further credibility to the hard currency policy, since it made a flexible exchange rate policy more expensive.

A similar 'third way' strategy was adopted towards the public sector. In order to avoid privatisation of public services, the growth of the public sector had to be halted (Premfors 1991: 91–2). One way of reducing the budget deficit was to control the payroll cost in the public sector. The government, therefore, attempted to stop the linkage between pay rises in the public with pay rises in the private sector. In 1983, the Metal Workers' Union, affiliated to the LO, had accepted a separate deal with the engineering employers. Instead of opposing this breach of the centralised solidaristic wage negotiations, the government supported this move. The way was open for increasing pay differentiation between the private and the public sector (Mahon, 1999: 136; Swenson, 1991: 383–7).

The original success of the 'third way' strategy was impressive. Sweden, at less than 2 per cent, maintained one of the lowest unemployment rates of the OECD countries and a 13 per cent budget deficit was transformed into a 1 per cent surplus. At the beginning of the 1990s, however, the economy faced the same problems as at the beginning of the 1980s. 'The growth rate was sluggish, wage increases outstripped those of international competitors, the current-account deficit began to grow again, and inflation was on the rise' (Sainsbury, 1991: 39). As it turned out, while the macroeconomic balance had been restored, the structural problems of the Swedish economy had not been solved. Consequently, 'productivity growth increased only slightly between 1982 and 1990 to an average annual increase of 1 percent' (Ryner, 1994: 396). Moreover, while unemployment had successfully been checked, inflation had not been brought under control by the one-sided adoption of a hard currency regime. At an average of 8.6 per cent, it was significantly higher than the German rate of 3 per cent (Notermans, 1993: 139; see also Glyn, 1995: 51–3). The abolition of foreign exchange controls in 1989 was one way of importing price stability from the outside. Nonetheless, even further measures were necessary in order to achieve wage moderation and, thereby, avoid inflation. In October 1990, the government put forward an emergency package, including a partial privatisation of the Swedish state sector (e.g. the telecommunications system and the electricity network) and a cut in the level of sickness benefits (Luif, 1996: 215). It was further concluded that a general expansive fiscal policy in order to counter rising unemployment was no longer possible. 'Social Democrats eventually saw no other way than to abandon their central policy goal [of full employment] and institute a policy regime which consciously created unemployment in order to restore price stability' (Notermans, 1993: 148). This was further highlighted through the declaration that the government intended to apply to the EU for membership, announced as a part of the economic crisis package (Bieler, 2000: 81–4).

It is frequently argued that the demise of the Swedish model was due to the rejection of it by Swedish capital (e.g. Wilks, 1996: 94). And correctly, from the mid-1970s onwards, Swedish capital started to oppose the various features of the Swedish model. It was especially the WIFs initiative component of the labour reform offensive in the 1970s that ran into fierce opposition from employers in that it threatened capital's prerogative over investment and management decisions as such. Unsurprisingly, the WIFs 'deeply antagonized employers in SAF, mobilizing and unifying the economic and political right to a degree highly unusual in Sweden' (Swenson, 1989: 176). The export-oriented capital fraction dominated over the home-market-oriented fraction in the mid-1970s and its members took over key leadership positions in the employers' associations (Olsen, 1991: 131). When Curt Nicolin became the Swedish Employers' Association's (SAF) new chairman in 1976, the association changed its policies towards neo-liberalism and started to transform itself from a wage bargaining institution into an ideologically motivated think tank, which offered the platform for 'organic intellectuals' to spread their neo-liberal message. It 'expanded into the political arena, where it ventured into "the marketing of capitalism" by establishing a range of publishing houses and by organising campaigns aimed at selected target groups to promote pro-capitalist ideology, particularly amongst the young' (Whyman and Burkitt, 1993: 607). This ideological offensive was backed up at the structural level through outward FDI and the related shift of production units predominantly to locations in the EU (see Chapter 3), illustrating the material structure of neo-liberalism in Sweden. Overall, the issue of the WIFs led to an increased class conflict and started the process towards the eventual break-up of the Swedish model.[2]

The SAF's efforts were at first directed against the WIFs. Then, the attack went against the solidaristic wage policy, corporatism and the welfare state (Olsen, 1991: 131–6). Central wage negotiations could temporarily be restored in the years after the separate deal between the engineering employers and the Metal Workers' Union in 1983, but eventually SAF as a whole left the system in the spring of 1990. 'The following winter, it withdrew from the system of corporatist representation on government bodies' (Pontusson, 1995: 39; see also Olsen, 1996: 5). The success of the SAF strategy has to be understood against the background of the increasing transnationalisation of production (see Chapter 3). Without the increase in structural power, resulting from these changes in the social relations of production, it would have been much more difficult for Swedish capital to carry out its strategy against trade unions and the SAP government. Nevertheless, the offensive by capital is only one part of the story. The SAP also contributed to it. It was via the Swedish 'third way' that neo-liberal ideas representing the interests of transnational capital became internalised in the Swedish form of state. The 'third way' never really represented a viable alternative to Keynesian and neo-liberal economic policies. By accepting some principles of neo-liberalism, the seeds were sown for the demise of the Swedish model. First, 'combined, the fixed exchange rate strategies and liberalized capital markets undermined what little monetary autonomy might have remained in the hands of [Swedish] policy-makers' (Moses, 1995: 342). When the economic crisis hit Sweden in 1989/1990, it had to adapt to the global economy, concentrating on price stability via austerity measures in order to avoid the flight of capital. Second, the SAP government actively supported export-oriented employers and unions in their quest for different inter-sectorial wage levels. However, as a result the eventual collapse of the total system of multi-sector centralised wage bargaining had been prepared.

The 'third way' with its neo-liberal ingredients was not the only option available to the SAP after its return to power in 1982. To adopt the 'third way' and to reject the alternative of WIFs was a conscious political decision:

> At the beginning of the 1980s, the Swedish state possessed the institutional requisites for a national economic policy. A good part of the story of the Third Road is the story of how these controls were dismantled, increasing the country's vulnerability to continental and global developments. Such vulnerability, in turn, became the standard rationale for unpopular decisions in the 1990s. (Mahon, 1999: 139)

Moreover, the substitution of price stability for the full employment policy at the beginning of the 1990s was not a necessity. Despite the structural changes since the early 1970s, the expansion of employment was still possible via negotiated wage restraint (Glyn, 1995: 55; Ryner, 2002: 48–54 and 142–4). The actual decisions taken by the SAP were also partly due to SAP-internal ideological changes (Olsen, 1996: 10). From 1976 onwards, the SAP leadership had only half-heartedly supported the LO initiative of WIFs. Additionally, after its electoral defeat of the same year, it had formed its own research unit under Kjell-Olof Feldt, later Finance Minister. 'Feldt and his advisors were determined to give priority to private-sector growth, profits and market forces' (Pontusson, 1995: 35). It was this group that formulated the 'third way' strategy and put it into practice after 1982. The LO, on the other hand, was significantly weakened. 'Intellectual authority had passed from its researchers to the policy unit of the party' (Pontusson, 1995: 28). Hence, neo-liberal economics had become internalised within core state institutions such as the Finance Ministry. Unsurprisingly, it was the Finance Ministry together with the Prime Minister's Office, which had been the driving force within the SAP government behind the decision to apply to the EU in 1990. Application was the attempt to refer a 'sound' economic policy to supranational restrictions and to have a scapegoat for harsh domestic policy measures (Bieler, 2000: 83).

Finally, another reason for the demise of the Swedish model was the division within the labour movement between national and transnational labour resulting from globalisation. For example, the separate wage agreement between the LO affiliate the Metal Workers' Union and the Engineering Employers' Association in 1983 had not only resulted in a conflict between SAP and LO, but also in an LO internal conflict between the Municipal Workers' Union, representing workers in the domestic public sector, and the Metal Workers' Union, organising workers in transnational manufacturing (Sainsbury, 1991: 41). This split became further visible in the debates around the referendum on EU membership in 1994. Transnational sector unions supported membership arguing that Sweden had to follow the de facto move to the EU by the TNCs via their FDI activities. National production sector unions, on the other hand, were concerned about the impact of the neo-liberal economic-political model of the EU on the Swedish model and here especially on the extensive public sector spending. Consequently, they argued for a 'no' in the referendum (Bieler, 2000: 102–7). It is investigated in Chapters 6 and 7 whether this split within the labour movement is also visible over the issues of EMU and European co-operation.

Collective bargaining experienced some revival in Sweden from 1997 onwards. This was not, however, at the multi-sector level, where talks failed in 1998 (Eironline, 28 January 1999, http://www.eiro.eurofound.eu.int/1999/01/inbrief/se9901135n.html; 07/12/2004), but at the sectoral level. In 1997, trade unions and employers' associations in private industry signed the so-called Industrial Agreement, renewed in 1999, which comprised the formulation of common assessments of the economic situation and an agreement on rules and procedures about collective wage bargaining at the sectoral national level. This included the imposition of an impartial Chair should negotiations stall with the intention 'to reach a new agreement with a balanced result before the old agreement expires' (Industrial Agreement, 1999: 2). It was soon followed by similar agreements in other sectors. In 2000, the Swedish government established a new Mediation Authority to support collective bargaining in those areas, not covered by separate sectoral agreements (Eironline, 28 May 2001, http://www.eiro.eurofound.eu.int/2001/05/feature/se0105195f.html; 07/12/2004). In sum, Swedish trade unions, while they lost their traditional central role and influence via multi-sector collective bargaining and corporatist state institutions, regained some impact within the structural selectivity of the Swedish form of state in the late 1990s due to the re-establishment of collective bargaining and be it at the sectoral level.

Conclusion

All five forms of state have clearly become transnationalised over the last two decades. This does not imply an institutional convergence. Due to the different way capitalism emerged historically in the five countries, the particular institutional set-up continues to differ from country to country. What can, however, be identified is a general move towards neo-liberal economic policies. Britain, already ahead as far as neo-liberal policies are concerned, has moved even further in this direction. France has retained its distinctive institutional set-up, but the identification of a shift to a state-enhanced model of capitalism is an expression of an increasing use of neo-liberal policies. Germany preserved its traditional model longer than others. While Britain and then also France started to change in the 1980s, the former more rapid than the latter, Germany opted for clearer neo-liberal policies only towards the end of the 1990s. Austria and Sweden too shifted towards neo-liberal economics, but on different time-scales. While Austria re-focused from the early 1980s onwards, in Sweden the decisive turn to neo-liberalism occurred in the early 1990s, although the 'third way' strategy of the 1980s had in many respects prepared this change of course. While neo-liberalism occurred in Austria initially within the established institutional set-up, the traditional corporatist institutions collapsed in Sweden in the early 1990s, before new corporatist arrangements were established from 1997 onwards. For the following investigation of trade unions' positions on EMU and European co-operation, two factors need to be kept in mind. First, despite a general shift towards neo-liberal economics within the individual forms of state, the degree of transnationalisation of the social relations of production and thus the nature of social forces differs from country to country (see Chapter 3). This needs to be referred to when dealing with the first hypothesis, introduced in Chapter 1:

> A labour movement's position on EMU depends crucially on its length and degree of exposure to the competitive pressures of globalisation. Unions, which represent workers in transnational production sectors, are more likely to support EMU, because they may support their companies – on which their own well-being depends – which benefit from a stable monetary environment and institutionalised free trade within the EU. Moreover, because they realise that they have lost control over capital at the national level, they are probably prepared to co-operate with other unions at the European level. National production sector unions, on the other hand, are likely to oppose EMU, since it undermines national policy autonomy and, thus, the support, on which their sectors depend. Relying on the state, they may also be less concerned about European co-operation.

Second, the continuing institutional diversity makes clear that trade unions are confronted with different structural possibilities in the individual countries. The extent to which they can influence policy-making at the national level, i.e. the structural selectivity of the particular form of state, may imply for some that a shift of focus towards the EU is the best way forward, while others are likely to continue placing an emphasis on domestic politics. This needs to be kept in mind in relation to the second hypothesis:

> Those trade unions, which have lost influence within the national institutional set-up, are probably more in favour of European co-operation and the establishment of an industrial relations system as well as social regulations at the European level to counter global pressures. By contrast, unions that still enjoy considerable impact on policy-making at the national level are likely to be less interested in European co-operation.

In the next part of this book, the positions of trade unions in the five case studies and at the European level on EMU and European co-operation will be assessed in close relation to these two hypotheses.

Notes

1 Additional weekly demonstrations in cities across Germany took place in July and August 2004 (Eironline, 6 September 2004, http://www.eiro.eurofound.eu.int/2004/09/inbrief/de0409204n.html; 04/11/2004).
2 The SAP's loss of power in 1976 prevented the establishment of WIFs. After their return to power in 1982, the fund system was implemented, but only in a watered-down version and with little reference to workers' control over capital and investment decision-making (Heclo and Madsen, 1987: 282).

Part III
Trade unions and their positions on EMU and European co-operation

5
Trade union confederations and the attempt at coherence

Introduction

This chapter analyses the positions of the trade union confederations on EMU and European co-operation in the five case studies. This does not relate directly to the first hypothesis, since confederations include both transnational and national forces of labour, but it provides a good first marker of the empirical situation in the countries under investigation. Trade union confederations' positions are also important because their affiliated sectoral unions are frequently either aligned with, or contrasted their positions to, the confederations. In turn, the latter were concerned to retain some degree of organisational unity. Importantly, the positions on EMU in themselves do not provide information about confederations' willingness to engage in European level co-operation. Hence, the latter issue will be dealt with in a separate sub-section. Here it is important to see whether the second hypothesis of this book holds, i.e. are those unions, which have lost influence at the national level, more likely to engage in European level co-operation? Finally, when analysing trade unions' positions on EMU and European co-operation, additional attention will be placed on investigating whether these unions have accepted neo-liberal restructuring or not.

This chapter is organised in three parts. While there is only one confederation in Austria, Britain and Germany, there are several rival organisations in France and Sweden. More space is, consequently, allocated to the latter two countries. Hence, the first section will deal with the unions' positions on EMU and European co-operation of those countries that have only one confederation, i.e. Britain, Germany and Austria. The second section will analyse the French situation, where seven confederations are of importance, while the third section is dedicated to the three Swedish confederations. The conclusion will sum up the results of this chapter and provide an outlook on the subsequent empirical chapters.

Countries with one trade union confederation: the TUC in Britain, the DGB in Germany and the ÖGB in Austria

The confederations' positions on EMU

The British TUC discussed EMU from the Delors appearance at the 1988 congress onwards (Interview No. 17; London, 28/03/2001) and swung fully behind it in 1996 (Josselin, 2001: 61). This positive position was confirmed during the following years. EMU would imply that exchange rate uncertainty was overcome, helping especially export-oriented manufacturing, which was suffering from an over-valued Pound (Interview No. 17; London, 28/03/2001). Remaining outside EMU, on the other hand, could imply that Britain drifted further apart from the rest of the EU. 'The TUC is particularly concerned at the statements attributed to a number of leading inward investors that the strong pound and the uncertainty about the Euro are threatening long-term investment in the UK' (TUC, 2000: 7). There were also concerns about being squeezed with a relatively unimportant currency between the US Dollar bloc and the Eurozone. The political implications of non-membership would be the relegation to a secondary place in the decision-making process, when the twelve finance ministers of the Euro-countries took their economic and monetary decisions (Interview No. 17; London, 28/03/2001). 'Exclusion from the euro Group reduces the UK's ability to influence the course of events, but the outcomes will have a permanent effect on the UK, whether we are members or not' (TUC, 2002: 2). John Monks, then general secretary of the TUC, summarised the position as follows: '[E]very day that passes that we stay out, our position is weakened in the European Union. If you don't take part in one of the central elements in the European project, our influence on the other elements diminishes. And while we keep putting off the decision, inward investors don't put off theirs . . .' (Monks, 2001).

The Social Dimension was, however, regarded as an absolutely essential part of EMU. Thus, the TUC raised various elements it considered to be important including the Social Chapter, a flexible interpretation of the convergence criteria, more regional funds, a co-operative growth strategy and democratic accountability of the ECB (Verdun, 2000: 142, 155). This link between EMU and the further development of the Social Dimension was also expressed in the TUC's report *Preparing for the Euro*, published in January 1999, when a positive reference was made to the first multi-sector framework agreements at EU level (Sisson et al., 1999: 21). In its statement to the 2002 TUC Annual Congress, the TUC General Council emphasised the 'continuing balance between economic and social progress, enshrined within the European Social Model' (TUC, 2002: 1). Initially, the TUC had also stressed the importance of economic policy co-ordination with the goal of higher employment levels and more rapid economic growth. In 2001, the TUC was still in favour of a common economic policy and a larger EU budget, geared towards employment programmes. Since the transfer of resources to Brussels was, however, an unpopular issue, the TUC had not pressed this point very strongly any more. In contrast to some of its affiliated unions (see Chapter 7), the TUC was less worried about the potential damaging effects of the convergence criteria on public investment levels. The criteria themselves were not regarded as unreasonable, as long as they were interpreted in a flexible way, and they would not be a problem for Britain, since the Chancellor Gordon Brown applied even tougher targets aiming for national debt below 40 per cent of GDP (Interview No. 17; London, 28/03/2001).

Accordingly, in its report to the Treasury Select Committee on the Euro in January 2003, the TUC argued that the SGP, continuing the enforcement of the convergence criteria, should not be unduly regarded as a big obstacle to (1) national economic policy autonomy and (2) public sector investment. First, because 'remaining outside the Euro does not free the UK from its obligations to observe and help enforce the guidelines, including the country specific policy recommendations' (TUC, 2003a: 3). Outside the Pact, actions to adapt would have to be even faster and more drastic. Second, the SGP as such would not oblige members to cut back on public sector investment. It would only say something about how public spending was financed. Moreover, relevant data would suggest that the three countries outside EMU, Britain, Denmark and Sweden, had cut back public spending more severely than EMU members. Of course, the TUC was in favour of some reform of the SGP including more emphasis on growth as well as allowing countries with debt levels clearly below 60 per cent to invest more in the public sector. Nonetheless, the Commission's recommendations on reform would already include this as they suggested to calculate the deficit in line with the economic cycle.

In relation to criticisms raised against the ECB too, the TUC adopted a moderate approach. In comparison with the ECB, the Bundesbank would always have been similarly tough on price stability, but the advantage now was that the ECB had to take its decisions in light of the interests of all EMU members, not only Germany. Moreover, despite its tough anti-inflationary statements, the ECB was deemed to have conducted a more pragmatic course, attempting to stimulate growth via interest rate cuts. As for the reform of the ECB, the TUC recommended, first, 'to increase transparency by publishing a summary of the debate within the ECB Council when interest rate policy is being decided' (TUC, 2003a: 11). Second, growth should play a stronger role through adopting the 2 per cent inflation target as a symmetrical target, i.e. undershooting the target should be regarded as much as a problem due to its deflationary implications as overshooting it. Additionally, the setting of an inflation target should be subject to a Commission recommendation to the Council as part of the annual BEPG, thereby introducing political input in monetary policy-making. Overall, the TUC favoured early entry in line with its view 'that the economics [of British EMU membership] are as about right now as they ever will be' (TUC, 2003a: 12). Thus, the TUC was a strong supporter of EMU membership. It pushed for the further development of the Social Dimension, but was not too concerned about the implications of the SGP, ECB independence and the related price stability policy. While this was understandable against the background of more restrictive domestic policies, it also indicated a rather accommodationist position vis-à-vis neo-liberal restructuring. At the same time, the TUC also had to take into account the divisions among its affiliates over EMU membership (see Chapters 6 and 7). Hence, in its statement on Britain and the Euro for the 2003 TUC congress, the TUC General Council argued that

> the central considerations identified by Congress in relation to membership of the single currency are the achievement of a sustainable exchange rate between the pound and the Euro and the need for stability conducive to attracting foreign direct investment and sustaining a solid manufacturing base; a consolidation and expansion of the European Social Model rather than moves towards US free market approaches; and assurances regarding any repercussions of entry on public expenditure, notably through a harmful application of the Stability and Growth Pact. (TUC, 2003b: 2)

The DGB was leading the discussions on EMU within the German labour movement from the early 1990s onwards (Verdun, 2000: 180). It did not have a problem with EMU. Germany's export-oriented economy, often hampered by an appreciation of the Deutschmark (DM), would benefit from stable exchange rates within the EU (DGB, 1995: 26; DGB, 1997a: 2). A postponement of EMU was regarded as a danger to the German economy in this respect. 'Postponing EMU', it was argued, 'does not contribute to an active employment policy. The DGB, instead, is rather worried that a delay of monetary union will lead to a significant appreciation of the DM and, therefore, does not only endanger jobs dependent on export, but could also cause another economic recession' (DGB, 1996: 4). Moreover, the examples of France and Sweden in the 1980s would show that demand management macroeconomic policies at the national level would no longer be feasible in a situation of increasing interdependence of European economies. EMU would create the conditions for regaining economic policy autonomy at the European level (DGB, 1997a: 5).

Nevertheless, the DGB's support was not without conditions, indicating its opposition to neo-liberal restructuring. First, the DGB demanded a further development of the Social Dimension. Most importantly, social minimum standards should be established at the EU level to avoid the competition between different economic locations (Interview No. 10; Berlin, 06/02/2001). Second, the union realised that the convergence criteria forced a budget austerity policy. Hence, the DGB initially demanded an additional employment target and a stronger co-ordination of national employment policies. Full employment as a goal should be written into the revised treaty at Amsterdam (DGB, 1995: 11; DGB, 1996: 4). Additionally, the criterion of 3 per cent budget deficit of GDP should not be regarded as an absolute, but be interpreted flexibly to allow for the stimulation of demand during recession (DGB, 1996: 3). Moreover, the deepening of the Internal Market through EMU was likely to lead to further restructuring, affecting especially small- and medium-sized companies and including the possible loss of jobs. National and European structural policies should take this into account and support these companies. 'This does not only affect social and ecological minimum standards, which need to be expanded further. It will be decisive that the employment and structural policy (industrial and regional policy) will be strengthened at the European level beyond the existing support by the EU structural funds' (DGB, 1997a: 4). Finally, the European institutions such as the Commission, European Parliament (EP) and Economic and Social Committee (ESC) had to be strengthened to provide an institutional counter-weight to the ECB (DGB, 1996: 5). At a meeting of the general executive on 8 April 1997, the DGB confirmed its support for EMU on the following condi-tions: a flexible interpretation of the convergence criteria, especially the 3 per cent budget deficit criterion; a commitment not to cut back further the welfare state and public investment; a stronger focus on employment within the EU; and European-wide investment to modernise infrastructure and to create employment and economic growth (DGB, 1997b). Unsurprisingly, the DGB was not satisfied with the SGP. In its current form, it would represent a structural obstacle to growth and employment in the Euro-zone. The 3 per cent budget deficit criterion could not be justified economically and especially public invest-ment in areas such as education, R&D policies should not be taken into account in the calculation of this criterion considering their importance for future economic growth (DGB, 2005: 2). Not high labour costs, but the lack of domestic demand, argued Michael Sommer, the president of the DGB, would be the main cause of Germany's low economic growth and high unemployment levels. Hence, low wage increases and public austerity budgets should be rethought, when the necessary formulation of a new comprehensive macroeconomic policy took place (DGB, 2004: 3). Again, this clearly indicates the DGB's continuing criticism of neo-liberal economics.

Initially in 1992/1993, EMU was not regarded as a problem by the ÖGB, as it was clear that Austria, at that time not an EU member yet, would comfort-ably fulfil the convergence criteria. Moreover, the Commission's plans for a European-wide infrastructure investment programme in 1993, which intended to half unemployment by 2000, gave further reason for optimism (Tüchler, 1997: 1). Of course, the ÖGB was disappointed about the missing Social Dimension in the convergence criteria, but this was taken as a reason for being even more in favour of membership, as only this would allow participation in the decision-making processes (ÖGB, 1991). This included the possibility of demanding the adding of an unemployment criterion, as raised by several voices within the Austrian labour movement (Bieler, 2000: 91). Additionally, it was also considered to be rather unlikely that EMU would ever come about in view of the economic difficulties of the EMS in 1992/1993 (Interview No. 26; Wien, 19/03/2002). First criticisms arose from 1995 onwards against the background of a difficult budgetary situation to become stronger with the SGP in 1997. Here, EcoFin was perceived to set a fiscal framework, which would be more like a straightjacket. Through its requirement of a balanced budget over the medium term, it would intensify the convergence criteria even further. The next problem was the position of the ECB, which exclusively concentrated on price stability (Interview No. 26; Wien, 19/03/2002). In Austria, it was clear that public invest-ment levels had declined due to the convergence criteria and their one-sided focus on price stability. Hence, there was an increasing demand for an unemployment criterion, based on the assumption that labour market deregulation in combination with a policy of price stability would not lead to more employment (Interview No. 25; Vienna, 18/03/2002). 'If the criterion for employment is not incorporated into the convergence programme, there is the danger that unemployment will continue to rise dramatically' (ÖGB-News, 1997).

The ÖGB argued that a European economic policy must be more than monetary policy. Full employment had to be the core focus (Tüchler, 1997: 2–3). The identification of full employment as a goal in the Lisbon strategy was welcomed, but the political and institutional primacy of a stability oriented economic and monetary policy by the EU and ECB was heavily criticised (AK, 2001: 1–2). Additionally, the ÖGB demanded together with the ETUC that the ECB operated more like the US Federal Reserve Bank, which also had to pay attention to employment and growth levels and had, therefore, used cuts in interest rates as a tool of demand stimulation in a much more aggressive way than the ECB (Interview No. 25; Wien, 18/03/2002). This should also include a re-definition of inflation, which was deemed as too low with a value between 0 and 2 per cent to generate enough demand and, thereby, economic growth (AK, 2001: 92). Furthermore, wage agreements should be in line with inflation plus productivity increases, in order to ensure that there was enough demand to stimulate growth (Interview No. 26; Wien, 19/03/2002). This did not signify that EMU was completely rejected by the ÖGB. It was accepted that the single currency implied greater levels of economic stability due to the loss of changing exchange rates (ÖGB-News, 1997). The fundamental basis of EMU, however, had to be changed. Instead of neo-liberal oriented economic and social policy-making, a social and employment union was needed.

In sum, all three confederations endorsed EMU. All three, however, had also continued to criticise its neo-liberal rationale embodied especially in the convergence criteria, with perhaps the TUC slightly less worried about the general neo-liberal implications than the other two. The TUC and DGB argued that the criteria should be interpreted flexibly, the DGB and ÖGB demanded an additional unemployment criterion. All three demanded a further development of the Social Dimension as well as a stronger commitment towards employment policies. The latter should also include demand-side components with the TUC advocating a common economic policy geared towards employment programmes, the DGB and ÖGB supporting European-level investment into infrastructure programmes. The TUC and DGB demanded to make the ECB democratically accountable, while the ÖGB argued that the ECB should use the tool of interest rate cuts more forcefully in order to stimulate demand. For the same purpose, wage increases should be in line with inflation plus productivity increase. Hence, none of the three confederations supported neo-liberal restructuring in Europe, but they felt for a range of different reasons that EMU should be accepted. What needed to be changed would be its underlying rationale. These positions were not accepted by all affiliated unions. The various differences within the Austrian, British and German labour movements and whether they fall along the division between national and transnational production sectors, as envisaged in the first hypothesis, will be dealt with in Chapters 6 and 7. The next sub-section assesses whether the conditional support for EMU by the confederations was combined with a willingness to co-operate along this line at the European level.

The issue of European co-operation

In general, the TUC was very positive about the Social Dimension and its development. In contrast to sectoral social dialogue, the ETUC-UNICE multi-sector social dialogue was deemed to be a real success. Guaranteeing direct union involvement, the multi-sector framework agreements would be a good way of obtaining general standards while leaving enough room for manoeuvre for implementation in the very different national circumstances. The TUC combined this emphasis on social dialogue at the European level with a push for collective negotiations/bargaining as a better way of implementing directives in the UK instead of government legislation. From a UK point of view, the agreements of the social dialogue had brought considerable improvements of the working conditions and workers' rights in Britain. The TUC maintained a small office in Brussels, but it did not approach the Commission directly on its own. It was closely integrated in the ETUC and almost all initiatives went via the ETUC (Interview No. 17; London, 28/03/2001). In general terms, the TUC regarded this point in time as a defining moment in relation to the future European model of capitalism. In the words of the General Secretary Brendan Barber,

> on the one hand is the American model – deregulation, casual hire and fire, minimal levels of social welfare, long working hours, an economy in which trade unionism is under constant attack from corporate leaderships desperate to deny working people a voice . . . ; the alternative, for which we have to be the standard bearer, which is a hugely important battle of ideas, is the model which we have developed here in Europe, based on secure welfare states, social partnership, a strong framework of rights, both for citizens and workers. (TUC Annual Congress, 2004)

EU membership including EMU membership was for the TUC part of the struggle for a European social model of capitalism.

One needs to understand this positive attitude towards European integration against the background of the British labour movement's experience with the Thatcher governments during the 1980s. Traditionally, the TUC and British unions in general were one of the fiercest opponents to EU membership. In 1972, the TUC declared its opposition to EU membership in principle. 'The result of the 1975 referendum saw the British union movement commencing its participation in the advisory committee structure, but official policy continued to oppose UK membership of the [EU]' (Rosamond, 1998: 133). Large parts of the labour movement supported the so-called Alternative Economic Strategy (AES) in the early 1980s, based on 'the socialist regeneration of the British economy upon the reclamation of full economic sovereignty' (Rosamond, 1993: 430). This would clearly have been incompatible with EU membership. Nevertheless, after the Labour Party's electoral defeat in 1983 and the failure of the French socialist experiment of the Mitterand government in 1983, there was a shift away from the AES criticised for its nationalist overtones and exclusion of international solutions to British workers' problems. The view that international competitiveness and stable domestic demand could be maintained via flexible exchange rates was abandoned (Strange, 1997: 18; Strange, 2002a: 343–4). From then onwards, trade union and leftwing political goals were perceived as feasible within the European arena. Important in this re-orientation was Jacques Delors', then president of the Commission, appearance at the TUC Congress in 1988, lobbying for a positive attitude towards European integration. In more concrete terms, the emerging Social Dimension around the Social Charter in 1989 and the Social Chapter of the Maastricht Treaty in 1991 as well as the concrete improvements for British workers resulting from the first EU directives, which were negotiated by the ETUC and UNICE, against the background of the Conservative government's onslaught on unions, 'laid the basis for positive connotations of European integration to become embedded in British trade union discourse' (Rosamond, 1998: 142). Becoming a member of EMU, John Monks argued at a TUC conference in May 1999, 'would strengthen the influence of the "European social model" on UK industrial relations' (Sisson et al., 1999: 21). The main strategy forward was located at the European level in the form of Euro-Keynesianism, 'in which the traditional post-war emphasis on the management of national demand by the nation-state has been replaced by a new emphasis on the co-ordinated management of the European economy through European level mechanisms of governance and economic control' (Strange, 1997: 18; see also Strange, 2002b: 352–60).

Since the arrival of Labour in power in 1997, the TUC's approach had been more even-handed between the European and national level. The minimum wage and new union recognition laws were put forward as positive results of domestic level lobbying of the UK government. The slightly more intensive focus on the national level was also an appreciation of the fact that there would currently be less and less enthusiasm for more re-regulation at the European level. For the next years, the TUC assumed that it would be involved more in the defence and consolidation of the achieved conditions than progressing into new areas (Interview No. 17; London, 28/03/2001). Clearly, this confirms the second hypothesis that very good access to policy-making at the national level is likely to make the European level less relevant to unions. While trade unions were under frontal attack by Conservative governments, the European avenue was pursued more forcefully. With Labour back in power, there was a further re-adjustment of strategy, putting more emphasis again on the national level. Whether this remains the case considering New Labour's continuing neglect of core trade union concerns is an open-ended question.

For the DGB, the most important European task was the establishment of social minimum standards across the EU to avoid competition between different countries over which was the most attractive economic location. This echoed its position on the Internal Market in the late 1980s/early 1990s (Markovits and

Otto, 1993: 46). Not much had, however, happened yet in this respect, it was argued. The EU level was regarded as important, but decisions would still be taken by the Council of Ministers and European Council. Hence, the DGB had tended to put more pressure on the national government. The co-ordination of wage bargaining at the European level (see Chapter 8) was considered to be possible to some extent, but European-wide collective wage bargaining was regarded as illusionary. National systems would simply be too different (Interview No. 10; Berlin, 06/02/2001). Thus, on the one hand, the DGB was supportive of European integration. The neo-liberal rationale of EMU and European integration in general was criticised, but the demands for change such as the further development of the Social Dimension, further European restructuring assistance and a strengthening of European institutions as a counterweight to the ECB (see above) emphasised further European integration, not retaining sovereignty at the national level. In short, there was clearly a positive attitude towards the EU. One has to see this against the specific German historical background. Similar to general German support for European integration after World War Two, German unions saw no alternative to closer European ties. EMU was regarded as an important further step of European integration towards political union and the DGB as well as its affiliated unions almost regarded it as their historical duty to support it (Interview No. 8; Stuttgart, 01/02/2001; Interview No. 9; Hannover, 05/02/2001; Interview No. 10; Berlin, 06/02/2001). 'A failure of the monetary union project would imply a high risk for the future political development of Europe. The return to nationalism is not only for Germany, but also for others a real danger' (IG Metall, 1996: 1). Thus, the DGB is part of 'an ideological world in the Federal Republic that perhaps more than ever advocates Germany's integration into a strong European framework lest suspicions about Germany's "Sonderweg" and "Schaukelpolitik" once again become manifest' (Markovits and Otto, 1993: 67; see also Josselin, 2001: 71).

On the other hand, the DGB was realistic in its assessment of the possibilities at the European level in comparison with its capacities at the German level. The historical background of tripartite decision-making in Germany (see Chapter 4) and especially the coming to power by a Social Democratic and Green Party coalition government in 1998 suggested at least initially that avenues of influence would be much more concrete at the national level than within the European arena. Similarly to the TUC in the UK, the DGB therefore re-oriented its attention to the German level (Interview No. 10; Berlin, 06/02/2001). This confirms again the second hypothesis that unions with better access to policy-making at the national than the European level are likely to prioritise the former over the latter. For how long the DGB continues this strategy considering the unilateral neo-liberal restructuring course of the Social Democratic-Green government and the Social Democratic-Christian Democratic government since 2005 remains to be seen.

In Austria during the process leading towards the country's EU membership, both the AK and the ÖGB supported accession to the EU in the late 1980s/early 1990s. Both felt unable to suggest an alternative way of how to revive the Austrian economy other than by EU membership and the related opening up and restructuring of the sheltered sectors of the economy. After the end of the Cold War, the emergence of new competitors in CEE further focused trade union leaders' minds on the EU. In addition to retaining neutrality, however, it was demanded that full employment was the EU's key goal in its economic and social policy. This positive position also needs to be seen in the light of the French failure between 1981 and 1983 to pursue Keynesian policies at the national level. It was the European level that would provide better possibilities to control TNCs in times of globalisation (Bieler, 2000: 59–60). In short, the ÖGB considered the EU to be the better level to influence policy-making, thereby placing specific emphasis on the Social Dimension as a counterweight to EMU. Similar to the controls on fiscal national policy, the implementation of social policy should also be monitored (Interview No. 26; Wien, 19/03/2002).

In practical terms, however, it was realised since membership in 1995 that this had not materialised yet. Social dialogue in itself was deemed very good and here the multi-sector and sectoral levels were considered to be preferable to the EWCs level for EU bargaining. Otherwise, some workers would gain a privileged status, while the majority suffered from cut-backs. Nevertheless, the Commission was criticised for not having been very active here over the last years and the ÖGB had noticed the employers' reluctance in this respect (Interview No. 25; Wien, 18/03/2002). The latter would have blocked the establishment of social minimum standards and rejected the implementation of the so-called voluntary multi-sector agreements on telework and work-related stress in Austria (ÖGB, 2004: 2). In short, the development of the Social Dimension to date was regarded as a disappointment. Finally, the ETUC would need to be restructured in order to become more effective. Overall, against the background of successful bargaining at the Austrian level for decades and a general fear of loss of power, the transfer of competencies was still regarded as less likely. One needs to remember, however, that the AK had had its own office in Brussels for some time and had increasingly attempted to lobby the Commission directly (Interview No. 26; Wien, 19/03/2002). Moreover, the more recent onslaught on tripartism in Austria by the ÖVP-FPÖ coalition government and the related deteriorating possibilities of unions within the changing structural selectivity of the Austrian form of state (see Chapter 4) may make the European level further attractive in the future.

In sum, all three confederations were supportive of European-level co-operation, the extent of which, however, strongly depended on the possibilities at the national level in line with the second hypothesis of this study. Despite the recent re-orientation to the national level, the TUC was clearly the most enthusiastic supporter of European-level co-operation having experienced the curtailing of its national power base by Conservative governments during the 1980s and early 1990s. This may also explain why it was least worried about the neo-liberal implications of EMU. The DGB and ÖGB also appreciated the possibilities of the European level. Their concrete strategies, however, were still very much focused on the national level, where they had enjoyed strong involvement in economic and social decision-making in corporatist institutions over decades. The more recent undermining of these national avenues to policy-making may, however, induce a future re-direction of strategy.

Trade union confederations in France

French confederations and EMU

A focal point of discussion in France was the referendum on the Treaty of Maastricht in September 1992. The CFDT came out strongly in favour of the Treaty. It was considered to be an historic step of European integration in that for the first time countries decided voluntarily to give up their own currency (Interview No. 55; Paris, 12/09/2002). This endorsement, however, did not imply an uncritical acceptance of neo-liberal restructuring. The CFDT criticised the Treaty of Maastricht for its one-sided focus. 'The Treaty of Maastricht,' it was argued 'remains inspired by too liberal a vision at the economic and monetary level' (Prouteau, 1992: 6; see also 8). Market forces and economic growth alone would not automatically result in more employment. Rather, employment itself needed to be retained as an objective with specific policies devised in this respect (Raiga, 1990: 10). If the CFDT supported a 'yes' in the referendum, then it did so despite the neo-liberal underpinning of EMU. The hope was that it would only be the starting-point towards a social as well as political union. As Jean Kaspar, then general secretary of the CFDT, outlined, 'this ratification is necessary to start a new stage for Europe, especially at the social level' (Kaspar, 1992: 7). In this respect, the fact that the social partner agreement between the ETUC and UNICE of 31 October 1991 was integrated into the Treaty and that QMV was partly introduced for social policy issues, making it thus easier to achieve further integration in the social policy area, was highlighted as a positive step towards a social union (Kaspar, 1991: 3; Kaspar, 1992: 7; Prouteau, 1992: 7).

Since the referendum, the CFDT had concentrated on lobbying for a common economic policy at the European level. Additionally, it questioned whether the SGP should not be made more flexible to allow the accommodation of national emergencies such as large-scale flooding in Germany in 2002 (Interview No. 55; Paris, 12/09/2002). The Euro was perceived as a logical next step of European integration. Considering the geopolitical situation with regional integration projects around the Dollar being pushed forward elsewhere in the world, there would be no alternative to monetary union in Europe. Only together could small European countries make their voices heard at the international level (Bass, 1997: 29; CFDT, 1997: 3–4; Réau, 1997: 12). The convergence criteria themselves or the independent status of the ECB, however, were not regarded as a problem. It was argued that because the national level could no longer provide alternatives, public deficits must not be allowed to grow further. It was only questioned whether the cuts had to be necessarily in the public sector. An independent ECB was welcomed, because it would prevent economic policy from becoming an election issue (Interview No. 55; Paris, 12/09/2002). The CFDT did not pay too much attention to a possible link between unemployment and the single currency, although it was accepted that the latter implied job losses. The Treaty of Amsterdam was regarded as a positive step forward, since it included the employment chapter, which forced governments to co-ordinate better national employment policies within the Luxembourg employment strategy. A common, more active employment policy at the European level would be welcomed, but it was accepted that this was currently unlikely in a climate where states generally refused to transfer more money to Brussels (Réau, 1997: 11; Interview No. 55; Paris, 12/09/2002). In sum, there was strong support for EMU as long as it was combined with further progress in the area of the Social Dimension. This, together with a focus on active employment programmes, indicates that the CFDT had not fully accepted neo-liberal restructuring. Nevertheless, by not criticising the convergence criteria and the independent status of the ECB, the CFDT had adopted some neo-liberal policy aspects.

In contrast to the CFDT, the CGT recommended a 'no' for the referendum on the Treaty of Maastricht in 1992. This was, however, neither a rejection of the EU, nor an objection of the idea of an economic union. The 'no' was due to the monetarist contents around the convergence criteria. Rather than having criteria that allowed the integration of the social aspects of the economy, the latter would be forced to adapt to the neo-liberal criteria (Interview No. 60; Paris, 13/09/2002). In short, the CGT rejected EMU initially for three major reasons:

> First, the convergence criteria were deemed too restrictive and likely to lead to a multi-speed Europe, with inherent risks of instability. Second, the establishment of a European central bank independent from political authority would reinforce the power of financial markets. Third, once the autonomy of national monetary and budgetary policies had been curtailed, the burden of adjustment would fall on wage earners, in the form of lower wages or higher unemployment. (Josselin, 2001: 60–1)

Once France had become an EMU member, the CGT mainly criticised the SGP and its budgetary constraints (Durand, 2002). Additionally, the ECB was criticised for concentrating almost exclusively on price stability. The US Federal Reserve Bank, which had employment and economic growth amongst its objectives, was presented as an alternative. Moreover, the ECB should not only lower interest rates more radically, but one should also think about steering credit allocation towards the creation of production facilities. Economic union as such was deemed necessary nowadays and a much stronger industrial policy at the European level, for example in the area of R&D, demanded. The Luxembourg process of employment policy co-ordination and the Lisbon strategy, on the other hand, were not regarded as satisfactory in their present form, since social and economic policies were not integrated. In sum, as France was now a member of EMU, it should remain inside, but try to change its rationale (Interview No. 60; Paris, 13/09/2002). Thus, while accepting EMU as a reality now, the CGT, in contrast to the CFDT, not only demanded a stronger focus on the further development of the Social Dimension, but it also wanted to change the rationale underlying EMU to date. 'We cannot', the CGT argued, 'be content with a mere assessment that the construction of Europe is mainly organised around a monetary and financial approach. There is a legitimate feeling that we need a Europe that offers social cohesion, through links of solidarity between its inhabitants' (CGT, 2002: 5).

Adhering to its commitment to political neutrality, the FO only outlined the different positions before the 1992 referendum and left it to its members to decide on how to vote. As such, however, the FO heavily criticised the Maastricht convergence criteria. They would imply financial cut backs in the public sector, resulting in job losses and lower quality services. The ECB's sole focus on price stability was also criticised. FO accepted the referendum outcome but continued to criticise the economic rationale as it was represented in the convergence criteria and the SGP (Interview No. 58; Paris, 12/09/2002; see also Josselin, 2001: 61). Along this line, the FO criticised the ECB in 1999 for the increase in interest rates by 0.5 per cent. This would only put pressure on wage negotiations and lead towards more precarious and temporary employment, while it did not improve the purchasing power of the public and, thus, general demand levels (FO, 1999). There would simply be an uneven priority between economic and social issues. 'Integration is mainly economically and financially driven, while the EU still considers the social sphere to be a sub-product of the economy' (FO, 2000: 558; see also FO, 2002a). The FO had no illusions about the Amsterdam employment chapter, since 'employability, competence, flexibility and adaptability are the main words in this new chapter' (FO, 2000: 560). Although full employment was mentioned in the Lisbon strategy, the required macroeconomic policy would still be missing. Unemployment and deindustrialisation, it was argued, had actually accelerated and the Lisbon strategy had failed in that there was persistent mass unemployment and precarity. Under the guise of full employment, the Lisbon strategy would push for the 'reform' of the labour market, of the social security and pension systems and the public services more generally (FO, 2004). Overall, FO perceived a clear danger that the EU adopted a neo-liberal, Anglo-American model of capitalism (Interview No. 59; Paris, 13/09/2002). Instead, FO requested a better distribution of wealth in tandem with national and EU policies towards full, high-quality employment leading to the development of a European social model, which guaranteed national pension and social security systems (FO, 2003). In this respect a return to a more Keynesian policy of demand management via higher wage agreements and budget deficit spending at the national and European level was demanded (Interview No. 58; Paris, 12/09/2002). This strategy must further include a fundamental revision of the SGP towards an economic policy favourable to growth via consumption and public investment and a better distribution of wealth as well as the creation of employment (FO, 2002b; FO, 2004). In sum, similar to the CGT, FO accepted EMU as a reality, but it criticised the underlying neo-liberal rationale.

The CFTC had traditionally had a positive position on European integration and, therefore, officially recommended a 'yes' in the 1992 referendum on the Treaty of Maastricht. There were, however, big internal discussions about this position and it was anything but generally accepted. Especially the convergence criteria were deplored, because they implied a predominant focus on monetary stability. At its 1996 congress in Nantes, strong criticism of the ECB was voiced and its reform demanded towards more democratic accountability. Moreover, instead of being exclusively concentrated on price stability, full employment should also be made part of its overall objectives similar to the Federal Reserve Bank in the US. It was further demanded that the international financial markets should be regulated through methods such as the Tobin Tax (Interview No. 61; Paris, 13/09/2002). In a context of strong economic competition, the priorities would rest on competitiveness, while social aspects were too often relegated to a secondary place (Bailacq, 1999a: 14). This deregulation and deconstruction of the social acquis would be, it was further argued, against the original idea of the EU's founding fathers. Hence, Europe should be re-focused on the social core of the originally federalist message, including a new language of economic and social policy different from monetarism and traditional dirigism alike (Arondel, 2001: 11–14). Thus, 'in order to be able to counterbalance the monetary federal power of the ECB, in order to determine a policy of change for the Euro and avoid thereby that the markets are in charge instead of politics, it is, therefore, necessary to support a true federal power in Brussels, and at least an economic government' (Arondel, 1997: 10; see also Arondel, 1998: 13–14).

Rather than focusing exclusively on price stability, what would be needed was a more expansive fiscal policy, co-ordinated at the EU level including a larger EU budget. Devaluations would be no longer possible, but in order to make a Keynesian demand-oriented policy possible the SGP should be interpreted more flexibly and the ECB should set the interest rates lower (Interview No. 61; Paris, 13/09/2002). In order to boost employment, fiscal policies should be harmonised in a way that takes into account different national situations, but also makes fiscal dumping impossible. The lowering of taxes should not only affect employers, but also employees and 'the policy of big public works at the European level is equally a way forward, which the CFTC often underlines' (Heitz, 1999: 15). Moreover, in a context of economic growth, it would be justified to increase wages after two decades of wage moderation. Resulting additional demand would further boost more employment (Kapamadjian, 2000: 12, 14). Finally a defensive strategy based on commercial rules and social clauses was deemed necessary in order to protect those industrial sectors that are most exposed to foreign competition (Heitz, 1999: 14–15). In sum, EMU was supported as a part of further European integration, but the underlying neo-liberal rationale was deplored. Europe's future was perceived to be a clear choice over the future model of capitalism. Nobody could accept in this respect that the single currency would only be used as a Trojan horse to press for a restructuring of the European social model along neo-liberal lines (Arondel, 1998: 14).

The CFE-CGC had been a strong supporter of EMU and its monetary policy focusing on price stability. Rather than regarding it as endangering the European social model, the CFE-CGC considered EMU to be a way of securing it in the face of the global liberal market. Public spending restrictions, resulting from the convergence criteria, would not be a huge problem for France. This position was very similar to the union's positive assessment of globalisation. The global market as such would be a good thing, but needed more management and control of the distribution of the resulting benefits. Its underlying basis should be worldwide labour minimum standards to avoid wage dumping and unfair competition. The union's suggestion for an employment policy focused on supply-side measures and here especially better training policies (Interview No. 77; telephone interview, 13/02/2003). This was, however, combined with a focus on the demand side including issues such as a reduction of working time and larger domestic demand levels via higher wage increases. The CFE-CGC pointed to 'the evidence according to which there can be no growth in the absence of a strong domestic demand component, within which employees play a key role' (Cazettes, 2000: 1).

Amongst the new French trade unions that emerged in the late 1980s/early 1990s, UNSA viewed EMU in a very similar way to the CFDT and CFTC. Thus, EMU was regarded as an important aspect of further European integration. As the Internal Market, it was pointed out, had already been established, EMU was beneficial in that it provided a greater level of economic stability with the abolition of exchange rates. 'We take a position in favour of the Euro, which puts an end to monetary chaos' (UNSA, 1999: 2). This support for European integration in general and EMU in particular, was, however, combined with strong criticism of the underlying neo-liberal rationale of EMU. As a counterweight, more steps needed to be undertaken to strengthen social integration. As early as 1995, UNSA pointed out that the single currency needed to be accompanied by social Europe arguing also that public services could not be accommodated within the logic of the market (UNSA, 1995: 1). Europe, it was argued, had not yet chosen its future social model. In the choice between the neo-liberal model, where higher employment levels were obtained at the price of increasing inequality and deteriorating public services, and a Scandinavian model characterised by social dialogue and high levels of employment, UNSA clearly supported the latter (Olive, 2002: 103).

Hence, UNSA demanded the implementation of social convergence criteria as a counterweight to the monetary criteria (UNSA, 1999: 1, 3). In any case, the convergence criteria should be interpreted politically and, considering the current economic recession, be interpreted in a more flexible way (Interview No. 67; Paris, 17/12/2002). Public services were regarded as a key element of social Europe, as were a minimum wage and fundamental rights such as the right to accommodation and the right to a professional education. The employment chapter should be put into practice with the reduction of working time as one of the core elements of an employment strategy (UNSA, 1999: 3–5). Additional steps should include a move towards the harmonisation of fiscal and tax policies, which in turn would have positive implications for a further development of common social policies leading to an overall balance between economic and social progress (UNSA, 2002: 19). In relation to the ECB, UNSA argued that its powers needed to be balanced by a common economic government. In addition to the co-ordination of national budgets in favour of more employment, a proper European budget as part of the common economic government should focus on creating employment through trans-European infrastructure projects (UNSA, 1999: 3). The Lisbon 2000 European Council summit specified full employment as a goal, but a proper European common policy would be necessary to achieve this objective. In short, UNSA accepted that EMU and here especially the convergence criteria and the role of the ECB were problematic. Nevertheless, this should be taken as a sign that more European integration towards a proper political and social Europe was necessary rather than taking EMU as a reason for opposing the EU. UNSA, thus, was the only French union that openly demanded a move towards a federal union (Interview No. 67; Paris, 17/12/2002).

G10-Solidaires, on the other hand, made up of unions such as SUD-PTT, which emerged at the end of the 1980s through a split with moderate unions, was more critical of the EU. The problems G10-Solidaires had with EMU were the implications for public finances, which were limited due to the convergence criteria, as well as the independent status of the French central bank and the ECB. The convergence criteria had had a negative consequence for public investment and went against G10-Solidaires' conviction that education and health should not be part of the market. The French central bank and the ECB were outside any political control and accountability. A political choice over economic policy, consequently, was not possible (Interview No. 65; Paris, 16/12/2002). Overall, however, G10-Solidaires maintained that the currently negative EU policies should not imply a general rejection of the EU and EMU. 'At the European level, we need to take into account that Europe is a fact, a reality. But this European construction is not neutral; it is inscribed in a precise neo-liberal political project' (G10-Solidaires, 2002: 96). European integration as part of a general progressive, non-nationalist policy was supported, as was the single currency as a technical instrument. What was rejected, however, was the underlying neo-liberal economic rationale (Interview No. 65; 16/12/2002). Instead of a neo-liberal Europe based on economic competition that puts social policies in EU member states under downward pressure, G10-Solidaires supported a Europe that was based on the co-operation between people (G10-Solidaires, 2002: 96–7). The EU could potentially play a role in combating unemployment. So far, however, the impact was deemed to have been negative in that the EU contributed to the flexibilisation of the labour market and increasing precariousness of job contracts. Again, it was not the EU as such, but its current neo-liberal policies, which were rejected. To protect existing employment, G10-Solidaires demanded legislation, which made it impossible for profitable companies or companies subsidised by public money to make workers redundant. The public sector in general should not lay-off employees. Hence, more public investment and a stop to further privatisation was seen as a crucial way forward in the struggle against unemployment (Interview No. 65; Paris, 16/12/2002).

Overall, there was a division in the French labour movement over EMU. On the one hand, the CFDT, CFTC and UNSA, although critical of the underlying neo-liberal rationale, supported EMU. It was regarded as a fact, a logical step forward, but a change to its contents was demanded. On the other hand, FO and G10-Solidaires were much more drastic in their criticism of EMU, linking it to a more general criticism of the EU as a whole. The CGT took a position in the middle in that it was very critical of the neo-liberal rationale of EMU, but slightly more hopeful about the possibilities to change the basis of EMU within the current institutions of the EU. Importantly, however, all unions with the slight exception of the CFDT, continued to be highly critical of neo-liberal restructuring as embodied in EMU. The only union with a different position here was the CFE-CGC, which endorsed the focus on price stability. This overall rather positive and less critical assessment of EMU reflects the fact that the union represents mainly executives and managers in the private sector, i.e. high-level employees often in charge of neo-liberal restructuring. It can be related back to the second expected split between a core labour force on the one hand, which may benefit from neo-liberal restructuring, i.e. the employees represented by the CFE-CGC, and, on the other hand, workers employed in the periphery of the labour market in precarious conditions (see Chapter 2). The next section will analyse whether these different positions have had an impact on the individual unions' positions on European-level co-operation.

French confederations and European co-operation

The CFDT's strong support for EMU, regarding it as an important step towards a social and political union, indicated its generally strong support for European integration and co-operation at the supranational level. Considering TNCs' global strategies, the unions too would have to concentrate on the international level in their organisation and strategies (Interview No. 55; Paris, 12/09/2002). The EU was seen here as the right level to control and manage globalisation (CFDT, 1998: 20). 'Europe had seemed, in our eyes, to be one of the essential vectors for a controlled system which – such as no other – could procure a counterweight against the excesses of the free market' (CFDT, 2002: 2; see also 6). The CFDT's overall goal for Europe is a balanced model, which paid attention to economic competitiveness as well as fundamental social needs, cohesion and solidarity (CFDT, 1999: 81; CFDT, 2002: 15). In this respect, the development of the Social Dimension to date was evaluated positively. Multi-sector bargaining agreements had been important and it was here as well as at the sectoral level and within EWCs that further efforts by the unions were deemed necessary to establish a balance of force with the employers. It was the culture of negotiations that would determine to a large extent unions' capacities to develop a new European social model that paid equal attention to competitiveness and social solidarity (CFDT, 1998: 27). In order to be more successful, first, social dialogue must take place outside, and in addition to, initiatives by the European Commission (CFDT, 2002: 10). Second, trade unions themselves must co-ordinate better their positions and be prepared to transfer competencies to the ETUC in order to strengthen European trade unions, able to balance capital within the EU. This claim was frequently put forward at CFDT congresses (CFDT, 1998: 27; CFDT, 1999: 81). The CFDT itself was prepared to transfer competencies to the ETUC at the European level and had welcomed the adoption of QMV by the ETUC at its congress in 1999 (Interview No. 55; Paris, 12/09/2002). Third, social dialogue must be backed up by a strong show of force. 'Recent European demonstrations, in Porto, Nice and Brussels illustrate the mature nature of European trade unionism, which has the capacity to bring together 80–100,000 persons calling for a greater Europe in the field of jobs as well as improved social regulations' (CFDT, 2002: 4). In sum, while areas such as the public sector would still require a strong national focus, the EU had become increasingly important for the CFDT's strategies (Interview No. 55; Paris, 12/09/2002).

In the course of the 1990s, the CGT had dropped its principled rejection of the EU. The clearest expression of this change in strategy was its accession to the ETUC in 1999 (Eironline, 28 March 1999, http://www.eiro.eurofound.eu.int/1999/03/inbrief/fr9903167n.html; 05/09/2002). This indicates that social dialogue and collective bargaining were no longer as fiercely rejected as before. This change can be regarded as a result of the CGT's recognition that the Internal Market 'raised the issue of labour rights. The introduction of the Euro makes it even more urgent to deal with labour and social issues in Europe' (CGT, 2000: 41). What was required would be a Europe of social cohesion and solidarity and the CGT emphasised the European level in the search for solutions in this respect. 'The construction of new links of solidarity and new forms of democracy required a political and institutional debate on tax harmonisation within Europe, the development of a Community budget and jointly-devised economic policies' (CGT, 2002: 6). The CGT further demanded the increase of QMV for social policy except for social protection and the general expansion of community competencies in the area of social policy-making including pay and especially minimum pay (CGT, 2002: 15). Wage bargaining at the EU level may be a solution in some sectors one day, but this must not lead to a harmonisation at lower levels. The co-ordination of national wage bargaining was definitely a project in which the CGT would be prepared to participate, but it had only started to discuss the issue of transferring competencies to the ETUC. In short, while working within the ETUC and at the European level, the CGT relied less on the effectiveness of this strategy. It was recognised that the social dialogue alone was not enough to achieve results. The governments also needed to be involved. In the end, the success of the Social Dimension would really depend on workers' capacity to influence its development and there should be no hierarchy of different levels (Interview No. 60; Paris, 13/09/2002). Close to its traditional roots, the CGT was always prepared to back up its negotiations with demonstrations and industrial action. It was, hence, no surprise that the CGT was well represented in large demonstrations at the Nice European Council summit on 6 December 2000 (Eironline 2001, 28 January 2001, http://www.eiro.eurofound. eu.int/2001/01/feature/fr0101122f.html; 05/09/02).

Although a founding member of the ETUC in 1973, the FO had become an increasingly reluctant member since its Congress in 1989. First, because 'FO remains fixed upon a bread-and-butter wages and hours unionism which, for treaty reasons, cannot exist at the European level' (Daley, 1999: 191). Second, because it had translated its criticism of the neo-liberal convergence criteria (see above) into criticism of European integration and here the role of the ETUC itself. Since the SEA in 1987, the FO had become critical of the ETUC and its then President Emilio Gabaglio's strategy to put Europe as such above everything else. The ETUC had made the mistake, the FO alleged, not to criticise Maastricht from the very beginning for the ECB's lack of a focus on employment and for the convergence criteria. This criticism had been raised now, but this would be too late. Thus, the ETUC had proven to be unable to construct a union force at the European level. It would have focused too much on federalism instead of organising the national movements into a coherent force. This implied the danger that the ETUC became de-linked from its basis, the workers (Interview No. 59; Paris, 13/09/2002). Caught by its support for the Euro and by the embarrassment that its policies had no impact on the ECB or national governments, the ETUC would have now signed up to an employment chapter that institutionally integrated unions into a policy that subordinated social issues to economic priorities (FO, 2000: 568–9). FO had voted against the ETUC's conditional acceptance of the employment chapter and argued that 'we need to remind ourselves that it is the foremost role of trade unions to demand a better distribution of wealth for the benefit of active, unemployed and retired workers' (FO, 2000: 605). The social dialogue would have had only very little concrete results. Due to the lack of European social regulations, national systems had competed with each other since the Internal Market programme, making the national level the most important one for the defence of workers' rights (Interview No. 59; Paris, 13/09/2002; FO, 2000: 564). The co-ordination of national wage bargaining as, for example, envisaged by the Doorn initiative (see Chapter 8) was welcomed and co-ordination of wage bargaining at the sectoral level to counter social dumping was favoured (FO, 2000: 564, 590). Hence, the European level as such was not rejected as a strategic arena. Rather, it was the concrete strategies, pursued to date by the EU in general and the ETUC as far as the labour movement was concerned in particular, which were criticised.

Against the background of its general positive attitude towards European integration (see above), it is not surprising that the CFTC strongly supported further co-operation at the European level. The construction of a political Europe must include in the eyes of the CFTC a strengthening of European-level trade union co-operation (Deygas, 2001: 10). However, the confederation was not impressed by the results to date. In practice, the multi-sector agreements would be a lot of empty words without concrete consequences for France. The following points were identified as the core problems: (1) different positions by social partners from different countries due to different social and cultural back-grounds; (2) UNICE, while accepting the principle of negotiations, often used social dialogue to delay decisions; (3) EWCs were too often confronted with fait accompli situations; and (4) the sectoral social dialogue was underdeveloped (Bailacq, 1999a: 14–15). In order to counter the dominant competitiveness discourse, unions should develop the social dialogue tool further. The EWCs directive should be revived in order to clarify the notion of consultation towards more union impact on company decision-making and the employers needed to be convinced of the necessity to construct jointly a Europe that was not only economic but also social (Bailacq, 1999b: 21). In any case, however, the much more fundamental issue of what kind of social Europe was desired should be discussed first. While the Lisbon strategy identified full employment as one of the core objectives, the way it was supposed to be achieved would resemble closely the Anglo-American model of capitalism. Moreover, one should ask what kind of employment one wanted to create. The quality of jobs would be too easily overlooked. Importantly from the CFTC's point of view, the ETUC in 2001 finally made the step and argued that wage moderation across the EU should stop in order to increase domestic demand. Wage bargaining co-ordination following the Doorn initiative was regarded as a good thing, but would need stronger support by the ETUC. In order to strengthen the ETUC in these efforts, the CFTC was prepared to transfer more competencies (Interview No. 61; Paris, 13/09/2002).

The CFE-CGC was a founding member of the Confédération Européenne des cadres (CEC), not the ETUC, although the CEC was in close discussions with the latter. 'As an interprofessional organisation representative of European Executives and Managerial staff, CEC takes part in the European social dialogue in all its forms (information, consultation, standing committee for employment, social collective bargaining). CFE-CGC is deeply involved in CEC actions, in the field of collective bargaining and in the processes of consultation' (CFE-CGC, 2001). This was the result of an agreement with EUROCADRES in 1999, which also represents professional and managerial staff in the EU and is associated to the ETUC (Cazettes, 2002: 41–6; CFE-CGC, 2002). The confederation had accepted that against the background of European and worldwide restructuring of companies, the French level was no longer sufficient for union activities. Hence, the commitment was made 'by the whole of the managerial team to reposition the confederation in a permanent, resolutely European perspective' (CFE-CGC, 2000: 15). The European level and here especially the European Commission had become more important for the confederation, affecting all aspects of its work at the national level, and was likely to become even more so in the future. The CFE-CGC emphasised the importance of higher minimum standards across the EU covering also the future members from CEE. Only higher wage levels in Eastern Europe would guarantee a fair share of the profit for these workers as well as make it possible for industry in Western Europe to continue production. Social dumping must be avoided in the European as well as global market place. The negotiation of wages at the European level was likely to occur in the future, and it had to be the task of trade unions to engage in this development (Interview No. 77; telephone interview, 13/02/2003). Social dialogue at all decision-making levels in companies was regarded as the best way forward in this respect (CFE-CGC, 2000: 15; Cazettes, 2000: 3). The confederation, consequently, demanded the increase of EWCs' power towards a consultative and negotiating role (Cambus, 2000: 37).

UNSA had been a member of the ETUC since 1999. Forming a joint delegation with the CFDT, both confederations have got one vote together within the ETUC (Eironline, 28 May 1999, http://www.eiro.eurofound.eu.int/1999/05/inbrief/fr9905186n.html; 05/09/2002). UNSA had recognised that Europe was already a fact in that the big companies, as well as many medium-sized companies, had already Europeanised and macroeconomic policy was increasingly decided at the European level (Olive, 2002: 101–2). As big European companies already had a transnational, European dimension, a European labour law would be required in tandem with the existing EWCs in order to balance these new realities (UNSA, 1999: 1–2). UNSA regarded social Europe as absolutely essential. It needed to be preserved also in order to sustain the individual national social models. The confederation accepted that the achievements so far were rather modest. Nevertheless, it pointed out that over time it was possible to see that from treaty to treaty social Europe had been strengthened, be it via agreements between the ETUC and UNICE, or be it via Council of Ministers directives. Importantly, in order to push the Social Dimension forward, it would be necessary to build a 'rapport de force'. The ETUC had started doing this by organising demonstrations at the Nice summit in 2000 as well as the summit in Barcelona in 2002. The organisation of further demonstrations across the EU in support of the European social model were planned for the next years. In short, the combination of demonstrations and negotiations was regarded by UNSA as the best way forward towards a proper social Europe. The emerging European-wide trade union consciousness as a result of these activities should now be translated into a European awareness at the workplace (Interview No. 67; Paris, 17/12/2002). For this purpose, the European movement of reformist trade unions must speak with one voice through the ETUC (UNSA, 2002: 19). UNSA supported the restructuring of the ETUC along federal lines, making it able to co-ordinate national activities and negotiate with employers in Europe at the multi-sector as well as sectoral level. It, thus, accepted the democratic delegation of sovereignty to the ETUC (UNSA, 1999: 5–6). UNSA fully adopted ETUC resolutions as its points of reference and supported ETUC policies towards fundamental social rights, negotiations with employers at the sectoral and multi-sector level, a proper budget for the EU for an active macroeconomic policy and the reduction of inequality between European regions (Olive, 2002: 102).

According to G10-Solidaires, European integration had concentrated on the establishment of a free market, full competition and a single currency. It had not been a social project. Rather, its policies had been anti-social leading towards wage reductions and social dumping by individual member states in order to attract FDI. Nevertheless, the union acknowledged the importance of the European level. Considering that the employers were already organised European-wide, trade unions needed to follow, it was argued. At the same time, there was still room for manoeuvre for national governments and, hence, efforts would have to concentrate on the national level, too. In Europe, G10-Solidaires worked together with other ideologically leftwing, non-reformist unions such as the metal workers' unions the German IG Metall and the Italian Federazione Impiegati Operai Metallurgici (FIOM), but also the British National Union of Rail, Maritime and Transport Workers (RMT). Similar to the FO, however, G10-Solidaires heavily criticised the ETUC for its reformist tendencies, relying on lobbying instead of direct action (Interview No. 65; Paris, 16/12/2002). The problem was that the ETUC would refuse to criticise the political basis of the European construction. It would demand a more social Europe, but lagged behind organisations such as Euromarches, which had organised unemployed people across the EU against neo-liberal Europe, and other social movements in mobilising people for demonstrations (G10-Solidaires, 2002: 97–9). Hence, G10-Solidaires had increasingly emphasised co-operation with other social movements within the annual World Social Forum and European Social Forum, the meetings of world and European anti-neo-liberal globalisation movements. Especially the defence of the public sector in Europe but also beyond was expected to lead to joint union-social movement activities (Interview No. 65; Paris, 16/12/2002). 'The encounters of the World Social Forum of Porto Alegre confirm the emergence of a new internationalism' (G10-Solidaires, 2002: 99), and it was this internationalism outside of the established European trade union structures around the ETUC, on which G10-Solidaires was concentrating its efforts. Thus, the union recognised that neo-liberal exploitation had gone beyond issues of the workplace. 'It is, therefore, necessary to operate in relation to all these consequences in partnership with social movements, which also struggle on this terrain' (G10-Solidaires, 2002: 29–30; see also G10-Solidaires, 1998). Chapter 9 will explore this area further.

In sum, the division of French trade unions over EMU becomes even more pronounced when assessing unions' positions on European-level co-operation. As all confederations represent workers across a whole range of different industrial sectors, although they are, of course, stronger in some sectors than in others (see Chapters 6 and 7), this split cannot be related directly back to the production structure, but indicates a fundamental ideological difference over the best strategy forwards. This goes right back to the traditional division of French unions along ideological lines. On the one hand, the CFDT, CFTC, CFE-CGC and UNSA supported collective bargaining and the social dialogue as the proper trade union strategy in order to represent the interests of their members. This was still combined, however, in true French tradition with an emphasis on the mobilisation for demonstrations. Additionally, they recognised the limited impact on decision-making they enjoyed within the structural selectivity of the French form of state. Consequently, they strongly supported trade union involvement in European integration through the social dialogue, echoing to some extent the second hypothesis of this study. There was an additional sub-division of this group in that the CFE-CGC endorsed neo-liberal restructuring and the CFDT accepted it to some extent, while the CFTC and UNSA continued to oppose it. On the other hand, the strong criticism by the FO and G10-Solidaires of the neo-liberal rationale underlying EMU was translated into a criticism of the ETUC itself, accused of sustaining neo-liberal restructuring through its involvement with the Commission. As a result, both looked for alter-native ways of co-operation. While the FO concentrated on the workplace at the French level, G10-Solidaires attempted to forge alternative European-level alliances outside the ETUC structures. It, therefore, expanded its co-operation with other social movements dedicated to a challenge of neo-liberal economics. The CGT, finally, occupied somehow a middle position. It clearly rejected neo-liberal restructuring, but had shifted from more radical actions towards a stronger focus on collective bargaining and European-level co-operation. This was com-bined with an openness towards co-operation with other social movements in a very similar way to the G10-Solidaires in order to expand the social basis of resistance. Here too, an increasingly impotent position within France may have induced a strategic rethinking towards the European level, confirming the second hypothesis of this study. The ideological tensions within the French labour movement were not unique. Elsewhere too trade unions were confronted with internal ideological divisions. Nevertheless, while these tensions were accom-modated within trade unions in other countries, in France the fragmented labour movement provided the basis for an institutional expression of this split.[1]

Rival confederations in Sweden

Swedish trade union confederations and EMU

In Sweden, EMU was initially kept outside the debate over EU membership in 1994 (Bieler, 2000: 91). A referendum on EMU on 14 September 2003, however, brought the issue to the fore. In the event, 56 per cent of the electorate voted against membership, and 42 per cent in favour (http://www.sweden.gov.se/sb/d/2757/a/15436;jsessionid=agLhq2_EezUa; 28/02/2005). On the basis of an internal report on EMU (LO, 1996), the LO executive board decided against member-ship in February 1997. It was concerned about the potentially deflationary impli-cations of EMU. 'The timetable is rigid and the convergence criteria doubtful. According to estimates the convergence criteria will cost many jobs and be a contributory reason for recession in Europe' (LO, 1996: 10; see also Bieler, 2000: 103). Hence, it was stated that 'if a monetary union is to be discussed at all, in our opinion it must be balanced by an equally strong employment union' (LO, 1996: 64). In order to make monetary union acceptable, the co-ordination of fiscal policies at the European level with a focus on Keynesian policies across borders was demanded. This would involve some kind of transfer mechanism within the EU budget as well as the provision of common funding 'through the EU issuing "Union Bonds" to finance public sector investments without increasing the member states' national debt' (LO, 1996: 69–70). Fiscal expansion would need to be supported by a monetary policy that did not solely focus on low inflation. Inflation of 3 to 4 per cent would be a more realistic target than 2 per cent inflation in this respect (LO, 1996: 80; see also Bieler, 1999: 34–5). In general, employment policy needed to be equally included in the macroeconomic framework of the EU and institutionally, labour and finance ministers should be combined in one council within the EU for this purpose (LO, 1996: 82–3).

At the LO congress in 2000, however, the position was re-assessed and a conditional 'yes' formulated. Politically, the strongest concerns were voiced about the danger of remaining outside the inner decision-making circle of the EU as a non-EMU member (LO, 2000: 3). Economically, membership would help the Swedish economy to retain competitiveness as it most likely implied slightly lower interest rates in the long-term and even more room for a national fiscal policy (LO, 2000: 4–5). LO was still concerned about the convergence criteria and their neo-liberal orientation as well as the undemocratic nature of the ECB. Nonetheless, outside EMU Sweden may have to pursue an even tighter monetary policy and the ECB would imply that some supranationality was the price to be paid for increased political influence within the EU (LO, 2000: 3, 5). The most important conditions for the union's support for EMU dealt with the possibilities of how to counter asymmetric shocks within EMU, once adjustment via a free floating currency was no longer possible. Membership should only be an option, if a stable wage formation system was secured in Sweden and so-called buffer funds established by the government that could be used in times of economic recession to stimulate domestic demand. The establishment of a structural council, including representatives from trade unions and employers' associations, responsible for the economic policies in times of asymmetric shocks, was considered to be necessary as an institutional safeguard in this respect (Interview No. 43; Stockholm, 25/06/2002). Finally, 'if Swedish membership of monetary union is to be regarded as legitimate, it must be preceded by a referendum' (LO, 2000: 7). The conditional pro-EMU conference decision in 2000, however, neither referred to the idea of an employment union of 1996, nor did it mention the further development of the Social Dimension (LO, 2000). Of course, the Social Dimension was evaluated positively and EU-wide employment policies were supported (Interview No. 47; Stockholm, 27/06/2002). Nevertheless, progress in these areas was not made a precondition for EMU support. If at all, EMU would require less co-ordination of economic stimulation policies and more national room for manoeuvre to facilitate the stabilisation of the national economy once the exchange rate had been lost (Interview No. 43; Stockholm, 25/06/2002). On Monday 7 April 2003, the LO executive council decided that its preconditions for EMU support and here especially its demands for buffer funds had not been fully met by the government and that as a confederation it would, therefore, adopt a neutral position in the referendum campaign (LO, 2003). This implied that a 'yes' in the referendum was less likely. It did not, however, change the shift in LO's position on EMU from the mid- to the late 1990s and the related general change in the union's macroeconomic outlook.

As in 1994, differences between and within unions affiliated to the TCO prevented an official position by the confederation. A TCO committee considered EMU in 1996. It was split fifty/fifty and since then, partly at least in order to avoid an open split of the union, the TCO had frequently made clear that it would not take a position. 'Remaining outside the EMU entails both risks and opportunities, and the TCO affiliates differ in their evaluation of these risks. TCO as an organisation takes no stance on the issue of Swedish membership of the EMU' (TCO, 2001: 13). EMU should be decided at the political level and be put to the Swedish people in a referendum (Interview No. 37; Stockholm, 20/06/2002; Interview No. 44; Stockholm, 25/06/2002). The majority of unions affiliated to the TCO followed the latter's stance and did not take an official position. Similar to Swedish public opinion in general, union members were deeply divided over EMU and the outcome of the referendum was anything but clear. Especially within TCO unions, there were concerns over splitting the membership by taking a decisive stance on EMU (see Chapters 6 and 7).

SACO, finally, was the confederation that most strongly supported EMU. As early as 1997, SACO recommended its members to support Swedish EMU membership from the start, without linking this endorsement to a range of conditions. Remaining outside, it was argued, implied that Sweden lost the possibility to participate in the formation of the rules of monetary policy-making. Moreover, to increase employment levels, economic stability resulting from EMU membership was regarded as essential. 'A risk with being outside EMU is that the stability is easily disturbed by different market reactions, which in turn makes it even more difficult to achieve that kind of trustfulness and stable capital costs that business and households need' (SACO, 1997 [translation by Åke Zettermark]). SACO was not worried about the convergence criteria. Rather, it criticised Sweden's big spending on labour market policies, which were regarded as too costly and ineffective. In order to boost the economy, Sweden should lower taxation levels to the EU average and widen the wage structure, thereby making Sweden economically more attractive. In general, a more market-oriented system was demanded, which provided people with incentives towards more education and risk-taking (Interview No. 45; Stockholm, 26/06/2002). The preconditions for LO support for EMU membership and the non-position by the TCO can be explained by different positions of the various affiliated unions from different production sectors. The strong, unconditional support for EMU membership by SACO, however, can be related back to the second split within the labour movement identified by Cox (1981: 235). As the French CFE-CGC (see above) SACO represents employees with academic degrees and, therefore, the most educated parts of the Swedish workforce. Its members are frequently in positions that require technical expertise and carry more responsibility, i.e. those workers with established positions at the core of the labour market. They lose out most due to the compressed Swedish wage structure resulting from the relatively high progressive taxation levels. Neo-liberal restructuring, as demanded

by SACO, introducing more flexibility, lower taxes and larger wage differences
are likely to benefit SACO's members most.

Swedish union confederations and European co-operation

During the EU membership referendum campaign in 1994, all three Swedish
trade union confederations did not adopt an official position. The LO and TCO,
because their affiliated unions were deeply divided over the issue risking a split
in case of endorsing one or the other side. SACO, because it considered EU
membership to be an issue of foreign policy and, therefore, outside its remit
(Bieler, 1999: 33–8). Since Sweden's accession to the EU in 1995, however, they
had developed positions on the extent to which they were willing to co-operate
at the European level. Interestingly, all three Swedish trade union confederations were slightly reluctant in relation to European-level co-operation. LO was
still the most positive one in this respect. It saw the general development of the
Social Dimension as very positive and emphasised especially the social dialogue
component, where LO had been very active in the ETUC-UNICE negotiations.
In order to retain Swedish social levels, it was deemed important to help others
to raise their own standards. Of course, the directives agreed to date would only
establish minimum standards, but Sweden would benefit from them indirectly
in that they made social dumping increasingly less possible, while also allowing Sweden to retain its higher standards at the same time (Interview No. 47;
Stockholm, 27/06/2002). For the Social Dimension to become a successful counterpart to EMU, LO had pushed the demand for a right to sympathy strikes in
Europe. Only this would really give trade unions the same level of power as
employers (Interview No. 43; Stockholm, 25/06/2002).

   LO's European-level engagement was driven by the realisation that more and
more aspects of labour market regulation were decided at the European level.
Hence, LO decided that it had to respond at this level. Along the same lines,
in order to counterbalance capital and to protect Swedish workers, the union,
it was felt, had to operate at the same level as the increasingly transnationalised
employers. What would be problematic, however, was the lack of employer
counterparts especially for the sectoral social dialogue and the Commission's
unwillingness to push employers towards this dialogue (Interview No. 47;
Stockholm, 27/06/2002). Nevertheless, while the EU had become more important, it was not regarded as the most important level. Especially in social policy
matters, the national level would require priority. The same was correct in
relation to collective bargaining. While the ETUC-UNICE negotiations would
already imply in practice the transfer of sovereignty to the ETUC, LO had not
pushed for EU-wide bargaining. National economies and labour markets would
simply be too different. What was, however, important and occurring was
the increasing exchange of information on productivity increases and employer
strategies in the various countries. This had been helped by the establishment
of the EWCs as well as collective bargaining co-ordination within the European
Metalworkers' Federation (see Chapter 8). Interestingly, the latter, it was argued,
relied on the same principle, according to which LO had operated for decades,

i.e. wage increases calculated as productivity increase plus inflation (Interview No. 43; Stockholm, 25/06/2002). Thus, there was a clear need perceived to intensify the co-ordination of national bargaining in order to avoid the downward competition between different national systems. In contrast to the TCO and SACO, LO accepted the ETUC initiative for the co-ordination of national bargaining rounds at the 1999 ETUC Congress in Helsinki. The ETUC recommendations to demand productivity increase plus inflation as wage increase and to focus on the lowest income levels and the continuing difference between male and female salaries in their bargaining rounds at the national level was subsequently passed on as general recommendation within the LO-internal co-ordination of sectoral bargaining in Sweden (Interview No. 47; Stockholm, 27/06/2002).

The TCO, similar to its position in 1994 prior to the EU referendum (see Bieler, 1999: 33–5), argued that global restructuring necessitated stronger European-level engagement and a further development of the Social Dimension. 'The increasing pressure by globalisation makes it necessary to defend and develop the Swedish model, and we can use Europe as a platform in this work' (TCO, 2001: 11). Together with the LO and SACO, it received money from the Swedish government to establish an information office in Brussels. It is a member of the ETUC and thus TCO representatives participated in the social dialogue with UNICE. Nevertheless, it was not thought that the Social Dimension had been developed into a counterpart to EMU. It was the Commission that drafted the initial statements, often giving the social partners little time to work through them and make their own changes. Problems were also perceived with the set-up of the ETUC, which was partly financed by the Commission. There was a concern that this would compromise the ETUC in its possible criticism of neo-liberal restructuring in general and EMU in particular. The results of the multi-sector social dialogue were deemed to be very minimal and sectoral social dialogue was not regarded as very effective. Trade union interests in the various European countries would simply differ too much for successful European-level initiatives (Interview No. 44; Stockholm, 25/06/2002). Hence, both the TCO and SACO rejected in 1999 the ETUC initiative to co-ordinate national collective bargaining at the European level (Interview No. 37; Stockholm, 20/06/2002).

SACO had started later with its European activities than the LO and TCO. In 1996, SACO joined the ETUC and in 1997 the joint Swedish union information office in Brussels. Co-operation amongst the different unions was deemed to be good there. SACO viewed as its main task informing members more clearly how important the EU was for Swedish legislation. The Social Dimension was regarded as very important by SACO and the confederation was committed to participating in the social dialogue between the ETUC and UNICE. Hence, the EU level had become more important for SACO, which recognised that this was the level where it had to attempt to influence directives that were then to be implemented at the national level later on. Nevertheless, collective bargaining at the European level was opposed. The confederation had accepted to collect and distribute information about the different national negotiations.

Co-ordination of bargaining may be a possibility, depending on how one defines 'co-ordination'. Within EMU, however, it was argued that one could either have a fully centralised bargaining system or a completely decentralised system, where bargaining was devolved to the company level. Considering the differences from sector to sector and from country to country, only decentralisation was really an option in SACO's view. Productivity increases, where achieved, should be translated into higher wages. This, again, would require a higher wage disparity. In other words, the centralisation of wage bargaining was opposed by the confederation (Interview No. 45; Stockholm, 26/06/2002).

This positive endorsement of the decentralisation of bargaining, a core demand of neo-liberal economics in order to increase flexibility, demonstrates yet again how SACO, representing employees in privileged positions in the labour market, had accepted core neo-liberal concepts in its trade union strategies. This clearly separates it from the other two Swedish confederations as well as the vast majority of other European unions and yet again confirms this potential split between employees in core positions of production, and employees on the periphery of the labour market. In general, it can be concluded that Swedish unions were least interested in active European-level co-operation of all the confederations analysed here. In accordance with the second hypothesis, this can be explained through a reference to the continuation of good possibilities of influencing policy-making at the national level. As it was outlined in Chapter 4, collective bargaining, for example, was re-established at the sectoral level in Sweden in 1997. Against the background of an improving structural selectivity of the Swedish form of state, co-operation at EU level had become slightly less urgent.

Conclusion

Several main conclusions can be drawn from this chapter. First, the clear majority of confederations supported EMU. Only the French union G10-Solidaires was openly opposed, while the FO was highly critical. The Swedish LO and TCO remained neutral. This did not, however, imply that unions had generally accepted neo-liberal restructuring. On the contrary, it was widely demanded that monetary integration needed to be followed by political and social integration. The latter should include a more active position on creating employment as well as protection of the public sector. Some unions demanded the addition of an unemployment and/or social criterion. In general, monetary integration needed to be counterbalanced by social integration. Only the Swedish union SACO and the French union CFE-CGC indicated support for the neo-liberal principles underlying EMU with perhaps the French union CFDT showing a tendency in a similar direction by accepting the convergence criteria and ECB independence. In general, these findings cannot be related to the first hypothesis of a split between national and transnational sector unions, since all confederations organise workers across domestic and transnational sectors. Only when looking at the affiliated unions in Chapters 6 and 7, will it be possible to come back to this issue. What is interesting here, however, is the indication of a confirmation of the second split in the labour movement, as identified by Cox, between established labour in privileged, core employment positions on the one hand, and workers on atypical contracts in the periphery of the labour market on the other (see Chapter 2). Both SACO and CFE-CGC organise highly educated employees in positions with management responsibilities, who either carry out or benefit most from neo-liberal restructuring. They are, therefore, much more likely to become allies of transnational capital and its neo-liberal restructuring project. Unsurprisingly, in contrast to the other unions, they endorsed EMU including its neo-liberal rationale.

Moreover, as envisaged in the second hypothesis, there is a difference between the various confederations and their emphasis on European level co-operation. This can be related back to different degrees of influence unions enjoyed at the national level within the structural selectivity of the various forms of state. While the British TUC showed a strong emphasis on the European level especially during the years of Conservative governments in the 1980s and 1990s, the Swedish confederations, which continued to play a strong role at the national level, were much more reluctant. In Germany and Austria, where the DGB and ÖGB were traditionally pro-European, but less active in European-level co-operation due to their strong position at the national level, one has to see whether recent limitations of trade union influence will result in a stronger focus on the EU. In France, finally, those unions that accepted social dialogue and collective bargaining had strongly participated in European-level co-operation in view of the lack of influence at the national level, again in line with the second hypothesis. Even G10-Solidaires, rejecting the ETUC, was increasingly focusing on European and international level co-operation, while the FO's focus on the workplace can be explained by its rejection of any involvement in political issues. The next chapter will analyse transnational sector unions in the five countries, to be compared with the positions on EMU and European co-operation by national sector unions in Chapter 7.

Note

1   The ideological split in the French labour movement was also apparent in the 1995 strikes over the welfare state restructuring of the Juppé plan (Daley, 1999: 189). Those unions focusing on social partnership were pushed by their members towards more radical action (Jefferys, 1996: 17; Mouriaux, 1996: 301 and 305). Similarly, this split could be identified in relation to the more recent attempts by EU institutions to integrate trade unions into the reform process through concertation (Gordon and Mathers, 2004).

6

Transnational social forces of labour and their support for EMU

Introduction

In accordance with the first hypothesis, this chapter concentrates on the transnational sector unions in the five countries and their positions on EMU and European co-operation. As it was hypothesised in Chapter 2,

> *Hypothesis 1*: . . . unions, which represent workers in transnational production sectors, are more likely to support EMU, because they may support their companies – on which their own well-being depends – which benefit from a stable monetary environment and institutionalised free trade within the EU. Moreover, because they realise that they have lost control over capital at the national level, they are probably prepared to co-operate with other unions at the European level.

As it was also argued, however, whether unions have actually adopted positions in line with this hypothesis is a matter for empirical enquiry. Trade unions' strategies cannot simply be read off from their location in the production process. Production shapes actors' behaviour, but it does not determine it. Neo-Gramscian perspectives, as a historical materialist approach, give explanatory primacy to the social relations of production, but they do not adopt a position of economic determinism (see Chapter 2). Importantly, there are some sectors that are transnationalised across the EU such as the metalworking and chemical industry sectors. Other sectors may be transnationalised in one country such as construction in Germany, but still very much domestic in another as, for example, construction in Britain. When assessing trade unions in the individual case studies, this will, therefore, also include a brief outline of the relevant production structures.

The labour movement of a country, the production structure of which is more transnationalised such as Britain and Sweden, will inevitably be discussed to a greater extent in this chapter than the labour movement of a country, where production is hardly transnationalised such as in Austria. Finally, as in

Chapter 5, whatever unions' positions are on EMU and European-level co-operation, their stances on neo-liberal restructuring needs to be addressed as a related, yet separate, analytical issue. Hence, while discussing unions' positions on EMU and European-level co-operation, specific emphasis will be placed on the rationale, the social purpose underlying their particular positions.

Transnational production sector unions and their positions on EMU

British transnational sector unions and EMU

As expected in the first hypothesis, transnational sector unions in Britain shared the TUC's positive position on EMU. The Amalgamated Engineering and Electrical Union (AEEU) strongly pushed for early membership of EMU. Considering that the vast majority of the AEEU's members are in export-oriented or transnational manufacturing sectors, which had suffered from exchange rate fluctuations in recent years, EMU membership was deemed to be absolutely necessary. This direct relationship between the sectoral position of the AEEU's members and the union's position on EMU, as well as more generally in relation to other unions' positions, was directly acknowledged by Bernie Hamilton, an AEEU representative, in evidence given to the Treasury Select Committee on the Euro on 10 February 2003 (AEEU-AMICUS, 2003: Question 629). Moreover, a great number of job losses in manufacturing were directly linked to the launch of EMU in 1999 by the AEEU. As Maureen Rooney stated on behalf of AEEU, then already re-named as AMICUS, at the TUC Annual Congress in 2002, 'in the past 18 months we have lost 250,000 jobs in manufacturing, and when the Engineering Employers' Federation talk to us they are saying that the threat of job losses are not threats but they will become a reality before we have a refer-endum, if we put it off for much longer' (TUC Annual Congress, 2002; see also AEEU-AMICUS, 2003: Question 625). Moreover, key investment decisions by foreign companies would be made on the basis of whether Britain participated in EMU or not. Finally, it was asked in what way the UK could continue to be a full EU member without actually being also a member of EMU. The conver-gence criteria were not feared, since public investment levels were at an all-time low anyway. There would also be some room for increased public investment within the criteria. The ECB was asked to consider more strongly employment levels in its monetary decisions, but one should not forget that unemployment was not necessarily due to EMU, but due to restructuring in times of global-isation. New jobs should be the result of a strong economy, not created by the government for the sake of creating jobs (Interview No. 20; Hayes/Kent, 23/05/2001; see also Mulhearn, 2004: 305). Together with four other unions organising workers predominantly in transnational and export-oriented sectors, i.e. the GPMU, the community union ISTC, organising workers in the steel and metal industries, the General, Municipal and Boilermakers' Union (GMB) and the National Union of Knitwear, Footwear and Apparel Trades (KFAT), the AEEU formed the movement Trade Unionists for Europe (TUfE). It was pointed out that even outside EMU 'Britain is already subject to the Stability and Growth Pact, the EU's common rules for government borrowing' (TUfE, 2000: 11). Britain fulfilled the criteria comfortably and, therefore, did not have to fear that EMU membership would require public sector cuts. The lack of political influence outside EMU was also bemoaned. Britain 'will see EU guidelines and policies drafted with the needs of the Euroland states placed first . . .' (TUfE, 2000: 13).

UNIFI, organising around 150,000 members in the highly transnationalised finance sector including banks, insurance companies, building societies and finance houses, also endorsed EMU membership. At its annual conference in 2001, the union decided that it 'supports UK entry into a single currency in circumstances where the Chancellor's five tests are met – particularly those related to the finance sector, UK employment, growth and stability' (UNIFI, 2003: 1).[1] Exchange rate stability resulting from the Euro would stabilise the UK economy in its relationship with the rest of the EU, which was Britain's most important market (Mulhearn, 2004: 304). UNIFI was concerned about the possible impact of the SGP on public spending, but argued that cut-backs in other countries were the result of political decisions, not the Pact itself. Hence, UNIFI demanded reassurances by the government on public spending in relation to EMU membership. Overall, and very similar to the AEEU's line of argument,

> UNIFI believes that the implications of UK entry into the Euro are positive. UNIFI believes that the economic benefits of joining a successful single currency will have a positive impact on growth, stability and employment in this country. In particular from our point of view representing workers in the finance sector, a successful UK economy means a successful UK finance sector, which is good for UNIFI members. (UNIFI, 2003: 2)

This position was re-iterated by Ed Sweeny on behalf of UNIFI at the TUC Annual Congress in 2002: 'If the tests have been met and a sustainable exchange rate between the Pound and the Euro can be achieved, it is the clear intention of my union to campaign and persuade other like minded affiliates to support a "yes" vote in a referendum' (TUC Annual Congress, 2002). The Communications Workers' Union (CWU) organises workers in the telecommunications and postal sectors. Telecommunications in Britain, characterised by the presence of TNCs and the forming of international partnerships, is fully transnationalised, while the postal service has just started to become more transnational in the wake of national deregulation and European liberalisation. The CWU had not taken a decision yet, but unsurprisingly it was expected that the workers in the transnational telecommunications sector were more likely to be in favour of EMU than the postal workers (Interview No. 14; London, 27/03/2001).

This positive position by transnational social forces of labour on EMU can also be identified in those general unions, the majority of their members being from transnational sectors. Being a part of the TUfE movement, the GMB executive supported by a majority of its members working in transnational manufacturing favoured EMU membership at an early date. The problem of the convergence criteria for high employment levels was acknowledged, but the main worries of the union were related to the job losses in manufacturing due to the overvalued Pound. As John Edmonds, then general secretary of the GMB, argued in a debate on Europe at the TUC Annual Congress in 2002,

> the cost of the over valued pound has been colossal: over half a million manufacturing jobs lost since the 1997 election; a quarter of a million lost since the launch of the Euro. This year more than 3,000 a week every week with no sign of respite – clothing, steel, cars, ships, electronics, high tech, untold misery. That is the price of government uncertainty over the Euro. So do not talk to me about saving the pound; our priority is saving the jobs of our members in manufacturing industry. (TUC Annual Congress, 2002)

It was also pointed out that at least as far as Britain was concerned there would be quite a bit of room for manoeuvre within the criteria (Interview No. 16; London, 28/03/2001). As Steve Pickering argued on behalf of GMB at the TUC Annual Congress in 2002, the British chancellor's rules for public spending would be tougher than the SGP rules and EMU membership, therefore, would actually imply more flexibility for public spending (TUC Annual Congress, 2002). Hence, at its congress in June 2001, the Central Executive Council of the union put forward a statement that pointed to the problems of the current exchange rate for manufacturing, the potential loss of FDI in the future and lack of political influence on decision-making in the EU, while remaining outside EMU (GMB, 2001a). The union Manufacturing Science Finance (MSF) supported an AEEU motion in favour of EMU membership at the 1996 TUC annual conference (Strange, 1997: 16). It argued that membership was desirable provided it was done at the right time in the right economic circumstances. Pushed by the manufacturing sector workers of the union and supported by the financial sector members, it was pointed out that only membership would help Britain to overcome the problems related to the high Sterling exchange rate (Interview No. 13; London, 26/03/2001).

Importantly, being in favour of EMU did not automatically imply that these unions had accepted the neo-liberal logic of deregulation and liberalisation. All unions stressed the importance of a further development of the Social Dimension as a counterpart to EMU. A difference in the degree of criticism of neo-liberalism was, however, noticeable. The AEEU and CWU, for example, did not directly criticise the neo-liberal drive of EMU, nor did they advocate active employment programmes. Instead, they demanded the further development of the Social Dimension as a way of countering the job losses and lower work standards resulting from neo-liberal restructuring (Interview No. 14; London, 27/03/2001; Interview No. 20; Hayes/Kent, 23/05/2001). This also reflected the AEEU's uncritical endorsement of New Labour's supply-side-oriented labour market and employment policy with its focus on labour mobility and employability. Thus, despite an 'almost exclusive focus on neo-liberal interpretations of micro-economic flexibility, the AEEU welcomed the Amsterdam employment chapter without qualification' (Strange, 2002a: 346). Along this line, the TUfE movement accepted the inevitability of restructuring European industry as a result of the Internal Market and EMU, but highlighted the corrective dimension of EU social policy. 'A common European social safety net, to give everyone at least the same basic standards of social protection and rights at work, can stop structural change from turning industrial casualties into social outcasts' (TUfE, 2000: 15; see also 16). Restructuring was not opposed, but social policies were demanded to make it acceptable. The EU was regarded as the only game in town by pro-EMU unions, since the alternative, the Anglo-American model, lacked comparable social policies. As Tony Dubbins, the general secretary of the Graphical, Paper and Media Union (GPMU), said at the TUC Annual Congress in 2002, 'the EU remains the only trading block with a Social Dimension. In the age of globalisation, we should be seeking to develop and expand that Social Dimension' (TUC Annual Congress, 2002).

At the same time, the GPMU was slightly more critical of neo-liberal restructuring than the AEEU and the TUfE movement as a whole and demanded clear commitments in exchange for its support for the Euro. Thus, Tony Dubbins made clear that 'any campaign to join the Euro will only be supported by the GPMU if it is accompanied by a clear and unambiguous commitment to maintain investment in our public services and to support the continued development of the European social model' (TUC Annual Congress, 2003). Similarly, UNIFI too demanded that the UK government committed itself to not cut back public spending, indicating a slightly more critical position (UNIFI, 2003: 1). Out of those supporting EMU, the GMB was the most outspoken union contra neo-liberalism. The European social model was its main goal and support for EMU was conditioned on this model. 'A single currency cannot succeed unless it is accompanied by a broad package of EU reforms aimed at encouraging a competitive European economy and a stable European society' (GMB, 2001a: 3). Moreover, the union was strongly in favour of employment creating programmes at the national and European level, especially via European-wide infrastructure projects. It supported a larger budget for the EU to finance these projects and was generally in favour of a more expansive fiscal policy. If this implied going beyond the limits set by the convergence criteria, the GMB would not be worried. The non-acceptance of neo-liberalism was most visible in the GMB's rejection to participate in the *Britain in Europe* campaign for EMU membership, since the union's analysis of why Britain should join and what had to be done afterwards differed significantly from Michael Heseltine's and Kenneth Clarke's views, both former Conservative ministers and high profile members of this campaign (Interview No. 16; London, 28/03/2001).

Support for EMU by German internationally oriented, transnational sector unions

The 'yes, but' position by the DGB in Germany (see Chapter 5) characterised also the position of most of its affiliated unions, which organise workers in export-oriented, transnational sectors. As in the case of the DGB, this position indicated that neo-liberalism had not been accepted. Especially the positions of the Commerce, Banking and Insurance Workers' Union (Handel, Banken, Versicherungen; HBV) and the Postal Workers' Union (Deutsche Postgewerkschaft; DPG) illustrated this. The HBV organises workers in the finance and retail sectors. In Germany, since the deregulation of financial markets in the early 1990s, all major banks and insurance companies have rapidly transnationalised their activities and even the retail sector has recently moved towards a transnational structure due to mergers and company purchases across borders (Interview No. 2; Düsseldorf, 22/01/2001). The DPG organises workers in telecommunications and postal services. Telecommunications is fully transnationalised as in Britain, but even the German postal sector has started to develop transnational production links as a result of recent liberalisation. Moreover, through the purchase of the Postbank, the Deutsche Post Worldnet emphasised its transnational aspirations (Interview No. 4; Frankfurt, 25/01/2001). Margret Mönig-Raane, general secretary of the HBV, considered EMU to be necessary, since exchange rate fluctuations damaged international trade, provided the possibility for currency speculation, put national central banks under pressure and made demand management policies at the national level impossible (Mönig-Raane, 1997: 3). EMU would, therefore, be part of the logic of the internationalisation of the economy and the issue would not be whether to support EMU or not, but how to structure it (HBV, 1998: 2). Both unions criticised the neo-liberal implications of the convergence criteria, which were considered to hinder a European social model and inhibit the combat of unemployment. They favoured active employment policies at the national and European level, even if this implied a change of the convergence criteria. The DPG demanded that the convergence criteria were corrected and amended. It argued that EU funds such as the social and regional funds should be increased and national state spending should be raised to achieve full employment (Interview No. 4; Frankfurt, 25/01/2001). At the national level, the HBV demanded larger public investment especially in infrastructure programmes. At the European level, a larger EU budget would be required and one should also think about an independent tax income for the EU leading towards a common economic policy (Interview No. 2; Düsseldorf, 22/01/2001). The main line would have to be against the neo-liberal economic-political model and towards a social union (Interview No. 4; Frankfurt, 25/01/2001; HBV, 1998: 2). This was to be achieved via a democratisation of the EU by giving the EP control over all key decisions and making the ECB democratically accountable (Interview No. 4; Frankfurt, 25/01/2001; DPG, 1997: 188). A social Europe would only be possible in the form of a democratic Europe (Mönig-Raane, 1997: 3).

The IG Metall organises workers in the fully export-oriented and increasingly also transnationalised manufacturing sector (Interview No. 6; Frankfurt, 30/01/2001). Despite hesitating initially, the IG Metall supported EMU. It pointed to the problems resulting from an appreciating DM for the export-oriented German economy. This would be overcome through EMU at least within the Euro-zone. Additionally, EMU could help to counter financial speculations, since Europe would have a greater weight with the single currency on the international financial markets (IG Metall, 1996: 1). The acceptance of EMU was, however, linked to a range of demands, which challenged neo-liberalism. The convergence criteria were criticised for focusing too much on price stability, while employment was neglected. In order to generate economic growth, public investment should be increased at the national and European level, carrying out the European-wide infrastructure projects as suggested by Delors in the White Paper on 'Growth, Competitiveness, Employment' in 1993. Moreover, the ECB was asked to lower interest rates to facilitate new investment, and collective bargaining should lead to wage rises along the formula of productivity increase plus inflation rate to generate consumer demand (IG Metall, 1999a: 6–8). Additionally, taxes should be harmonised to avoid competition between EU members and the working time should be reduced from forty-eight to forty-four hours with a long-term goal of thirty-five hours per week to create new jobs (IG Metall, 1999b: 24–5). In short, one should concentrate more on demand management in a Keynesian way, even if this implied a larger budget deficit than 3 per cent of GDP. The Social Dimension, at least as it had been developed so far, could not provide a counterweight to EMU (Interview No. 6; Frankfurt, 30/01/2001).

The Food Processing and Hotel Workers' Union (Nahrung-Genuss-Gaststätten; NGG) is strongly represented amongst workers in the transnationalised part of the tobacco and food processing industries (TNCs include Unilever, Nestle, BAT, Philip Morris and Japan Tobacco). EMU was regarded as a response to globalisation in that states could no longer manage their own economy and the European level may offer the best alternative vis-à-vis the USA/Japan but also international financial markets. It was accepted that in practice trade unions had made concessions to neo-liberalism and the DGB was criticised for accepting EMU too easily without putting forward more forcefully clearer preconditions such as the demand for a criterion on unemployment. As a small union, however, the NGG did not feel in a position to go against the emerging consensus within the DGB. The Social Dimension had developed slowly, the NGG accepted this, but there would be no alternative for unions than to push for its further development (Interview No. 12; Hamburg, 09/02/2001).

The Mine, Chemical and Energy Workers' Union (Industriegewerkschaft Bergbau, Chemie, Energie; IG BCE), which organises workers in the highly transnationalised chemicals sector, also supported EMU, which was deemed to strengthen the EU as an economic location. Moreover, 60 per cent of exports in the chemical industry go to Euro-countries and a single currency would remove exchange rate uncertainties. The convergence criteria were noticed critically and a balance demanded between austerity and employment, but a change or amendment of the criteria themselves was not sought. The IG BCE had been in favour of a European employment programme in the form of European infrastructure programmes to be achieved via an intensification of the macroeconomic dialogue. Instead of accepting increased budget deficits, however, a better use of existing resources was recommended (Interview No. 9; Hannover, 05/02/2001).

The Construction, Agricultural and Environmental Workers' Union (Industriegewerkschaft Bauen-Agrar-Umwelt; IG BAU) organises workers in the concrete and construction industries. While the former is fully transnationalised, the latter also shows an increasing degree of transnationalisation. Although there are still many small- and medium-sized domestic companies in construction, many German firms have started to buy affiliates in foreign countries and foreign companies have bought German construction firms. What is equally important for this sector is the internationalised labour market, characterised by illegal workers and posted workers, i.e. foreign companies carrying out jobs in Germany with their workforce. Especially workers from CEE, but also Britain, Greece, Ireland and Portugal have come to Germany in one of these two ways (Interview No. 5; Frankfurt, 29/01/2001; Menz, 2005a: 56, 58). The IG BAU was the only union within the DGB that rejected EMU and demanded through its General Secretary Wiesenhügel in 1997 to postpone the starting-date of EMU. Considering that the union represents workers in the transnational construction sector, this case contradicts the first hypothesis of this study. The union, however, was not against EMU and a single currency as such. In a presentation in 1998, Bernd Schütt from the IG BAU accepted that a single currency was necessary (Schütt, 1998: 1). It was the neo-liberal economic rationale and the one-sided focus on low inflation that the IG BAU had been worried about. The construction sector relied very much on public infrastructure projects and due to the general austerity course in order to meet the criteria, they were at their lowest level since 1945. Some construction projects in the rail sector, for example, were postponed or cancelled in the run-up to EMU to keep the budget deficit within the criteria (Interview No. 5; Frankfurt, 29/01/2001; see also Menz, 2005a: 58). It was this reliance on public investment at the national level that explains the union's negative position on EMU despite the transnationalised character of its production sector. Moreover, against the background of high unemployment, it was argued that EMU and the concomitant wage transparency would force workers to accept wage restraint and welfare cut-backs. According to Wiesenhügel, this was exactly what employers, big industry and banks had in mind when they supported the Euro (Wiesenhügel, 1997: 3). The union demanded to add a criterion on unemployment and further asked for an active employment policy at the European level concentrating on European-wide infrastructure projects, even if this implied that budget deficits were higher than 3 per cent of GDP. Additionally, a demand strategy concentrating on necessary services was called for (Schütt, 1998: 8). Finally, the Social Dimension was regarded as completely insufficient. The core aspects of economic and social policy would have remained untouched and the social partners would still not be consulted on crucial questions such as the WTO negotiations about the liberalisation of services (Interview No. 5; Frankfurt, 29/01/2001).

French internationally oriented and transnational labour's position on EMU
In France, it is mainly the public sector that has remained an almost exclusively domestic production sector, while private industry has been to a large extent

internationally oriented and transnationalised. As the unionisation level is extremely low and confederations are comparatively small, it is rather difficult to identify the positions of even smaller affiliated federations, which frequently do have not enough resources to develop their own positions in the first place. Hence, I will also refer back to French confederations in this as well as the next chapter. While the CFDT had a majority of its members in the public sector with 53 per cent vis-à-vis 47 per cent in the private sector in 1988, this had turned around by 2001. Then, 56 per cent of its members were in the private sector, while 44 per cent worked in the public sector (CFDT, 2001: no page). In short, the union's strong support for EMU and relatively mild criticism of neo-liberal restructuring, having accepted the convergence criteria and the independent status of the ECB (see Chapter 5), can at least partly also be explained through its predominance in the private internationally oriented or transnational sectors. Similarly, the CFTC is more presented in the private than the public sector and here especially the big retail chains and banks. This may have contributed to the union's endorsement of EMU in addition to the union's general pro-European integration outlook (Interview No. 61; Paris, 13/09/2002) (see Chapter 5). Again, however, it needs to be remembered that union's positions on EMU cannot be read off from the production structure. The Banking and Financial Institute Federation (Fédération des banques and societés financières; CFDT-Banques), affiliated to the CFDT, organises employees in the highly transnationalised banking sector. In contrast to its confederation, CFDT-Banques supported a 'no' in the Maastricht referendum in 1992. This was not a 'no' to the EU, but to its purely financial construction. Europe, it was alleged, was built by and for finance, not the people. The convergence criteria would be indicative of the financial construction, especially considering that they did not include a criterion on unemployment. Negative deflationary policies in France were perceived as a result of the efforts to meet the criteria (Interview No. 54; Paris, 11/09/2002).

The CGT, as outlined in Chapter 5, had recommended its members to vote 'no' in the 1992 referendum on Maastricht, mainly because of its rejection of the neo-liberal rationale underlying EMU. This negative position was also supported by the affiliated unions organising workers in transnational production sectors. The Chemical Workers' CGT federation (Fédération Nationale des Industries Chimiques; FNIC-CGT), organising workers in the transnational chemical sector, argued that its task was not to formulate positions on macroeconomic questions. This would be the role of the confederation CGT and its position was also the position of FNIC-CGT (Interview No. 53; Paris, 11/09/2002). The Construction Sector Federation of the CGT (Fédération Nationale des Travailleurs de la Construction; CGT-construction) organises workers in a sector characterised by world-leading construction and construction material companies and a large number of small companies often acting as sub-contractors (Menz, 2005a: 53–5). It also endorsed the official CGT position. While not opposing the common currency as such, the union strongly criticised the convergence criteria, which had led to job losses in the construction industry as well as public sector due to lower public investment. What would be needed instead, were the creation of conditions for full employment via public finance. Full employment would clearly be a matter of political will (Interview No. 57; Paris, 12/09/2002).

The Financial Sector Federation of the CGT (Fédération Nationale CGT des Personnels des Secteurs Financiers; CGT-finance), organising workers in the highly transnationalised finance sector, initially rejected EMU and the single currency mainly because of the neo-liberal convergence criteria. Now, with EMU having become a reality, the union, in line with the CGT position, would work towards improvements from within (Interview No. 51; Paris, 09/09/2002). Finally, the Metal Workers' Federation of the CGT (CGT-metallurgie), organising workers in transnationalised manufacturing, as the CGT, rejected the Maastricht Treaty because of the convergence criteria. The union's main problem was that the whole construction of Europe focused on a neo-liberal macro-economic system organised around the Internal Market and EMU. The SGP and the convergence criteria were not acceptable to the CGT-metallurgie. They would engender low growth levels, lead to high unemployment throughout Europe and were dangerous especially in view of enlargement, when more flexibility would be required. The general emphasis had to shift more towards social policy. Nevertheless, EMU was now a reality. Again similar to the CGT and other affiliates, the union worked for change from within. This should imply tackling unemployment through higher domestic demand based on wage increases and further investment in public services via budget deficit spending (Interview No. 52; Paris, 11/09/2002). In short, as already indicated in Chapter 5, in addition to the nature of the production structure, the ideological rift has to be taken into account in France. Transnational sector unions, affiliated to the CGT, opposed EMU because of its neo-liberal implications and despite the nature of their production structure.

The confederation FO was extremely critical of the neo-liberal rationale underlying EMU (see Chapter 5). Here too, it can be seen that the Communication Workers' Federation of FO (FO de la Communication), despite the partially transnational character especially of the telecommunications sector, supported this sceptical position vis-à-vis EMU. The union regarded the prioritisation of economic policy over social policy as the main problem of European integration. The convergence criteria would be too restrictive and increased the problems for states to subsidise companies in difficulty and, thus, to protect jobs. The second problem would be the ECB, which mainly focused on inflation and generally set the interest rates too high in marked contrast to the US Federal Reserve Bank. Instead of greater labour market flexibility, a stronger focus on public investment was needed to combat unemployment (Interview No. 66; Paris, 17/12/2002).

Finally, the Postal and Telecommunications Workers' Federation of Solidarity, Unity, Democracy (Solidaires, Unitaires et Démocratiques; SUD-PTT) organises workers in the postal services, which is still a state corporation, but also telecommunications, which has developed into an at least partially transnationalised sector. Prior to the 1992 referendum on Maastricht, SUD-PTT had its own internal referendum, in which a majority rejected EMU. Since then, the union had accepted that it had to live with the new reality of EMU membership. Hence, it concentrated on achieving changes within EMU. In general, SUD-PTT opposed privatisation and austerity budgets and, thus, of course also the convergence criteria (Interview No. 63; Paris, 16/12/2002). Its rejection of EMU may be explained partly by the fact that the postal services are still a domestic production sector. Partly, however, being a member of G10-Solidaires, this negative position, similar to the critical positions by the CGT transnational federations and the FO de la Communication, may also result from the union's ideologically more critical position vis-à-vis neo-liberal restructuring.

Internationally oriented labour and EMU in Austria

The Austrian production structure is strongly export-oriented in some sectors, but hardly transnationalised (see Chapter 3). Only two unions can be identified that organise workers almost exclusively in these areas, the Metal and Textile Workers' Union (Gewerkschaft Metall-Textil; GMT) and the Chemical Workers' Union (Gewerkschaft der Chemiearbeiter; GdC). The former represents workers in the following sectors: mining, oil, electrical supplies, metal working and textile, clothes and leather. These sectors are predominantly export-oriented as, for example, the suppliers of car manufacturers, but there are also increasingly foreign TNCs operating in Austria such as GM and BMW as well as in the textile and electrical goods sector (Interview No. 29; Wien, 20/03/2002). The GdC organises blue-collar workers in the chemical industry, paper, glass and oil, i.e. sectors that are all export-oriented and to some extent transnationalised in that some foreign TNCs are present and some Austrian companies in the paper sector, for example, have got affiliates abroad (Interview No. 32; Wien, 21/03/2002). The GMT was positive about EMU. The Internal Market would require a monetary union and the convergence criteria as such were not regarded as a problem. The real problem would be the way the Austrian government tried to achieve a balanced budget. Hence, the union demanded that the full room for manoeuvre within the criteria was used to cope with economic recession. Moreover, the co-ordination of national employment programmes through the Luxembourg process was not deemed sufficient. Rather, a common employment and industrial policy should be established at the European level. Finally, the union criticised the lack of participatory possibilities in monetary and more general economic policy-making to strengthen the Social Dimension. Europe would need a legally established industrial relations system (Interview No. 29; Wien, 20/03/2002). The GdC regarded EMU as a positive step forwards, because it strengthened the EU in the competition with the USA and Japan. As such, it was argued, there was nothing wrong with the convergence criteria. It would, however, be important to have a common tax system to create equal conditions for competition in the Internal Market. As for the creation of employment, the state was not necessarily a good employer, it was pointed out. Instead of creating employment, one should attempt to make Austria more attractive as a production location (Interview No. 32; Wien, 21/03/2005). Thus, the position of both the GMT and the GdC confirms the first hypothesis that unions organising internationally oriented and transnational forces of labour are likely to be in favour of EMU. Interestingly, the position of both unions did not exhibit a strong criticism of neo-liberal restructuring in that both were not worried about the convergence criteria. At least the GMT, however, demanded a stronger focus on employment creation at the European level and a deepening of the Social Dimension.

Swedish transnational labour and EMU

In Sweden, it was the Metal Workers' Union affiliated to LO, which came out first in favour of Swedish EMU membership. At its congress in 1997, out of 300 delegates, 80 per cent endorsed a pro-EMU position. The Metal Workers' Union represents workers in the transnationalised manufacturing sector, dominated by TNCs such as Ericsson, Electrolux and Volvo. Considering that the union's sector depended on TNCs, which operated on the European and even global level, the union argued that it simply had to follow capital to the European level to re-establish a balance between capital and labour lost at the national level (Interview No. 38; Stockholm, 20/06/2002). This argument echoed very much the union's position on EU membership in 1994 (Bieler, 1999: 36). The convergence criteria were not considered to be a problem. If at all, they had a positive impact on Sweden, forcing it to focus on low levels of inflation and a consolidated budget, putting it now with a budget surplus of 2 per cent in a position to employ more people in the public sector. The establishment of buffer funds as a safeguard against asymmetric shocks was rejected. It would make no sense to take money out of the economy in times of stable budgets. The LO condition of buffer funds was regarded as a concession to those unions in LO, which were opposed to EMU (Interview No. 38; Stockholm, 20/06/2002).

This position was supported by the Industrial Workers' Union (Industrifacket) and the Paper Workers' Union (Pappers) within LO. The former organises workers in the chemical, textile and clothing sectors, but also pharmaceuticals, plastics and refineries. The majority of the union's members work in TNCs and even the large amount of small companies in these sectors are often in foreign ownership. On the basis of a union internal report in 1999, the executive committee of Industrifacket adopted a pro-EMU position as union policy, provided that membership was submitted to the population in a referendum. EMU membership was supported because a single currency would be better for smaller enterprises, since increased competition would have beneficial implications in the long run, and because it would push higher Swedish price levels down to EU averages. Considering the current Swedish budget surplus of 2 per cent and the fact that inflation was under control, the convergence criteria were no longer a worry. As long as wage formation was under control, the budget surplus would be enough as a buffer (Interview No. 39; Stockholm, 24/06/2002). Pappers organises workers in the pulp and paper industry. Some 80 per cent of production is for the export, out of which 80 per cent goes to locations in

EMU countries. With 90 per cent of union members working in cross-border companies, the sector is to a large extent transnationalised. The executive board of the Pappers decided on a 'yes' to EMU membership in December 2000. Politically, it was argued, non-membership had damaging implications for Sweden's influence in the EU. Economically, with a majority of exports now going to EMU countries and in view of companies' decisions on where to invest, the Euro and EMU had become increasingly important. Finally, Swedish wage increases were still slightly above the EU average and EMU membership would put further pressure on, and thus help with, staying in line with wage developments elsewhere (Interview No. 40; Stockholm, 24/06/2002).

The majority of unions affiliated to the TCO followed the latter's position and did not take an official stance. Within TCO unions, there were concerns about splitting the membership by taking a decisive position on EMU. Nevertheless, a pro-EMU decision by transnational sector unions can be identified. The executive committee of the Finansförbundet, representing employees in the financial sector dominated by four large, transnationally operating Swedish banks, decided in 1997 in favour of EMU. It was accepted that the convergence criteria were problematic and that the disappearance of the SKr implied the loss of jobs in the financial sector. Overall, however, it was assumed that EMU membership would strengthen the competitiveness of the efficient large Swedish banks and, thus, of the Swedish financial sector as a whole (Interview No. 50; Stockholm, 28/06/2002). The Swedish Union of Clerical and Technical Employees in Industry (Svenska Industritjanstemannaförbundet; SIF), the TCO affiliate organising white-collar workers in transnational manufacturing, had not adopted an official position on EMU. Regarding itself as independent from the SAP and having many members who are also members in other political parties including the Green and Left Parties, which were both opposed to EMU, SIF had decided that EMU was an issue that its members should decide upon independently in a referendum. It was still expected, however, that amongst its members as well as the executive board, there was a majority in favour of EMU, thus reflecting the transnational production structure. Similarly to the LO Metal Workers' Union, buffer funds were not considered to be feasible. Instead, labour costs needed to be kept under control and a budget surplus was deemed to be the best possible buffer for times of economic recession (Interview No. 49; Stockholm, 28/06/2002).

In short, as expected in the first hypothesis, Swedish transnational sector unions were in favour of Swedish EMU membership. An analysis of the contents of transnational labour's arguments shows that neo-liberalism was no longer fully criticised. The acceptance of the neo-liberal convergence criteria and related low inflation policies, as well as the recognition that wage development was a core factor of economic stability, indicated that some neo-liberal concepts had been accepted or were at least no longer considered to be a danger. In a way, the discussion on EMU, similar to the LO's position, had been de-linked from considerations on a further development of the EU Social Dimension. This could be seen as an indicator that transnational Swedish labour may no longer be interested in Swedish model-type solutions at the European level in contrast to its position during the EU referendum campaign in 1994 (Bieler, 2000: 106–7). The next section will look at the various unions' positions on European-level co-operation in more detail.

Transnational production sector unions and their position on European co-operation

British transnational sector unions and European co-operation

It is the transnational sector unions that were most involved in European-wide co-operation in Britain, thereby confirming the first hypothesis. The CWU was actively participating in the sectoral dialogue in both telecommunications and postal services and frequently made direct presentations to the Commission or via its European confederation Union Network International-Europa (UNI-Europa). Moreover, it was in principle in favour of European-wide collective bargaining, although this was not deemed very realistic at the moment due to the refusal by employers (Interview No. 14; London, 27/03/2001). UNIFI, although it did not see immediate pressures towards cross-border bargaining, had recognised that a European-level response would be required in the medium-term and had been participating in the online collective bargaining network by its EIF UNI-Europa. The latter also had plans 'to organise a four-year programme for the development of European-level collective bargaining' (Mulhearn, 2004: 308; see also Chapter 8). As Margaret Hazell made clear, speaking on behalf of UNIFI at the TUC Annual Congress in 2003, 'the trade union movement nationally and across Europe must continue to work together to ensure that the Social Dimension of the EU is strengthened wherever possible' (TUC Annual Congress, 2003). The AEEU, moreover, was strongly involved with the European Metal-workers' Federation (EMF) and its attempts to co-ordinate national collective wage bargaining. It had an additional close relationship with the IG Metall of the district Lower Saxony, although the exact nature of this co-operation still had to be specified (Interview No. 20; Hayes/Kent, 23/05/2001). The GMB with its majority of members from transnational manufacturing went furthest in its direct involvement in Brussels. The EU level was considered to have become increasingly important and the union had maintained its own presence in Brussels for over ten years. It lobbied the Commission directly and had a close relationship with the Commissioner for Employment and Social Affairs. The GPMU was the only other British union present in Brussels, sharing the GMB's office. The Commission frequently turned to these two unions for a British union perspective on individual issues (Interview No. 16; London, 28/03/2001). Finally the TUfE movement demanded the further development of the European social dialogue into a proper European industrial relations system, ensuring trade union involvement in the management of restructuring processes, which resulted from the Internal Market and EMU (TUfE, 2000: 16).

Support for European co-operation by German unions

German internationally oriented and transnational sector unions were equally supportive of co-operation at the European level. The DPG, representing workers in transnational telecommunications and finance and internationally oriented postal services, pointed out that a policy within national boundaries was no longer able to achieve union objectives. Hence, trade union organisation, strategies and collective bargaining needed to be Europeanised (DPG, 1997: 188; Sattler, 1996: 22). European-wide collective bargaining was, however, difficult in practice, since the employers' associations had not developed into negotiating partners (Interview No. 4; Frankfurt, 25/01/2001). The HBV, representing workers in transnational finance and the internationally oriented retail sector, was strongly in favour of European-wide bargaining and co-operation with other unions. In order to bring about change to the neo-liberal logic of integration in times when states had lost their economic policy, autonomy and decisions were taken at the supranational level in Brussels, and unions too would need to integrate at the European level. Thus, the European trade unions would have to involve themselves more strongly as part of a European-wide social movement, which co-determined social conflicts (HBV, 1998: 2). The HBV, as a member of UNI-Europa, had been actively participating in the first sectoral social dialogues in its sectors, which had led to joint declarations (Interview No. 2; Düsseldorf, 22/01/2001).

The IG Metall accepted that the EU was now the most important level in many policy areas and acknowledged that it perhaps still relied too much on the national level in its attempts to influence policy-making. At the European level it was a member of the EMF. Sectoral social dialogue was, however, impossible, because employers refused to participate. The most important development had, therefore, been the co-ordination of national collective bargaining via the EMF. Considering the different national industrial relations systems, productivity growth rates and general economic development, this co-ordination might be the best and only feasible way forward. Additionally, the various IG Metall districts had started to build up relations with the metal workers' unions of neighbouring countries to improve the understanding of each others' systems through the exchange of personnel and information (Interview No. 6; Frankfurt, 30/01/2001; Interview No. 7; Stuttgart, 31/01/2001; see Chapter 8).

The NGG demanded social dialogue in its sectors, but the problem was that these sectors were faced with seventy-three different European employers' associations. Issues had been discussed in the sugar, cigarette and catering industries, and there was an agreement about the working time in agriculture (Interview No. 12; Hamburg, 09/02/2001). The IG BAU actively supported European co-operation. As stated earlier, the construction sector is not only transnationalised as far as production is concerned, but also in relation to the labour market in that it is characterised by a large number of illegal workers, posted workers and foreign contract companies, which carry out projects in Germany with their own workers. This made national collective bargaining agreements almost unenforceable and highlighted the importance of the international level. The IG

BAU had, therefore, been taking part in the co-ordination of wage bargaining and the exchange of each others' wage conditions within the European Federation of Building and Woodworkers (EFBWW), concentrating on issues such as working time, and length and payment of holidays. Nevertheless, despite these activities, the IG BAU did not consider the European level more important than the national level. One should not forget that it was national governments that eventually made the decisions in the EU (Interview No. 5; Frankfurt, 29/01/2001). This can again be explained by the fact that the construction industry relies to a considerable extent on public infrastructure projects.

The IG BCE did not consider the European level to be more important than the national one despite the high degree of transnationalisation of production in its sector. Social dialogue at the European level was not taking place in the union's sectors, mainly due to the refusal by employers, and European bargaining co-ordination had no impact on the IG BCE's collective bargaining at the German level (Interview No. 9; Hannover, 05/02/2001). The main focus of the union was on EWCs as the decisive level for the development of European industrial relations (IG BCE, 2000: 14). After a crucial defeat of the union in 1971, the union had purged its radical wing and accepted the co-operation offered by the employers in exchange for industrial peace. Since then, the IG BCE had had a very close social partnership arrangement with the highly centralised employers' association at the national level (Behrens and Jacoby, 2004: 103). In line with the second hypothesis, these very good possibilities to influence policy-making within the structural selectivity of the national form of state made the European level less attractive despite the union's transnationalised chemical production sector.[2] It also, however, reflects the general European-level situation where the European Mine, Chemical and Energy Workers' Federation (EMCEF), the EIF of the unions in the chemicals sector, was much less involved in independent activities than, for example, the EMF, organising workers in the highly trans-nationalised manufacturing sector across the EU (see Chapter 8).

French internationally oriented and transnational unions and European co-operation

The previous section showed that despite the transnational production structure of their sector, a whole range of French unions, in contrast to the expectations of the first hypothesis, opposed EMU in line with their confederation's position (see here the CGT transnational sector affiliates) or even in opposition to their own confederation (see here the CFDT-Banques). When analysing these unions' positions on European-level co-operation, however, their strong emphasis on regional co-operation brings them back in line with the second part of the first hypothesis. Now that EMU was a reality, the CFDT-Banques tried to adapt its actions to this new situation and became more active in matters of European co-operation. The national level would still be more important due to the contin-uing importance of different national regulations in areas such as the retail activities of banks. The transfer of competencies to European union organisa-tions would be difficult, but should bargaining become a European issue, the union would be prepared to do this, as long as this process was under its control. Nevertheless, while the union was cautious in relation to the concrete possibilities of European-level co-operation, in contrast to its confederation CFDT, it had always had a global vision. Bernard Dufill, the union's president, was a founding member of ATTAC-France (Association pour la Taxation des Transactions Financiers pour l'Aide aux Citoyens) (see Chapter 9), and the union had actively participated in the World Social Forums in Porto Alegre (Brazil), the world-level meeting of anti-neo-liberal globalisation movements, as well as the preparations for the related first European Social Forum in Florence in November 2002 (Bieler and Morton, 2004b). Trade unions, it was argued, simply had to open up themselves to other actors in order to push through counter-neo-liberal projects such as the Tobin Tax on international currency speculations (Interview No. 54; Paris, 11/09/2002).

Similar to the CGT confederation, the transnational sector affiliates of the union had accepted to participate in European-level co-operation within the official institutional set-up. Being sceptical of the possibilities, however, the unions did not rely exclusively on this strategy. The FNIC-CGT put emphasis on the future construction of social Europe, including social security, workers rights and the right to work, allowing the EU to develop a system different from the USA. As a member of EMCEF, the exchange of information at the European level was regarded as very important, but European collective bargaining was deemed unlikely due to the different national systems. Co-ordination similar to the EMF would not be possible yet. Hence, like other chemical workers' unions such as the German IG BCE and the Austrian GdC (see below), the union considered the transfer of competencies to the European level as unlikely and argued that the main co-operation across borders would take place in EWCs (Interview No. 53; Paris, 11/09/2002). The CGT-construction demanded a social union and here the further development of the Social Dimension. Sectoral social dialogue in the union's sector would, however, be difficult due to different national positions, cultures and industrial relations systems. Finally, the production structure in construction would be less transnationalised and more mobile than in the metal working sector and the co-ordination of national wage bargaining therefore not possible. As a result, the transfer of competencies was deemed difficult, especially also because French unions were comparatively weak to other unions and could be outvoted or not heard at the European level (Interview No. 57; Paris, 12/09/2002). The CGT-finance accepted that the strengthening of European-level co-operation was increasingly important in order to give the social union priority over monetary union. Nevertheless, the results of the Social Dimension were considered to be meagre and there had been hardly any sectoral social dialogue in the union's areas. The union was also sceptical about the possibility to overcome the various national differences and deemed the national level to remain more important, thereby excluding also the transfer of competencies to European-level union organisations (Interview No. 51; Paris, 09/09/2002). Due to the transnational organisation of production in its sector, the CGT-metallurgie regarded European co-operation as absolutely essential. The co-ordination of national wage bargaining via the EMF was deemed to be a positive step forwards but so far it had not had an impact on wage bargaining in France. The union had also participated in the exchange of observers in other countries' collective bargaining rounds, which was very informative. The transfer of competencies was, however, a difficult issue. The problem would be that there were no good European-level agreements that could encourage unions and workers to look more at the European level (Interview No. 52; Paris, 11/09/2002).

FO de la Communication, perhaps partly due to its more transnational production structure, was more positive about European-level co-operation than its confederation. Clearly, the union was sceptical about the Commission's argument that the Social Dimension should be developed via the social dialogue, since it would generally be the Commission that had been behind the full-scale liberalisation and privatisation of the European economies, going back to the Internal Market programme of the mid-1980s. Nevertheless, the union demanded further sectoral social dialogue to prevent social dumping. The transfer of competencies would currently not be an issue, but the union had to operate increasingly transnationally due to the changing production structure. Unfortunately, joint union responses would still often be hampered by internal disagreements between different national unions. There were, therefore, no attempts at the co-ordination of national wage bargaining at the time (Interview No. 66; Paris, 17/12/2002).

SUD-PTT, finally, supported supranational co-operation. Similar to its confederation G10-Solidaires, however, it rejected the ETUC for being unable to organise cross-border actions and, therefore, concentrated on organising alternative cross-border networks with unions such as the Italian Comitati di Base (COBAS) and Sindacato intercategoriale dei comitati di base (SINCOBAS). Its networks, however, also included other social movements such as Euromarches and the various 'sans' groups (see below) (Interview No. 63; Paris, 16/12/2002; SUD-PTT, 2002: 7–8). During the widespread public sector strikes in 1995 and 1996, SUD-PTT gained mobilising potential. Together with other, like-minded radical unions within the G10-Solidaires confederation the union increasingly attempted to bridge the gap with other social movements that also organised resistance against neo-liberal restructuring. As Waters (2003) outlines, during the 1990s France experienced the return of the social question and the emergence of a whole range of social movements, fighting for the social rights of those on the margins of society. At the forefront were the so-called 'sans' groups such as the 'sans-employ' (unemployed), the 'sans-abri' (homeless) and the 'sans-papiers' ('illegal' immigrants). Traditional trade unions often found it difficult to engage with these groups constructively, but it was the SUD unions, including SUD-PTT, which actively co-operated and, thereby, emerged as a new force of resistance against neo-liberal economics (Waters, 2003: 21). In Chapter 9, the possibilities of union-social movement co-operation will be looked at in more detail.

Austrian internationally oriented labour and European co-operation

The strong focus on European-level co-operation by the Austrian GMT confirms the first hypothesis that internationally oriented and transnational forces of labour are likely to support stronger international co-operation. The union was a strong supporter of the EMF's attempts to co-ordinate national bargaining rounds at the European level ensuring that all affiliated unions demanded wage rises in line with inflation plus productivity increases (see Chapter 8). In this respect, the GMT accepted that national diversity was no longer an obstacle to European-level co-ordination with other unions. As a next step, intra-union co-operation needed to be intensified further at the European level and negotiations with employers sought more actively. Ultimately, a union merger at the European level was considered to be necessary in order to push successfully for the Social Dimension to become a counterpart to EMU. EWCs were also deemed important, but one should be careful that they stayed outside collective bargaining in order not to undermine the structural power of unions at the sectoral level (Interview No. 29; Wien, 20/03/2002).

The GdC argued that the European co-ordination of national bargaining would be important and did not even exclude the possibility of transnational wage bargaining as well as common environmental standards. In concrete terms, however, the union was rather pessimistic. National interests would still dominate individual unions' agendas and EMCEF, the union's EIF, was evaluated as having achieved very little as far as a social dialogue with employers was concerned as well as in relation to intra-union co-operation. Due to these overriding national interests, often also stifling the work of EWCs, one would simply be powerless vis-à-vis TNCs (Interview No. 32; 21/03/2002). In sum, while indicating a willingness to co-operate more at the European level, in practice the GdC was much less involved than the GMT. This reflects clearly the different levels of supranational activities between the EMCEF on the one hand, and the EMF on the other respectively (see Chapter 8).

Swedish transnational labour: little enthusiasm for European co-operation

Interestingly and in contrast to other transnational sector unions, Swedish transnational forces of labour were much more reluctant about European-level involvement. The Metal Worker's Union argued that a balance between capital and labour needed to be re-established at the European level and hoped that the Lisbon strategy with its commitment to full employment, developed at the European Council summit in Lisbon in 2000, may offer a way of breathing new life into the Social Dimension. Nevertheless, it asserted that lobbying the Swedish government was still the most important way of influencing policy-making. European-wide collective wage bargaining was rejected and the attempts of co-ordinating the different national wage bargaining rounds at the European level by the EMF (see Chapter 8) would play no role in collective bargaining in Sweden (Interview No. 38; Stockholm, 20/06/2002). Industrifacket acknowledged the positive developments of the Social Dimension, but pointed out that the multi-sector social dialogue agreements between the ETUC and UNICE were minimum agreements, which had no concrete impact on Swedish conditions. Wage bargaining or the co-ordination of national bargaining at the European level were not considered to be feasible. Wage formation systems, tax systems, social security systems and bargaining cultures as well as the various languages would simply be too different (Interview No. 39; Stockholm, 24/06/2002). The Pappers echoed this position. While the importance of increased co-operation at the European level was emphasised, collective bargaining of wages or other material interests was still considered to be impossible due to the different interests by various national unions in the pulp and paper industries (Interview No. 40; Stockholm, 24/06/2002).

Finally, the transnational sector TCO affiliates were similarly reluctant about European co-operation. For influence on policy-making, the Finansförbundet still deemed the national level to be more important in practical terms and the transfer of competencies to European unions was not on the agenda (Interview No. 50; Stockholm, 28/06/2002). SIF too continued to concentrate on the national level and, similarly to its LO counterpart the Metal Workers' Union, pointed out that the wage bargaining co-ordination attempted by the EMF had had no impact on its bargaining with the employers at the Swedish level (Interview No. 49; Stockholm, 28/06/2002). In general, the willingness to engage in stronger European co-operation by transnational sector unions in Sweden was an intention for the future at best and the further development of the Social Dimension or other measures in the area of a European employment policy were not put forward as a precondition for EMU support. The explanation for this interesting position needs to be sought by looking at the domestic institutional set-up. It was the transnational sector unions, white-collar as well as blue-collar, which signed in 1997 the Industrial Agreement, updated in 1999, with their counterparts of the employers covering all private sector industries (see Chapter 4). This Industrial Agreement was path-breaking in that it re-co-ordinated collective bargaining at the sectoral level, with one trade unionist hailing it as the new Saltsjöbaden agreement (Interview No. 39; Stockholm, 24/06/2002).[3] Hence, in line with the second hypothesis of this study, Swedish transnational sector unions emphasised the national level in their activities due to renewed possibilities within the structural selectivity of the Swedish form of state.

Conclusion

As outlined in this chapter, the vast majority of transnational sector unions in the five countries supported EMU as expected in the first hypothesis of this study. Monetary union was considered to ensure a stable economic environment necessary for growth in these sectors, thereby securing employment of the unions' members. Nevertheless, unions' positions on EMU cannot be read off from their location in the production process. Theoretically, this would imply a position of economic determinism, empirically it would simply be incorrect.

Those transnational sector unions strongly critical of neo-liberal restructuring as, for example, the various CGT affiliates, CFDT-Banques, FO de la Communication and SUD-PTT also rejected EMU because of its neo-liberal rationale as embodied in the convergence criteria and the related SGP. Unsurprisingly, these unions are to be found in France, where the ideological split is expressed in the large number of different trade unions in the first place. On the other hand, however, several though not all unions, which strongly supported EMU, were also the ones least critical of the neo-liberal implications of EMU. The British AEEU and CWU, the Austrian GMT and GdC, the Swedish transnational unions affiliated to the LO and TCO and to a lesser extent the German IG BCE, while demanding a strengthening of the Social Dimension, were all less worried about the neo-liberal convergence criteria and the independent status of the ECB.

Similarly, in relation to European-level co-operation most of the transnational sector unions were positive, even if their concrete activities differed from sector to sector. Interestingly, however, while metal workers' unions favoured very much strong co-operation expressed especially in the EMF attempt to co-ordinate national collective bargaining at the European level, chemical workers' unions were less supportive of European-level co-operation. If they did support it, then they were mainly thinking in terms of EWCs, but not sectoral co-operation. This different focus will be revisited in Chapter 8, when the activities of the related EIFs are assessed. Most notable, however, was the reluctance by Swedish transnational sector unions to emphasise more co-operation at the European level. In line with the second hypothesis of this study, the explanation for this can be sought in the revival of sectoral collective bargaining at the national level since 1997. This strong possibility to influence policy-making at the national level made the EU much less attractive. The German IG BCE is a similar case due to its rather specific tight relationship with the respective employers' association. The next chapter will analyse the positions of national production sector unions on the same issues.

Notes

1   The five tests were developed by the Chancellor Gordon Brown to assess the right moment for UK entry into EMU. The five tests are as follows: (1) 'Are business cycles and economic structures compatible so that we and others could live comfortably with Euro interest rates on a permanent basis?'; (2) 'If problems emerge is there sufficient flexibility to deal with them?'; (3) 'Would joining EMU create better conditions for firms making long-term decisions to invest in Britain?'; (4) 'What impact would entry into EMU have on the competitive position of the UK's financial services industry, particularly the City's wholesale markets?'; (5) 'In summary, will joining EMU promote higher growth, stability and a lasting increase in jobs?' (HM Treasury, 2003: 2).

2   I am indebted to Dr Michael Fichter, Freie Universität Berlin, for this observation (06/02/2001).

3   In 1938, Saltsjöbaden was the place of a famous agreement between the central organisations of capital and labour, preparing the way for industrial peace and the establishment of the Swedish model.

7
National social forces of labour: the reluctance to engage in European co-operation

Introduction

This chapter concentrates on the national sector unions in the five case studies and their positions on EMU and European co-operation. According to the first hypothesis, it is expected that

> *Hypothesis 1*: ... national production sector unions are likely to oppose EMU, since it undermines national policy autonomy and, thus, the support, on which their sectors depend. Relying on the state, they may also be less concerned about European co-operation.

As in the case of transnational sector unions, however, the production sector does not determine the ideological outlook of a union. Hence, domestic sector unions' positions on neo-liberal restructuring has to be analysed separately. Finally, the length of discussion of the individual labour movements depends again on the countries' production structure. As Austrian production is hardly transnationalised, there are still many unions that operate in domestic production sectors, resulting in a comparatively larger analysis.

National forces of labour and their positions on EMU

British national sector unions: clear opposition to EMU

British unions in domestic production sectors fiercely opposed EMU. UNISON is the biggest British public sector union. Its criticism of EMU was threefold. First, the convergence criteria and, since the launch of EMU in 1999, the SGP would limit what countries could spend on public services due to their neo-liberal rationale and exclusive focus on price stability. On behalf of UNISON, Jane Carolan made this clear at the TUC Annual Congress in 2002: 'The fundamental part of the Growth and Stability Pact is that the only goal of European economic policy is price stability, a policy based on tight control of interest rates and public expenditure' (TUC Annual Congress, 2002). Second, as a result, EMU would have a negative effect on employment and growth levels in that it limited public spending on the public sector. Simply to add a criterion on unemployment could not counter the general neo-liberal, monetarist policy course. Instead of cutting back public spending, the public sector, it was argued, would be in an excellent position for active employment policies. Jobs would be quick to create, relatively cheap due to low pay and provided an immediate reward for society through better service provisions (Interview No. 19; London, 02/05/2001). Finally, EMU was rejected because of the ECB's lack of democratic accountability and its exclusive focus on price stability and low inflation. Again Jane Carolan, this time at the TUC Annual Congress in 2003:

> From Galway to Greece the Euro economies are no longer run by democratically elected governments; they are run by the European Central Bank. The economic criteria applied by that Bank are strictly monetarist based on inflation targets and interest rates. The effect of this is deflation requiring countries to cut budgets and reduce public sector debt, and we can look at the results of that. (TUC Annual Congress, 2003)

In short, EMU is criticised for its underlying neo-liberal rationale and the concomitant restriction of an active employment policy. Rather than concentrating solely on low inflation, Britain would need strong investment in the public sector to create further employment (see also Strange, 1997: 17).

The RMT, which organises workers in a predominantly domestic railway sector, decided to oppose EMU membership and strongly favoured an early referendum. Most importantly, the RMT was worried about the potential restriction of spending programmes by the British government due to the convergence criteria. As it was argued by Greg Tucker on behalf of the union at the TUC Annual Congress in 2002,

> for us the Stability and Growth Pact, the Instability and Lack of Growth Pact, the essential part of the Euro process, is about forcing countries inside the Eurozone to impose huge spending cuts attacking welfare provision and social spending in the interests of big business. The Pact exacerbates recession across Europe, stifling growth to less than two per cent in the last two successive years. Unemployment is rising to nine per cent, but the Pact forbids the extra spending required in a downturn. (TUC Annual Congress, 2002)

One year later at the same occasion, Bob Crow the RMT's general secretary briefly summed up the position of his union and stated 'that we should not go into the Euro because we believe it will be at the expense of jobs' (TUC Annual Congress, 2003). EMU was also rejected because of the transfer of monetary policy authority to the independent and supranational ECB. The RMT welcomed the government announcement about increased investment in infrastructure after the re-election of Labour in 2001, but demanded additionally that more jobs were created in the rail industry to increase staff levels and, thereby, security especially in the evening (Interview No. 18; London, 29/03/2001). The Union of Construction, Allied Trades and Technicians (UCATT), which organises workers in the predominantly domestic construction sector in Britain, discussed EMU from the mid-1990s onwards. It had not made an official decision yet, but a clear negative tendency was noticeable. UCATT feared cuts in benefits and job losses due to the anti-inflationary bias of EMU. Workers in the construction sector relied very much on public infrastructure projects and the convergence criteria were perceived to endanger this (Interview No. 21; London, 29/05/2001).

The resistance to EMU membership by domestic production sector unions could also be identified in Britain's general unions. As stated in Chapter 6, the GMB, with a majority of its members employed in transnational manufacturing, supported early UK membership in EMU. Nevertheless, about a third of the GMB members are employed in the public sector and this wing of the union opposed EMU. The GMB intended to bridge this gap by demanding a guarantee from government that EMU membership would not lead to lower public investment levels (Interview No. 16; London, 28/03/2001). Similarly, MSF also experienced the emergence of a position opposed to membership. Its public sector members argued that the convergence criteria were too narrow and too restrictive, implying a negative impact on the welfare system (Interview No. 13; London, 26/03/2001). Consequently, although the overall sentiment was positive, the union's document on the single currency only intended to provide a basis for further discussion by outlining both positions (MSF, 2000: 1).

Finally, the Transport and General Workers' Union (T&G) had not taken a decision yet. At its biannual conference in 1997, the T&G put forward a sceptical line in relation to the neo-liberal convergence criteria and stated that 'Conference believes that trying to meet the criteria, without adequate economic convergence, poses a real threat to jobs and services' (T&G, 1997). It was in favour of a referendum and argued that Britain had to meet the five economic tests set out by the Chancellor Gordon Brown (Interview No. 15; London, 27/03/2001). In its memorandum to the Treasury Select Committee on the Euro in January 2003, the union outlined its sceptical position, regarded as a 'third way' between those who rejected EMU membership on principle and those who favoured early entry at any cost (T&G, 2003: 1). Due to the high economic interdependence with the other EU members and considering that the EU was Britain's most important export market, EMU membership potentially implied significant economic gains. Nevertheless, this should not be regarded as a panacea for the problems of Britain's manufacturing sector either. Structural problems required, for example, more spending on R&D and increased investment in skills and training. They could not be remedied via devaluation of the currency as part of adopting the Euro. In general, the timing of membership would have to be right. In the words of Bill Morris, then general secretary of the T&G, at the TUC Annual Congress in 2003: 'Yes, I support the long-term aim of joining the Euro at the right time and on the right conditions' (TUC Annual Congress, 2003). And in this respect, T&G rejected membership for the parliamentary period of 2001 to 2005, because membership could prevent, it was argued, the government's programme of public sector renewal. Chancellor Gordon Brown's Comprehensive Spending Review 2002 had announced an additional £63 billion in government spending on public services by 2005–2006 and this was the union's priority for this period. The T&G's criticism was mainly directed against the SGP. In contrast to the chancellor's 'Golden Rule', which distinguished between borrowing for investment and borrowing for funding short-term spending, making the former possible, and which applied a budget deficit target over the whole period of an economic cycle instead of an annual basis, the SGP would be too inflexible to deal with changing economic circumstances. Several countries would have had to cut back public investment due to the SGP and the criticism of Gordon Brown's spending plans by the Commission in January 2002 indicated that Britain would have to do the same as an EMU member. As Bill Morris argued at the TUC Annual Congress in 2002, 'you can choose the Euro or you can choose to re-build vital public services. Under the Growth and Stability Pact I have to tell you, you cannot have both' (TUC Annual Congress, 2002).

Additionally, the T&G criticised the ECB, first, for its deflationary rationale resulting from its asymmetrical inflation target, which only tackled the overshooting, but not the undershooting of the inflation target and, more generally, for its primary focus on price stability. This left it in contrast to the US Federal Reserve Bank without any tools to promote growth and employment. Second, the ECB was criticised for the lack of accountability and transparency. Hence, the T&G demanded the reform of the ECB along the lines of the Bank of England including

> measures such as replacing the asymmetric inflation target with a symmetrical target; widening the ECB remit to include jobs and growth; the publication of ECB minutes; the introduction of a mechanism of democratic scrutiny and accountability; and the putting in place of clearer lines of authority and co-ordination between the European Commission, national governments, Eurozone central banks and the ECB. (T&G, 2003: 9)

This overall hesitant position with a strong emphasis on the requirements of the public sector may reflect the fact that the T&G represents workers in the transnationalised food processing industry and parts of manufacturing, notably the engineering and chemical sectors, while being at the same time strongly represented in the public service and local government sectors. In overall membership terms, over a quarter of a million members work in public and private services and thus make up about one-third of the union (T&G, http://www.tgwu.org.uk/Templates/Internal.asp?NodeID=89369; 08/04/2005). The T&G may not press the issue of EMU membership in order to avoid an open internal split.[1] In relation to the first hypothesis of this study, this confirms again that national forces of labour are more likely to oppose EMU membership.

The criticism by the T&G of the SGP and the one-sided commitment by the ECB on price stability clearly implied a rejection of the neo-liberal logic underlying EMU. The rejection of EMU by UNISON, the RMT and most likely UCATT indicated a similar position opposed to neo-liberalism. All three demanded active employment programmes via public investment at the national level (see above), which challenged directly the neo-liberal assumption that employment was the automatic result of a competitive economy. Moreover, UNISON made clear that despite the Social Dimension, EMU and the ECB still remained democratically unaccountable (Interview No. 19; London, 02/05/2001). UCATT pointed out that EMU itself needed to be changed for a fundamental correction of policy. The Social Dimension alone could not provide a counterpart to EMU (Interview No. 21; London, 29/05/2001).

The 'yes, but' position by German domestic labour

In contrast to Britain and the case of UNISON, there was no clear rejection of EMU by the public sector unions in Germany. The vast majority of the Public Services, Transport and Traffic Union's (Öffentliche Dienste, Transport und Verkehr; ÖTV) members are in the public service sector, i.e. a clearly domestic production sector. On the basis of the initial experience with EMU, the ÖTV regarded it as the correct answer to globalisation. The union pointed to the low rate of inflation in the EU and the advantage Germany's export industry received from stable exchange rates (ÖTV, 2000: 153; Ladwig, 2000: 7). The ÖTV was initially extremely sceptical about the convergence criteria and their exclusive focus on price stability and low inflation. Public austerity policies due to these criteria, it was pointed out, had mainly had a negative impact on the public services sector. Similar to the DGB position, however, it was thought that a critical support of EMU gave the union more influence than a straightforward rejection. In a climate of general acceptance of the neo-liberal logic, the widespread sentiment in Germany to secure a strong Euro similar to the DM and the dominance of conservative parties in the EU, it was perceived to be difficult, if not impossible, to argue for the creation of jobs via budget deficit spending. Similarly, to ask for a change of the criteria was considered to be unrealistic. Instead, states should be more active within the available space of the criteria and interpret them in a flexible way (Interview No. 8; Stuttgart, 01/02/2001). In general, however, EMU could only be accepted if it was part of a process towards political union based on the European social model and a further development of the democratic and social aspects of integration. Only if the EP and national parliaments were strengthened and the EU institutions in general democratised, could they operate as a counterweight to the ECB (ÖTV, 1997: 35–36; ÖTV, 2000: 153).

Before its merger with other unions into Ver.di in 2001 (see Chapter 1), the German Salaried Employees' Union (Deutsche Angestellten-Gewerkschaft; DAG) was an independent white-collar union, which organised employees predominantly in the public sector. The union regarded EMU as a positive response to globalisation. The EU would clearly be the better level now to exert influence in that it presented a good possibility to defend the European social model based on co-operation against the conflictual and competitive-based Anglo-American model of capitalism. EMU was also seen as a positive step towards political union (Interview No. 11; Hamburg, 09/02/2001). Nevertheless, it was highlighted that Maastricht continued the neo-liberal policies of the Internal Market and led to job losses through the enforced policy of budget austerity and the related stifling of economic growth (DAG, 1997: 8). To counter this tendency, the union demanded active employment programmes at the national level, to be co-ordinated by the EU. In accordance with the Maastricht Treaty, the convergence criteria should be interpreted in a flexible way (DAG, 1997: 19). Finally, the DAG expected the ECB to pursue a more expansive policy through lower interest rates in the light of recent moderate wage agreements (Interview No. 11; Hamburg, 09/02/2001; DAG, 2000: 4).

The German Civil Servants' Federation (Deutscher Beamtenbund; DBB), being especially well represented within the 'Beamten' (civil servants) group in the public sector, accepted EMU similar to the other public sector unions. Its criticism of neo-liberalism was, however, less developed. The Social Dimension was welcomed as a way towards a social market economy and the Anglo-American model of capitalism was rejected. Nevertheless, the German budget, it was argued, had to be consolidated in any case and the convergence criteria were, therefore, not regarded as a problem (Interview No. 1; Bonn, 22/01/2001). The German Railway Workers' Union (Transnet) organises workers mainly in the rail sector, which is dominated by the predominantly domestic Deutsche Bahn AG. While the Deutsche Bahn AG has started to transnationalise its activities to some extent, only a few small regional rail companies have been taken over by foreign companies. Transnet did not reject EMU either. The union pointed out that job losses in its sector were due to necessary restructuring, not to EMU. The convergence criteria were welcomed as a way of consolidating the budget, but the further development of an accompanying Social Dimension was demanded in order to defend the European social model (Interview No. 3; Frankfurt, 25/01/2001).

In short, unlike in Britain, the first hypothesis of a split between national and transnational forces of labour is not confirmed in the case of Germany. Both internationally oriented/transnational and national sector unions predominantly supported the DGB's 'yes, but' position. Several reasons can be put forward in this respect. First, with the increasing privatisation and liberalisation of telecommunications, postal services, rail and energy sectors in the 1990s (Jacobi et al., 1998: 228–9), all German public sector unions are now also representing workers in the often transnationalised private service sector. The ÖTV, for example, has been affected by privatisation and resulting partial transnationalisation in the postal, rail, telecommunications and energy sectors as well as an increasing liberalisation of the local public transport sector (Interview No. 8; Stuttgart, 01/02/2001). The DAG, in addition to the public sector, was also present in private services in the banking sector, insurance companies, the retail sector, telecommunications and the so-called new industries in the IT area, again areas with signs of increasing transnationalisation (Interview No. 11; Hamburg, 09/02/2001). In short, there are hardly any purely nationally oriented production sectors left and this results in these unions' more international outlook. Nevertheless, as argued in Chapter 2, unions' positions cannot be read off directly from their location in the production process. The historical formation of economic-political strategies including economic as well as political and moral concerns need to be taken into account by a neo-Gramscian analysis.[2] Similar to the DGB's general support for European integration since World War Two (see Chapter 5), nationally oriented unions considered it to be their historical duty to support EMU as a further step towards political union (Interview No. 8; Stuttgart, 01/02/2001).

The support for EMU, however, did not imply support for neo-liberal restructuring. Especially the ÖTV and DAG continued to criticise the neo-liberal rationale underlying EMU. Both demanded a flexible interpretation of the criteria, the ÖTV asked for a further democratisation of EU institutions to balance better the ECB and the DAG requested national employment programmes plus a more expansive policy by the ECB through lower interest rates. The less critical position by the DBB can be explained by the fact that this union represents civil servants and, thus, employees in the core of the labour market, who cannot be made redundant by law and are, therefore, hardly affected by neo-liberal restructuring. This relates back to the split between established workers and workers on the periphery of the labour market, introduced in Chapter 2, and echoes the positions of the French CFE-CGC and the Swedish SACO (see Chapter 5).

French national forces of labour and EMU

In Chapter 6, it was argued that the French confederations CFDT and CFTC were dominated by internationally oriented and transnational production sector members and that this could at least partly explain their support for EMU and European level co-operation. The confederations FO and UNSA, on the other hand, are more prominent in the public and, therefore, domestic production sector. FO's 'strongest federations are in public services, health, white-collar and professional work, the post office, engineering and transport' (Goetschy, 1998: 363). This traditional stronghold of the FO in the public domestic production sector explains to some extent the union's very critical position on EMU. Within FO, the public sector federations were much more critical of EMU and the EU in general due to the deregulation resulting from liberalisation directives and the convergence criteria, yet again confirming the first part of the first hypothesis (Interview No. 59; Paris, 13/09/2002). As already mentioned several times, however, the position of trade unions cannot be read off from their location in the production structure and in France an ideological split between unions can be frequently identified. Initially, UNSA had been almost exclusively a public and, thus, national sector confederation. Only in the December 2002 industrial tribunal elections did it obtain a roughly equal amount of votes from both public and private sectors (Interview No. 67; Paris, 17/12/2002). While very critical of neo-liberal restructuring, due to a more moderate outlook and an endorsement of collective bargaining, social dialogue and the EU more generally, the union supported EMU albeit with misgivings (see Chapter 5).

Similarly, UNSA-Education, organising predominantly teachers and related social workers in schools, i.e. a purely domestic production sector, nonetheless supported EMU. Historically, the union had always been in favour of European integration and the move towards federalism. The Euro was viewed as representing an opportunity to develop further the common market. UNSA-Education, therefore, recommended a 'yes' in the Maastricht referendum in 1992. The union was not too worried about the convergence criteria, first, because education was a national policy area. Second, since the European Council summit in Lisbon in 2000, the creation of the knowledge economy had been declared to be more important than the convergence criteria (Interview No. 56; telephone interview, 12/09/2002). Nevertheless, and yet again the ideological split within the French labour movement becomes apparent, the other French education union Unitary Union Federation (Fédération Syndicale Unitaire; FSU) is the rival, bigger union organising workers in the same area. Both unions UNSA-Education and the FSU had emerged in 1992 as a result of the split of the old education union Fédération de l'éducation nationale (FEN). When still part of the FEN, the future members of FSU had been sceptical about European integration in general and EMU in particular. Maastricht included the first two articles on education policy. They were accepted in that they favoured national exchanges and retained education at the national level. In this sense, the Treaty of Maastricht was supported. The unions' criticism, however, was mainly directed against the underlying general economic rationale. Most importantly, the future FSU criticised the one-sided convergence criteria and demanded additional criteria in relation to employment and social protection levels. As they were, the criteria would translate the Washington consensus on neo-liberal economics into EU policy-making (FSU, 2002: 109).[3] Second, the independent status of the ECB and its sole focus on price stability were severely criticised (Interview No. 68; Paris, 18/12/2002). Finally, and here FSU differed most obviously from UNSA-Education, while the union also recognised that education policy was still a national policy, it had become increasingly worried about the impact of the EU and here especially the Commission on the shaping of the wider framework of education policy. It was precisely the way, in which education had been included in the Lisbon strategy in 2000, which was a cause for concern. Through a strong focus on the notion of 'employability', it was training and education that were made responsible for unemployment. 'One reduces education to a large extent to an instrument in the service of competitiveness of the European economy' (FSU, 2002: 127; see also Weber, 2002: 12). Instead, education should also be understood in its importance for personal development and the 'formation of active citizens at the heart of democratic societies' (Baunay, 2002: 17). In short, the production sector alone cannot explain these unions' positions on EMU. While UNSA-Education was rather relaxed about the convergence criteria and supported EMU, the FSU was fiercely opposed to the neo-liberal implications of monetary union.

Austrian national sector unions and EMU

Two Austrian domestic production sector unions, the Union of Local Government Employees (Gewerkschaft der Gemeindebediensteten; GdG) and the Railway Workers' Union (Gewerkschaft der Eisenbahner; GdE), opposed EMU membership. The GdG organises blue- and white-collar workers within the public sector at the local government level. EMU was discussed from the accession debate onwards, but the union accepted that it had not been aware of the consequences at the time and here in particular the related liberalisation and privatisation pressures. As such, the GdG accepted that it had missed the right point for opposing EMU and had to deal now with adapting to the new requirements. It was assumed that the majority of its members opposed EMU mainly as a result of the convergence criteria. Local governments would attempt to meet the convergence criteria via the sub-contraction and privatisation of services. In many sectors such as energy this would have led to a lack of invest-ment. EMU itself, it was argued, had become a reality. Within this new environment, the GdG, therefore, concentrated on ensuring that local govern-ments were given the right to decide themselves how social services were provided, whether they wanted to privatise them or not. Moreover, the whole process needed to pay more attention to employment levels, it was demanded. Finally, the high social standards must be retained in instances of privatisation. Of course, an additional unemployment criterion would be good, but it was not considered feasible in the current political climate (Interview No. 23; Wien, 18/03/2002). The GdE, organising railway workers in an almost exclusively domestic production sector with hardly any private companies, argued that due to the union's opposition to the Commission's liberalisation drive in the trans-port and especially the railway sector, the majority of its members would be opposed to the EU in general and EMU membership in particular. Overall, the union was critical of EMU especially considering the Austrian government's aim of a balanced budget within the SGP. An unemployment criterion, similar to the ÖGB's position (see Chapter 5), was deemed as absolutely essential and the bringing forward of public infrastructure projects was demanded (Interview No. 28; Wien, 20/03/2002).

Two further unions organise workers in predominantly domestic production sectors. The Commerce, Transport and Traffic Workers' Union (Gewerkschaft Handel, Transport, Verkehr; HTV) organises blue-collar workers in social services, commerce and transport. In general, these sectors are hardly trans-nationalised in Austria. In contrast to the two other unions, EMU was evaluated as positive in the long run. It was hoped that the resulting higher transparency of collective bargaining would facilitate the introduction of common minimum standards at the European level. While the convergence criteria were evaluated negatively, it was pointed that, first, many problems as for example in the health service were home-made. Second, one should not forget that the room for manoeuvre within the criteria was not fully used by the Austrian govern-ment, which had a balanced budget as its most important target. It would be very well possible to bring forward infrastructure projects and remain within the criteria, and this was one of the union's core demands (Interview No. 22; Wien, 18/03/2002). The Public Services Trade Union (Gewerkschaft Öffentlicher Dienst; GÖD), finally, organises state employees at the federal as well as *Land* level, including the various chambers and semi-official institutions. The union had dealt with EMU since the Treaty of Maastricht in 1991 and concentrated on the impact of EMU on the public sector. In general, EMU was considered to be a positive step of further integration, but the GÖD identified limitations due to its sole focus on price stability and low inflation as embodied in the convergence criteria. In many instances, it was alleged, states had manipulated budgets to meet these criteria. For example, state responsibilities were sub-contracted so that the financial burden could be lifted off the budget. In Austria, this affected areas such as the air traffic control system. The union also criticised the related reduction in public investment in infrastructure projects and resulting job losses. Due to sub-contracting and restructuring, the public sector had lost 15,000 jobs alone between 2000 and 2002. Hence, while not rejecting EMU as such, the union demanded that the state must accept its public responsibilities and invest in infrastructure projects at the national and, together with other EU members, European level. This should go hand in hand with investment in better training and further education. The overall goal had to be full employment. This would not imply softening the criteria, which already permitted a room for manoeuvre allowing in Austria for public investment in infrastructure projects via new public borrowing (Interview No. 34; telephone interview, 14/05/2002). In short, while the GdG and the GdE linked their rejection of EMU to a strong criticism of its neo-liberal rationale, the HTV and GÖD, while critical of the convergence criteria, were more positive about EMU and mainly demanded to use the room for manoeuvre available within the criteria. At least in the case of the GÖD, this more reluctant criticism can be linked to a different ideological background, based on the fact that it is the Christian union fraction and not the socialist fraction, which dominates this ÖGB affiliate (see Chapter 1).

Prior to EU membership in 1995, Austria had had a large domestic production sector protected against international competition. As a result of accession to the EU and general globalisation pressures, traditionally domestic production sectors have become increasingly internationally oriented and partly even transnationalised (see Chapter 3). Five further unions organise workers in sectors particularly strongly affected by these restructuring processes. The Agricultural and Food Processing Workers' Union (Gewerkschaft Agrar-Nahrung-Genuss; ANG) is the best example in this respect. Prior to EU membership it had organised workers in the agricultural and food processing industries, which were fully protected against international competition. As a result, the union was highly sceptical about EU membership and could only be brought on a pro-EU course through the promise of funds for the retraining of workers in these sectors (Bieler, 2000: 61). Inevitably, since membership protectionism has had to be abandoned and these sectors are now generally export-oriented as well as supplying the domestic market. Foreign TNCs have started to invest in the Austrian food processing sector leading to the closure of many companies. Overall, due to restructuring and the related job losses in the wake of EU membership, the ANG lost about 10,000 members. The ANG had worked a lot on the issue of EU membership in the early 1990s and this included an assessment of EMU. The union's survey of employers in its sectors made clear that membership would be negative. By 2002, however, the ANG had accepted EMU as a matter of reality. The lack of stronger union criticism of the convergence criteria at the national and European level was deplored as well as unions' acceptance of the related budgetary austerity course. The unemployment criterion would be demanded by unions on paper, but in reality the necessary lobbying for this would not happen (Interview No. 33; Wien, 22/03/2002).

The Construction and Wood Workers' Union (Gewerkschaft Bau-Holz; GBH) is another union, which still organises a predominantly domestic construction sector dominated by small- and medium-sized companies that, however, shows increasing signs of transnationalisation since the mid-1990s (Menz, 2005a: 51). Especially German firms operate in Austria and some Austrian companies carry out contracts abroad. The wood and stone-ceramic sectors are very much export-oriented and to some extent even transnationalised (Gewerkschaft Bau-Holz, 2001: 8). In principle, the union supported EMU, but Europe, it was pointed out, should also become a social union. 'The competitiveness of Europe is important, but more important is that the special characteristics of the European social model and of the broad democracy of EU members are not dropped' (Gewerkschaft Bau-Holz, 2001: 12). This reflects closely the ÖGB's 'yes, but' position (see Chapter 5). While accepting EMU, the convergence criteria and SGP were strongly criticised for their insufficient focus on employment. The decline of jobs in the construction sector would have been the result of the postponement or even cancellation of public infrastructure projects, which resulted from the obligation to meet the criteria in the first place. The Austrian government's attempts to achieve a balanced budget would make things worse. Hence, the GBH demanded an additional unemployment criterion as well as the introduction of obligatory employment targets at the European level. The ECB was urged to pursue an anti-cyclical policy instead of dampening growth through its predominant focus on price stability (Interview No. 30; Wien, 20/03/2002; see also Menz, 2005a: 53). 'The hesitant and little developed policy of the ECB and European Commission contributes to the intensification of the economic situation in Europe. The self-imposed constraints through the Maastricht criteria prevent an effective anti-cyclical economic and fiscal policy by the EU' (Gewerkschaft Bau-Holz, 2001: 14).

This 'yes, but' position was also adopted by the Hotel, Catering and Personal Services Workers' union (Gewerkschaft Hotel, Gastgewerbe, Persönlicher Dienst; HGPD), the Postal and Telecommunications Workers' Union (Gewerkschaft der Post- und Fernmeldebediensteten; GPF) and the Union of Private Sector Employees (Gewerkschaft der Privatangestellten; GPA). The HGPD organises mainly blue-collar workers in the private services sector encompassing tourism, hairdressers, cleaning companies, etc. Tourism and cleaning companies are transnationalised to some extent, while the labour market is even more transnationalised. Two-thirds of all employees are foreigners, mainly from CEE and Turkey. The union welcomed EMU, since it abolished the loss of currency exchange, which tourists could then spend on their holidays in Austria. The convergence criteria were, however, criticised and the ECB was asked to react, similar to the US Federal Reserve Bank, faster to economic recession through reducing interest rates to stimulate the economy. This should be combined with employment programmes at the European level. Co-ordinating national employment policies alone would not be enough (Interview No. 31; Wien, 21/03/2002). The GPF organises workers in the postal and telecommunications sectors. Privatisation in telecommunications started in 1996, leading to the transnationalisation of this sector. Postal services and buses are still 100 per cent in public hands, but there is an increasing tendency towards liberalisation in the postal services in order to prepare the sector for market competition. This has already led to significant job cuts. The union argued that the convergence criteria should be strictly adhered to, as they ensured economic stability, but demanded in line with the ÖGB that an unemployment criterion was added. Moreover, the union demanded public infrastructure projects to create jobs (Interview No. 27; Wien, 19/03/2002).

Finally, the GPA, similarly to the DAG in Germany, organises white-collar workers across the whole economy including the industrial sectors such as metal, financial services and the banking system, but also commerce. These are all sectors that have experienced an increasing transnationalisation since EU membership. Similarly to the ANG, the GPA had been highly sceptical of EU membership in 1994, but was prevented by the ÖGB from going public with its criticism (Bieler, 2000: 61, 98). This position was also expressed in the union's view of EMU. Especially the convergence criteria were criticised. As early as 1992, the general secretary of the union Hans Sallmutter pointed to the possibly negative consequences of national austerity budgets to meet the convergence criteria. To avoid this, 'full employment should become a part of the general EU goals. At the same time, it is necessary to examine the convergence criteria and add other criteria such as a low rate of unemployment' (Sallmutter, 1993: 166). The establishment of social Europe was the main concern for the GPA and European collective agreements were demanded in order to avoid social dumping. In line with the ÖGB's 'yes, but' position, EMU as a guarantor of a stable economy was not opposed. A single currency, Sallmutter argued in 1997, would be the logical consequence of the Internal Market and its four freedoms. The increasing internationalisation and globalisation would further require that economic policy tools such as monetary policy were conducted at a supranational level. The task however would be to develop monetary union into an instrument of a co-ordinated growth and employment-oriented economic policy. 'Such a concept would secure broad support by trade unions' (Sallmutter, 1997: 7). The ECB was criticised for its exclusive focus on price stability and its lack of democratic accountability. Austria had been used to a hard currency policy, but this relied on close involvement of the social partners including trade unionists on the governing board of the Austrian National Bank. The third stage of EMU implied, however, that this governing board was transformed into a supervisory board without any real competencies (Reischl and Sykora, 1997: 47).

Alternatively, there could be a broad discussion between institutions and social partners over monetary policy leading towards a policy of full employment and economic growth. Monetary policy should be in the service of employment policy. Employment programmes should be carried out at the national level, supported by EU social funds. EU infrastructure projects could further sustain a high employment level policy. Nevertheless, the union recognised that an unemployment criterion should have been demanded prior to Austria's acceptance of EU membership. Now, it would be too late. The SGP and the goal of a balanced budget by the Austrian government would go even further in their restrictive nature than the criteria (Interview No. 24; Wien, 18/03/2002).

In short, similarly to Germany, the increasing transnationalisation of sectors implied that there were fewer and fewer predominantly domestic production sector unions in Austria. The increasingly export-oriented sectors, however, regarded the Euro as a cause for economic stability. Additionally, the core European debate in Austria had been over EU membership. The Euro hardly generated additional discussions. Having been an EMU member, unions started to adapt to the new reality and pushed for the adoption of an additional unemployment criterion. More radical changes or open opposition to EMU were not voiced. In short, the fact that Austria was an EMU member and the increasing transnationalisation of traditionally domestic production sectors go a long way to explain the lack of open opposition to EMU by Austrian unions. In relation to unions' position on the related neo-liberal restructuring, it was mainly the GdG, the GdE and the GPA, which raised strong objections, while the other unions had started to accept basic neo-liberal assumptions such as assuming that the convergence criteria would ensure a stable economy. The latter was, however, still combined with calls for a full employment policy. The ECB should move away from an exclusive focus on price stability, an unemployment criterion be added and employment programmes carried out at the national and European level.

Swedish domestic sector unions and EMU

In Sweden, very similar to the situation in Britain and as expected in the first hypothesis, domestic production sector unions opposed accession to EMU. The Union of Commercial Employees (Handels) and the Transport Workers' Union (Transportarbetareförbundet), both affiliated to LO, opposed Swedish EMU membership. They have experienced some transnationalisation within their sectors, in the appearance of some large chains in the retail and wholesale sectors in the case of the former, and the areas of transport and the security industry in the case of the latter. Overall, however, the majority of members of both unions still work for small domestic companies and shops, indicating a predominantly domestic production structure. Handels took its first view of expression on EMU in 1997. Politically, the union was concerned about the loss of influence on monetary policy vis-à-vis the democratically unaccountable ECB. Economically, higher Swedish wage increases due to near full employment would require a fluctuating exchange rate to counter asymmetric economic shocks.

Moreover, the convergence criteria would cause mass unemployment and the ECB would stifle economic growth due to its unnecessarily high interest rates (Interview No. 35; Stockholm, 20/06/2002). This position was echoed by the Transportarbetareförbundet, the executive board of which had decided to recommend its members a 'no' in the referendum. The way the ECB was set up and ran monetary policy was alleged to be undemocratic. The convergence criteria would hamper economic growth and had been used by the Swedish government to justify unpopular measures. EMU was likely to intensify this tendency. Finally, remembering the 1992 Swedish currency crisis, when the rigid peg of the SKr to the ECU had cost about 200,000 jobs in Sweden, the exchange rate was considered to be absolutely necessary for the stabilisation of the economy in times of recession. The idea that buffer funds and/or a budget surplus would be enough was not regarded as realistic (Interview No. 46; Stockholm, 26/06/2002).

Very clearly, the rejection of EMU by Handels and the Transportarbetareförbundet was a sign of their continuing resistance to neo-liberal restructuring. The convergence criteria were considered to endanger economic growth and jobs, while the decision-making by the ECB in the area of monetary policy was deemed undemocratic. This was in stark contrast to Swedish transnational sector unions, which had started to accept some neo-liberal principles (see Chapter 6). However, not all national production sector unions adopted the same strong anti-EMU, anti-neo-liberal position. The Municipal Workers' Union (Kommunal) represents blue-collar workers in the public sector and some workers in public transport. Similar to the campaign around the referendum on EU membership, the union decided in 2000 not to adopt a position on EMU, but to distribute information to its members prior to a referendum so that they could make their own decision. Nevertheless, it was assumed that a majority of members was opposed to EMU membership, while the board of the union was split. It was accepted that the union could have adopted a 'no' position, but then members would have the chance anyway to have their say in the referendum (Interview No. 41; Stockholm, 24/06/2002). The lack of a position by Kommunal partly reflected the attempt to avoid a split within the union. Partly, however, it may have also been an indicator of the union's more relaxed attitude towards neo-liberal restructuring. Even outside EMU, it was argued, Sweden would have to adopt policies similar to the convergence criteria to keep inflation down. Public sector expansion to combat unemployment would no longer be feasible. To ensure high levels of employment, it was considered absolutely necessary that Swedish wage formation did not deviate from other European countries. Employment programmes should concentrate on more training to reduce structural unemployment. Public investment was not precluded by EMU, as long as the budget was in balance or in surplus (Interview No. 41; Stockholm, 24/06/2002).

The Building Workers' Union (Byggnads) organises workers in the predominantly domestic construction sector. Large companies and here especially the well-known TNCs Skanska and NCC control 60 per cent of the market share in construction, but it is only recently that they have started to become active internationally and there are no significant activities by foreign construction companies in Sweden (Menz, 2005a: 61). There was no discussion on EMU at the union's congress in 2002 and Byggnads mainly supported the LO position, i.e. a 'yes' to EMU membership provided certain preconditions such as buffer funds were fulfilled. Similar to its confederation, convergence criteria were not regarded as a problem especially considering that Sweden's healthy budget implied that there had been no cut-backs in public infrastructure projects. Only in the case of uneven economic growth in the EU would the criteria result in problems and for these instances buffer funds would be required. In any case, the key question in relation to employment was wage formation for Byggnads. Wage increases had traditionally been too large in Sweden only to be crowded out by higher inflation levels afterwards. EMU would provide additional incentives to keep inflation low through wage restraint. This in return would then assure that lower nominal wage increases still implied real wage increases (Interview No. 36; Stockholm, 20/06/2002). Both Kommunal's and Byggnads' positions demonstrate that while no position on EMU had been taken by these unions, similar to transnational sector unions some national production sector unions too had started to accept neo-liberal principles. The convergence criteria and related low inflation policies were deemed to be necessary anyway and wage formation, in which wage increases were moderate and not above other European bargaining agreements, were regarded as the core aspect of a full employment policy. The idea that wage increases were important to maintain domestic demand levels was not put forward.

Several TCO domestic production, public sector unions were sceptical of EMU similar to Handels and the Transportarbetareförbundet, although none came out openly against EMU membership in order to avoid an internal split. The Union of Civil Servants (Statstjänstemannaförbundet; ST), organising state employees at the national level, for example, was worried about the impact of the convergence criteria on public services and feared that EMU could prevent the necessary expansion of the public sector after years of restructuring and job cuts (Interview No. 42; Stockholm, 25/06/2002). Similarly, the Swedish Teachers' Union (Lärerförbundet), organising teachers in the domestic education sector, acknowledged that the convergence criteria posed a threat to the funding of public education. Individual members of the union's executive board had made strong statements against EMU and it was assumed that a majority of members shared this position (Interview No. 37; Stockholm, 20/06/2002). Again, in both cases this scepticism indicated opposition to neo-liberalism.

Nevertheless, similar to the slight divide within LO domestic production sector unions, there were some national sector unions affiliated to the TCO, which were less critical of EMU. The Swedish Union of Local Government Officers (Sveriges Kommunaltjänstemannaförbund; SKTF) organises members in local government. Due to the privatisation of public services, 15 per cent of the union's members are now employed in the private sector, but the employers in these areas such as waste, water, energy, etc. are still predominantly Swedish. As the other two TCO unions, SKTF did not make a recommendation to its members of how to vote in the referendum. As the union was not aligned to a political party, adopting positions on issues such as EMU was not regarded as the union's task. Nevertheless, in contrast to the other two TCO unions, SKTF was not worried about the impact of the convergence criteria. Sweden had experienced an increase in real wages since about 1995 thanks to a responsible and moderate wage formation and even lower inflation levels, and in relation to this successful economic policy the convergence criteria had actually helped. Thus, Sweden would have already had an EMU-type policy, which in itself was not a problem. Again, it is clear that a Swedish domestic production sector union had started to accept core neo-liberal principles. This had also been increasingly visible in SKTF's position on decentralising wage bargaining, where it had moved towards endorsing individual bargaining between employer and employee within a framework set by sectoral collective bargaining (Interview No. 48; Stockholm, 27/06/2002). Finally, even in SACO, although no individual union affiliated to SACO had taken an official stance on EMU, while the confederation had endorsed membership early on (see Chapter 5), there were signs that especially female members working in the public sector were more likely to oppose EMU membership (Interview No. 45; Stockholm, 26/06/2002). This also reflects the opposition by national forces of labour to EMU.

National forces of labour and their positions on European-level co-operation

British national labour and European co-operation

Against the background of consecutive Conservative governments over the 1980s and early 1990s, the vast majority of British unions moved towards a pro-EU position. This is, however, sometimes misinterpreted as a general willingness to co-operate strongly at the European level (e.g. Mulhearn, 2004: 307–9). My argument is that the division between transnational and national sector unions on EMU was mirrored in a different emphasis placed on the importance of European co-operation. UNISON considered both the national and European levels important for exerting influence, but had concentrated on Britain since Labour's return to power in 1997 (Interview No. 19; London, 02/05/2001). The RMT acknowledged the important impact the Social Dimension had had on Britain, but European co-operation was limited to the exchange of information and experience. It regarded as its main task the lobbying of the British government to implement EU directives fully (Interview No. 18; London, 29/03/2001). UCATT strongly supported the Social Dimension and especially welcomed the working time directive, which had ensured that construction workers received the right to a paid holiday for the first time. It too, however, argued that the national level was currently more important due to the new Labour government (Interview No. 21; London, 29/05/2001). Finally, all three unions were in favour of active employment programmes in Britain, which further indicates that they concentrated on the national level.

The T&G had been very positive about the Social Dimension. As the British social security and welfare levels were lower than in other EU countries, the multi-sector agreements between the ETUC and UNICE had generally implied an upgrading of conditions. Similar to the TUC, the T&G pushed for the European social model of capitalism and European integration was regarded positively in this respect. In relation to concrete co-operation at the European level, T&G members, who were representatives in EWCs, received training from the union. Nevertheless, unlike the AEEU, the T&G had not had much involvement in cross-border co-operation with other trade unions or sectoral social dialogue. Moreover, the union was not really prepared to hand over competencies to European negotiation teams. The various national cultures and industrial relations systems would simply be too different for successful co-operation (Interview No. 15; London, 27/03/2001). In short, in contrast to British transnational sector unions, domestic sector unions continued to concentrate on the national level in their policy-making efforts.

German national forces of labour and European co-operation

As it was outlined above, there was no split between transnational and national sector unions over EMU membership in Germany. They supported the DGB's 'yes, but' position. Acceptance of EMU was combined with demands for changes to its neo-liberal rationale. In relation to emphasis on co-operation at the European level, however, this split can be noticed. In contrast to German internationally oriented, transnational sector unions, national sector unions still focused on the domestic level in their efforts to influence policy-making. Theoretically, the ÖTV demanded that the sectoral social dialogues were further developed at the European level to establish a social Europe (ÖTV, 1997: 45). This should also imply the right to form coalitions and to strike (ÖTV, 2000: 152). Collective bargaining may be unrealistic at the moment, but national wage policies should be co-ordinated by the European Federation of Public Service Unions (EPSU) with a focus on public sector workers' participation in productivity increases and a parallel development of private and public sector wages (Ladwig, 2000: 13–14). In practice, however, the transfer of competencies in the area of employment policy to the EU was rejected and the union admitted that it was still concentrating its efforts on the national level. Social policy, it was argued, had reached high standards in Germany and the various national systems were deemed too different for a European-wide approach. In any case, the union's negotiation partners would be the German interior minister and the *Land* and local governments (Interview No. 8; Stuttgart, 01/02/2001).

The DAG was slightly more active at the European level. It was part of UNI-Europa and was also presented in a range of EWCs. The co-ordination of national productivity-oriented bargaining was considered to be the best way forward (DAG, 1997: 15) and the union demanded an improvement of the EWC directive to strengthen the various works councils in TNCs (DAG, 2000: 29). As a white-collar service union, despite its dominance within the public sector, it was also represented in the transnational banking and insurance sectors, as well as the retail sector and this may explain its slightly stronger international involvement. Less international activity was the case in the public sector and employment policy should remain a national matter, it was argued (Interview No. 11; Hamburg, 09/02/2001; DAG, 1997: 22). The DBB was in regular contact with the Commission. Nevertheless, many competencies would remain at the national level, as for example working times and salaries, and the public sector would have predominantly national characteristics, which made European co-ordination difficult. Similar to the other two public sector unions, the DBB pointed out that employment policy was a national task (Interview No. 1; Bonn, 22/01/2001).

In short, the specific national characteristics and national employers of the sector pushed these public sector unions towards prioritising the national level. Thus, in line with the first hypothesis, the level at which production is organised strongly influenced unions' strategies of where to direct their policy effort. Interestingly, Transnet, although operating within a largely national production sector, strongly favoured European-wide co-operation. Integration should be accompanied by social union, which included highly developed industrial relations, and lead towards political union based on democratic institutions and basic civil and social rights (Transnet, 2000: 16). The union demanded European-wide collective wage bargaining in the sense of a general framework agreement with an opening clause, which allowed for the fine-tuning at the various different national and regional levels. As explanation for this willingness to co-operate despite the national production sector, the union itself pointed out that transport policy was now increasingly made at the European level. Unions would need to respond to this (Interview No. 3; Frankfurt, 25/01/2001). The specific impact of EU level decision-making on trade union strategies will be addressed further in Chapter 8 on European-level trade union organisations.

French national sector unions and European co-operation

The comparison between the two French education unions, UNSA-Education and FSU, in the previous section demonstrated the ideological split. This ideological difference also surfaced in relation to international co-operation. Both unions were members of the ETUC-E. The way they evaluated however the Social Dimension and European-level trade union structures differed. On the one hand, UNSA-Education had accepted neo-liberalism as a reality and welcomed the Social Dimension as a way to counter the negative implications of EMU. Social dialogue with employers as the basis of the Social Dimension was appreciated and the agreements on nightwork and telework in multi-sector negotiations considered to be important improvements in a whole range of countries. Sectoral social dialogue in education would be difficult, because education was a national responsibility, but information should be exchanged especially in relation to the Bologna process and its objective to establish a European area of higher education by 2010. UNSA-Education also maintained some co-operation with other social movements, but argued that unions and social movements would often have different responsibilities, positions and concerns (Interview No. 56; telephone interview; 12/09/2002).

The FSU recognised the increasing importance of the European level due to the impact of decisions taken there on national policy-making as well as the possibilities to influence policy-making within the EU. Nevertheless, echoing the positions of the confederations FO and G10-Solidaires, the ETUC was severely criticised for being too much influenced by the Commission. Moreover, the ETUC would incorrectly understand states as an obstacle for progressive policies by default. Finally, similar to the Commission, the ETUC would have started to adopt the same language on education, focusing increasingly on issues of employability and market requirements (FSU, 2002: 121). In its attempts to influence policy-making, the FSU, therefore, concentrated on co-operation with other social movements. In the defence of education becoming a commodity due to European-level developments and the General Agreement on Trade in Services (GATS) negotiations, the union had sent delegates to the World Social Forum in Porto Alegre and the European Social Forum in Florence, Italy in November 2002, and some of its members were participating in the organising committee for the ESF in Paris in November 2003 (Interview No. 68; Paris, 18/12/2002; Charlot, 2001: 45–53) (see Chapter 9). In short, both unions concentrated on the national level in their policy-making efforts, because education was a national responsibility, but both recognised the increasing importance of international developments. Nevertheless, following the ideological split of French unions mentioned earlier, UNSA-Education focused on the structures of the ETUC at the European level, while the FSU sought co-operation with more radical social movements in Europe and beyond.

Austrian national forces of labour and European co-operation

Austrian domestic production sector unions, similar to other national forces of labour, continued to concentrate on the national level, where they perceived to have the best opportunities to influence decisions relevant to their members. The Social Dimension was not regarded as a success by the GdG. It was acknowledged that employment policy was now an EU topic, but without consequences at the practical level. The sectoral social dialogue led by the union's EIF EPSU in areas such as local public transport had started, but was mainly restricted to the exchange of information. Trade unions themselves would only be at the beginning of proper European-wide co-operation and the biggest challenge to move forward would be to overcome the huge national differences between them. The GdG was also sceptical about the possibilities at the European level, since the structures including the union movement would not be enough transparent. Furthermore, there was a lack of full participatory rights within the EU institutional set-up for trade unions. Hence, the GdG was not prepared to transfer competencies to the European level. Having said this, however, the union acknowledged that the more decisions were taken at the European level, such as liberalisation directives in the area of public services, the more important it would become to lobby in Brussels. Hence, a Europeanisation of trade unions, despite the current problems, was deemed necessary within the next ten years (Interview No. 23; Wien, 18/03/2002). The GÖD, the second Austrian public sector union, stressed the importance of social policies as a component of economic policies in a social market economy in German and Austrian tradition. Social policies should not be regarded as a counterpart to EMU. Also organising employees in postal services and telecommunications, the union had been involved in sectoral social dialogue and acknowledged the need to free up more resources for international activities. In general, however, the GÖD highlighted the importance of subsidiarity, ensuring that states accepted their responsibilities to deal with certain issues at the national level, rather than simply attempting to transfer tasks to the European level. The same would be valid for unions and this implied a continuing emphasis on the national level for the GÖD (Interview No. 34; telephone interview, 14/05/2002).

The HTV asserted that the national level remained the most important area for influencing policy-making. One should realise that employees work in particular geographical locations and the existing social standards of EU members would be too different to attempt the establishment of common norms. The union could not accept a lowering of Austrian standards in this respect. Nevertheless, while rejecting the transfer of competencies to EU level unions, the HTV acknowledged that issues in the area of the transport sector, for example, had an increasing European dimension and that as a member of the European Transport Workers' Federation (ETF), it would actively participate in sectoral social dialogue. Unions would be behind the employers in organising at the European level and needed to catch up in order to establish a balance of power (Interview No. 22; Wien, 18/03/2002). The ANG similarly recognised the increasing importance of the European level due to the amount of decisions taken in Brussels affecting its sectors. In practice, however, the sectors would still be characterised by national, egoistic behaviour. There was no collective bargaining, no social dialogue and no attempt to co-ordinate national bargaining at the European level. The union's EIF, the European Federation of Food, Agriculture and Tourism Trade Unions (EFFAT), would be too preoccupied with the consequences of its recent merger between the European agricultural union and the European food processing union. While emphasising the need to intensify European-level co-operation, the union accepted that the ceding of national competencies in areas such as collective bargaining was unlikely (Interview No. 33; Wien, 22/03/2002).

The GBH confirmed the increasing importance of the European level, but emphasised the continuing priority of the national level. The transfer of competencies to the European level was not regarded as an option. There was some sectoral social dialogue and the co-ordination of national bargaining was discussed, but the union's EIF, the EFBWW, had not moved very far in this respect. The visible lack of solidarity within EWCs would also raise doubts about the possible transnational solidarity at the sectoral level. The GBH was engaged in closer co-operation with Swiss, German and some Central European unions, but even this process was only at the beginning (Interview No. 30; Wien, 20/03/2002). The HGPD, while recognising the increasing importance of the European level due to the decisions taken there relevant to its sectors, accepted the difficulty in combining the various different national interests of unions. As a member of EFFAT and UNI-Europa, the union participated in sectoral social dialogue that, however, had mainly been concerned with the exchange of information. A co-ordination of national collective bargaining had not been developed beyond the exchange of information between unions. Moreover, the union was not prepared to give up competencies to European-level organisations as far as wage bargaining was concerned. Overall, however, it was envisaged that in the medium-term European-level bargaining would be on the agenda again and in time the union may be prepared to give up national competencies (Interview No. 31; Wien, 21/03/2002).

The GPF made clear that it wanted to see the Social Dimension developed into a counterweight to economic integration. So far, however, this would mainly consist of declarations of intention. Considering that more and more issues relevant to the union's sectors were discussed and decided in Brussels, European co-operation would become increasingly important, but negotiations with boards of directors would have to continue at the national level. Sectoral social dialogue would take place in the area of postal services and telecommunications to some extent, but the co-ordination of national bargaining had not been developed very far due to the different national systems. The acceptance of each other's education and training systems in relation to questions of social benefits and pensions would be the more fruitful way forward (Interview No. 27; Wien, 19/03/2002). The GPA demanded that Europe must become much more socially oriented to avoid the increasing social divisions. The union argued that a social model should include the following characteristics: (1) a functioning net of social security; (2) regulations of workplace conditions; and (3) institutionalised forms of trade union influence at the European level. To obtain such a model, the course within the EU would have to change drastically. The results of the social dialogue so far were deemed to be insubstantial consisting mainly of the exchange of opinions at the sectoral level. The structural problem would be that collective agreements could not be obtained without the European-wide right to strike. Hence, for concrete results, the national level would remain more important and, consequently, there would be no point in giving up competencies to the European level (Interview No. 24; Wien, 18/03/2002).

In short, the domestic production sector unions still focused predominantly on the national level in their activities, thereby confirming the first hypothesis. This also included those unions such as the ANG, GBH, HGPD, GPF and GPA, the sectors of which had become increasingly internationally oriented and transnationalised since Austria's accession to the EU. The change in these unions' production structure had not yet at least had an impact on their position on European-level co-operation. The continuing reluctance to transfer competencies to the European level, however, may also be a result of the historically strong possibilities within the structural selectivity of the Austrian form of state characterised by an institutionalised system of social partnership, as envisaged by the second hypothesis. It will be interesting to observe the developments over the next years, considering that these possibilities at the national level have been more and more undermined (see Chapter 4). Nevertheless, with the GdE there is one exception to this pattern. The union deplored that the commitment to the Social Dimension had not been backed up by concrete activities. Very similar to the case of the German union Transnet (see above), the GdE argued that due to the fact that most decisions in the transport sector were taken in Brussels now, the EU level had become the more important arena. Hence, the union increasingly shifted its attention and resources to the European level. As a member of the ETF, of which the GdE's president was also its president, the union had been strongly involved in sectoral social dialogue. This was regarded as a protection against the deregulation of the sector, focusing on issues such as security of services and the introduction of a European engine driving licence. In the area of security, it had actually been possible to go beyond the exchange of information with employers and obtain negotiated agreements. In addition to sectoral social dialogue, the GdE via the ETF was actively involved in co-ordinated lobbying of national governments, the Commission and MEPs in Brussels. Via the EP, for example, the ETF had been successful at throwing out a directive on the liberalisation of local transport. In general, the union's efforts were aimed at resisting liberalisation of the transport sector. The time of consensus would be over. Unions would have to stop, it was argued, to be co-opted into restructuring decisions they did not want. Importantly, the GdE demanded the right to European-wide strikes to ensure the possibilities for successful European co-operation with other unions. Moreover, unions needed to co-operate with like-minded NGOs on a project-by-project basis at the international level around meetings such as the European Social Forums (Interview No. 28; Wien, 20/03/2002) (see Chapter 9).

Swedish domestic labour and the emphasis on the national level

As expected by the first hypothesis and mirroring the position of other domestic production sector unions, Swedish national forces of labour continued to emphasise the national level in their activities. Handels could not make out any substantial, concrete results of the Social Dimension. More international co-operation was necessary, it was argued, but only in order to strengthen trade unions at the local and national level, since change had always come from below. Due to the different national labour legislation, tax systems and social insurance systems, the co-ordination of bargaining at the European level would be impossible. The transfer of union competencies to the European level was rejected outright (Interview No. 35; Stockholm 20/06/2002). From the perspective of the Transportarbetareförbundet, the social dialogue was valued too highly. The results would simply be too poor and the fact that there was no right to take industrial action at the European level would significantly weaken the potential role of unions (Interview No. 46; Stockholm, 26/06/2002). Kommunal showed not much enthusiasm either. The agreements achieved between the ETUC and UNICE were considered to be good, but had no practical impact on Sweden. In general, the union was strictly opposed to transfer any further competencies in areas such as education or health care to the EU. The worry was that this would lead to a lowering of Swedish standards. The EU level had increased in importance, but the national level clearly remained the more important one. The negotiation, even discussion of wages at the European level was rejected and Kommunal was also sceptical about the European-level co-ordination of national bargaining rounds. The transfer of competencies to the ETUC was not on the agenda (Interview No. 41; Stockholm, 24/06/2005). Byggnads supported the Social Dimension in that minimum standards in other countries would be of indirect benefit to Sweden, even if the multi-sector agreements had not had any direct positive impact on the country. The co-ordination of bargaining was deemed to be premature as was the transfer of competencies to European-level union organisations. Unions in other countries would often simply be too weak (Interview No. 36; Stockholm, 20/06/2002).

ST and the Lärerförbundet of the TCO both highlighted the need for a Social Dimension, but accepted that steps towards a social union had been limited so far. Both still considered the national level to be the most important one for their activities (Interview No. 37; Stockholm, 20/06/2002; Interview No. 42; Stockholm, 25/06/2002). SKTF, finally, regarded the development of the Social Dimension both as positive and necessary, but was worried about the idea of European collective bargaining because of the danger of having to lower the generally higher Swedish welfare levels. The union did acknowledge that the events in the medium-term would demonstrate that there was a need for closer co-operation between the unions at the European level, because more and more policies were decided at that level. Nevertheless, negotiations of wages were not considered to be an option, while the co-ordination of bargaining within the union's EIF EPSU may be feasible at some stage (Interview No. 48; Stockholm, 27/06/2002).

In short, as the other national sector unions, Swedish national forces of labour continued to concentrate on the national level in their efforts of influencing policy-making. The Social Dimension was welcomed but unions were suspicious about any further developments of co-operation because they were worried about downward pressure on the higher Swedish conditions. Proper European-level bargaining or the transfer of competencies to European unions were ruled out. Only some acknowledged that the co-ordination of national bargaining may be an option at the European level in the future (e.g. SKTF). The only slight exception to this rather sceptical view on European-level co-operation was that the Lärerförbundet (TCO) had maintained an office in Brussels since 1994. It was realised that EU-level policies on education had become national issues and that, consequently, the union's members needed to be better informed about EU developments (Interview No. 37; Stockholm, 20/06/2002).

Conclusion

In contrast to expectations of the first hypothesis, domestic production sector unions differed in their position on EMU. British and Swedish unions clearly opposed it. The neo-liberal rationale of the convergence criteria and the SGP as well as the ECB's focus on price stability would endanger jobs and economic growth. Furthermore, the way decisions were taken by the ECB lacked transparency and democratic accountability and was, therefore, unacceptable. Austrian, French and German domestic production unions, however, accepted monetary union as a reality and attempted to make the best out of this situation. Clearly, whether a country had already been an EMU member or not played a role in unions' positions on EMU. Domestic production sector unions in Austria, France and Germany were no longer faced with the question whether to be for or against EMU, but how to cope best with its realities. In Britain and Sweden, on the other hand, where a referendum on EMU was either held, i.e. Sweden, or still forthcoming, i.e. Britain, the line of division with transnational sector unions was much sharper, since a position had to be formulated. Additionally, at least in the Austrian and German cases, the increasing transnationalisation of traditionally domestic production sectors further pushed these unions towards a position, which made them accept the reality of EMU. Some even regarded EMU as a way of ensuring economic stability. Generally, a critical position on EMU implied a rejection of neo-liberal restructuring. Nevertheless, the analysis indicated that several unions had accepted some neo-liberal principles such as the German DBB and Transnet, the French UNSA-Education, the Austrian HTV, GÖD and GPF and the Swedish unions Kommunal, Byggnads and SKTF. They all regarded the convergence criteria as necessary for economic stability, but demanded to use the room for manoeuvre within the criteria in full.

The first hypothesis was, however, confirmed, as far as European co-operation was concerned. There was a general reluctance of domestic production sector unions to co-operate at the European level. National industrial relations systems, tax and insurance systems as well as languages would simply be too different for extensive co-operation at the European level. Additionally, the relevant negotiation partners on the employers' side would be national associations. The only exceptions were the German and Austrian railway workers' unions, Transnet and GdE, which had acknowledged the increasing importance of European-level decision-making in this sector. Unions would have to respond via co-operation at the same level. This theme is further developed in the next chapter on the role of European-level trade union organisations.

Notes

1   On the T&G's hesitant position, see also Josselin, 2001: 62, Mulhearn, 2004: 301–3; Sisson et al., 1999: 24; and Strange, 1997: 16–17.
2   See Gramsci's point that political struggles go beyond economic interests, including also moral and ideological concerns of the superstructure (Gramsci, 1971: 181–2).
3   For the original definition of the so-called Washington consensus, see Williamson (1990).

8

European trade unions and EMU: the emergence of labour as a regional actor?

Introduction

In line with the overall topic of this study, this chapter will deal with European level trade unions and their positions on EMU and European co-operation. The two hypotheses developed in relation to domestic labour movements are adjusted as follows:

> *Hypothesis*: First, EIFs, which organise workers in transnational sectors, are likely to endorse EMU, assumed to benefit companies in their sectors, which rely on open borders. For similar reasons, they are likely to emphasise European-level co-operation with EIFs emerging as supranational actors in their own right responding to the transnational structure of their production sectors and the fact that unions have lost control over capital at the national level. On the other hand, EIFs, which organise workers in domestic production sectors across Europe, are expected to be opposed, or at least less supportive of monetary union, since workers in these areas still rely on state protection. For the same reason, they are also less likely to emerge as independent actors and operate more as secretariats with the task to organise international co-operation of their national members.

Moreover, as Ziltener outlines, understood as a system of multi-level governance, the EU institutional set-up constitutes a complex area for strategic-relational decision-making, a form of state with its own inherent structural selectivity (Ziltener, 2000: 78, 81). Clearly, trade unions' willingness to co-operate at the European level will also depend on their possibilities to influence policy-making within the EU institutional set-up. According to Greenwood, increasing EU competencies since the 1980s have made lobbying and working at the European level more attractive to interest groups (Greenwood, 2003: 33). This leads to the following second, adjusted hypothesis:

> *Hypothesis*: Trade unions are more likely to co-operate at the European level if they perceive such an engagement as furthering their influence on policy-making. In other words, those trade unions, where there are more

EU competencies and more decisions taken at the European level in their particular sector, are more likely to develop into supranational actors, even if their production structure is not transnational.

EMU as such had been less of a conflictual topic for trade unions at the European level. From the very beginning of the revival of European integration, the ETUC had been supportive of further European integration including the Internal Market programme and EMU. Bieling (2001: 100) identifies three core reasons as to why trade unions accepted the Internal Market. First, against the background of economic recession and the rise of the neo-liberal discourse in the early 1980s, unions had accepted that deregulation and privatisation were economically beneficial or at least unavoidable, already before the Internal Market programme was initiated in 1985. Second, there was an optimistic view that the Internal Market was a step towards political union including also a social union, comprising the necessary re-regulation at the European level. Third, the presence of Jacques Delors as president of the Commission and his emphasis on the necessity of a social counterpart to economic integration including the participation of trade unions in European policy-making convinced unions to support the Internal Market. Acceptance of EMU and the institutionalisation of neo-liberalism in the convergence criteria and the SGP together with the establishment of the ECB, its focus on price stability and the lack of democratic control was more difficult for unions. The ETUC supported EMU from 1990/1991 onwards, but always regarded it as a next step towards political union including a social union. The latter was deemed essential to provide a balance to monetary union. For the ETUC, the market needed to be regulated at the European level. Moreover, the ETUC accepted that some criteria were necessary, but it strongly argued for a more flexible interpretation of the SGP with a specific emphasis on growth. This implied, first, that a consultative committee should be established to push the ECB towards accepting more its responsibilities for growth and not only low inflation. While the ECB's independent status was not challenged, there was a clear demand for making it politically accountable. Additionally, the ETUC stressed the importance of demand creation via wage increases according to the formula inflation plus productivity. Finally, it asked for investment into trans-European infrastructure networks as well as social infrastructure development, again to stimulate demand (Interview No. 70; Brussels, 21/01/2003). These hopes were not fulfilled. In the end, however, considering unions' political weakness during the economic recession in Europe in the early 1990s and the small gains of the Social Chapter, European trade unions accepted the Treaty of Maastricht (Bieling, 2001: 105).

It is due to this endorsement of European integration by the ETUC, described at its inception as 'firmly capitalist' (van der Pijl 1984: 249), that some national trade unions such as the French FO and G10-Solidaires (see Chapter 5) and many commentators accuse the ETUC of having been co-opted into neo-liberal restructuring through their participation in a symbolic system of Euro-corporatism (e.g. Bieling and Schulten, 2003; Ryner and Schulten, 2003). As

Taylor and Mathers (2002a: 54) have put it, '"the social partnership" approach that dominates the thinking of leading members of the European labour movement amounts to a strategy that not only further abandons the autonomy of the labour movement but confirms the logic of neo-liberalism through "supply side corporatism" or "progressive competitiveness"'. In this process, the ETUC 'has promoted monetary stability, market flexibility and employability at both European and enterprise level' (Taylor and Mathers, 2002a: 49). Chapters 5 to 7 have already demonstrated that while a minority of unions may have accepted some neo-liberal concepts, the majority of unions, even if supportive of EMU, continued to oppose neo-liberal restructuring. In this chapter, it will also be analysed whether European-level trade unions, whatever their positions on EMU and European-level co-operation, had accepted neo-liberal restructuring or whether they continued to oppose it. The next section will assess the general structural selectivity of the EU institutional set-up from the perspective of trade unions. Then, several EIFs' positions on EMU will be assessed, before the issue of European-level co-operation is addressed.

The structural selectivity of the EU

When analysing the European form of state, in accordance with Jessop's strategic-relational approach (see Chapter 2), the focus has to be first on the current 'state project'. As outlined in Chapter 1, since the mid-1980s European integration has been revived around neo-liberal economics, embedded in the four freedoms and overall rationale of the Internal Market as well as the neo-liberal convergence criteria of EMU and the related focus on price stability and low inflation by the independent ECB. The transnationalisation of finance has been part of the Internal Market and the transnationalisation of European production partly drove the Internal Market project, but was also partly driven by it. Finally, the neo-liberal rationale was also behind the 1995 and 2004 EU enlargements. The new, neo-liberal form of state has been institutionally protected by removing monetary and economic policy-making from the wider influence of actors. First, in a depoliticisation move labelled 'new constitutionalism' by Gill (2001), monetary policy-making has been handed over to the ECB, made up of 'impartial' technocrats. Second, the core macroeconomic decisions are taken by the European Council, the meeting of heads of government and heads of state within the EU, which is largely outside lobbying pressures. In June of each year, the European Council passes the so-called BEPG as well as the Employment Policy Guidelines, which both must support the low inflation policy of the ECB. While full employment was made a goal by the Lisbon Council in 2000, employment policy itself remained subordinated to the objective of price stability and, therefore, concentrated on supply-side measures such as lifelong learning and labour market deregulation. In other words, 'European employment policy was made to fit the existing integration project and thus became one of the pillars of supply-side-oriented neo-liberal restructuring' (Tidow, 2003: 78).

The multi-level nature of governance in the EU provides trade unions as other interest groups with easy access to supranational decision-makers, but with a related much lower chance of making an impact on the outcome of policy-making (Greenwood, 2003: 29, 73). 'The Commission's role in drafting legislation, together with its interdependencies with outside interests, make it the foremost venue for outside interests' (Greenwood, 2003: 30). This is also the case in relation to trade unions, which have a particularly close contact to the Directorate General (DG) for Employment and Social Affairs, formerly DG V. Overall, however, the Commission has twenty-three DGs, and not all DGs are equally important. The DG for Competition and the DG for Economic and Financial Affairs are more decisive within the EU. Together with the DG Internal Market and DG Trade, they are the hard core of the Commission (Interview No. 72; Brussels, 22/01/2003), driving the neo-liberal project through the discourse of competitiveness (Rosamond, 2002). Trade unions' focus on the DG for Employment and Social Affairs has often marginalised them within the Commission internal decision-making process. On the one hand, other DGs do not feel responsible for social policy. On the other hand, 'DG V has little voice in other DG's measures . . . and cannot require them to take their social implications into account, so there is no forum where that must be done' (Martin and Ross, 1999b: 333). In short, trade unions have been too reliant on the DG for Employment and Social Affairs without receiving enough in return (Greenwood, 2003: 47, 151, 170).

The EP has become a focus of interest groups, since it can amend and co-decide legislation. For the ETUC, a monthly meeting with the trade union intergroup of the EP is the most crucial contact point. There are also close links between the Socialist Party and the European trade union leaders. 'ETUC has been able to table amendments in the Parliament through this route' (Greenwood, 2003: 159). The overall position of the EP within the EU decision-making process, however, remains weak. The ESC has proven to be ineffective for trade unions. 'The ESC is a frozen legacy of a constellation of factors that, in an earlier era of corporatist interest intermediation, seemed an appropriate way forward. Rapidly, however, it became anachronistic and is now more or less irrelevant' (Jeffery, 2002: 345). The influence on policy-making via the lobbying of supranational EU institutions is doubtful, but making a difference through the lobbying of intergovernmental institutions is even less likely. Both the European Council and the Council of Ministers are to a large extent outside trade union lobbying. Some interest groups of transnational capital may be able to lobby effectively the Council Presidency, but interest groups in general tend to concentrate on the lobbying of individual national governments (Hayes-Renshaw and Wallace, 1997: 229). This is further cemented by the fact that interest groups have only a limited role in intergovernmental grand treaty negotiations, such as Maastricht in 1991, when EMU was agreed upon (Greenwood, 2003: 27–8).

Multi-sector social dialogue is one of the core avenues for the ETUC to influence policy-making in the EU. As mentioned in Chapter 1, the Commission has had the possibility to give a negotiation mandate to the ETUC and their employers' counterpart UNICE since the Treaty of Maastricht in 1991. The Treaty further extended the EU competencies to social policy issues and introduced QMV for decision-making in this area. Overall, however, as already indicated in Chapter 1, the significance of the social dialogue should not be exaggerated. To date, it has concluded only few agreements establishing minimum standards (Greenwood, 2003: 68) and the agreements on telework and work-related stress are based on voluntary implementation by the social partners. Hence, the comprehensive implementation of the latter two is doubtful and they should not be mixed up with the initial three agreements on parental leave, part-time work and fixed-term contracts, which were transferred into Council directives (Keller, 2003: 415–17). Moreover, the areas covered by the social dialogue are compartmentalised and do not include issues of the general macroeconomic direction of the EU. More fundamental issues such as the right to strike, the right to association and wage bargaining have been excluded from European competencies (Greenwood, 2003: 150; Schulten, 1999: 200–1). In other words, the social dialogue is in no position to effect fundamental change of the current neo-liberal drive in the EU.

Some social dialogue has also been started at the sectoral level between EIFs and their employers' counterparts. This, however, has often been limited to the exchange of information and the formulation of common positions and joint statements. Hardly any substantial, binding agreements have resulted from it, also because employers' associations do not want to engage in negotiations. Partly, because they benefit from the competition in an unregulated area and a related further decentralisation of bargaining, partly because they are too weak vis-à-vis their national members (Keller and Sörries, 1999: 335–6; Martin and Ross, 1999b: 331–2). Hence, 'on the whole, the European sectoral social dialogue has so far failed to fulfil the original goal set by the European Commission, namely that it contribute to the development of a European system of industrial relations and the formulation of European collective agreements at sectoral level' (Weber, 2001: 129; see also Keller, 2003: 418–23). Here it is problematic that the EU is not a fully fledged state. It is, thus, prevented from 'endowing groups with authority as representative entities charged with public policy functions, as is common in countries with corporatist features such as much of Germanic Europe' (Greenwood, 2003: 20).

Finally, there are currently about 650 EWCs, which had to be established by European TNCs since 1994. Some are worried that they could develop into a double-edged sword in that they drive a wedge between privileged core workers of TNCs and workers in the periphery of the labour market on atypical, temporary contracts, supplying TNCs (Martin and Ross, 1999b: 343–4). Moreover, an increasing number of cross-border agreements at company level, it is argued, undermines further national multi-sector or sectoral agreements, thereby contributing to the tendency towards a decentralisation of bargaining (Schulten, 1996: 320). Others are more optimistic and regard them as the main building block of a future European industrial relations system (e.g. Marginson and Sisson,

1998). Wills argues that by developing EWCs further, EIFs could be strength-ened, if they are given the role to service and support EWCs. 'In addition, EWCs could be used to foster social movement-type unionism within companies and communities' (Wills, 2004: 99–100). Nevertheless, she too has to admit that to date EWCs have not developed enough transnational solidarity necessary for more progressive steps along these lines.

It is sometimes suggested that on the basis of the general nature of multi-level governance in the EU, we also witness the emergence of a multi-level industrial relations framework (Marginson and Sisson, 2004: 26). Especially the related 'Open Method of Co-ordination' (OMC) decision-making procedure, in which national decision-makers respond to European guidelines, would give actors such as trade unions additional opportunities for influence. An analysis of the European Employment Strategy (EES) by Mathers and Taylor, however, indicates that OMC did neither push labour movements towards new forms of networked trade unionism nor did it give unions more influence at the national level. The EES 'seems to have involved unions in countries most where there was already an established tradition of social consultation with little, if any, evidence of it producing significant new developments in member states without such a tradition' (Mathers and Taylor, 2005: 20). Contents wise, OMC did not engender any alternatives to neo-liberalism either. While it may lead to stronger rights for workers, it could equally 'be used as a vehicle of "competitive harmon-ization" around a neo-liberal agenda' (Sisson et al., 2003: 27). In sum, there are limited structural possibilities for trade unions within the EU institutional set-up. The EU is characterised by a neo-liberal 'state project' and the actual institutional set-up disadvantages trade unions. Nonetheless, the strategic-relational approach to the form of state does not only focus on the structural environment. It also concentrates on the choice of strategies by agency within specific structural conditions. The section on European-level co-operation below will analyse trade unions' concrete activities at the European level and investi-gate whether, and if so how, they overcome these structural limitations.

EIFs and their positions on EMU

The European Metalworkers' Federation (EMF) organises workers in one of the most transnationalised sectors in Europe, including many TNCs in consumer electronics, car manufacturing and machinery production. Politically, the union supported EMU, regarded as an important step of further European integra-tion. Economically, considering that the companies in this strongly trans-nationalised sector benefited from the Euro, the single currency was also important for the EMF. Thus, the union's 'yes' mirrored the position of the employers in this respect. Nevertheless, this 'yes', and here it becomes clear that EMU support did not imply support for neo-liberal restructuring, had always been a 'yes, but'. The EMF strongly criticised the convergence criteria for being too strict. The resulting austerity in the EU member countries would also fall back on workers in the metalworking sector in the form of wage restraint. Special social pacts along this line had been concluded in Ireland and Finland, Belgium was given a new formula requiring negotiation results not to be higher than in the neighbouring countries, and bargaining agreements in Germany were low in practice. Instead of low inflation policies, unemployment would need to be tackled by a policy-mix of lower interest rates by the ECB combined with European-level co-ordination of national collective bargaining (see below) to ensure stable wage formation and sufficient demand levels. Other elements should be lifelong learning, a further reduction of working time and European employment programmes in the form of European-wide infrastructure projects (Interview No. 76; Brussels, 23/01/2003).

The EMCEF organises workers especially in the chemical sector. After a period of extensive restructuring including increasing productivity rates as well as job losses during the 1990s, the chemical industry is the most transnationalised sector in the EU (Le Queux and Fajertag, 2001: 123–4). EMCEF had been supportive of EMU from the very beginning of the related discussion. TNCs, it was argued, had already had a common European-wide accounting system since the early 1990s. A single currency was the final logical step in the chemical sector. In contrast to the EMF, however, the criticism of neo-liberal restructuring was less pronounced. The convergence criteria, for example, were not deemed to be of any concern for EMCEF. National federations should tackle this in national bargaining rounds. The same can be said in relation to employment policy. The reduction of working time was still mentioned, but otherwise the union focused on supply-side measures such as the right for employees to lifelong learning. To improve workers' employability the European-wide recognition of national training certificates was another item on the union's agenda. European employment programmes, however, were not demanded (Interview No. 73; Brussels, 22/01/2003).

Education on the other hand is a purely national sector. The European Trade Union Committee for Education (ETUC-E) co-ordinates the activities of its national member federations at the European level. The union was less critical of the EU's neo-liberal direction. The convergence criteria were not criticised, since a policy of price stability was deemed essential for a strong economy. Unemployment should be combated with the help of better education and training as well as structural reforms of labour markets and further support for the private sector. Nevertheless, it was acknowledged that the ETUC-E's national member federations and here especially education unions from Northern Europe were some of the most outspoken opponents of EMU. Hence, in order to avoid an internal split over EMU, the union refrained from adopting an official position (Interview No. 75; Brussels, 22/01/2003). The ETUC-E, to sum up, was perhaps one of the unions that had accepted aspects of neo-liberal restructuring due to its involvement with EU institutions. Nevertheless, it did not adopt an official position on EMU, partly also because education was a strictly national policy area with national unions having the biggest say.

The European Federation of Public Service Unions (EPSU) organises workers in the civil service from local to European government as well as in the health sector and general utilities such as energy and water. In short, it organises workers in all those sectors that were traditionally part of the public sector with a clear national production structure. As EMU was regarded as a further important step of European integration, EPSU did not oppose the single currency. Nevertheless, various features of its exact form were a problem for the union. The union developed its first position on EMU in 1992. It perceived very clearly the neo-liberal contents of the convergence criteria. As a result of the requirement of meeting the criteria, national governments had to adopt deflationary policies. Hence, 'after the continuing ideological attacks on the public sector in a whole range of European countries during the 1980s, EMU seems to constitute a new basis for pressure on this sector' (Public Services International, 1992: 4). Especially between 1996 and 2000, budgetary cuts undermined the public sector in a range of member states. A paper commissioned by EPSU drew a direct link between the Internal Market, EMU, the related necessary policies of cutting public debt and a policy of deregulating the public sector. 'This is leading to further restructuring of the public sector as profitability criteria, contracting-out and privatization are introduced. The changes are particularly affecting key sectors such as electricity, gas, transport and telecommunications' (Jacobi, 1997: 6). In this process, the traditional public sector had been increasingly eroded.

In more concrete terms, the main problem would be the SGP and its inflexible interpretation. 'The tight limits of the Stability and Growth Pact could lead to budget cuts at a moment of economic slowdown and thus contribute to a further increase in unemployment' (EPSU, 2004b: 2). As an alternative macro-economic policy, the ECB should go beyond its focus on price stability and emphasise more the growth aspect of the SGP via further cuts in interest rates and a generally faster response to economic developments. EPSU also supported an active EU employment policy including European employment programmes via public investment. It had been hopeful about the Lisbon strategy, but bemoaned the fact that the focus shifted towards a neo-liberal agenda with an emphasis on a flexibilisation of the labour market under the cover of 'modernisation'. And this, although 'unemployment increases while labour markets have become more flexible, which questions the argument that states that the rigidity of labour markets causes unemployment' (EPSU, 2004b: 1). In practice, EU co-ordination of economic policy would have led to wage moderation in 1992 and 1993 in the public sector and the same was happening again in 2002 and 2003. To counter these tendencies, the union acknowledged that due to EMU, it had to focus on the co-ordination of national wage bargaining (see below) to secure workers their part of increasing productivity. 'Maintaining purchasing power and a fair share of productivity increases will contribute towards sustaining demand and thus growth, employment and social protection' (EPSU, 2004b: 2). Finally, EPSU demanded more rights for the EP in relation to EMU in order to guarantee the democratic accountability of monetary policy (Interview No. 72; Brussels, 22/01/2003). Again, similar to the EMF, these policies demonstrate that EPSU despite its support for EMU was strongly opposed to neo-liberal restructuring.

As assumed in the introduction to this chapter, due to the fact that EIFs had been confronted with the realities of EMU at the European level for several years, there was a much more homogeneous response to it. The transnational sector unions EMF and EMCEF strongly emphasised the economic importance of the single currency for their sectors, but the national sector unions ETUC-E and EPSU did not oppose EMU either. As one interviewee pointed out, the differences between the EIFs was not so much about EMU, regarded as an inevitable step of further Europeanisation, but about the extent to which they followed the trend and Europeanised themselves (Interview No. 76; Brussels, 23/01/2003). The next section looks at this issue in more detail.

EIFs and trade union co-operation at the European level

In accordance with the first hypothesis of this study, the emphasis here will be on transnational sector unions on the one hand, and national sector unions on the other. It will be assessed whether EIFs have developed into independent actors at the supranational level.

Transnational sector unions

In response to transnationalisation, affecting especially workers in its sectors, the EMF argued that it had to follow and internationalise its structure and activities. The crucial turning-point was the early 1990s. 'Under the influence of the opening-up of the European borders, growing international competition, complete Europeanisation of the economy and massive unemployment in Europe, [the EMF] had noticed a distinct tendency towards a competition-driven collective bargaining policy' (EMF, 2001: 1). Plans for EMU further implied the danger of social dumping through the undercutting of wage and working conditions between several national collective bargaining rounds (EMF, 1998b: 1–2). In short, the EMF realised that wage bargaining was no longer a national issue in its sector, characterised by an increasing transnationalisation of production. In response, the EMF started restructuring itself and began to discuss the potential of co-ordinating wage bargaining (Interview No. 76; Brussels, 23/01/2003; see also Schulten, 2004: 284–94). The EMF co-ordination strategy has three main pillars (EMF, 2001: 1): first, a sophisticated system for the exchange of information about national collective bargaining rounds has been established, the so-called European Collective Bargaining Information Network (EUCOB@) (Schulten, 2001: 315). Second, this exchange of information is further supported through the establishment of cross-border collective bargaining networks including the exchange of observers for collective bargaining rounds (Gollbach and Schulten, 2000: 166–76; Schulten, 2001: 316–19). While EUCOB@ was generally considered to be a success, the performance of the cross-border networks differed from network to network. Notably, the Nordrhein Westfalen-Belgium-Netherlands network had not only exchanged observers, but also obtained speaking rights for the visiting observers (Interview No. 76; Brussels, 23/01/2003). The third area of co-operation deals with the adoption of common minimum standards and guidelines. Wage bargaining co-ordination is an important aspect of it, but only one of several. In 1998, the EMF adopted the 1750 hours working time per year charter (EMF, 1998a). This led to the reduction of the working time in four countries with only a few EU members left, where metal workers are still working more hours. A vocational training charter was adopted in 2001 – there has been a limited success in this area because not all member unions regard this as a core issue – and the EMF worked on a social charter of minimum standards in the areas of pensions and sick pay.

The co-ordination of national wage bargaining was approved in 1998 and the EMF tried to ensure that national unions pursue a common strategy of asking for wage rises along the formula of productivity increase plus inflation rate (EMF, 1998b: 3; Schulten, 2001: 304–7). As far as data is concerned, although national negotiators did not refer to the EMF guidelines, the actual bargaining results were pretty much within the formula until 2001 (Interview No. 29; Wien, 20/03/2002). After 2001, the results were more out of line with the formula, but importantly the guidelines were increasingly used as a political bargaining tool. When there was a strike in Germany during the 2002 bargaining round, seventeen presidents of metal workers' unions went to Frankfurt during the strike and defended the IG Metall claims through reference to the EMF co-ordination formula (Interview No. 76; Brussels, 23/01/2003). The main goal of the co-ordination of collective bargaining was to avoid the downward competition between different national bargaining rounds and to protect workers against the related reduction in wages and working conditions. Thus, 'a coordinated European collective bargaining policy will play a major role in intensifying and reinforcing the social dimension of European unity' (EMF, 1998b: 1). Along the same lines, 'the EMF reconfirms its rejection of wage policies geared towards further redistribution in favour of profits derived from capital. Such policies reduce purchasing power, destroy jobs and undermine the European social and welfare model' (EMF, 2003: 3).

In order to implement this strategy of collective bargaining co-ordination, the EMF restructured its institutional set-up. Most important here was the re-orientation of the Collective Bargaining Committee in the early 1990s from a forum, which had met twice a year and where unions could report the results of national collective bargaining, into an institution, where common collective bargaining objectives were debated. Additionally, a Select Working Party was created, responsible for the preparation of Collective Bargaining Committee meetings including the formulation of new initiatives within the area of collective bargaining (Schulten, 2001: 314). Moreover, the EMF changed its statute in 1999, giving itself a proper negotiating role. Finally, the institutional changes went hand in hand with an expansion of members of staff. In 1989, the EMF had four full time members of staff, in 2003 it employed thirteen (Interview No. 76; Brussels, 23/01/2003). At the second EMF congress in Prague on 13 and 14 June 2003, internal decision-making was further facilitated. The statutes of the EMF were changed to allow the Executive Committee to delegate decision-making power to the EMF policy committees including the Collective Bargaining Committee. In turn, the Executive Committee can adopt recommendations from the policy committees by a two-thirds majority. At the same time, the affiliated unions agreed on an increase of membership fees to allow for the employment of six more permanent staff.[1] Overall, the EMF clearly developed into an independent actor at the European level in accordance with the hypothesis that transnational sector unions are more likely to engage in co-operation at the European level.

The focus on union internal co-ordination did not mean that the EMF was not interested in sectoral social dialogue. It had demanded European framework agreements, although not on wages, since 1996. For years, employers had generally been reluctant to engage with the EMF (Interview No. 76; Brussels, 23/01/2003; see also Martin and Ross, 1999b: 332). It was only more recently that social dialogue was forthcoming in the shipbuilding sector (Eironline, 11 November 2003, http://www.eiro.eurofound.eu.int/2003/11/inbrief/eu0311203n. html; 27/01/2004). The example of the EMF highlights that trade unions are structurally disadvantaged within the EU form of state. Sectoral social dialogue had almost no substance and the impact on EU institutions was limited. Nevertheless, when assessing the possibilities of labour within the EU form of state, a strategic-relational analysis also focuses on the strategies of labour and how they are related to the structural selectivity of the EU. The co-ordination of bargaining provided a good, alternative way forward in this situation, characterised by the following three advantages: (1) it did not rely on an employers' counterpart, which had not been willing to engage in meaningful social dialogue; (2) the disadvantaged position within the EU institutional framework was of no consequence, since inter-union co-ordination did not rely on the compliance of EU or national institutions; and (3) this strategy allowed national differences to be taken into account, often cited as the core reason of why European-wide union co-operation would be impossible. If productivity was lower in one country than another, then the wage increase demands in the former country would be lower than in the latter accordingly. Finally, the EMF was prepared to back up its European activities with industrial action. On 25 January 2001, for example, it organised a European day of action in support of the Vauxhall workers in Luton, UK against the closing down of their company (Eironline, 21 March 2002, http://www.eiro.eurofound.eu.int/2002/03/feature/eu0203203f. html; 27/01/2004). This relates to the EMF's general demand 'that the trade unions must be able to initiate joint transnational action, demonstrations and strikes in order to establish a European wage and collective bargaining policy' (EMF, 2003: 6).

The main hypothesis that transnational sector unions are more likely to become independent European actors is also confirmed by the social dialogue activities of various transnational sector branches of UNI-Europa. This included a review of sectoral social dialogue progress and discussion of a new work programme in telecommunications (Eironline, 03 December 2002, http://www. eiro.eurofound.eu.int/2002/12/inbrief/eu0212203n.html; 27/01/2004), a joint declaration on lifelong learning in the banking sector (Eironline, 17 December 2002, http://www.eiro.eurofound.eu.int/2002/12/feature/eu0212207f.html; 27/01/2004) as well as a joint statement on corporate social responsibility in the commerce sector (Eironline, 18 December 2003, http://www.eiro.eurofound.eu. int/2003/12/feature/ eu0312208f.html; 27/01/2004). Nevertheless, in line with the neo-Gramscian, historical materialist perspective of this book, the production structure itself only creates the possibility of action, it does not determine it. There is no automatic, economic deterministic correlation between a transnational production structure and intensive European level co-operation. EMCEF, organising workers in the highly transnationalised chemical industry, is a good example in this respect.

Commission initiatives pushed EMCEF towards joint responses with the employers at the European level. In November 2003, EMCEF and the European Chemical Employers' Group (ECEG) signed a joint statement on the future of the chemical sector in response to a new draft EU regulation for this sector (e.g. Eironline, 9 December 2003, http://www.eiro.eurofound.eu.int/2003/12/ inbrief/eu0312202n.html; 27/01/2004). In September 2004, one year later, EMCEF and ECEG declared their willingness to propose to the Commission the establishment of a formal social dialogue committee for the chemical industry. A new joint position paper on 'Education, Vocational Training and Lifelong Learning' was also adopted (ECEG-EMCEF, 2004). It is the issue of co-ordinating collective national bargaining, however, which shows the difference between the EMF and EMCEF best.

In 1997, EMCEF formed a Euro Working Group, which became responsible for the exploration of the possibility of European collective bargaining. The results were guidelines for collective bargaining in the Euro-zone adopted by the EMCEF conference in November 1999. 'These include the common objective to safeguard workers' purchasing power, the convergence of working time within a European corridor and the limitation of overtime, and a sector-based control of variable pay schemes introduced by MNCs' (Le Queux and Fajertag, 2001: 129). Nevertheless, these guidelines were not supposed to lead to a harmonisation of national bargaining claims and, thus, fell short of the EMF's ambitions. The latter was considered to be wishful thinking. Only the exchange of information on the different ways of bargaining in individual countries, including the exchange of bargaining observers, was deemed a realistic possibility. Nevertheless, EMCEF too recognised that globalisation put stronger pressure on Europe-wide co-ordination. European integration and especially the single currency added further pressure. As a result, 'in the long term, there needs to be greater agreement on trade union collective bargaining policy' (EMCEF, 2004a: 4). Hence, it was also in the process of establishing a new internal structure reflecting and adapting to specific European themes, moving beyond a simple, co-ordinating role (Interview No. 73; Brussels, 22/01/2003). The 3rd EMCEF Congress in Stockholm from 8 to 10 June 2004 adopted a new structure with four committees, dedicated to (1) Industrial Policy, Health, Safety and Environment, (2) EWCs, (3) Collective Bargaining, and (4) Social Dialogue (EMCEF, 2004b; EMCEF, 2004c).

Additionally, a motion was passed on the future work of the Collective Bargaining Committee. Nevertheless, although co-ordination was frequently mentioned, practicalities concentrated on a better collection and exchange of information (EMCEF, 2004d: 1–2). Inflation rates and productivity gains were mentioned in relation to wage bargaining, but only in relation to the development of benchmarks (EMCEF, 2004d: 3). They were not put forward as a general formula for national bargaining rounds. Overall, this analysis of EMCEF confirms the earlier finding of the German IG BCE and the Austrian GdC, which both despite their transnationalised production structure relied nonetheless on influence at the national level (see Chapter 6). It will be interesting to see whether EMCEF develops into a more independent European actor in the future.

National sector unions

Education is clearly a domestic production sector. There are no common EU positions or competencies in this area. Social dialogue took place between the ETUC-E and employers' associations on the lack of teachers in the EU. Progress had, however, been hampered by the fact that the employers' side, state level and local government, were either not interested or not organised at the European level. In 2002, the Chief Negotiators' Electronic Network was launched to improve the exchange of information (ETUC, 2002: 37). The co-ordination of national collective bargaining at the European level was, however, deemed to be unfeasible (Interview No. 75; Brussels, 22/01/2003; see also Schulten, 2002: 19). Overall, the case of the ETUC-E confirms the first hypothesis that trade unions in national production sectors are unlikely to develop strong co-operation initiatives at the European level. There were some concerns over the draft European Constitution including education as part of the competencies within the Common Commercial Policy and, thus, subject to possible privatisation within a future GATS framework (ETUC-E, 2003). In its defence of education as part of the public sector, however, the ETUC-E's main focus was on ensuring that education policy remained subject to unanimity voting within the Council, preserving education as a national level competency (ETUC-E, 2004: 2). A European-level defence of education as a public sector was not attempted.

Another example of a national production sector EIF is the European Graphical Sector branch of Union Network International (UNI-EGS). 'In general, the European printing and publishing industry remains a collection of national industries, and this holds for the graphical sector in particular' (Leisink 2002: 110). The vast majority of companies are small with fewer than twenty employees and there is no European labour market and relatively little export and import activity. Unsurprisingly, considering the national production structures, the respective employers' association had no interest in a formal social dialogue at the European level. On the other hand, however, the UNI-EGS Collective Bargaining Committee, initially set up in 1990, intensified its efforts at bargaining co-ordination in 1997. This led to the adoption of a formal agreement at a collective bargaining conference in November 2000. 'As a guideline for establishing bargaining demands, the agreement stipulates that wages plus cost-effective aspects should at least be equal to the rate of inflation plus gains in national productivity, while 1750 hours per year are the standard working hours' (Leisink 2002: 113; see also Schulten 2002: 17). Hence, the resistance by the employers' association to co-operate had been successfully side-stepped through intra-union co-operation. The actual impact of these co-ordination attempts remains to be seen, but it is clear that even in national production sectors labour may emerge as a European actor.

This is even more so the case with EPSU, which organises workers across the public services as well as formerly public, now privatised sectors, with predominantly domestic production structures. EPSU had become increasingly active as an independent actor at the European level since the 1990s. Confronted with intensified neo-liberal restructuring, it struggled to preserve a system of integrated public services within EU members. In order to explain EPSU's increased activity, one needs to refer to the second hypothesis, shaping the enquiry of this study. Especially the amount of decisions taken at the European level concerning the public sector put pressure towards more European-level activities. EMU in general, it was pointed out by EPSU, had intensified the need for closer co-ordination of national bargaining. It provided a common European framework for the public sector, even if the production structures remained largely national. A study by the European Trade Union Institute (ETUI) confirmed that national preparations for EMU with a focus on meeting the convergence criteria had negatively affected collective bargaining in the public sector (Hoffmann and Jacobi, 1999: 11). The study concluded that if EPSU was to be put in a position able to respond to these pressures on behalf of its member associations, 'then the responsibilities and competencies of the EPSU must be extended and its human, technical and financial resources increased' (Hoffmann and Jacobi, 1999: 17). More specifically in relation to the public sector, it was the drive for deregulation and liberalisation of traditionally domestic production sectors such as energy and public procurement, driven by the Commission, which had made the international, European level more relevant for trade union activity. In a letter to EPSU's affiliated unions, the General Secretary Carola Fischbach-Pyttel herself pointed to the decisions in relation to public services to be taken at the European level in 2003. This included the Commission's position on GATS negotiations, the report by the working group on social Europe within the Convention on the Future of Europe, and a Green Paper by the Commission on Services of General Interest (see Commission, 2003). The discussion by the EP of draft directives on public procurement and a further opening of the electricity and gas markets was also expected. Finally, a general push by the DG Internal Market towards more deregulation of services of general economic interest would have to be considered (EPSU, 2003a).

According to EPSU, the 'liberalisation policies of the European Commission with the majority support of the European Council are undermining public services' (EPSU, 2002b). The union regarded public services as the basis of a 'humane and fair society', guaranteeing fundamental rights such as the rights to training and education, health care and social protection, minimum levels of income, etc. Within the EU, 'the ability of public services to guarantee and deliver these rights to citizens has been under pressure from liberalisation, deregulation and privatisation. New forms of service delivery are booming: concessions, public-private partnerships, and private enterprise aiming for profit rather than fulfilling human needs' (EPSU, 2000a: 1). Additionally, EPSU considered the public sector to be a core element of a co-ordinated European strategy of full employment and sustainable development. This clearly demonstrates EPSU's continuing resistance to neo-liberal restructuring despite its reluctant acceptance of EMU. The Commission was especially criticised for giving 'priority to the internal market and competition rules over other objectives within a socially balanced market economy' (EPSU 2003d: 3). EPSU criticised the Commission's strategy to apply private sector criteria of management and evaluation to the public sector, based on the assumption that the former would be automatically more efficient than the latter. The Commission would, thereby, provide a rationale for the introduction of liberalisation measures in the public sector and the application of strict budgetary constraints on public spending in line with the single currency and SGP. EPSU needed to challenge this neo-liberal economic orthodoxy, it was argued (EPSU, 2004a: 2–3). Unsurprisingly, the union was highly sceptical of the Commission's conclusion in its White Paper on Services of General Interest, published in 2004, that 'the pursuit and achievement of public policy objectives with competitive objectives are reconcilable' (EPSU, 2004c: 2).

EPSU attempted to stop these moves towards further deregulation, privatisation and the related dangers of undermining the guaranteed access for everybody to services of general interest. In response to neo-liberal restructuring, EPSU engaged to some extent in sectoral social dialogue in the electricity industry, now the most transnationalised sector within the remit of EPSU (Eironline, 8 November 2002, http://www.eiro.eurofound.eu.int/2002/11/inbrief/eu0211203n.html; 27/01/2004; and Eironline, 6 July 2004, http://www.eiro.eurofound.eu.int/2004/07/inbrief/eu0407201n.html; 27/10/2004). Moreover, a new social dialogue committee in the local and regional government sector was established in January 2004, adopting a joint statement on telework as its first measure (Eironline, 23 March 2004, http://www.eiro.eurofound.eu.int/2004/03/feature/eu0403203f.html; 27/10/2004). Social dialogue may follow in the gas industry. In general, however, results had remained below the ones in the multi-sector social dialogue, also because public sector employers' associations at the European level either did not exist or emphasised national differences (Interview No. 72; Brussels, 22/01/2003; see also EPSU, 2000b: 4; and EPSU, 2004b: 4–5). First attempts had also been made at European-level co-ordination of national bargaining. At its congress in 2000, 'EPSU adopted a declaration of principles regarding collective bargaining in public services' (Schulten, 2002: 18). Similar to the EMF, it was argued that 'a joint wage policy for public sector unions should ensure that the rate of inflation is compensated and that workers maintain an appropriate share of productivity increases' (EPSU, 2000b: 3; see also EPSU,

2004b: 2–3). In 2002, the executive committee of EPSU adopted a bargaining information exchange system similar to the EMF and appropriately called it EPSUCOB@. An annual collective bargaining conference was also established. Overall, however, collective bargaining co-ordination was far less developed than by the transnational sector union EMF (Interview No. 72; Brussels, 22/01/2003).

A third strategy employed by EPSU had been the lobbying of EU institutions. GATS highlighted the importance of the European level in international trade agreements, because the Commission was in this instance the EU's main negotiator. EPSU was concerned that EU public services had become bargaining chips for the Commission in its attempt to open up other countries for European services exporters (EPSU, 2003a). It, therefore, demanded that 'the exclusion of health, education, culture, social services and water from any [GATS] trade obligations must be made unequivocal' (EPSU, 2004a: 4). Reservations were expressed by EPSU in a meeting with the Commissioner Pascal Lamy of DG Trade on 17 February 2003 in relation to the tightness of GATS safety clauses, allowing countries to maintain their own regulations, and the secret nature of the negotiations. The pressure applied by institutions such as the World Bank on developing countries to move towards liberalisation in these areas as well as the rights of foreign citizens carrying out contract work within the EU were also discussed (EPSU, 2003b). In a letter to Lamy, summing up the results of the meeting, the EU's role in pressuring developing countries towards deregulation was criticised and it was demanded that Lamy seeks 'withdrawal of the requests to developing countries to open public services such as waste water treatment, postal services and others by the European Union' (EPSU, 2003c: 2). Hence, at its Congress in Stockholm in June 2004 EPSU called 'on the European Commission to tailor its WTO-GATS negotiating position to the principles of the European Social Model' (EPSU, 2004a: 5).

The most innovative strategy was, however, EPSU's increasing co-operation with other social movements. In relation to GATS, additionally to its direct lobbying of the Commission, EPSU had participated in demonstrations organised by Belgian unions and ATTAC on 9 February 2003 to keep public services out of GATS. Furthermore, it took part in the European day of national action on GATS and public services organised by the European Social Forum on 13 March as well as the ETUC European day of national action for a social Europe on 21 March 2003 (EPSU, 2003a). Finally, via its international federation Public Services International, EPSU signed up to the campaigns 'Stop the GATS Attack' and 'Shrink or Sink' (Interview No. 72; Brussels, 22/01/2003). The link with other social movements was also visible in relation to public procurement. EPSU and several other EIFs co-operated with a range of environmental and other social movements such as Greenpeace Europe and the Social Platform, itself a network of European NGOs promoting the Social Dimension of the EU, in lobbying the EU Council of Ministers to amend the Draft Directive on Public Procurement towards the inclusion of social, ecological and fair trade criteria in the award of public procurement contracts (Coalition for Green and Social Procurement's Amendment, 2002; Interview No. 72; Brussels, 22/01/2003).

Finally, the drafting and debating of the Convention on the Future of Europe including a working group on 'social Europe' inspired EPSU, as part of a broad public service coalition including unions and social movements, to demand that 'the social and economic value of services of general economic interest are protected and formally enshrined in any new constitutional framework in Europe' (EPSU, 2002a; see also EPSU, 2002b). Co-operation with social movements was supported by research of the Public Services International Research Unit (http://www.psiru.org), which was widely used by the NGO community in their own publications. Finally, this openness to co-operation with other social movements was backed up by a commitment to strike action, if necessary. Hence, EPSU demanded that the EU was 'to recognise transnational rights including the right to transnational industrial action along with the right to strike. Sympathy strikes and solidarity action should be allowed' (EPSU, 2000b: 6).

In sum, the increasing involvement by the EU in general and the Commission in particular in moves of actual or potential future deregulation and liberalisation of national public services had intensified EPSU's engagement at the European level with the aim to counter these measures. The case of EPSU demonstrates again that trade unions are disadvantaged within the structural selectivity of the EU form of state, but also that there are strategies available, which may help to overcome these disadvantages. EPSU had been engaged in sectoral social dialogue. It had started developing the co-ordination strategy following the lead of the EMF and lobbied directly EU institutions. Additionally, however, in all its activities against the further privatisation of public services, EPSU formed close alliances not only with other trade unions, but also wider social movements, accepting that 'social Europe is the bridge that connects Europe to the citizen' (EPSU, 2002b). Hence, a separate 'social discourse' emerged in the EU and EPSU had successfully used it to broaden its social basis for the struggle against neo-liberal restructuring of the public sector, thereby increasing its impact on EU policy-making (see also Greenwood, 2003: 150, 155–8).

Agriculture was another sector, where the EU through the Common Agricultural Policy exercised a lot of power at the European level. Similar to EPSU, the EFFAT had increasingly become an independent actor at the European level. In December 2002, it signed an agreement on vocational training with the employers, to be implemented by the social partners at the national level (Eironline, 20 January 2003, http://www.eiro.eurofound.eu.int/2003/01/inbrief/eu0301203n.html; 27/01/2004). Additionally, it negotiated and signed a voluntary code of conduct in relation to corporate social responsibility with employers in the sugar industry in February 2003 (Eironline, 5 March 2003, http://www.eiro.eurofound.eu.int/2003/02/feature/eu0302204f.html; 27/01/2004). The ETF organises workers in national transport systems, however with increasingly transnational implications due to cross-border transport links. The only two sectoral framework agreements, one in maritime transport and one in railways, were signed in this sector in 1998 (Keller, 2003: 418). The fact that this occurred mainly due to Commission pressure confirms again the importance of the amount of decisions taken at the European level for social partner inter-action. Additionally, the ETF participated in sectoral social dialogue as, for example, preparing 'negotiations on establishing a European licence for drivers and working conditions of staff on international transport services' (Eironline, 14 May 2003, http://www.eiro.eurofound.eu.int/2003/03/feature/eu0303101f. html; 27/01/2004). In general, however, it took the consequences from the fact that only few results could be expected from lobbying national and EU institu-tions or sectoral social dialogue. Bargaining results, it was argued, depended on the structural power of unions. Hence, the first important issue was to drive forward the organisation of workers in those areas that had not been unionised yet. Only the show of force at the international level via cross-border strikes would ultimately be able to push through unions' demands. In January 2003, for example, the ETF organised a European-wide strike against the EU direc-tive on the flexibilisation of dock workers through an opening of market access to port services (Eironline, 11 February 2003, http://www.eiro.eurofound.eu.int/ 2003/02/inbrief/eu0302201n.html; 27/01/2004). Partly thanks to the ETF's actions, the directive was rejected by the EP in its final reading in November 2003 (Eironline, 9 December 2003, http://www.eiro.eurofound.eu.int/2003/12/ inbrief/eu0312203n.html; 27/01/2004). Moreover, since 2000 the ETF had actively participated in the organisation of annual international days of action highlighting especially the danger of rail liberalisation in Europe for passenger safety (Eironline, 8 April 2003, http://www.eiro.eurofound.eu.int/2003/04/ inbrief/eu0304202n.html; 27/01/2004). It was this kind of concrete collective action, the union wanted to focus on. This was combined with a strong effort at engaging with other social movements, similar to EPSU. Trade unions would have a clearer level of representation, but co-operation with social movements was considered to be essential by the ETF because their members would often have a stronger commitment and greater mobilisation potential. Furthermore, they would also conduct a broader information campaign. It came as no surprise that the ETF took actively part in the European Social Forum (ESF) in Florence from 6 to 10 November 2002, when anti-globalisation movements from all over Europe met to discuss current problems and how to overcome them (Interview No. 74; Brussels, 22/01/2003; Bieler and Morton 2004b) (see Chapter 9). This strong focus on European-level activities despite the national production struc-ture also reflected the increasing amount of decisions taken at the EU level, something that was also mentioned by the German Transnet and the Austrian GdE as a reason for their strategic prioritisation of Europe (see Chapter 7).

Conclusions

EMU, generally regarded as an inevitable step of further Europeanisation/ European integration, was not a controversial issue for EIFs. The EMF and EMCEF highlighted the economic benefits for their sectors, but the ETUC-E and EPSU did not openly reject it either. Nonetheless, this chapter also showed that in accordance with the first hypothesis, those trade unions with a more transnationalised production structure were more likely to engage in intensive European level co-operation with some EIFs emerging as independent actors. The EMF and its co-ordination of national collective bargaining strategy demonstrated this. National sector unions, on the other hand, saw less a need of European-level activities. The ETUC-E served as an example here. Nevertheless, the production structure does not determine unions' behaviour. It only creates the possibility for particular actions. EMCEF, a transnational sector union, had developed the European level much less, while EPSU, representing national public sector workers, had increasingly intensified its independent activities within the EU. Following the second hypothesis, the latter could be explained by the European form of state and specifically the increasing amount of decisions taken at the European level, which affected the delivery of services of general interest. As it was also shown, the EU form of state structurally disadvantages unions. Nevertheless, what is important are the ways unions' strategies relate to the structural selectivity of a form of state. Here it was shown that inter-union co-ordination of national collective bargaining – see here the EMF – and the wider co-operation with other social movements – see here especially EPSU – plus a focus on collective action across borders along the examples of the ETF were good ways forward within the structural selectivity of the EU form of state.

Following the critical theory dimension of the neo-Gramscian perspective underpinning this book, the analysis of the social purpose underlying trade unions' activities made clear that these activities were mainly directed against neo-liberal restructuring. For EPSU, it was the defence of public services against further liberalisation that was at the top of its agenda. For the EMF, the fight against a downward competition between different national bargaining rounds including further liberalisation of the labour market was the main goal. The ETF, finally, was mainly concerned about the safety of rail travel. Two points are important in relation to the future trade union development at the European level against neo-liberal restructuring. First, in summer 1999, the ETUC adopted the co-ordination of collective bargaining as one of its four main tasks and established an ETUC Collective Bargaining Committee (Schulten, 2002: 21–2). In December 2000, the ETUC then adopted a recommendation on the co-ordination of collective bargaining at the European level, which had as its main component the formula of inflation rate plus productivity plus some extra factors, if appropriate. The main goal was to stop the fall of wages as a percentage of GDP based on the understanding that a further fall of workers' real income would damage domestic demand levels across the EU (Mermet, 2001: 52–61 and 181–2). The ETUC, thereby, followed closely the example of the EMF as well as the so-called Doorn declaration in September 1998, when the Belgian, Dutch, German and Luxembourg trade union confederations and major sectoral unions in metalworking, chemicals, construction and private and public services agreed to co-ordinate their national collective bargaining along the lines of 'the sum total of the evolution of prices and the increase in labour productivity' in order to prevent downward competition on wages and working conditions under EMU (Eironline, 28 October 1998, http://www.eiro.eurofound. eu.int/1998/10/feature/de9810278f.html; 17/03/2005; Schulten, 2004: 280–3). The ETUC's main task had been the compilation of an annual collective bargaining report, in which it compared national bargaining results with the ETUC co-ordination formula (see ETUC, 2002). This was judged to have been a success (Interview No. 70; Brussels, 21/01/2003), also because some national confederations made reference to the ETUC formula in recent national bargaining rounds in France, Portugal and Spain (Interview No. 71; Brussels, 21/01/2003; Schulten, 2004: 304). Second, the ETUC had also increasingly engaged in co-operation with other social movements and was well presented at the ESF in Florence in November 2002 (Bieler and Morton, 2004b). An analysis of the ETUC campaigns on the European Charter of Fundamental Rights and the Convention of the Future of Europe by Taylor and Mathers too indicated that the ETUC, despite continuing limitations, had started to move beyond a focus on social partnership towards a strategy of intensified co-operation with other social movements (Taylor and Mathers, 2004). The potential of this co-operation will be discussed further in Chapter 9. The ETUC's commitment to wider action was also expressed in its organisation of large-scale demonstrations at EU summits such as Nice in 2000 and Barcelona in 2002. This was backed up with its demand to the right to strike at the European level (Interview No. 70; Brussels, 21/01/2003).

Only if these strategies are pursued further, will the ETUC be able to develop a position of strength, from which it can make effective use of tripartite discussions offered by the macroeconomic dialogue and the more recently institutionalised tripartite social summit for growth and employment, bringing together the social partners and EU institutions on the eve of the annual spring Economic and Social Council (Eironline, 8 April 2003, http://www. eiro.eurofound.eu.int/2003/04/inbrief/ eu0304201n.html; 27/01/2004). To conclude, the ETUC had increasingly emerged as an actor in its own right at the European level, because of its involvement in the multi-sector social dialogue, but also because of its increasing initiatives in the area of co-ordinating national collective bargaining and co-operation with other social movements. This was internally backed up through the introduction of QMV in 1999, making it easier to operate as a coherent actor (Interview No. 70; Brussels, 21/01/2003). While the ETUC had made many compromises in its support of European integration including EMU, the allegations that it had succumbed to neo-liberal restructuring and been co-opted into a new elite at the European level were unfounded. The ETUC continued to criticise neo-liberalism and, therefore, needs to be taken into account when thinking about resistance to neo-liberal restructuring in the EU and beyond.

Note

1   E-mail message by the EMF deputy general secretary on 23/06/2003.

Part IV

What future Union?
The struggle for a social Europe

9
Trade unions and the future of the European model of capitalism

Introduction

The purpose of this book was to analyse trade unions' positions on EMU and European co-operation in order to assess their perceptions of how to represent best the interests of their members in times of global restructuring. Related to this was the concern of whether in the process of dealing with EMU, trade unions had accepted neo-liberal restructuring or whether they were still attempting to oppose it and, therefore, to what extent they play a role in the resistance to neo-liberal globalisation. In Chapter 2, a neo-Gramscian historical materialist perspective was developed that was able to comprehend the historical specificity of capitalism as well as to conceptualise the current capitalist stage of transnational class formation and, as a consequence, labour as a potential international actor. Globalisation was understood as the transnationalisation of production and finance at the material level and the shift from Keynesianism to neo-liberal ideas at the ideological level. As a result, it was argued that there are now also transnational class fractions of capital and labour. While globalisation is not a uniform process across the world, European integration is clearly a part of globalisation. The transnationalisation of production partly drove and was partly driven by the Internal Market programme and revived European integration included the formation of an integrated European financial space. The 'state project' underlying this revival was neo-liberal as expressed in the four freedoms and the common competition policy of the Internal Market, the independent ECB, the convergence criteria and the SGP of EMU as well as the rationale driving the 1995 and 2004 EU enlargements. Against the background of this new structural framework of the partial transnationalisation of production and the shift towards neo-liberal economics at the global as well as the European level, the following hypothesis was formulated in respect of trade unions' positions on EMU and co-operation at the European level:

> *Hypothesis*: A labour movement's position on EMU depends crucially on its length and degree of exposure to the competitive pressures of globalisation. Unions that represent workers in transnational production sectors

are more likely to support EMU, because they may support their companies – on which their own well-being depends – which benefit from a stable monetary environment and institutionalised free trade within the EU. Moreover, because they realise that they have lost control over capital at the national level, they are probably prepared to co-operate with other unions at the European level. National production sector unions, on the other hand, are likely to oppose EMU, since it undermines national policy autonomy and, thus, the support, on which their sectors depend. Relying on the state, they may also be less concerned about European co-operation.

As it was, however, also argued, social forces continue to operate within and through national forms of state. As a result of the different historical development of capitalism in the five countries under investigation and despite similar restructuring pressures related to globalisation, a continuing divergence of national institutional set-ups was identified. Hence, while trade unions still enjoyed considerable impact on policy-making within the structural selectivity of the Swedish form of state, for example, their rights had been drastically cut back in Britain. This led to the following second hypothesis:

Hypothesis: Those trade unions that have lost influence within the national institutional set-up are probably more in favour of European co-operation and the establishment of an industrial relations system as well as social regulations at the European level to counter global pressures. By contrast, unions that still enjoy considerable impact on policy-making at the national level are likely to be less interested in European co-operation.

Throughout this study, in line with the first hypothesis, the main focus was on the potential division between transnational and national labour, rather than on a country-by-country comparison, also in order to avoid the implicit emphasis on national differences inherent in the latter strategy. This conclusion will, however, first present an overview of the empirical results focusing on the different situations within the countries as well as the European level. In a second move, consideration will be given to possible alternatives to neo-liberalism as exemplified by EMU, before possible strategies to achieve these alternatives are reflected upon.

Trade unions vis–à–vis EMU and European co-operation in Austria, Britain, France, Germany, Sweden and the EU

Split between transnational and national labour in Britain

The TUC led the pro-EMU membership debate within the British labour movement. Introducing the Euro would save manufacturing jobs and ensure the continuation of inward FDI. It would, moreover, allow Britain to be at the heart of decision-making within the EU and imply a continuing positive impact of the European social model on British domestic politics. The TUC was less worried about the impact of the convergence criteria and SGP on public spending, since British fiscal policy would be even tougher. In short, EMU membership had clear economic and political advantages in the eyes of the TUC. This position was strongly supported by affiliated unions who organise workers in transnational finance (e.g. UNIFI), and transnational production (e.g. AEEU, CWU). They all stressed the negative impact of a high Sterling in relation to the Euro and exchange rate instability, leading to drastic job losses especially in manufacturing. This position was also confirmed by the pro-EMU position of the transnational manufacturing sections within the general unions GMB and MSF. Nevertheless, the opposition to EMU by sections linked to domestic production sectors within the general unions indicated the general split between national forces of labour and transnational forces of labour over EMU as envisaged by the first hypothesis. Domestic production sector unions such as UNISON, RMT and UCATT rejected EMU membership for its neo-liberal rationale expressed in the convergence criteria and the SGP. It would put pressure on cutting back public spending and, therefore, prevent the renewal of British public services as well as the creation of public sector jobs. If at all, EMU membership would actually imply job losses in the public sector. Additionally, these unions criticised the ECB for its exclusive focus on price stability expressed in its asymmetrical inflation target, for example, and its lack of transparency and accountability. The tensions resulting from the split between national and transnational forces of labour was perhaps most visible in the position of the T&G, organising members in the domestic public as well as transnational manufacturing sector. While the union accepted that EMU membership would bring economic benefits to Britain in the medium- to long-term, it opposed membership for the period of 2001 to 2005, because the SGP would prevent the much-needed renewal of the British public sector.

This division between transnational and national labour was also visible over co-operation at the European level. While the TUC – its former General Secretary John Monks became the ETUC general secretary in 2003 – and transnational sector unions as well as especially the general union GMB pushed for increasing co-operation at the European level, national sector unions continued to concentrate on the national level with their policy-making efforts. Nevertheless, this division should not make us overlook the fundamental shift of British labour (national and transnational) towards a pro-EU position. This generally positive attitude towards the EU, including also those unions that are opposed to EMU, can be related to the second hypothesis. Against the background of a Conservative onslaught on trade union rights during the 1980s and 1990s, British unions had generally moved towards a positive position on the EU as such. They tried to further the interests of their members at the supranational level, since they had been weakened within the transformed structural selectivity of the British form of state. With the Labour Party's return to power in 1997, there was a temporary re-orientation to the national level and party – union co-operation intensified especially prior to general elections.[1] Nevertheless, this could not mask unions' increasing sense of disillusionment with 'New' Labour and its policies. Especially the government's intention to facilitate private sector involvement in the provision of public services via PFI had already led to union backlashes. The GMB announced on 17 July 2001 that it would cut up to £1 million from its contribution to the Labour party over the next four years in protest of continuing privatisation of public services (GMB, 2001b). At UNISON's annual conference in June 2001, delegates demanded a review of the union's multi-million Pound support of the Labour Party with potential future cuts in mind (Guardian, 22 June 2001). The following year at the Labour annual conference on Monday, 30 September 2002, a union motion for the review of PFI schemes was backed by a majority of union activists with the support of constituency delegates against the will of the Labour leadership (Guardian, 1 October 2002). In short, a renewal of the stronger focus on Europe may occur in the future.[2]

The rejection of EMU membership due to its neo-liberal bias clearly indicated the opposition to neo-liberal restructuring by domestic labour in Britain. Transnational sector unions, too, however, continued to oppose neo-liberalism. Here a sub-division could be identified. On the one hand, there was a group of unions around the TUC and AEEU that was not worried that the SGP would have a negative impact on public spending. The Social Dimension should be further developed to accommodate restructuring, but the underlying rationale of EMU could remain the same. On the other hand, unions such as the GPMU, UNIFI and GMB were concerned about the implications on public spending levels and demanded a government commitment not to cut back public spending in case of EMU membership in exchange for their active support in a future referendum on the Euro. The GMB's demands for a larger EU budget and European employment programmes indicated clearly the union's support for a change of the rationale underlying EMU towards more demand-oriented employment policies. As the confederation, the TUC attempted to maintain a line that would guarantee maximum possible unity of the British labour movement. Hence, in addition to emphasising the importance of the Euro for manufacturing and inward FDI, the TUC General Council argued in its report to the 2003 TUC Annual Congress that an expansion of the social model as well as assurances that EMU membership would have no detrimental impact on public investment were equally important (TUC, 2003b: 2). In the event, this statement could not overcome the resistance of those unions, opposed to EMU membership (TUC Annual Congress, 2003).

Support for EMU but division over European co-operation in Germany
In Germany, the DGB's 'yes, but' position was dominant amongst its affiliated unions, whether they organise internationally oriented/transnational or national sector workers. Hence, in contrast to Britain, there was no split over EMU in the German labour movement. The vast majority of unions supported EMU, partly because it would remedy the problems of an appreciating DM for German exports and partly because it was regarded as an important step of further European integration, representing an essential part of German foreign policy

after World War II. Additionally, in line with the general focus on the social relations of production advocated by the neo-Gramscian perspective central to this book, it was asserted that there are hardly any purely domestic production sectors any longer in Germany in the wake of the liberalisation and privatisation of large parts of the public sector. Finally, it was noted that EMU was already a reality, when research for this project was carried out. Hence, unions had accepted EMU and focused on how to cope best with its implications rather than thinking about how to prevent it as in the case of British and Swedish unions. At the same time, however, German unions criticised the neo-liberal implications of EMU as represented in the convergence criteria and the ECB's exclusive focus on price stability. Unions generally demanded active employment policies at the national and European level, a more flexible interpretation of the convergence criteria, with some even wanting to add an unemployment criterion to demonstrate a stronger emphasis on employment and growth. Some unions also mentioned wage increases in line with inflation and productivity increases in order to ensure domestic demand as well as tax harmonisation to avoid regime competition within the EU as additional steps. The goal had to be a further development of the Social Dimension in order to obtain a social model of capitalism in contrast to the market-oriented model of the USA. This would also imply an additional democratisation of the EU through more power for the supranational institutions in order to make the ECB accountable.

The IG BCE was a slight exception in that it accepted EMU, but was less critical of its neo-liberal implications. This indicated a more accommodationist position, also visible in the union's focus on agreements with employers at the national level at the expense of intra-union co-ordination at the European level. The IG BAU was a further exception. Although construction is a transnational sector in Germany, it relied heavily on public investment in infrastructure projects. The IG BAU, consequently, rejected EMU and demanded that at least its start was postponed. Neo-liberal restructuring had led to cut backs in public investment and the union's members were directly affected by this. Finally, it was shown that the DBB and Transnet were less critical of neo-liberal restructuring as represented by EMU exhibiting a similar position to the IG BCE. At least in the case of the DBB, this could be explained as a result of it representing a more privileged clientele within the German public sector, i.e. the 'Beamten'. As they cannot be made redundant, they are immune against the negative impact of neo-liberal restructuring on the public sector. Only in relation to the issue of co-operation at the European level could a division be observed in Germany. While transnational sector unions, with perhaps the exception of the IG BCE, were heavily involved in European-level efforts, domestic public sector unions continued to concentrate predominantly on the national level in their efforts to influence policy-making. The latter argued that the public sector had mainly national characteristics and national employers as the unions' counterpart. Transnet was the slight exception here. Due to the increasing number of EU regulations in transport, the union emphasised the increasing importance of European-level activities.

The ideological split of the French labour movement

There was a clear split in the French labour movement, which ran along ideological lines rather than production sector differences. On the one hand, the confederations CFDT, CFTC, CFE-CGC and UNSA supported EMU as well as stronger co-operation at the European level with an emphasis on social dialogue and collective bargaining. While CFTC and UNSA, however, strongly opposed the underlying neo-liberal structure, the CFE-CGC endorsed the focus on price stability very similar to the Swedish union SACO, and the CFDT accepted neo-liberal principles to some extent in that it did not reject the convergence criteria and the independent status of the ECB. On the other hand, FO and G10-Solidaires strongly criticised EMU for its neo-liberal rationale. The transfer of this criticism into a more general criticism of European integration also implied that both unions were not in favour of co-operation within the existing EU institutions via the ETUC. FO instead concentrated on the workplace while G10-Solidaires attempted to forge alternative alliances at the European level, including also new social movements. The CGT occupied a middle position. While it vigorously criticised neo-liberal restructuring, this was combined with a strategy that included collective bargaining and European-level co-operation. With the exception of FO, this focus on the European, international level could be explained through a reference to the second hypothesis. Due to a lack of impact on policy-making within the French form of state – similar to British unions although in a different way – French unions saw the regional level as the best way forward.

The ideological division between unions became also apparent in the analysis of French transnational sector unions. The CGT transnational federations in line with their confederation rejected EMU despite the transnational nature of their sector, while the CFDT-Banques also rejected EMU, but this time in opposition to its confederation. The CFDT, dominated by members in the private and often transnationalised sector, itself supported EMU. FO de la Communication, again, despite its transnational production sector, heavily criticised EMU in line with its confederation. The first hypothesis, however, was at least partly confirmed in relation to its second part. As expected, these various transnational sector unions, even if they rejected EMU, favoured stronger European-level co-operation. This was frequently justified with the increasingly transnational character of their production sectors. The practice of these intentions, of course, differed from union to union, reflecting also the different level of co-operation within the EIFs. Thus, the CGT-metallurgie participated in the co-ordination of wage bargaining within the EMF, while the FNIC-CGT concentrated on co-operation across borders in EWCs. Importantly, both CFDT-Banques and SUD-PTT also increasingly focused on co-operation with other social movements in their struggle against neo-liberal restructuring.

Two education unions and, thus, domestic production sector unions were analysed and the ideological split could be observed there too. While UNSA-Education supported EMU despite misgivings about its neo-liberal principles, the FSU strongly opposed EMU for its neo-liberal contents. Both unions concentrated on the national level in their efforts to influence policy-making considering that education policy is predominantly a national matter. When engaging in European-level co-operation, UNSA-Education worked through the ETUC-E and was generally positive about the European-level trade union structures. FSU, by contrast, strongly criticised the ETUC for its lack of opposition vis-à-vis neo-liberal restructuring. Hence, it put more effort into co-operation with other social movements.

Austrian trade unions and the reality of EMU

The ÖGB set the tone of the general debate in Austria. It accepted that EMU and the single currency were beneficial in that they implied greater levels of economic stability. Nevertheless, the underlying basis of EMU, its neo-liberal rationale, needed to be changed, it was argued. EMU should have full employment as its core focus and a related unemployment criterion was demanded in this respect. Moreover, the ECB should be asked to concentrate on growth and employment in addition to price stability, following here the US Federal Reserve Bank. This should also imply a redefinition of the inflation target. Finally, the ÖGB demanded that in order to ensure domestic demand within the EU, wage agreements should follow the formula of productivity increase plus inflation. As a result of Austria's comparatively less transnationalised production structure, only two unions represent workers in clearly internationally oriented and transnational production sectors, the GMT and GdC. Both supported EMU and both were in favour of European-level co-operation as expected in the first hypothesis. In relation to European co-operation, however, only the GMT was strongly involved, while the GdC saw fewer opportunities within the less active EIF EMCEF. Importantly, the support for EMU went hand in hand with a lack of critical engagement with neo-liberal restructuring. Especially the GdC was little concerned about the neo-liberal implications of monetary union.

Four unions organise workers in almost exclusively domestic production sectors, the GdG, GdE, HTV and GÖD. The former two rejected EMU due to its neo-liberal rationale. At the same time, however, they accepted that it was too late for open opposition, since Austria had become an EU as well as EMU member in 1995. Thus, the fact that Austria was already an EMU member at the time of the research for this study had an impact on these unions' positions very similar to the German case. The HTV and GÖD were more positive about EMU, but demanded that the room for manoeuvre within the criteria was used for public investment and employment programmes. In the case of the GÖD, a small ideological rift with the other unions could be discerned, considering that the GÖD is dominated by the Christian union fraction, not the socialist fraction unlike the other ÖGB affiliates. Five Austrian unions, the ANG, GBH, HGPD, GPF and GPA, organise workers in domestic production sectors with an increasingly internationally oriented/transnational aspect since EU membership in 1995. These unions were critical of EMU and neo-liberal restructuring, but this was now regarded as a matter of fact to which unions had to adapt. Hence, similar to the ÖGB position, EMU was accepted, partly even welcomed as a guarantee for a stable economy, but a change in its neo-liberal rationale was sought. Demands included an additional unemployment criterion, employment programmes at national and European level and an anti-cyclical monetary policy by the ECB through more rapid cuts in interest rates. In relation to European-level co-operation, Austrian domestic sector unions, including those organising workers in increasingly export-oriented and transnational production sectors, continued to concentrate on the national level in their policy-making efforts. This had to be seen in close relation to the traditionally extremely strong position within the structural selectivity of the Austrian form of state. As expected in the second hypothesis, unions in such a situation were much less prepared to shift competencies to the regional level. The future will tell whether the increasing undermining of these possibilities at the national level (see Chapter 4) will result in a change in Austrian unions' outlook. Only the GdE, very similar to the German union Transnet, had increasingly shifted its efforts to the European level. Considering that so many decisions on transport were taken in Brussels, the European level was deemed to have become increasingly important.

The Swedish labour movement and the focus on the domestic arena
As expected in the first hypothesis, transnational forces of labour, the companies of which were directly affected by the single currency, were supportive of EMU, while national labour opposed it. In the case of the latter, the two unions that openly rejected EMU, Handels and the Transportarbetareförbundet, linked their opposition to EMU to a clear rejection of neo-liberal restructuring, perceived to be embodied in the convergence criteria and the role of the independent, undemocratic ECB. Nevertheless, several of the national sector unions that had not adopted a position on EMU, i.e. Kommunal and Byggnads from LO and SKTF from the TCO, were less critical of neo-liberal restructuring or, indeed, had adopted some neo-liberal principles. For example, they accepted the low inflation policy as well as the role of moderate wage development in maintaining economic stability. This was even more visible in the positions of the transnational sector unions and the changed position by LO. In general, the whole debate in Sweden about EMU prior to the 2003 referendum wavered around the question of how to stabilise the national economy as an EMU member in times of economic recession. Transnational sector unions argued that a budget surplus was enough, some argued in favour of additional buffer funds, and the two LO unions opposed to EMU argued that retaining the exchange rate was essential. The possibilities of how to generate economic growth and jobs at the European level were not explored in the discussion on EMU (Interview No. 40; Stockholm, 24/06/2002).

Interestingly, there was no split of unions over European co-operation parallel to the split over EMU. The focus of national labour on the domestic level of policy-making could still be explained through a reference to the first hypothesis. In order to explain the reluctance of Swedish transnational labour as well as union confederations to co-operate more extensively at the European level and to demand a concrete further development of the Social Dimension as a major precondition for EMU support, it was necessary to turn to the structural selectivity of the Swedish form of state. Since 1997, transnational labour and capital had successfully co-operated in sectoral collective wage bargaining. In line with the second hypothesis, it was this strong influence on policy-making at the national level, which had made Swedish transnational labour reluctant to engage more strongly in co-operation at the European level.

Finally, SACO organising employees in managerial positions had come out strongly in favour of EMU from early on and even demanded neo-liberal policies such as a greater wage disparity as the best way forward to make the Swedish economy more competitive. As in the case of the French CFE-CGC and to some extent the German DBB, SACO's position could be linked back again to the first hypothesis. The neo-Gramscian perspective adopted here does not only expect a division between national and transnational labour, but also between established labour at the core of the labour market and workers on atypical contracts in the periphery. SACO clearly organises highly skilled, well-trained and flexible members of the workforce often in managerial positions. It was its members, who were likely to gain most from neo-liberal restructuring as expressed by EMU, which it consequently supported. In summary, there had, first, been a shift away from positions critical of neo-liberal restructuring in Sweden and second, the European level had drastically lost attraction. As a result, it is less likely that Swedish labour will play a leading role in European efforts to resist neo-liberal restructuring in the near future.

The different intensity of EIFs' independent activities at the European level

In relation to EMU, there was no open split between transnational sector and national sector EIFs. Of course, transnational sector unions such as the EMF and EMCEF welcomed EMU also for economic reasons, since the companies in their sectors benefited from a single currency and had to some extent already operated with European-wide common currency accounting systems. National sector unions and here especially EPSU, on the other hand, were clearly worried about the implications of the austerity budgets for the public sector resulting from the convergence criteria. The traditional public sector had been undermined due to job cuts and measures of deregulation, liberalisation and privatisation, often driven by EU directives. Nevertheless, EIFs generally viewed EMU as an important step of further European integration, leading eventually also to a social union.

In relation to the intensity of European-level co-operation and the related independent actor capacity of EIFs, however, differences were identified. In line with the first hypothesis of this study, transnational sector unions such as the EMF had clearly developed European-level activities, in this case with a strong emphasis on the co-ordination of national collective bargaining. National sector unions such as the ETUC-E, by contrast, had hardly developed beyond the stage of an international secretariat with the task of organising meetings of its national member unions. Nevertheless, the production structure does not determine unions' strategies. EMCEF, organising workers in the highly transnationalised

chemical sector, had developed its capacities much less than the EMF, while
EPSU had become increasingly active as an independent actor at the European
level. The latter could be mainly explained with reference to the second hypothesis and the increasing amount of decisions initiated by the EU in the area of
public services. The EMF with the co-ordination of national collective bargaining
and EPSU in the co-operation with other social movements both succeeded in
developing strategies, which allowed them to overcome unions' disadvantages
within the structural selectivity of the EU form of state. The EMF's focus
on the preservation of wages and working conditions across the EU and EPSU's
defence of public services demonstrate these unions' continuing resistance to
neo-liberal restructuring. Importantly, the ETUC itself moved beyond an exclusive focus on social partnership and also started to support the co-ordination
of national collective bargaining as well as to co-operate with other social
movements.

Alternatives within EMU and beyond

The analysis of trade unions' positions on EMU has made clear that while there
were some trade unions that had accepted neo-liberal concepts or were more
relaxed about them, the vast majority of unions, whether they supported
EMU or not, continued to reject neo-liberal restructuring. Many domestic
production sector unions that rejected EMU did so because of its neo-liberal
underlying rationale. The support for EMU by transnational production sector
unions did not, however, imply that they supported neo-liberal economics
either. Rather, although to a different extent, in the vast majority of cases support
for EMU was linked to demands of changing its neo-liberal implications. This
understanding, that a single currency could be combined with a non neo-liberal,
more employment-oriented policy, is also reflected in scholarly assessments (e.g.
Strange, 2002b: 351–60). EMU and a single currency by themselves do not imply
neo-liberal restructuring, but could be filled with a completely different contents.
Rather than being a problem, 'the incorporation of the separate European economies within a large, relatively closed regional economy with a single currency
could provide a degree of insulation from disturbances in the international
economy' (Martin and Ross, 2004: 3). The problem with EMU, therefore,
is not the single currency as such, but the related policy by the ECB with its
exclusive focus on price stability as the only primary goal in an overall restrictive macroeconomic policy-mix (Hein and Truger, 2005: 23–48). Martin outlines that the EU needs a sustained growth spurt to bring unemployment down
to pre-recession levels. The ECB, however, 'denies that demand management,
particularly monetary policy, has any direct responsibility for growth and
employment' (Martin, 2004: 25). Hence, when there was the opportunity for
such a sustained growth spurt in early 2000, the ECB quickly raised the interest
rate to 4.75 per cent. It was not prepared to accept temporary slightly higher
levels of inflation, necessary according to Martin in order to bring unemployment down. Instead, the ECB identified apparently rigid labour markets as the

core reason for high unemployment and, as a result, implicitly demanded that national forms of state were restructured to become more in line with the Anglo-American model of capitalism. This is not the only way, however, to explain the persistent high unemployment levels in the EU:

> An alternative view offers evidence that the primary reason why unemployment has been higher in Europe than in the US since the early 1980s, and higher in some European countries than others, is not that labor markets are more rigid but that macroeconomic policy, especially monetary policy, has been more restrictive, resulting in lower growth in output and employment and hence higher unemployment. (Martin, 2004: 27)

Again, the problem is not EMU as such, but the way it is interpreted by the ECB as well as the policy-makers, which set it up in the first place. In short, what is needed is a macroeconomic policy-mix, in which price stability, economic growth and employment are equally important goals, instead of the current situation, where price stability overrides all other objectives. In the next section, I will concentrate on what such a policy-mix could look like, in which monetary policy, fiscal policy and wage formation all play an important role.

A growth and employment-oriented macroeconomic policy-mix

Clearly, nobody wants to return to the 1970s and early 1980s when inflation reached double digit figures in several European countries. In my view, price stability has to remain one objective of the macroeconomic policy-mix. Beyond low inflation levels, however, monetary policy also needs to be demand oriented. In times of economic downturns, similar to the US Federal Reserve Bank, the ECB should cut interest rates much more drastically in order to stimulate higher investment levels into new production facilities. This was called for by many unions across the case studies. Additionally, the need for economic growth and related higher employment levels may on occasions make it imperative to accept slightly higher inflation rates, especially during periods of a sustained growth spurt after economic recessions. As Martin outlines, this will lead to lower unemployment levels without causing permanently higher inflation rates (Martin, 2004: 33). Here, the demand made by several British unions to use a symmetrical inflation target is relevant (see also Hein and Truger, 2005: 53). The ECB should react not only when inflation overshoots but also undershoots its target, since the latter implies the danger of demand contraction and, therefore, lower growth and higher unemployment levels.

Monetary policy alone, however, cannot end a recession. Fiscal policies and wage formation play an equally important role in a closely co-ordinated macroeconomic policy-mix (Hein and Truger, 2005: 48–9). As for fiscal policies, the SGP needs to be reformed so that it makes national as well as joint European-level public investment in infrastructure projects as well as human capital possible. A distinction needs to be made between borrowing for investment in social and economic infrastructure and borrowing for funding short-term spending, where the former is not part of a deficit calculation. The fact that countries such as France and Germany preferred not to meet the requirements of the SGP over facing the intensified class struggle with labour, which would have resulted from a strict implementation of the Pact (Bonefeld, 2004), indicates that reform of the Pact is a possibility as long as labour is prepared to mobilise for it. Of course, price stability must not be overlooked by fiscal policy. EU member states cannot spend their way out of recession, since the resulting high inflation rates would crowd out whatever initial gains such a free spending strategy would make. Nonetheless, my argument is that slightly higher temporary inflation rates in times of expansion after recession should be acceptable, if it implies higher growth levels. Again, public employment programmes at the domestic and European level and a re-definition of the inflation target were frequent demands by trade unions.

Finally, there is the importance of wage formation. In the EU during the 1990s, one of the core characteristics was wage moderation, where wages did not increase as much as inflation plus productivity gains. Trade unions had partly participated in these policies in national social pacts. As a result, they were often put in situations of competitive deregulation with workers in other countries, without, however, gaining concrete concessions such as, for example, investment-driven employment growth in exchange (Dølvik, 2004: 283–4). In Chapter 1, this was described as a shift from social to competitive corporatism. As a result, as indicated by several unions, overall demand levels could not be maintained due to the high unemployment levels as well as wage increases, which did not keep up with productivity gains. In a new macroeconomic policy-mix, while wage increases need to be controlled, they also need to imply the full potential of inflation plus productivity increase in order to give workers their fair share as well as ensure domestic demand levels, necessary for sustained economic growth and employment generation (Mermet, 2001: 60). 'Wage dumping between member states is ... as much to be avoided as inflationary settlements which call for restrictive intervention from the central bank' (Hein and Truger, 2005: 51–2). This is again a demand that many trade unions put forward and informs, most prominently, the EMF's co-ordination approach.

Such a change from neo-liberal economics towards a new macroeconomic policy-mix is neither automatic, nor can it be expected that suddenly enlightened governments and employers accept it. Politics is class struggle and trade unions are at the forefront of this struggle for a negotiated model of capitalism in the EU. Trade unions need to ensure that in exchange for keeping wage increases within the formula inflation plus productivity gains they receive concessions by governments, employers and the ECB in the areas of monetary and fiscal policies as indicated above. The further development of intra-union collective bargaining co-ordination at the European level is a first positive step into this direction, because it does not rely on the co-operation by employers and governments. It could potentially lead to a more general 'internal social dialogue', 'in which the trade unions would develop their autonomous cooperation amongst each other and search for shared alternative political projects for which they can jointly mobilize support in the European working class' (Hein et al., 2005: 16). This co-ordination should be supported by increasing co-operation in industrial conflicts across borders. Workers' influence within corporatist structures depends on their capacity to take common industrial actions. This requires the right to European-wide strikes, demanded by a whole range of unions in the five case studies. It also, however, puts pressure on unions themselves to put in place the necessary institutional structures, which make these joint actions organisationally possible in the first place. In a second step, demands should include that the macroeconomic dialogue is re-formed into a proper corporatist institution, able to offer specific monetary policies and a more general focus on growth and employment as equally important goals as price stability in exchange for wage moderation (Hein and Truger, 2005: 60; see also Watt, 2005: 251–7). Moreover, the multi-sector social dialogue needs to be restructured so that it allows the discussion of much more fundamental macroeconomic issues related to the overall policy-mix. In short, sustained pressure by trade unions should focus on the establishment of tripartite institutions at the European level along the traditional lines of social corporatism. This also implies the removal of ECB independence. In order to reduce the high unemployment levels across Europe, this is not only a possible, but also a necessary strategy forward.

As outlined above, this strategy is feasible, because it combines the core demands of unions across the EU. Nevertheless, while it would improve the overall situation from a labour perspective in that it rolled back neo-liberalism, this strategy does not question capitalism in general and the private ownership of the means of production in particular. Hence, while it constitutes a viable strategy in the short-term, able to achieve concrete improvements for people across the EU, my argument is that it should be regarded not as an endpoint, but as the first stage of a more radical, medium- to long-term strategy in what Gramsci labelled a 'war of position', in which the foundations for a more fundamental change are slowly built from within a well established civil society (Gramsci, 1971: 238). In other words, the struggle for a new macroeconomic policy-mix can provide the platform for mobilising workers more widely in support for more far-reaching developments. A further step in this transformation strategy, in my view, is a renewed push for economic democracy.

Economic democracy as a challenge to capitalism

Economic democracy signifies system change in that it challenges capital's prerogative over the ownership of the means of production as well as investment and company employment decisions. By attacking the private ownership of the means of production, economic democracy tackles the source of exploitation and inequality. In the 1970s, the Swedish labour movement had gone furthest in its demand for economic democracy. Employers understood this clearly in Sweden. As shown in Chapter 4, it was especially the moment of the WIFs initiative that Swedish capital mobilised for a neo-liberal, market-oriented policy, thereby breaking the national class compromise with labour.

In the tumultuous 1980s and 1990s, characterised by neo-liberal offensives across the world, trade unions were on the defensive desperately trying to preserve as many rights as possible. Debates about economic democracy went quiet. In my view, now is a good moment to revive these discussions. Neo-liberal economics has led to a situation, where shareholder values have increasingly become the most important economic goal. The analysis of the various forms of state projects in Chapter 4 indicated that even in those countries, where traditional tripartite institutions had been retained to some extent such as Austria, Germany and Sweden, there was a shift towards neo-liberal restructuring. Capitalism in the current phase is increasingly characterised by institutional ownership of the means of production, where pension funds, insurance companies and investment funds control large parts of production through the stock market. Lindberg raises two crucial questions in this respect. 'The first is how do we want the money that belongs to [workers], but which is deposited in banks, insurance companies and pension funds to be used' (Lindberg, 2005: 12)? He demands that a strategy is developed, which ensures that workers are represented in the leadership of these funds. This could be a first step towards a more general, full democratic control of FDI and private domestic investment as demanded by Panitch (2001: 381). Second, Lindberg asks 'who is best suited to decide the organisation of labour and production – the shareholders or the employees' (Lindberg, 2005: 12)? In the increasingly knowledge-driven production processes, employees are frequently in a better position to decide flexibly how production is organised best. Technological development may have led to a situation in which the current ownership and power structures have become obsolete. In sum, economic democracy requires a two-pronged strategy. First, the demand needs to be made that the big pension and investment funds come under popular control ensuring a collective ownership of the means of production from above. Second, from below, the demand that employees decide themselves over how the production process is organised and investment is allocated at the plant level has to be made.

Of course, whether a strategy of economic democracy could be successful is again a matter of class struggle and, thus, open-ended. Above, it was already outlined that intensified intra-union co-operation across Europe is one way of constructing a counter-neo-liberal offensive. For more drastic changes beyond the capitalist social relations of production, however, a broader alliance of social forces is required. In many respects, this links to the possibilities of more intensive co-operation between trade unions and social movements in the resistance to neo-liberal restructuring. This study demonstrated that several unions had already expanded the social basis for their counter-neo-liberal struggle through co-operation with other social movements. At the European level, it was especially EPSU that pursued this strategy, but national unions too such as the French G10-Solidaires, SUD and FSU had started to focus on wider struggles and forged alliances with groups, which represented conflicts beyond the workplace. The final section will look more closely at the possibilities of this co-operation and concentrate on recent developments around the ESF.

The co-operation with new social movements within the ESF

The current wave of worldwide protests against capitalism is frequently associated with the emergence of a transnational civil society, re-establishing control over global market forces, freed from national shackles. Optimistic assessments treat the emergence of global civil society as transcending nation-state structures and providing the basis, by default, of opposition to neo-liberal globalisation through the establishment of some form of cosmopolitan social democracy (Held et al., 1999: 449–52; Held and McGrew, 2002: 135–6; Scholte, 2000a: 285, 291). As critics have pointed out, however, transnational civil society is to a large extent shaped by states (Chandler, 2003: 336) and transnational civil society actors potentially strengthen national borders instead of overcoming them (Colás, 2002: 172). Similarly, instead of resisting global neo-liberal restructuring, some transnational actors may actually further it. Business associations as representatives of transnational capital are frequently regarded as being the driving force behind neo-liberal globalisation (Gill, 1995). In short, there is no automatic link between transnational civil society on the one hand, and the erosion of national borders and increasing political control of market forces at the global level on the other. Moreover, these generally reformist suggestions vis-à-vis global capitalism overlook the fact that the source of inequality and exploitation is not to be found in the lack of political authority and control, but in the way capitalist social relations are organised. They fall 'into the trap of fetishizing the political expressions of global capitalism by assuming that the political forms of rule it throws up can be transformed in isolation from the social relations that underpin this system' (Colás, 2002: 160). By contrast, in line with the neo-Gramscian approach employed in this study, political developments related to this wave of worldwide protests are analysed as a result of class struggle around exploitation. As outlined in Chapter 2, the focus on exploitation implies that class struggle is not reduced to confrontations at the workplace. As a consequence of the extension of exploitation within the sphere of social reproduction by neo-liberal globalisation, the struggle by progressive environmental and social movements also needs to be understood as an instance of class struggle (van der Pijl, 1998: 46–8). It is in this sense that the potential co-operation between trade unions, as representatives of the various working class fractions, and social movements, organising those progressive forces that resist the neo-liberal restructuring of the sphere of social reproduction, is analysed within the historical specificity of the capitalist social relations of production.

From 6 to 10 November 2002, European anti-neo-liberal globalisation movements including trade unions and other social movements, gathered in Florence, Italy for the first European Social Forum (ESF). During 400 meetings ranging from small group workshops to large plenary discussions, around 32,000 to 40,000 delegates from all over Europe, plus 80 further countries, debated issues related to the three main themes of the Forum: 'Globalization and [neo-]liberalism', 'War and Peace', as well as 'Rights-Citizenship-Democracy' (Bieler and Morton, 2004b). The extent to which this led to co-operation between social movements and trade unions should not be exaggerated, because first only a selection of trade unions was present. While high level representatives attended from Southern European unions including the French CGT and several EIFs such as the ETF, big Northern European unions were absent. Missing were, for example, the German unions IG Metall and Ver.di, as were all the British unions except for the RMT. Swedish unions were almost completely absent, while Austrian unions, although strong on the ground as far as rank-and-file participation in the Forum was concerned, had not sent high-level representatives either. The small, more radical unions, on the other hand, such as the French SUD unions, its confederation G10-Solidaires, the FSU as well as the Italian COBAS were actively involved in the proceedings. As it was discussed in Chapters 5 and 6, G10-Solidaires and SUD unions had already had a history of co-operation with other social movements in their attempt to build a progressive national and international anti-neo-liberal movement.

Unsurprisingly, there were clear tensions between established unions on the one hand, and these new, more radical unions on the other. While established trade unions continued to focus on 'social partnership' with employers and state representatives in order to assert the demands of their members, radical trade unions emphasised the importance of bottom-up organisation with a focus on strikes, demonstrations and co-operation with other social movements to broaden the social basis of resistance. Hence, the latter frequently accused the former of having let themselves being co-opted into neo-liberal restructuring due to their involvement within the EU institutions. Social movements too are a rather mixed group of organisations ranging from groups such as ATTAC, which generally concentrated on influencing politics through research and lobbying, extra-parliamentary action groups such as the Italian *disobediente*, single-issue movements such as Habitat International Coalition and its commitment to secure housing for everybody, to Euromarches organising the unemployed across Europe. It was partly also this diversity of groups that made trade unions wary of closer co-operation, questioning the representativeness and internal accountability of these movements. In turn, the latter were rather sceptical of trade unions' hierarchical internal organisation and queried their willingness of confronting neo-liberal restructuring.

These differences, however, should not make us overlook the commonalities and resulting possible joint activities. Despite different structures and strategies, all movements present at the ESF identified neo-liberal globalisation as the main target for resistance. This included the economic as well as militaristic dimension, as embodied in the war on Iraq, of globalisation. And despite all the differences between unions and social movements as far as their internal structure, history and strategies are concerned, it was this common rejection of neo-liberal globalisation that prepared the ground for a range of common projects and activities. First, it was at the ESF that anti-war organisations agreed to hold European – and in the event worldwide – demonstrations against the impending war on Iraq on 15 February 2003. Second, neo-liberal restructuring of the public sector within the EU – pushed by the European Commission and the Lisbon European Council summit conclusions in 2000 – and the GATS negotiations at the global level, was perceived as the main threats to peoples' livelihoods and the focal point for joint struggles. The consensus was that public services must not become a new realm for capital accumulation. As a result of the interaction at the ESF, demonstrations in Brussels were organised by Belgian unions and ATTAC, on 9 February 2003, to keep public services out of GATS followed by a day of national action, on 13 March 2003, linked to the same theme. Similar co-operation efforts were initiated and/or deepened in relation to the demand for a European minimum income, the combat of tax evasion, as well as the co-ordinated demands for the introduction of a Tobin Tax on currency speculations (Bieler and Morton, 2004b: 316–19).

Hopes of an intensification of co-operation between unions and social movements were dented by the second ESF in Paris in November 2003. In contrast to the ESF in Florence, the ETUC organised its own forum prior to the ESF on 11 and 12 November 2003. No high-ranking ETUC official participated on panels of the ESF itself. In other words, rather than participating in an open-ended process of discussion facing potentially critical questions, a format of debate was chosen, which could be controlled by the trade union hierarchy. The concluding demonstration on 15 November 2003 further reflected the low profile of trade unions. In contrast to Florence, where the Italian Confederazione Generale Italiana del Lavoro (CGIL) had mobilised the masses, French unions, although present, had not turned out in the same number. An impression was created that established trade unions intended to put the breaks on developments, which they found increasingly unable to control. The Paris ESF as a whole was described by one commentator as a cultural happening, which had lost its political edge (Tormey, 2004). On the positive side, neo-liberal globalisation and here especially the threatened restructuring of the public sector remained the common ground of all groups present. Additionally, increased participation by groups from CEE gave reason for hope in relation to an expansion of resistance within the EU.

The third ESF in London in October 2004 became crucial as a sign of what future direction the ESF would take. Although smaller than the previous two ESFs, London was reassuring as far as the co-operation between social movements and trade unions was concerned. Instead of organising their own event, the ETUC was again present at the main Forum. Other unions represented by leading officials were the German IG Metall and Ver.di, the Austrian GdE, and especially British unions came out in force for the first time including UNISON, the GMB, the T&G as well as the CWU. The defence of the public sector against privatisation and the introduction of market principles was at the forefront of the debate more than ever. In short, London proved to be a positive step forward (Bieler and Morton, 2006).

As for the overall impact of the ESF, a lot depends on the extent of joint initiatives, which are carried out as a result of the gathering. The Forum provides a meeting place for different groups, it provides the space to establish common positions and identify other groups with similar strategies for joint activities.

The activities themselves have to be implemented after the ESF. A positive sign is the dissemination of the idea to hold social forums itself. The ESF was inspired by the World Social Forums, held for the first time in Porto Alegre/Brazil in 2001. In turn, the ESF has inspired social forums at the national and sub-national level. For example, in May 2004 German social movements and trade unions, including the IG Metall, Ver.di and the IG BAU organised a conference with the task to identify alternatives to neo-liberalism (Eironline, 10 June 2004, http://www.eiro.eurofound.eu.int/2004/06/inbrief/de0406202n.html; 04/11/2004). It was at this conference that an agreement was reached on organising the first German Social Forum in Erfurt from 21 to 24 July 2005 (http://sozialforum 2005.de/; 01/08/2005). In short, the importance of the ESF is not only the event itself, but also the various processes that are initiated as a result.

Interestingly, criticism of the draft EU Constitution,[3] already voiced at the second ESF in Paris, came more prominently to the fore in London as a line of possible criticism of neo-liberal restructuring. At the same time, this issue also demonstrated the continuing tensions within the labour movement. At its annual spring meeting in Brussels on 22 and 23 March 2005, the European Council decided to send back the highly controversial EU directive on the provision of services in the Internal Market for further revisions (Eironline, 30 April 2005; http://www.eiro.eurofound.eu.int/2005/04/feature/eu0504201f.html; 31/07/2005). This was hailed by the ETUC as a major success of its campaign against the restructuring of the public sector. In turn, the ETUC then strongly argued in favour of a 'yes' in the various national referenda on the Constitution, as this 'is the most pro-Social Europe treaty that Europe has ever had' (ETUC, 2005). By contrast, some members of the no-camp in France criticised the Treaty for not including fundamental rights, the implicit threat of the liberalisation of public services, its defence component and the continuing democratic deficit (Le Monde diplomatique, May 2005: 5). Especially Part III of the Constitutional Treaty was singled out as enshrining the predominance of neo-liberal economics within the EU (Cassen, 2005: 30–1). Unsurprisingly, the no-camp in the French referendum campaign included radical trade unions such as the G10-Solidaires, which argued that 'this "constitution" sets in stone an anti-democratic institutional mechanism, the primacy of competition law, the weakening of public services. The principles of an economic liberalism without limits is the backbone of the text and makes free and unhindered competition the supreme value of the European Union' (G10-Solidaires, 2005). Similarly, FO openly defied the ETUC and rejected the Constitution as yet another example of how economic interests would be the predominant driving force behind European integration (FO, 2005). The important role by ATTAC-France in the no-camp (Cassen, 2005), itself consisting of several unions such as SUD-PTT and FSU (Interview No. 64; Paris, 16/12/2002; and Interview No. 68; Paris, 18/12/2002) plus other social movements, illustrated the possible union-social movement co-operation over this issue. Nevertheless, these contradictory positions with the ETUC indicate that rather than providing common ground for joint resistance, the Constitutional Treaty split trade unions and social movements.[4]

Equally disturbing was the rift between Western and Eastern European labour over the 2004 EU enlargement. It was the former, and here especially the German DGB and the Austrian ÖGB, which pushed successfully for a transition period of up to seven years in relation to the free movement of labour in fear of the consequences of the large income gap between East and West on Western European labour markets. As Bohle and Husz make clear, this political victory, based on a lack of transnational solidarity, may turn out to have disastrous consequences for labour in general in that it may result in regime competition between the Eastern and Western labour movements. 'Thus, paradoxically, the political victory of Western labour in the accession negotiations is likely to contribute to the weakening of the position of labour and a further strengthening of the position of capital within the enlarged EU' (Bohle and Husz, 2003: 32). Trade unions are not automatically part of a resistance movement and especially the closer integration between Western and Eastern Europe proves to be a challenge.

Tensions between Southern and Northern labour movements could make it equally difficult to forge a successful counter-hegemonic alliance. Similarly to Eastern Europe's subordinated position to Western Europe in transnational production structures, inequalities between North and South in transnational production structures may imply conflicting interests between the labour movements of the two hemispheres. Combined but uneven development and even the development of underdevelopment in the South (Frank, 1969) implied that gains by Northern trade unions in the post-war decades were often paid for with intensified exploitation of workers in the South. It is an important challenge for trade unions in the North that successful transformation in Europe is not counterproductive for Southern labour movements' struggles against capitalist exploitation. In a way, it is Northern labour movements, which can learn a lot from their Southern counterparts about the successful formation of global social movement unionism, where 'unions move beyond their traditional workplace boundaries to form alliances with other civil society movements within the nation state, whilst at the same time creating a new global union form' (Lambert and Webster, 2001: 46; see also Lambert, 2002).

The open-ended struggle for a social Europe

As exploitation is rooted within the capitalist social relations of production organised around the private ownership of the means of production and wage labour, trade unions, which are by default at the core of exploitation within production, are of primary importance for successful resistance. As Panitch makes clear, 'unless a very substantial part of the labour movement becomes involved, no fundamental socio-economic change is realizable' (Panitch, 2001: 368). The continuing rejection of neo-liberal restructuring by trade unions as expressed in their positions on EMU does indicate that trade unions are potentially willing to play a significant role in the wider opposition movement against neo-liberal globalisation. Potentially successful avenues for organising include especially intra trade union co-ordination at the European level as well as an emphasis on wider co-operation with other social movements critical of neo-liberal globalisation. Importantly, the latter also requires union internal restructuring to become more inclusive ethnic and gender wise organisations, in which all members have the opportunity to participate much more directly in decision-making. 'The challenge is to discover ... how to build fully inclusive labour movements which are democratically structured in such ways as to encourage the development of the capacities of all members of the working class in as many facets of their lives as possible' (Panitch, 2001: 370). A successful form of new organisation could be what some have called 'a transnational "social movement unionism" that links diverse groups and networks in opposition to neo-liberal globalization' (Taylor and Mathers 2002b: 94). This internal restructuring is clearly one of unions' biggest challenges. If they fail to achieve this, strategies of resistance beyond the short-term objective of a new macroeconomic policy-mix will be impossible.

Once transformed into more inclusive organisations, it will be crucial that trade unions work together with social movements in order to stem the shift towards an Anglo-American, neo-liberal economic model in the EU and beyond. Strategically, the labour movement together with new social movements needs to work on a new vision for society. A focus on a macroeconomic policy-mix with an emphasis on growth and employment is initially important. In the longer run, economic democracy, challenging capitalism directly, may be the next step forward. Combined with demands for a wider democratisation of society, as expressed in the third theme of the ESF in Florence, such a strategy has got the potential to transform capitalism more fundamentally. In order to have a chance of success, the various activities need to take place at multiple levels including the company, local, national, European and international level. It may involve a combination of tactics, recognising that co-operation in corporatist institutions may be as necessary as more radical forms of opposition. While the former is often the only way of making gains in the short-term, necessary to maintain support, the latter is essential in view of more drastic change in the medium- to long-term. The experience of SUD unions, which despite their radical, confrontational orientation have been pushed to strike deals with employers, when the latter's proposals converged with workers' interests (Damesin and Denis, 2005: 25–7), demonstrates that the two strategies are not mutually exclusive (Schulten, 2004: 324). The tensions within the labour movement over the Constitutional Treaty, eastward EU enlargement and the potential North-South divide, indicated above, show that success is not automatic. Nevertheless, the ESF, to take place in Athens in 2006 next, possibly provides the framework to overcome these tensions through the hopefully increasing participation of Eastern European social forces as well as its focus on global justice. The increasingly militaristic form of neo-liberal domination expressed in the 'global war on terror', relying more and more on coercion instead of consent, indicates in my opinion that this is a potentially historical moment, in which resistance to neo-liberal restructuring has chances of success. Trade unions are in a good position to play a crucial role in these struggles.

Notes

1 For example, in view of the 2005 general elections, unions and 'New' Labour concluded the so-called Warwick agreement in July 2004, when trade union leaders held talks with Labour government ministers at the Labour party's National Policy Forum at Warwick University, UK. The resulting agreement included gains such as the promise to end the two-tier workforce in the public sector, where outsourcing had led to less good conditions for new employees, the extension of statutory holidays to a minimum of four weeks in addition to eight days bank holiday, as well as issues such as the inclusion of pensions into the remit of pay negotiations in unionised workplaces (Eironline, 6 September 2004, http://www.eiro.eurofound.eu.int/2004/09/inbrief/uk0409102n.html; 27/07/2005). Unions participating in the agreement praised it as an important step forward (e.g. Amicus, 2004; UNISON, 2004). Other unions were more sceptical and pointed out that 'even if the agreement was implemented in full there could still be an opt-out on the 48 hours legal working week cap, the link between state pension and wages would remain unrestored, 1980s anti-union laws would still be on the statute books after 13 years in power, and there would be more PFI investment projects and further privatisation' (UNIFI, 2004). More critical commentators even regarded the agreement as a strategy by New Labour to co-opt unions in exchange for little concrete concessions (Socialist Review, 2004).
2 Unions are divided over the best way forward vis-à-vis the Labour Party. While the majority focuses on reclaiming the party, some unions such as the RMT have cut their links with Labour (Charlwood, 2004: 391–2).
3 The European Convention, established under the leadership of the former French President Valerie Giscard d'Estaing in February 2002, adopted a 'Draft Treaty establishing a Constitution for Europe' in July 2003. After sometimes conflictual discussions within the European Council, an agreement on the Constitutional Treaty was reached at its meeting on 18–19 June 2004. Nevertheless, the Treaty still had to be ratified by the twenty-five EU members, including via referenda in several countries. On 29 May, the French population rejected the Treaty. The Dutch followed three days later and rejected the Treaty by an even larger margin (Le Monde diplomatique, June 2005: 2).
4 Taylor and Mathers identify a similar division within the trade union movement in relation to the European Charter of Fundamental Rights, discussed by the Nice European Council summit in December 2000 (Taylor and Mathers, 2004: 274–5).

Bibliography

For reasons of clarity, the bibliography is divided into interviews, primary sources and secondary sources. Primary sources inlude official documents by trade unions as well as statements by union officials. All other references are included in secondary sources. Material by the *European Industrial Relations Observatory Online* (http://www.eiro.eurofound.eu.int/) is clearly referred to in the text through the exact date and specific web site of the individual documents. It is not, therefore, additionally listed in this bibliography.

Interviews

Interview No. 1: Director of the section International and European Affairs, Head of the International Department, Deutscher Beamtenbund (DBB); Bonn, 22 January, 2001.

Interview No. 2: Political Officer, Section for General Politics and International Affairs, Gewerkschaft Handel, Banken und Versicherungen (HBV); Düsseldorf, 22 January, 2001.

Interview No. 3: Political Officer, Section for Economics, Transport and International Affairs/Trade Union Secretary, Transnet; Frankfurt, 25 January 2001.

Interview No. 4: Political Officer, Section for International Relations, Deutsche Postgewerkschaft (DPG); Frankfurt, 25 January 2001.

Interview No. 5: Political Officer for General and International Affairs, IG Bauen-Agrar-Umwelt (IG BAU); Frankfurt, 29 January 2001.

Interview No. 6: Economist, Department for Economy, Technology, Environment, IG Metall; Frankfurt, 30 January 2001.

Interview No. 7: Member of collective bargaining negotiation team, IG Metall, Regional District Baden-Württemberg, Regional Headquarters Stuttgart; Stuttgart, 31 January 2001.

Interview No. 8: Political Officer, Central Office for General Affairs, Section for Economic and Financial Policy, Gewerkschaft Öffentliche Dienste Transport und Verkehr (ÖTV); Stuttgart, 1 February 2001.

Interview No. 9: Political Officer, Section for Europe and International Relations, IG Bergbau, Chemie, Energie (IG BCE); Hannover, 5 February 2001.

Interview No. 10: Secretary of the Central Executive, Head of the Section for Economic Policy and Collective Wage Bargaining, Deutscher Gewerkschaftsbund (DGB); Berlin, 6 February 2001.

Interview No. 11: Political Officer, Section for Economic Policies, Deutsche Angestellten-Gewerkschaft (DAG); Hamburg, 9 February, 2001.

Interview No. 12: Political Officer, Head of the Section for Economics, Gewerkschaft Nahrung-Genuss-Gastätten (NGG); Hamburg, 9 February 2001.

Interview No. 13: International Officer, Research Department, Manufacturing, Science, Finance (MSF); London, 26 March 2001.

Interview No. 14: Head of Research, Communication Workers' Union (CWU); London, 27 March 2001.

Interview No. 15: Specialist Tutor, Education and International Department, Transport and General Workers' Union (T&G); London, 27 March 2001.

Interview No. 16: General Secretary, General, Municipal and Boilermakers' Union (GMB); London, 28 March 2001.

Interview No. 17: Senior Economist, Trade Union Congress (TUC); London, 28 March 2001.

Interview No. 18: Political Officer, National Union of Rail, Maritime and Transport Workers (RMT); London, 29 March 2001.

Interview No. 19: Head of Policy, UNISON; London, 2 May 2001.

Interview No. 20: International Officer, Amalgamated Engineering and Electrical Union (AEEU); Hayes (Kent), 23 May 2001.

Interview No. 21: Research Officer, Union of Construction, Allied Trades and Technicians (UCATT); London, 29 May 2001.

Interview No. 22: President/General Secretary, Gewerkschaft Handel, Transport, Verkehr (HTV); Wien, 18 March 2002.

Interview No. 23: Senior Political Officer, Gewerkschaft der Gemeindebediensteten (GdG); Wien, 18 March 2002.

Interview No. 24: Head of International Relations, Gewerkschaft der Privatangestellten (GPA); Wien, 18 March 2002.

Interview No. 25: Political Officer, Section for Economic Policy, Österreichischer Gewerkschaftsbund (ÖGB); Wien, 18 March 2002.

Interview No. 26: Economist, Arbeiterkammer (AK); Wien, 19 March 2002.

Interview No. 27: Deputy General Secretary, Gewerkschaft der Post- und Fernmeldebediensteten (GPF); Wien, 19 March 2002.

Interview No. 28: President, Gewerkschaft der Eisenbahner (GdE); Wien, 20 March 2002.

Interview No. 29: Senior Political Officer, Gewerkschaft Metall-Textil (GMT); Wien, 20 March 2002.

Interview No. 30: Secretary of the Chairman, Gewerkschaft Bau-Holz (GBH); Wien, 20 March 2002.

Interview No. 31: President, Gewerkschaft Hotel, Gastgewerbe, Persönlicher Dienst (HGPD); Wien, 21/03/2002.

Interview No. 32: International Officer, Gewerkschaft der Chemiearbeiter (GdC); Wien, 21 March 2002.

Interview No. 33: Political Officer, Gewerkschaft Agrar-Nahrung-Genuss (ANG); Wien, 22 March 2002.

Interview No. 34: Head of Section for Public Relations, Organisation and Economics, Gewerkschaft Öffentlicher Dienst (GÖD); telephone interview, 14 May 2002.

Interview No. 35: Economist, Union of Commercial Employees (Handels/LO); Stockholm, 20 June 2002.

Interview No. 36: Head of Research Department/Researcher, Building Workers' Union (Byggnads/LO); Stockholm, 20 June 2002.

Interview No. 37: International Secretary, Swedish Teachers' Union (Lärerförbundet/ TCO); Segelbåtsvägen 15, Stora Essingen; Stockholm, 20 June 2002.

Interview No. 38: EU-co-ordinator, Research Department, Metal Workers' Union/LO; Stockholm, 20 June 2002.

Interview No. 39: Researcher/Researcher/Union Officer, Negotiator/International Secretary, Industrial Workers' Union (Industrifacket/LO); Stockholm, 24 June 2002.

Interview No. 40: Head of Research, Paper Workers' Union (Pappers/LO); Stockholm, 24 June 2002.

Interview No. 41: International Secreatary/Political Officer, Municipal Workers' Union (Kommunal/LO); Stockholm, 24 June 2002.

Interview No. 42: Deputy General Secretary, Statstjänstemannaförbundet (ST/TCO); Stockholm, 25 June 2002.

Interview No. 43: International Economist, Landsorganisationen (LO); Stockholm, 25 June 2002.

Interview No. 44: Chief Economist, Tjänstemännens Centralorganisation (TCO); Stockholm, 25 June 2002.

Interview No. 45: International Secretary, Svenska Akademikers Centralorganisation (SACO); Stockholm, 26 June 2002.

Interview No. 46: International Secretary, Transport Workers' Union (Transportarbetareförbundet/LO); Stockholm, 26 June 2002.

Interview No. 47: Deputy Head, International Department, Landsorganisationen (LO); Stockholm, 27 June 2002.

Interview No. 48: National Officer, Sveriges Kommunaltjänstemannaförbund (SKTF/ TCO); Stockholm, 27 June 2002.

Interview No. 49: Senior Economist, Svenska Industritjanstemannaförbundet (SIF/TCO); Stockholm, 28 June 2002.

Interview No. 50: Research Officer/Assistant General Secretary, Finansförbundet/TCO; Stockholm, 28 June 2002.

Interview No. 51: Sécretaire Fédérale; CGT des Personnels des Secteurs Financiers (CGT-finance); Montreuil/Paris, 9 September 2002.

Interview No. 52: Member of the Federal Bureau, Officer for European Affairs and representative in the EMF, Fédération des Travailleurs de la Métallurgie (CGT-metallurgie); Montreuil/Paris, 11 September 2002.

Interview No. 53: International Officer, Fédération Nationale des Industries Chimiques (FNIC-CGT); Monetreuil/Paris, 11 September 2002.

Interview No. 54: Jean-Marie Roux, Banque de France, member of the CFDT-Banques council, CFDT-Fédération des banques and societés financiers (CFDT-Banques); Paris, 11 September 2002.

Interview No. 55: International Officer, Confederal Secretariat, Confédération française démocratique du travail (CFDT); Paris, 12 September, 2002.

Interview No. 56: General Secretary, UNSA-Education; telephone interview, 12 September 2002.

Interview No. 57: Jacques Vallet, Fédération Nationale des Travailleurs de la Construction (CGT-construction); Montreuil/Paris, 12 September 2002.

Interview No. 58: Confederal Secretary, Economic Affairs, Force Ouvrière (FO); Paris, 12 September 2002.

Interview No. 59: Confederal Secretary, member of the executive board and Head of the European and International Department, Force Ouvrière (FO); Paris, 13 September 2002.

Interview No. 60: Economics Department, Confédération générale du travail (CGT); Paris, 13 September 2002.

Interview No. 61: European Officer/Economic Researcher, Confédération française des travailleurs chrétiens (CFTC); Paris, 13 September 2002.

Interview No. 62: International Economist, Landsorganisationen (LO); telephone interview, 6 December 2002.

Interview No. 63: Federal Secretary, Postal and Telecommunications Workers' Federation of Solidaires, Unitaires et Démocratiques (SUD-PTT); Paris, 16 December 2002.

Interview No. 64: Member of the Administration Council of ATTAC-France and representative of the union SUD-PTT; Paris, 16 December 2002.

Interview No. 65: General Delegate (Secretary), Group of 10-L'Union syndicale Solidaires (G10-Solidaires); Paris, 16 December 2002.

Interview No. 66: National Federal Secretary, International Affairs, Force Ouvrière de la Communication; Paris, 17 December 2002.

Interview No. 67: National Secreatary, responsible for European and international affairs, Union nationale des syndicats autonomes (UNSA); Paris, 17 December 2002.

Interview No. 68: President of Research Institute of Fédération Syndicale Unitaire (FSU) and member of the ATTAC-France Administration Council; Paris, 18 December 2002.

Interview No. 69: Research Officer, Finansförbundet/TCO; telephone interview, 17 January 2003.

Interview No. 70: Political Officer, European Trade Union Confederation (ETUC); Brussels, 21 January 2003.

Interview No. 71: Economist-Research Officer, European Trade Union Institute (ETUI); Brussels, 21 January 2003.

Interview No. 72: Deputy General Secretary, European Federation of Public Service Unions (EPSU); Brussels, 22 January 2003.

Interview No. 73: General Secretary, European Mine, Chemical and Energy Workers' Federation (EMCEF); Brussels, 22 January 2003.

Interview No. 74: General Secretary, European Transport Workers' Federation (ETF); Brussels, 22 January 2003.

Interview No. 75: General Secretary, European Trade Union Committee for Education (ETUC-E); Brussels, 22 January 2003.

Interview No. 76: Deputy General Secretary, European Metalworker's Federation (EMF); Brussels, 23 January 2003.

Interview No. 77: General Secretary, Confédération française de l'encadrement-Confédération générale des cadres (CFE-CGC); telephone interview, 13 February 2003.

Primary sources

AEEU-AMICUS (2003) 'Treasury Select Committee on the Euro – Examination of Witnesses (Questions 624–639)'; http://www.publications.parliament.uk/pa/cm200203/cmselect/cmtreasy/187/30210a09.htm; accessed 08/04/2005.

AK (2001) *Strategie von Lissabon. Eine Analyse der Bundeskammer für Arbeiter und Angestellte,* Wien: Bundeskammer für Arbeiter und Angestellte.

Amicus (2004) 'Report from the Forum'; http://www.amicustheunion.org/default.aspx?page=985; accessed 27/07/2005.

Arondel, P. (1997) 'Euro: politique d'abord?', *Questions Economiques et Sociales,* 50: 8–10.

Arondel, P. (1998) 'Euro: le saut dan l'inconnu?', *Questions Economiques et Sociales,* 57: 11–14.

Arondel, P. (2001) 'Europe: une orthodoxie libérale suicidaire?', *Questions Economiques et Sociales*, 96–7: 11–14.

Bailacq, S. (1999a) 'Dialogue social européen: des enjeux à bien saisir', *Questions Economiques et Sociales*, 65: 13–15.

Bailacq, S. (1999b) 'Comités d'entreprise européens: un nouvel outil pour l'action syndicale', *Questions Economiques et Sociales*, 69: 20–1.

Bass, J. (1997) 'Ne pas manquer le train de l'Euro', *CFDT Magazine*, 224: 28–9.

Baunay, Y. (2002) 'Réflexions sur le tournant Lisbonne-Barcelone', *Nouveaux Regards: Éducation-Recherche-Culture*, 17: 16–17.

Cambus, C. (2000) 'L'Europe à la page', *Encadrement Magazine*, 89: 36–7.

Cazettes, J.-L. (2000) 'Adresse à Lionel Jospin et à Martine Aubry dans le cadre des consultations relatives au sommet européen de Lisbonne', http://www.cfecgc.org/vignettes/sommet_Europe.pdf; accessed 26/11/2002.

Cazettes, J.-L. (2002) *Qu'est-ce que la CFE-CGC?*, Paris: l'Archipel.

Charlot, B. (2001) 'Forum Social Mondial de Porto Alegre', *Nouveaux Regards: Éducation-Recherche-Culture*, 16: 45–53.

CFDT (1997) 'L'Europe en poche, l'Europe en marche', *Brochure CFDT*, 133.

CFDT (1998) 'Le syndicalisme face au défi de la mondialisation. Lille – 44e congrès CFDT', *Syndicalisme hebdo*, 2709.

CFDT (1999) 'Lille – 44e congrès CFDT: la force des choix, la valeur des actes', *Syndicalisme hebdo*, 2725.

CFDT (2001) *Our Values*, Paris: CFDT.

CFDT (2002) *CFDT's International Policy. Nantes – 45e congrès CFDT*, Paris: CFDT.

CFE-CGC (2000) 'European Work Councils: Reports and Perspectives (Seminar 17, 18 February 2000, Paris)'; http:// www.cfecgc.org/vignettes/SeminaireCEEGB.pdf; accessed 26/11/2002.

CFE-CGC (2001) 'Involvement of C.F.E.-CGC at European and International Levels'; http://www.cfecgc.org/vignettes/implicationdelacgc.pdf; accessed 26/11/2002.

CFE-CGC (2002) 'Négociation européenne sur le télétravail'; http://www.cfecgc.org/vignettes/teletravail0702.pdf; accessed 26/11/2002.

CGT (2000) *Planete plein emploi: réfrome des institutions financiers internationales*, Paris: CGT.

CGT (2002) 'Initial Proposals for the Contribution to the Discussion on the Future of Europe'; http://www.cgt.fr/ei/html/rubrique/?id_parent=1288&aff_docref=1&aff_ensavoirplus=1; accessed 03/02/2005.

Coalition for Green and Social Procurement's Amendment (2002) 'Proposal for a Directive on the Co-ordination of Procedures for the Award of Public Supply Contracts, Public Service Contracts and Public Works Contracts'; http://www.epsu.org/projects/procure/CoalEN.pdf; accessed 30/01/2003.

Commission (2003) 'Green Paper on Services of General Interest (21/05/2003)'; http://europa.eu.int/eur-lex/en/com/gpr/2003/com2003_0270en01.pdf; accessed 17/06/2003.

DAG (1997) *Für mehr Beschäftigung und soziale Gerechtigkeit – die Europäische Wirtschafts- und Währungsunion (EWWU): Chancen, Risiken und Gestaltungserfordernisse*, Hamburg: Deutsche Angestellten-Gewerkschaft.

DAG (2000) *WIPO-Dienst, Juli 2000*, Hamburg: DAG.

Deygas, G. (2001) 'L'euro, notre monnaie', *Questions Economiques et Sociales*, 96–7: 8–10.

DGB (1995) 'Zur Europäischen Wirtschafts- und Währungsunion (EWWU)', *Informationen zur Wirschafts- und Strukturpolitik*, 11.

DGB (1996) 'DGB-Positionspapier zur europäischen Beschäftgungspolitik (Beschluss des DGB-Bundesvorstandes vom 01.10.1996)', *Informationen zur Wirtschafts- und Strukturpolitik*, 8.

DGB (1997a) 'Währungsunion ja – aber auf die Ausgestaltung kommt es an! Gewerkschaftliche Thesen zur europäischen Wirtschafts- und Währungsunion', *Informationen zur Wirschafts- und Strukturpolitik*, 3.

DGB (1997b) 'DGB: Zustimmung zur EWWU abhängig von Ausgestaltung und Umsetzung', http://www.dgb.de/idaten/ewwu.doc; accessed 06/08/2001.

DGB (2004) 'Michael Sommer, Vorsitzender – Begrüßungsrede anlässlich des Makroökonomischen Kongresses: Wege zu nachhaltigem Wachstum, Beschäftigung und Stabilität (25/11/2004)', *Wipo-Schnelldienst*, 17: 1–5.

DGB (2005) 'Stellungnahme des Deutschen Gewerkschaftsbundes (DGB) zu Anträgen bezüglich des Europäischen Stabilitäts- und Wachstumspakt', *Wipo-Schnelldienst*, 2: 1–3.

DPG (1997) *Das Soziale Europe verwirklichen. Anträge auf dem 18. ordentlichen Gewerkschaftstag, 26.–31. Oktober*, Bremen: DPG. pp. 178–8.

Durand, D. (2002) 'Le Pacte de stabilité en 10 questions', *Analyses & Documents Economiques*, 90: 79–81.

ECEG-EMCEF (2004) 'Press Release – European Chemical Industry Proposes Formalised Social Partner Dialogue (10/09/2004)'; http://www.emcef.org/Committees/SD/Che/2004/PR-20040910.pdf; accessed 28/10/2004.

EMCEF (2004a) *General Resolution for Congress 2004: On EMCEF's Policy*, Brussels: EMCEF.

EMCEF (2004b) 'Press Release – 3rd EMCEF-Congress: Enlarging Europe Socially'; http://www.emcef.org/news/PR-Congress2-en.pdf; accessed 28/10/2004.

EMCEF (2004c) *Motion for the Congress 2004: On Number of Mandates for New Committees*, Brussels: EMCEF.

EMCEF (2004d) *Motion for the Congress 2004: The Future Work of the Collective Bargaining Committee*, Brussels: EMCEF.

EMF (1998a) 'EMF Charter on Working Time', approved by the EMF General Assembly, Luxembourg, 1/2 July; http://www.emf-fem.org/index.cfm?target=/default.cfm; accessed 26/10/2004.

EMF (1998b) 'Collective Bargaining with the Euro', 3rd EMF Collective Bargaining Conference, Frankfurth, 9/10 December; http://www.emf-fem.org/index.cfm?target=/default.cfm; accessed 26/10/2004.

EMF (2001) 'EMF position on the European industrial relation system', adopted by the EMF Executive Committee, Luxembourg, 3/4 December; http://www.emf-fem.org/index.cfm?target=/default.cfm; accessed 26/10/2004.

EMF (2003) 'EMF Work Programme 2003–2007', adopted by the 2nd EMF Congress in Prague, 13/14 June; http://www.emf-fem.org/Info_press/workprog/workprog.cfm?printpage=1&CFID=755520&CFTOKEN=32437947#_Toc45894534; accessed 07/06/2005.

EPSU (2000a) *EPSU Policy Statement: Public Services for People in Europe. Adopted at the 6th General Assembly in Lisbon*, Brussels: EPSU.

EPSU (2000b) *EPSU Policy Statement: Public Service Trade Unions and Collective Bargaining in a European environment. Adopted at the 6th General Assembly in Lisbon*, Brussels: EPSU.

EPSU (2002a) 'Broad Public Service Coalition with One Voice. European Federation of Public Service Unions Press Release (05/12/2002)'; http://www.epsu.org/press/sgicoul.pdf; accessed 17/06/2003.

EPSU (2002b) 'Services of General Interest and the Convention on the Future of Europe – You Can Shape the Future of Europe! EPSU General Circular No. 13 (1712/2002)', http://www.epsu.org/Campaigns/sgi/gen13.cfm; accessed 17/06/2003.

EPSU (2003a) '2003: A Crucial Year for Public Services in Europe. Letter by the EPSU General Secretary Carola Fischbach-Pyttel to All Affiliated Unions'; http://www.epsu.org/gen1.cfm; accessed 30/01/2003.

EPSU (2003b) 'GATS, PSI-EPSU and Pascal Lamy'; http://www.epsu.org/Campaigns/GATS/Lamy.cfm; accessed 17/06/2003.

EPSU (2003c) 'Letter to DG Trade Commissioner Pascal Lamy – Subject: General Agreement on Trade and Services'; http://www.epsu.org/Campaigns/GATS/jointlet.pdf; accessed 17/06/2003.

EPSU (2003d) 'EPSU position on the Communication of the Commission on the Internal Market Strategy Priorities 2003–2006'; http://www.epsu.org/IMG/pdf/EN_FINAL_EPSU_position_IMS_SC.pdf; accessed 09/06/2005.

EPSU (2004a) 'Resolution R.1. Public Services – Europe's Strength (7th EPSU Congress, Stockholm, 14–17 June)'; http://www.epsu.org/IMG/pdf/Adopted_EN_Congress_Reso_PS_Europe_s_strength.pdf; accessed 09/06/2005.

EPSU (2004b) 'Resolution R.2. Collective Bargaining (7th EPSU Congress, Stockholm, 14–17 June)'; http://www.epsu.org/IMG/pdf/Adopted_EN_Congress_Reso_CB.pdf; accessed 09/06/2005.

EPSU (2004c) 'EPSU Statement on the White Paper of the European Commission on Services of General Interst, COM (2004) 374'; http://www.epsu.org/IMG/pdf/EN_Statement_white_paper.pdf; accessed 09/06/2005.

ETUC (2002) *Third Annual Report on the Coordination of Collective Bargaining in Europe*, Brussels: ETUC-Executive Committee.

ETUC (2005) 'ETUC Hails Victory over Bolkenstein and Calls for "Yes" Votes on the Constitution (23/03/2005)'; http://www.etuc.org/a/1018; accessed 25/03/2005.

ETUC-E (2003) 'Resolution – Change the Proposed New Constitutional Treaty: Education Not to Be Subject to Trade'; http://www.etuce.homestead.com/Statements/eng/resolution_trade_ENG.pdf; accessed 26/10/2004.

ETUC-E (2004) ETUC-E Newsletter, No. 5 (July); http://www.etuce.homestead.com/ETUCE_Newsletter/newsletter_en/5.04_en. pdf; accessed 26/10/2004.

FO (1999) 'La BCE joue contre la croissance et l'emploi. Communiqué Force Ouvrière (5 November)'; http://www.force-ouvriere.fr/; accessed 08/02/2005.

FO (2000) *Rapports 2000: XIX Congrès, Marseille, 6–10 Mars*, Paris: FO.

FO (2002a) 'FO à Barcelone le 14 mars 2002. Communiqué Force Ouvrière (5 March)'; http://www.force-ouvriere.fr/; accessed 08/02/2005.

FO (2002b) 'Barcelone le 14 mars 2002. Communiqué Force Ouvrière (13 March)'; http://www.force-ouvriere.fr/; accessed 08/02/2005.

FO (2003) 'Euromanif du 4 octobre. Communiqué Force Ouvrière (2 October)'; http://www.force-ouvriere.fr/; accessed 08/02/2005.

FO (2004) 'Europe – Sommet de printemps: réviser le pacte de stabilité et de croissance! Communiqué Force Ouvrière (30 March)'; http://www.force-ouvriere.fr/; accessed 08/02/2005.

FO (2005) 'Europe – FO confirme qu'elle n'est pas engagée par la position de la CES. Communiqué Force Ouvrière (21 January)'; http://www.force-ouvriere.fr/; accessed 08/02/2005.

FSU (2002) *Le nouvel ordre éducatif mondial: OMC, Banque mondiale, OCDE, Commission européenne*, Paris: Institut de Recherches de la FSU.

Gewerkschaft Bau-Holz (2001) *Herausforderung Europa aus der Sicht der Gewerkschaft Bau-Holz*, Wien: GBH.

GMB (2001a) *Statement on the European Union by the Central Executive Council of the GMB at the GMB Congress in June*, Brighton: GMB.

GMB (2001b) 'GMB to Cut Labour Party Funding by up to £1 Million'; http://www.gmb.org.uk/press_office/; accessed 07/08/2001.

G10-Solidaires (1998) 'Congrès Constitutif: Résolution Générale'; http://www.g10.ras.eu.org/; accessed 20/05/2003.

G10-Solidaires (2002) *Qu'est-ce que SUD Solidaires*, Paris: L'Archipel.

G10-Solidaires (2005) 'La Constitution européenne: une constitution libérale contre les peuples – votez NON! (23/02/2005)'; http://solidaires.org/article2170.html?var_recherche=Constitution; accessed 31/07/2005.

HBV (1998) *Überarbeitete Stellungnahme der Gewerkschaft HBV zur Europäischen Wirschafts- und Währungsunion (30. April)*, Düsseldorf: HBV.

Heitz, V. (1999) 'Les quinze devant leurs choix', *Questions Economiques et Sociales*, 69: 12–16.

HM Treasury (2003) 'The Five Tests Framework: EMU Study'; http://www.hm-treasury.gov.uk/media/1B6/AD/adcornwall03_389.pdf; accessed 18/07/2005.

IG BCE (2000) 'Internationale Zusammenarbeit: Informationsaustausch verzahnen', *Umschau: Fachzeitschrift der Industriegewerkschaft Bergbau, Chemie, Energie* (October/November).

IG Metall (1996) *Europäische Wärungsunion – Erläuterung, Einschätzung, Forderungen*, Franfurt: IG Metall.

IG Metall (1999a) *Europapolitische Forderungen der IG Metall*, Frankfurt: IG Metall.

IG Metall (1999b) *Europäische Beschäftigungspolitik: Konzepte, Instrumente, Forderungen*, Frankfurt: IG Metall.

Industrial Agreement (1999) *Agreement on Industrial Development and Wage Formation*, Stockholm: No publisher.

Kapamadjian, I. (2000) 'Salaires en Europe: la fin de la modération?', *Questions Economiques et Sociales*, 77: 12–14.

Kaspar, J. (1991) 'Maastricht: la volonté et la raison triomphent', *Syndicalisme*, 2384: 3.

Kaspar, J. (1992) 'Pour la ratification des accords de Maastricht', *Syndicalisme*, 2414: 7.

Ladwig, B. (2000) 'Problems and Possibilities for European Trade Unions after EMU'; paper presented at the conference *European Trade Unions 2000: Convergence and Renewal*; Centre of Social and Economic Research; University of Bristol, UK, 24 March.

LO (1996) *Wage Earners and EMU. A Report by the Economists of the Swedish Trade Union Confederation*, Stockholm: LO.

LO (2000) *This EMU: Summary of LO's View of the Economic and Monetary Union*, Stockholm: LO.

LO (2003) 'The LO Adopts a Neutral Standpoint in the EMU Issue'; http://www.lo.se/english/news/newsindex.htm; accessed 01/05/2003.

Monks, J. (2001) 'Euro Campaign Cannot Be Put Off. Speech to the Annual Conference of the AEEU in Blackpool; 12 June 2001'; http://www.tuc.org.uk/international; accessed 06/08/2001.

Mönig-Raane, M. (1997) 'Ein Gespenst geht um . . .', *Ausblick* (Juni): 3.

MSF (2000) *The Single Currency (April)*, London: MSF.

ÖGB (1991) 'ÖGB-Präsident Fritz Verzetnitsch: "Enttäuscht vom EG-Gipfel", ÖGB-Pressedienst; 12.12.1991', in G. Kunnert (1992) *Spurensicherung auf dem österreichischen Weg nach Brüssel*, Wien: Verlag der Österreichischen Staatsdruckerei. pp. 447–8.

ÖGB (2004) *EU-Verfassungsvertrag – Bewertung und Position des ÖGB*, Wien: ÖGB.

ÖGB-Bundesvorstand (2002a) 'Resolution des Bundesvorstandes (7 March 2002)'; http://www.oegb.or.at/content/bundesvorstand/bv070302/bv_070302.html; accessed 12/03/2002.

ÖGB-Bundesvorstand (2002b) 'Ergebnisse und Stand der Verhandlungen mit den Regierungsmitgliedern (7 March 2002)'; http://www.oegb.or.at/europa/content/news/index.htm; accessed 15/08/2002.

ÖGB-News (1997) 'ÖGB-Bundesvorstand: Kampf gegen die Arbeitslosigkeit ist oberstes Ziel (13/03/1997)'; http://www.oegb.or.at; accessed 13/08/2002.

Olive, A. (2002) *Qu'est-ce que l'UNSA?*, Paris: l'Archipel.

ÖTV (1997) 'Europäische Wirtschafts- und Währungsunion, Beschäftigtendaten der EU-Länder', *Wirtschaftspolitische Informationen*, 13 (Juni).

ÖTV (2000) *Für ein soziales und demokratisches Europa in West wie Ost. Entschliessungen auf dem 14. Gewerkschaftstag, 4.–10. November*, Leipzig: ÖTV. pp. 149–55.

Prouteau, F. (1992) 'Un traité nécessaire mais pas suffisant', *CFDT Magazine*, 174: 6–8.

Public Services International (1992) *L'union economique et monetaire: conséquences pour le service public et les employés du service public*, Zoetermeer: AbvaKabo.

Raiga, A. (1990) 'Nouveau passeport pour l'Uem', *Syndicalisme*, 2335: 9–10.

Réau, P. (1997) 'Dossier Europe: une histoire en marche', *Syndicalisme hebdo*, 2655: 9–12.

Reischl, I. and C. Sykora (1997) 'Alle Macht der Zentralbank?', in Gewerkschaft der Privatangetellten (ed.) *Hart, härter, EURO? Schlaglichter auf die Währungsunion, GPA Info-Dienst, Extra No.20a/97*, Wien: GPA. pp. 44–9.

SACO (1997) *Pressmeddelande: SACO-styrelsen – Ja till svenskt medlemskap i EMU från start (19/02/1997)*, Stockholm: SACO.

Sallmutter, H. (1993) 'Diskussionsstand in der GPA zur europäischen Integration', in GPA (ed.) *Der Countdown läuft: Österreichs Arbeitnehmer auf dem Weg nach Europa*, Wien: Gewerkschaft der Privatangestellten. pp. 161–7.

Sallmutter, H. (1997) 'Das Abenteuer Währungsunion', in Gewerkschaft der Privatangetellten (ed.) *Hart, härter, EURO? Schlaglichter auf die Währungsunion, GPA Info-Dienst, Extra No.20a/97*, Wien: GPA. pp. 5–8.

Sattler, H.-J. (1996) 'Globalisierung und Gewerkschaftsarbeit: Europaweit tätig werden', *Gewerkschaftliche Praxis*, 41/1–2: 21–2.

Schütt, B. (1998) *Der Euro – ein Weg zu mehr Beschäftigung?*, DGB: Darmstadt.

Socialist Review (2004) 'The Joker Returns' (October); http://www.socialistreview.org.uk/article.php?articlenumber=9050; accessed 27/07/2005.

SUD-PTT (2002) *Les Nouvelles du SUD. Journal aux adhérent-e-s numéro 124, octobre*, Paris: SUD-PTT.

TCO (2001) 'TCO – Swedish Confederation of Professional Employees'; http://www.tco.se; accessed 15/05/2002.

T&G (1997) *Executive Explanatory Statement on European Integration – New Europe, New Deal (covering motions 165–187 and 189, and amendments to 165 and 168). T&G Biannual Conference*, Brighton: T&G.

T&G (2003) 'Treasury Select Committee on the Euro – Memorandum submitted by the Transport and General Workers Union'; http://www.publications.parliament.uk/pa/cm200203/cmselect/cmtreasy/187/3020402.htm; accessed 08/04/2005.

Transnet (2000) *Globalisierung und soziale Gerechtigkeit. Anträge auf dem 16. ordentlichen Gewerkschaftstag, 26. November–1. Dezember 2000*, Magdeburg: Transnet. pp. 8–18.

TUC (2000) *Economic and Monetary Union: Memorandum to the House of Commons Treasury Committee (May)*, London: TUC.

TUC (2002) 'General Council Report 2002 – Chapter 6: Europe'; http://www.tuc.org.uk/congress/tuc-6413-f0.cfm; accessed 06/04/2005.

TUC (2003a) 'Treasury Select Committee on the Euro – Memorandum submitted by the TUC'; http://www.publications.parliament.uk/pa/cm200203/cmselect/cmtreasy/187/3012302.htm; accessed 08/04/2005.

TUC (2003b) 'TUC Euro Statement and Congress 2003 Agenda'; http://www.tuc.org.uk/congress/tuc-6892-f0.cfm; accessed 06/04/2005.

TUC Annual Congress (2002) 'Verbatim Report Wednesday, 11 September'; http://www.tuc.org.uk/congress/tuc-6858-f0.cfm; accessed 06/04/2005.

TUC Annual Congress (2003) 'Verbatim Report Monday, 8 September, morning session'; http://www.tuc.org.uk/congress/tuc-7133-f0.cfm; accessed 06/04/2005.

TUC Annual Congress (2004) 'Verbatim Report Monday, 13 September'; http://www.tuc.org.uk/congress/tuc-8767-f0.cfm?theme=congress2004; accessed 06/04/2005.

Tüchler, E. (1997) 'Hat der ÖGB anlässlich des EU-Beitrittes auch dem EURO zugestimmt? (05/05/1997)', *ÖGB-Internal Document*, Wien: ÖGB.

TUfE (2000) *A Trade Union Agenda for Europe. A joint report from AEEU, GMB, GPMU, ISTC and KFAT*, London: TUfE.

UNIFI (2003) 'Treasury Select Committee on the Euro – Memorandum Submitted by UNIFI'; http://www.publications.parliament.uk/pa/cm200203/cmselect/cmtreasy/187/187ap24.htm; accessed 08/04/2005.

UNIFI (2004) 'The Offer'; http://www.unifi.org.uk/lores/fusion/current_issue/offer.htm; accessed 27/07/2005.

UNISON (2004) 'UNISON Labour Link: A Third Term for Working People'; http://www.unison.org.uk/acrobat/B1634.pdf; accessed 27/07/2005.

UNSA (1995) 'Notre charte syndicale (1995)', 1er Congres National, Paris: UNSA.

UNSA (1999) *Charte sur l'Europe. Le conseil national précise les positions de l'UNSA sur l'Europe*, Paris: UNSA.

UNSA (2002) 'Résolution générale adoptée par le congrès – Lille 2002, 15 au 18 janvier', *UNSA Magazine*, 42: 18–24.

Weber, L. (2002) 'La longue histoire de l'Europe de l'éducation', *Nouveaux Regards: Éducation-Recherche-Culture*, 17: 10–12.

Wiesenhügel, K. (1997) 'Euro später!', *Die Quelle* (April): 3.

Secondary sources

Adler, E. (1997) 'Seizing the Middle Ground: Constructivism in World Politics', *European Journal of International Relations*, 3/3: 319–62.

Albert, M. (1992) *Capitalism vs. Capitalism*, New York: Four Walls, Eight Windows.

Amable, B. (2003) *The Diversity of Modern Capitalism*, Oxford: Oxford University Press.

Andersson, T., T. Fredriksson and R. Svensson (1996) *Multinational Restructuring, Internationalization and Small Economies: The Swedish Case*, London: Routledge.

van Apeldoorn, B. (2002) *Transnational Capitalism and the Struggle over European Integration*, London: Routledge.

van Apeldoorn, B. (2004) 'Theorizing the Transnational: A Historical Materialist Approach', *Journal of International Relations and Development*, 7/2: 142–76.

Armstrong, K.A. and S.J. Bulmer (1998) *The Governance of the Single European Market*, Manchester: Manchester University Press.

Baker, A. (2000) 'Globalization and the British "Residual State"', in R. Stubbs and G.R.D. Underhill (eds) *Political Economy and the Changing Global Order (Second Edition)*, Oxford: Oxford University Press. pp. 362–72.

Bakker, I. and S. Gill (eds) (2003) *Power, Production and Social Reproduction: Human In/Security in the Global Political Economy*, Basingstoke: Palgrave.

Balanyá, B., A. Doherty, O. Hoedeman et al. (2000) *Europe Inc.: Regional and Global Restructuring and the Rise of Corporate Power*, London: Pluto Press.

Barnard, C. and S. Deakin (1999) 'A Year of Living Dangerously? EC Social Rights, Employment Policy, and EMU', *Industrial Relations Journal*, 30/4: 355–72.

Barrat, O., C. Yakubovich and J. Maurice (2002) 'Evolution of Collective Wage Bargaining in France', in P. Pochet (ed.) *Wage Policy in the Eurozone*, Brussels: PIE-Peter Lang. pp. 255–81.

Behrens, M. and W. Jacoby (2004) 'The Rise of Experimentalism in German Collective Bargaining', *British Journal of Industrial Relations*, 42/1: 95–123.

van der Bempt, P. (1993) 'The Impact of Economic and Monetary Union on Member States' Fiscal Policies', in K. Gretschmann (ed.) *Economic and Monetary Union: Implications for National Policy-Makers*, Maastricht: European Institute of Public Administration. pp. 245–61.

Bieler, A. (1999) 'Globalisation, Swedish Trade Unions and European Integration: From Europhobia to Conditional Support', *Cooperation and Conflict*, 34/1: 21–46.

Bieler, A. (2000) *Globalisation and Enlargement of the European Union: Austrian and Swedish Social Forces in the Struggle over Membership*, London: Routledge.

Bieler, A. (2001) 'Questioning Cognitivism and Constructivism in IR Theory: Reflections on the Material Structure of Ideas', *Politics*, 21/2: 93–100.

Bieler, A. (2002) 'The Struggle over EU Enlargement: A Historical Materialist Analysis of European Integration', *Journal of European Public Policy*, 9/4: 575–97.

Bieler, A. (2003) 'What Future Union? The Struggle for a Social Europe', Queen's Papers on Europeanisation, No. 1; http://www.qub.ac.uk/schools/SchoolofPolitics InternationalStudiesandPhilosophy/FileStore/EuropeanisationFiles/Filetoupload,5271, en.pdf; accessed 13/08/2005.

Bieler, A. (2005a) 'European Integration and the Transnational Restructuring of Social Relations: The Emergence of Labour as a Regional Actor?', *Journal of Common Market Studies*, 43: 461–84.

Bieler, A. (2005b) 'Class Struggle over the EU Model of Capitalism: Neo-Gramscian Perspectives and the Analysis of European Integration', *Critical Review of International Social and Political Philosophy*, 8/4: 513–26.

Bieler, A. and A.D. Morton (eds) (2001a) *Social Forces in the Making of the New Europe: The Restructuring of European Social Relations in the Global Political Economy*, London: Palgrave.

Bieler, A. and A.D. Morton (2001b) 'The Gordian Knot of Agency-Structure in International Relations: A Neo-Gramscian Perspective', *European Journal of International Relations*, 7/1: 5–35.

Bieler, A. and A.D. Morton (2003) 'Globalization, the State and Class Struggle: A "Critical Economy" Engagement with Open Marxism', *British Journal of Politics and International Relations*, 5/4: 467–99.

Bieler, A. and A.D. Morton (2004a) 'A Critical Theory Route to Hegemony, World Order and Historical Change: Neo-Gramscian Perspectives in International Relations', *Capital & Class*, 82: 85–113.

Bieler, A. and A.D. Morton (2004b) '"Another Europe is Possible"? Labour and Social Movements at the European Social Forum', *Globalizations*, 1/2: 303–25.

Bieler, A. and A.D. Morton (eds) (2005) 'Special Issue on Images of Gramsci: Connections and Contentions in Political Theory and International Relations', *Critical Review of International Social and Political Philosophy*, 8/4: 383–574.

Bieler, A. and A.D. Morton (2006) 'Canalising Resistance: Historical Continuities and Contrasts of "Alter-Globalist" Movements at the European Social Forums', in A. Gamble et al. (eds) *Labour, the State, Social Movements and the Challenge of Neo-Liberal Globalisation*, Manchester: Manchester University Press, forthcoming.

Bieling, H.-J. (2001) 'European Constitutionalism and Industrial Relations', in A. Bieler and A.D. Morton (eds) *Social Forces in the Making of the New Europe: The Restructuring of European Social Relations in the Global Political Economy*, Basingstoke: Palgrave. pp. 93–114.

Bieling, H.-J. (2003) 'Social Forces in the Making of the New European Economy: The Case of Financial Market Integration', *New Political Economy*, 8/2: 203–23.

Bieling, H.-J. and F. Deppe (1999) 'Europäische Integration und industrielle Beziehungen – zur Kritik des Konzeptes des "Wettbewerbskorporatismus"', in H. Schmitthenner and H.-J. Urban (eds) *Sozialstaat als Reformprojekt: Optionen für eine andere Politik*, Hamburg: VSA-Verlag. pp. 275–300.

Bieling, H.-J. and T. Schulten (2003) '"Competitive Restructuring" and Industrial Relations within the European Union: Corporatist Involvement and Beyond', in A.W. Cafruny and M. Ryner (eds) *A Ruined Fortress? Neoliberal Hegemony and Transformation in Europe*, Lanham, MD: Rowman & Littlefield. pp. 231–59.

Bispinck, R. and T. Schulten (2000) 'Alliance for Jobs – Is Germany Following the Path of "Competitive Corporatism"', in G. Fajertag and P. Pochet (eds) *Social Pacts in Europe – New Dynamics*, Brussels: ETUI. pp. 187–217.

Bohle, D. (2000) 'EU-Integration und Osterweiterung: die Konturen einer neuen europäischen Unordnung', in H.-J. Bieling und J. Steinhilber (eds) Die Konfiguration Europas: *Dimensionen einer kritischen Integrationstheorie*, Münster: Westfälisches Dampfboot. pp. 304–30.

Bohle, D. and D. Husz (2003) 'Whose Europe Is it?'; paper prepared for the *Thematic Network EPOC – Workshop: EU Enlargement and Social Cohesion*; Budapest, 7–9 March; http://www.epoc.uni-bremen.de/publications/pup2003/publications2003.htm; accessed 29/05/2005.

Bonefeld, W. (2001) 'European Monetary Union: Ideology and Class', in W. Bonefeld (ed.) *The Politics of Europe: Monetary Union and Class*, Basingstoke: Palgrave. pp. 64–106.

Bonefeld, W. (2004) 'Krise der Währungsunion', *Wildcat*, 68: 55–8.

Braunerhjelm, P. and L. Oxelheim (1996) 'Structural Implications of the Investment Response by Swedish Multinational Firms to the EC 1992 Program', in S. Hirsch and T. Almor (eds) *Outsiders' Response to European Integration*, Copenhagen: Handelshøjskolens Forlag. pp. 99–118.

Braunerhjelm, P., K. Ekholm, L. Grundberg and P. Karpaty (1996) 'Swedish Multinational Corporations: Recent Trends in Foreign Activities', *The Industrial Institute for Economic and Social Research: Working Paper 462*, Stockholm: Industrial Institute for Economic and Social Research.

Breit, J. and D. Rössl (1992) 'Internationalisierung der Klein- und Mittelbetriebe', in W. Clement (ed.) *Neue Entwicklungen – neue Formen – neue Herausforderungen. Internationalisierung Band VI*, Wien: Signum Verlag. pp. 191–222.

Brown, W. (2004) 'Industrial Relations and the Economy', in R. Floud and P. Johnson (eds) *The Cambridge Economic History of Modern Britain (Volume 3): Structural Change and Growth, 1939–2000*, Cambridge: Cambridge University Press. pp. 399–423.

Brown, W., S. Deakin and P. Ryan (1997) 'The Effects of British Industrial Relations Legislation 1979–1997', *National Institute Economic Review*, 161: 69–83.

Brown, W., P. Margisson and J. Walsh (2003) 'The Management of Pay as the Influence of Collective Bargaining Diminishes', in P. Edwards (ed.) *Industrial Relations: Theory and Practise*, Oxford: Blackwell. pp. 189–213.

Burnham, P. (1995) 'State and Market in International Political Economy: Towards a Marxian Alternative', *Studies in Marxism*, 2: 135–59.

Burnham, P. (2001) 'New Labour and the Politics of Depoliticisation', *British Journal of Politics and International Relations*, 3/2: 127–49.

Cain P.J. and A.G. Hopkins (2002) *British Imperialism, 1688–2000 (Second Edition)*, London: Longman.

Cameron, D.R. (1995) 'From Barre to Balladur: Economic Policy in the Era of the EMS', in G. Flynn (ed.) *The Remaking of the Hexagon: The New France in the New Europe*, Boulder, CO: Westview Press. pp. 117–57.

Carchedi, G. (1997) 'The EMU, Monetary Crises, and the Single European Currency', *Capital & Class*, 63: 85–114.

Cassen, B. (2005) 'ATTAC against the Treaty', *New Left Review*, 33/II: 27–33.

Cecchini, P., E. Jones and J. Lorentzen (2001) 'Europe and the Concept of Enlargement', *Survival*, 43/1: 155–65.

Chandler, D. (2003) 'New Rights for Old? Cosmopolitan Citizenship and the Critique of State Sovereignty', *Political Studies*, 51/2: 332–49.

Charlwood, A. (2004) 'Annual Review Article 2003: The New Generation of Trade Union Leaders and Prospects for Union Revitalization', *British Journal of Industrial Relations*, 42/2: 379–97.

Clift, B. (2003) 'The Changing Political Economy of France: Dirigisme under Duress', in A.W. Cafruny and M. Ryner (eds) *A Ruined Fortress? Neoliberal Hegemony and Transformation in Europe*, Lanham, MD: Rowman & Littlefield. pp. 173–200.

Coates, D. (1999) 'Models of Capitalism in the New World Order: The UK Case', *Political Studies*, 47/4: 643–60.

Coates, D. (2000) *Models of Capitalism: Growth and Stagnation in the Modern Era*, Cambridge: Polity.

Coates, D. (2005) 'Paradigms of Explanation', in D. Coates (ed.) *Varieties of Capitalism, Varieties of Approaches*, Basingstoke: Palgrave. pp. 1–25.

Colás, A. (2002) *International Civil Society: Social Movements in World Politics*, Cambridge: Polity.

Coleman, W.D. (1997) 'The French State, Dirigisme, and the Changing Global Financial Environment', in G.R.D. Underhill (ed.) *The New World Order in International Finance*, Basingstoke: Palgrave. pp. 274–93.

Collier, R.B. (1999) *Paths toward Democracy: The Working Class and Elites in Western Europe and South America*, Cambridge: Cambridge University Press.

Compston, H. and J. Greenwood (eds) (2001) *Social Partnership in the European Union*, London: Palgrave.

Cox, R.W. (1981) 'Social Forces, States and World Orders: Beyond International Relations Theory', *Millennium: Journal of International Studies*, 10/2: 126–55.

Cox, R.W. (1983) 'Gramsci, Hegemony and International Relations: An Essay on Method', *Millennium: Journal of International Studies*, 12/2: 162–75.

Cox, R.W. (1987) *Production, Power and World Order: Social Forces in the Making of History*, New York: Columbia University Press.

Cox, R.W. (1989) 'Production, the State, and Change in World Order', in E.-O. Czempiel and J.N. Rosenau (eds) *Global Changes and Theoretical Challenges: Approaches to World Politics for the 1990s*, Lexington, MA/Toronto: Lexington Books. pp. 37–50.

Cox, R.W. (1992) 'Global *Perestroika*', in R. Miliband and L. Panitch (eds) *The Socialist Register: New World Order?*, London: Merlin Press. pp. 26–43.

Cox, R.W. (1993) 'Structural Issues of Global Governance: Implications for Europe', in S. Gill (ed.) *Gramsci, Historical Materialism and International Relations*, Cambridge: Cambridge University Press. pp. 259–89.

Cox, R.W. with T. Sinclair (1996) *Approaches to World Order*, Cambridge: Cambridge University Press.

Crouch, C. (2002) 'The Euro and Labour Market and Wage Policies', in K. Dyson (ed.) *European States and the Euro: Europeanization, Variation, and Convergence*, Oxford: Oxford University Press. pp. 278–304.

Cumbers, A. (2004) 'Embedded Internationalisms: Building Transnational Solidarity in the British and Norwegian Trade Union Movements', *Antipode*, 36/5: 829–50.

Daley, A. (1999) 'The Hollowing out of French Unions: Politics and Industrial Relations after 1981', in A. Martin and G. Ross (eds) *The Brave New World of European Labor: European Trade Unions at the Millennium*, New York/Oxford: Berghahn Books. pp. 167–215.

Damesin, R. and J.-M. Denis (2005) 'SUD Trade Unions: The New Organisations Trying to Conquer the French Trade Union Scene', *Capital & Class*, 86: 17–37.

Dølvik, J.E. (2000) 'Building Regional Structures: ETUC and the European Industry Federations', *Transfer*, 6/1: 58–77.

Dølvik, J.E. (2004) 'Industrial Relations in EMU: Are Renationalization and Europeanization Two Sides of the Same Coin?', in A. Martin and G. Ross (eds) *Euros and Europeans: Monetary Integration and the European Model of Society*, Cambridge: Cambridge University Press. pp. 278–308.

Dörfel, A., B. Eggl and A. Schubert (1993) 'Insider or Outsider? The Case of Austria', in K. Gretschmann (ed.) *Economic and Monetary Union: Implications for National Policy-Makers*, Maastricht: European Institute of Public Administration. pp. 115–46.

Dunn, B. (2004) *Global Restructuring and the Power of Labour*, Basingstoke: Palgrave.

Dyson, K. (1994) *Elusive Union: The Process of Economic and Monetary Union in Europe*, Harlow: Longman.

Dyson, K. (1996) 'The Economic Order – Still Modell Deutschland?', in G. Smith, W.E. Paterson and S. Padgett (eds) *Developments in German Politics 2*, Basingstoke: Palgrave. pp. 194–210.

Dyson, K. and K. Featherstone (1999) *The Road to Maastricht: Negotiating Economic and Monetary Union*, Oxford: Oxford University Press.

Eder, M. and K. Hiller (1998) 'Sektorstudie Sozialpolitik', in G. Falkner and W.C. Müller (eds) *Österreich im europäischen Mehrebenensytem: Konsequenzen der EU-Mitgliedschaft für Politiknetzwerke und Entscheidungsprozesse*, Wien: Signum Verlag. pp. 39–78.

Edwards, P., M. Hall, R. Hyman et al. (1998) 'Great Britain: From Partial Collectivism to Neo-liberalism to Where?', in A. Ferner and R. Hyman (eds) *Changing Industrial Relations in Europe (Second Edition)*, Oxford: Blackwell. pp. 1–54.

Esping-Andersen, G. (1985) *Politics Against Markets: The Social Democratic Road to Power*, Princeton, NJ: Princeton University Press.

Fajertag, G. and P. Pochet (eds) (2000) *Social Pacts in Europe – New Dynamics*, Brussels: ETUI.

Falkner, G. (1998a) *EU Social Policy in the 1990's: Towards a Corporatist Policy Community*, London: Routledge.

Falkner, G. (1998b) 'Österreichische Politiknetzwerke und EU-Mitgliedschaft: Ergebnisse und Trends', in G. Falkner and W.C. Müller (eds) *Österreich im europäischen Mehrebenensytem: Konsequenzen der EU-Mitgliedschaft für Politiknetzwerke und Entscheidungsprozesse*, Wien: Signum Verlag. pp. 221–47.

Ferner, A. and R. Hyman (eds) (1998) *Changing Industrial Relations in Europe (Second Edition)*, Oxford: Blackwell.

Ferner, A. and M. Varul (2000) '"Vanguard" Subsidiaries and the Diffusion of New Practices: A Case Study of German Multinationals', *British Journal of Industrial Relations*, 38/1: 115–40.

Flecker, J. and T. Schulten (1999) 'The End of Institutional Stability: What Future for the "German Model"?', *Economic and Industrial Democracy*, 20/1: 81–115.

Frank, A.G. (1969) *Capitalism and Underdevelopment in Latin America: Historical Studies of Chile and Brazil (Revised Edition)*, Harmondsworth: Penguin.

Frieden, J. (1991) 'Invested Interests: The Politics of National Economic Policies in a World of Global Finance', *International Organization*, 45/4: 425–51.

Gamble, A. (2001) 'Neo-Liberalism', *Capital & Class*, 75: 127–34.

Garrett, G. (1996) 'Capital Mobility, Trade, and the Domestic Politics of Economic Policy', in R.O. Keohane and H.V. Milner (eds) *Internationalization and Domestic Politics*, Cambridge: Cambridge University Press. pp. 79–107.

Garrett, G. and C. Way (2000) 'Public-Sector Unions, Corporatism, and Wage Determination', in T. Iversen, J. Pontusson and D. Soskice (eds) *Unions, Employers, and Central Banks*, Cambridge: Cambridge University Press. pp. 267–91.

Germain, R.D. (1997) *The International Organization of Credit: States and Global Finance in the World-Economy*, Cambridge: Cambridge University Press.

Gill, S. (1995) 'Globalisation, Market Civilisation, and Disciplinary Neoliberalism', *Millennium: Journal of International Studies*, 24/3: 399–423.

Gill, S. (2001) 'Constitutionalising Capital: EMU and Disciplinary Neoliberalism', in A. Bieler and A.D. Morton (eds) *Social Forces in the Making of the New Europe: The Restructuring of European Social Relations in the Global Political Economy*, London: Palgrave. pp. 47–69.

Gill, S. and D. Law (1988) *The Global Political Economy: Perspectives, Problems and Policies*, London: Harvester-Wheatsheaf.

Gilpin, R. (2001) *Global Political Economy: Understanding the International Economic Order*, Princeton, NJ: Princeton University Press.

Giordano, F. and S. Persaud (1998) *The Political Economy of Monetary Union: Towards the Euro*, London/New York: Routledge.

Glyn, A. (1995) 'Social Democracy and Full Employment', *New Left Review*, 211: 33–55.

Goetschy, J. (1998) 'France: The Limits of Reform', in A. Ferner and R. Hyman (eds) *Changing Industrial Relations in Europe (Second Edition)*, Oxford: Blackwell. pp. 357–94.

Gollbach, J. and T. Schulten (2000) 'Cross-Border Collective Bargaining Networks in Europe', *European Journal of Industrial Relations*, 6/2: 161–79.

Gordon, A. and A. Mathers (2004) 'State Restructuring and Trade Union Realignment: The Pensions Struggle in France', *Capital & Class*, 83: 9–18.

Gordon, P.H. and S. Meunier (2001) *The French Challenge: Adapting to Globalization*, Washington: The Brookings Institution.

Gourevitch, P. (1986) *Politics in Hard Times: Comparative Responses to International Economic Crises*, Ithaca, NY: Cornell University Press.

Grahl J. and P. Teague (1989) 'The Cost of Neo-Liberal Europe', *New Left Review*, 174: 33–50.

Gramsci, A. (1971) *Selections from the Prison Notebooks*, ed. and trans. Q. Hoare and G. Nowell Smith, London: Lawrence and Wishart.

Grant, W. (1995) 'Britain: The Spectator State', in J. Hayward (ed.) *Industrial Enterprise and European Integration: From National to International Champions in Western Europe*, Oxford: Oxford University Press. pp. 76–96.

Greenwood, J. (2003) *Interest Representation in the European Union*, London: Palgrave.

Hall, P.A. (1990) 'The State and the Market', in P.A. Hall, J. Hayward and H. Machin (eds) *Developments in French Politics*, Basingstoke: Palgrave. pp. 171–87.

Hall, P.A. and R.J. Franzese (1998) 'Mixed Signals: Central Bank Independence, Coordinated Wage Bargaining, and European Monetary Union', *International Organization*, 52/3: 505–35.

Hall, P.A. and D. Soskice (2001) 'An Introduction to Varieties of Capitalism', in P.A. Hall and D. Soskice (eds) *Varieties of Capitalism*, Oxford: Oxford University Press. pp. 1–68.

Hall, S. (1986) 'The Problem of Ideology – Marxism Without Guarantees', *Journal of Communication Inquiry*, 10/2: 28–44.

Hancké, B. (2003) 'The Political Economy of Fiscal Policy in EMU', *European Political Economy Review*, 1/1: 5–14.

Harding, R. (1999) 'Standort Deutschland in the Globalising Economy: An End to the Economic Miracle?', *German Politics*, 8/1: 66–88.

Harrod, J. (1987) *Power, Production and the Unprotected Worker*, New York: Columbia University Press.

Harrod, J. and R. O'Brien (eds) (2002) *Global Unions? Theory and Strategies of Organized Labour in the Global Political Economy*, London/New York: Routledge.

Hassel, A. (2003) 'The Politics of Social Pacts', *British Journal of Industrial Relations*, 41/4: 707–26.

Hassel, A. and T. Schulten (1998) 'Globalization and the Future of Central Collective Bargaining: The Example of the German Metal Industry', *Economy and Society*, 27/4: 486–522.

Haworth, N. and Hughes, S. (2002) 'Internationalization, Industrial Relations Theory and International Relations', in J. Harrod and R. O'Brien (eds) *Global Unions? Theory and Strategies of Organized Labour in the Global Political Economy*, London: Routledge. pp. 64–79.

Hay, C. (2000) 'Contemporary Capitalism, Globalization, Regionalization and the Persistence of National Variation', *Review of International Studies*, 26/4: 509–31.

Hay, C. (2004) 'Common Trajectories, Variable Paces, Divergent Outcomes? Models of European Capitalism under Conditions of Complex Economic Interdependence', *Review of International Political Economy*, 11/2: 231–62.

Hay, C. and M. Watson (2003) 'Diminishing Expectations: The Strategic Discourse of Globalization in the Political Economy of New Labour', in A.W. Cafruny and M. Ryner (eds) *A Ruined Fortress? Neoliberal Hegemony and Transformation in Europe*, Lanham, MD: Rowman & Littlefield. pp. 147–72.

Hayes-Renshaw, F. and H. Wallace (1997) *The Council of Ministers*, London: Palgrave.

Heclo, H. and H. Madsen (1987) *Policy and Politics in Sweden: Principled Pragmatism*, Philadelphia: Temple University Press.

Hein, E. and A. Truger (2005) 'Macroeconomic Coordination as an Economic Policy Concept – Opportunities and Obstacles in the EMU', in E. Hein, T. Niechoj, T. Schulten et al. (eds) *Macroeconomic Policy Coordination in Europe and the Role of the Trade Unions*, ETUI: Brussels. pp. 19–67.

Hein, E., T. Niechoj, T. Schulten et al. (2005) 'Introduction', in E. Hein, T. Niechoj, T. Schulten et al. (eds) *Macroeconomic Policy Coordination in Europe and the Role of the Trade Unions*, ETUI: Brussels. pp. 7–16.

Heinisch, R. (2000) 'Copoing with Economic Integration: Corporatist Strategies in Germany and Austria in the 1990s', *West European Politics*, 23/3: 67–96.

Held, D. and A. McGrew (2002) *Globalization/Anti-Globalization*, Cambridge: Polity.

Held, D., A. McGrew, D. Goldblatt and J. Perraton (1999) *Global Transformations: Politics, Economics and Culture*, Cambridge: Polity.

Helleiner, E. (1994) *States and the Reemergence of Global Finance: From Bretton Woods to the 1990s*, Ithaca, NY/London: Cornell University Press.

Higgott, R., G.R.D. Underhill and A. Bieler (eds) (2000) *Non-State Actors and Authority in the Global System*, London: Routledge.

Hirst, P. and G. Thompson (1999) *Globalization in Question: The International Economy and the Possibilities of Governance (Second Edition)*, Cambridge: Polity Press.

Hoffmann, R. and O. Jacobi (1999) *EPSU: On Course to Become a Competence and Coordination Centre*, Brussels: ETUI.

Holloway, J. and S. Picciotto (1977) 'Capital, Crisis and the State', *Capital & Class*, 2: 76–101.

Holman, O. (1992) 'Transnational Class Strategy and the New Europe', *International Journal of Political Economy*, 22/1: 3–22.

Holman, O. (2001) 'The Enlargement of the European Union towards Central and Eastern Europe: The Role of Supranational and Transnational Actors', in A. Bieler and A.D. Morton (eds) *Social Forces in the Making of the New Europe: The Restructuring of European Social Relations in the Global Political Economy*, Houndmills: Palgrave. pp. 161–84.

Howell, C. (1999) 'Unforgiven: British Trade Unionism in Crisis', in A. Martin and G. Ross (eds) *The Brave New World of European Labour: European Trade Unions at the Millennium*, New York/Oxford: Berghahn Books. pp. 26–74.

Hyman, R. (2001) *Understanding European Trade Unionism: Between Market, Class and Society*, London: SAGE.

Iversen, T. and J. Pontusson (2000) 'Comparative Political Economy: A Northern European Perspective', in T. Iversen, J. Pontusson and D. Soskice (eds) *Unions, Employers, and Central Banks: Macroeconomic Coordination and Institutional Change in Social Market Economies*, Cambridge: Cambridge University Press. pp. 1–37.

Jacobi, O. (1997) 'European Economic and Monetary Union and its Effects on the Public Services'; paper commissioned by the European Federation of Public Services Unions; Brussels: EPSU.

Jacobi, O., B. Keller, W. M_ller-Jentsch et al. (1998) 'Germany: Facing New Challenges', in A. Ferner and R. Hyman (eds) *Changing Industrial Relations in Europe (Second Edition)*, Oxford: Blackwell. pp. 190–238.

Jeffery, C. (2002) 'Social and Regional Interests: ESC and Committee of the Regions', in J. Peterson and M. Shackleton (eds) *The Institutions of the European Union*, Oxford: Oxford University Press. pp. 326–46.

Jefferys, S. (1996) 'France 1995: The Backward March of Labour Halted?', *Capital & Class*, 59: 7–21.

Jessop, B. (1990) *State Theory: Putting the Capitalist State in its Place*, Cambridge: Polity.

Jessop, B. (2001) 'Institutional Re(turns) and the Strategic-Relational Approach', *Environment and Planning A*, 33: 1213–35.

Jessop, B. (2002) *The Future of the Capitalist State*, Cambridge: Polity.

Jones, E. (2002) *The Politics of Economic and Monetary Union*, Lanham, MD: Rowman & Littlefield.

Jones, E., J. Frieden and F. Tores (eds) (1998) *Joining Europe's Monetary Club: The Challenges for Smaller Member States*, Basingstoke: Palgrave.

Joning, L. (1986) 'Financial Deregulation in Sweden', *Skandinaviska Enskilda Banken Quarterly Review*, 4: 109–19.

Josselin, D. (2001) 'Trade Unions for EMU: Sectoral Preferences and Political Opportunities', *West European Politics*, 24/1: 55–74.

Karazman-Morawetz, I. and G. Pleschiutschnig (1997) 'Wirschaftsmacht und politischer Einfluss', in H. Dachs, P. Gerlich, H. Gottweis et al. (eds) *Handbuch des Politischen Systems Österreichs: Die Zweite Republik (3., erweiterte und völlig neu bearbeitete Auflage)*, Wien: Manz. pp. 418–31.

Kassim, H. (1997) 'French Autonomy and the European Union', *Modern & Contemporary France*, 5/2: 167–80.

Katzenstein, P.J. (1985) *Small States in World Markets: Industrial Policy in Europe*, Ithaca, NY/London: Cornell University Press.

Keller, B. (2003) 'Social Dialogues – The State of the Art a Decade after Maastricht', *Industrial Relations Journal*, 34/5: 411–29.

Keller, B. and B. Sörries (1999) 'Sectoral Social Dialogues: New Opportunities or More Impasse', *Industrial Relations Journal*, 30/4: 330–44.

Keohane, R.O. and H.V. Milner (eds) (1996) *Internationalization and Domestic Politics*, Cambridge: Cambridge University Press.

Keohane R.O. and J.S. Nye (eds) (1971) *Transnational Relations and World Politics*, Cambridge, MA: Harvard University Press.

Keohane R.O. and J.S. Nye (1977) *Power and Interdependence*, Boston, MA: Little, Brown.

Keohane, R.O. and J.S. Nye (2002) 'Governance in a Globalizing World', in R.O. Keohane (ed.) *Power and Governance in a Partially Globalized World*, London: Routledge. pp. 193–218.

Kitschelt, H., P. Lange, G. Marks et al. (1999a) 'Introduction', in H. Kitschelt, P. Lange, G. Marks et al. (eds) *Continuity and Change in Contemporary Capitalism*, Cambridge: Cambridge University Press. pp. 1–8.

Kitschelt, H., P. Lange, G. Marks et al. (1999b) 'Convergence and Divergence in Advanced Capitalist Democracies', in H. Kitschelt, P. Lange, G. Marks et al. (eds) *Continuity and Change in Contemporary Capitalism*, Cambridge: Cambridge University Press. pp. 427–60.

Koll, W. (2005) 'Macroeconomic Dialogue – Developments and Intentions', in E. Hein, T. Niechoj, T. Schulten et al. (eds) *Macroeconomic Policy Coordination in Europe and the Role of the Trade Unions*, Brussels: ETUI. pp. 175–212.

Kresl, P.K. and S. Gallais (2002) *France Encounters Globalization*, Cheltenham: Edward Elgar.

Kurzer, P. (1993) *Business and Banking: Political Change and Economic Integration in Western Europe*, Ithaca, NY/London: Cornell University Press.

Lambert, R. (2002) 'Labour Movement Renewal in the Era of Globalization: Union Responses in the South', in J. Harrod and R. O'Brien (eds) *Global Unions? Theory and Strategies of Organized Labour in the Global Political Economy*, London: Routledge. pp. 185–203.

Lambert, R. and E. Webster (2001) 'Southern Unionism and the New Labour Internationalism', in P. Waterman and J. Wills (eds) *Place, Space and the New Labour Internationalisms*, Oxford: Blackwell. pp. 33–58.

Lane, C. (1995) *Industry and Society in Europe: Stability and Change in Britain, Germany and France*, Aldershot: Edward Elgar.

Lane, C. (1998) 'European Companies between Globalization and Localization: A Comparison of Internationalization Strategies of British and German MNCs', *Economy and Society*, 27/4: 462–85.

Lane, C. (2000) 'Globalization and the German Model of Capitalism – Erosion or Survival?', *British Journal of Sociology*, 51/2: 207–34.

Lane, C. (2003) 'Changes in Corporate Governance of German Corporations: Convergence to the Anglo-American Model?', *Competition & Change*, 7/2–3: 79–100.

Lauber, V. (1996) 'Economic Policy', in V. Lauber (ed.) *Contemporary Austrian Politics*, Boulder, CO/Oxford: Westview Press. pp. 125–50.

Leibfried, S. and P. Pierson (2000) 'Social Policy: Left to Courts and Markets?', in H. Wallace and W. Wallace (eds) *Policy-Making in the European Union (Fourth Edition)*, Oxford: Oxford University Press. pp. 267–92.

Leisink, P. (2002) 'The European Sectoral Social Dialogue and the Graphical Industry'. *European Journal of Industrial Relations*, 8/1: 101–17.

Le Queux, S. and G. Fajertag (2001) 'Towards Europeanization of Collective Bargaining: Insights from the European Chemical Industry', *European Journal of Industrial Relations*, 7/2: 117–36.

Lindberg, I. (2005) 'The Swedish Welfare State Model – Effects of Globalisation and Economic Restructuring. Discussion of Social Democratic and Union Strategies'; paper presented at the conference *Governance of Welfare for the 21st Century: New Social Rights and Renewal of Social Democracy*, Tokyo, 18–19 February.

Lipietz, A. (1991) 'Governing the Economy in the Face of International Challenge: From National Developmentalism to National Crisis', in J.F. Hollifield and G. Ross (eds) *Searching for the New France*, London: Routledge. pp. 17–41.

Ludlam, S. (1992) 'The Gnomes of Washington: Four Myths of the 1976 IMF Crisis', *Political Studies*, 40/4: 713–27.

Ludlam, S. and A. Taylor (2003) 'The Political Representation of the Labour Interest in Britain', *British Journal of Industrial Relations*, 41/4: 727–49.

Ludlam, S., M. Bodah and D. Coates (2002) 'Trajectories of Solidarity: Changing Union-Party Linkages in the UK and the USA', *British Journal of Politics and International Relations*, 4/2: 223–5.

Luif, P. (1994) 'Die Beitrittswerber: Grundlegendes zu den Verhandlungen der EFTA-Staaten um Mitgliedschaft bei der EG/EU', *Österreichische Zeitschrift für Politikwissenschaft*, 23/1: 21–36.

Luif, P. (1996) *On the Road to Brussels: The Political Dimension of Austria's, Finland's and Sweden's Accession to the European Union*, Wien: Braumüller.

Lütz, S. (2000) 'From Managed to Market Capitalism? German Finance in Transition', *German Politics*, 9/2: 149–70.

McIlroy, J. (2000a) 'New Labour, New Unions, New Left', *Capital & Class*, 71: 11–45.

McIlroy, J. (2000b) 'The New Politics of Pressure – the Trades Union Congress and New Labour in Government', *Industrial Relations Journal*, 31/1: 2–16.

Maclean, M. (1997) 'Privatisation, Dirigisme and the Global Economy: An End to French Exceptionalism?', *Modern & Contemporary France*, 5/2: 215–28.

Maclean, M. (2002) *Economic Management and French Business: From de Gaulle to Chirac*, Basingstoke: Palgrave.

Maclean, M., C. Harvey and J. Press (2001) 'Elites, Ownership and the Internationalisation of French Business', *Modern & Contemporary France*, 9/3: 313–25.

Mahon, R. (1999) '"Yesterday's Modern Times Are No Longer Modern": Swedish Unions Confront the Double Shift', in A. Martin and G. Ross (eds) *The Brave New World of European Labour: European Trade Unions at the Millennium*, New York/Oxford: Berghahn Books. pp. 125–66.

Marginson, P. and K. Sisson (1998) 'European Collective Bargaining: A Virtual Prospect?', *Journal of Common Market Studies*, 36/4: 505–28.

Marginson, P. and K. Sisson (2004) *European Integration and Industrial Relations: Multi-Level Governance in the Making*, Basingstoke: Palgrave.

Marin, B. (1985) 'Austria – The Paradigm Case of Liberal Corporatism?', in W. Grant (ed.) *The Political Economy of Corporatism*, Basingstoke: Palgrave. pp. 89–125.

Markovits, A.S. and A. Otto (1993) 'West German Labour and Europe '92', in C.F. Lankowski (ed.) *Germany and the European Community: Beyond Hegemony and Containment?*, Basingstoke: Palgrave. pp. 45–70.

Martin, A. (2000) 'Social Pacts, Unemployment and EMU Macroeconomic Policy', in G. Fajertag and P. Pochet (eds) *Social Pacts in Europe – New Dynamics*, Brussels: ETUI. pp. 365–400.

Martin, A. (2004) 'The EMU Macroeconomic Policy Regime and the European Social Model', in A. Martin and G. Ross (eds) *Euros and Europeans: Monetary Integration and the European Model of Society*, Cambridge: Cambridge University Press. pp. 20–50.

Martin, A. and G. Ross (eds) (1999a) *The Brave New World of European Labor: European Trade Unions at the Millennium*, New York/Oxford: Berghahn Books.

Martin, A. and G. Ross (1999b) 'In the Line of Fire: the Europeanization of Labor Representation', in A. Martin and G. Ross (eds) *The Brave New World of European Labor: European Trade Unions at the Millennium*, New York/Oxford: Berghahn Books. pp. 312–67.

Martin, A. and G. Ross (2004) 'Introduction: EMU and the European Social Model', in A. Martin and G. Ross (eds) *Euros and Europeans: Monetary Integration and the European Model of Society*, Cambridge: Cambridge University Press. pp. 1–19.

Mathers, A. and G. Taylor (2005) 'Trade Union Participation in European Multi-Level Governance: Towards Networked Trade Unionism?'; paper presented at *Frontiers of Sociology: The 37th World Congress of the International Institut of Sociology*, Stockholm, Sweden, 5 to 9 July.

Menz, G. (2005a) *Varieties of Capitalism and Europeanization: National Response Strategies to the Single European Market*, Oxford: Oxford University Press.

Menz, G. (2005b) 'Old Bottles – New Wine: The New Dynamics of Industrial Relations', *German Politics*, 14/2: 1–12.

Mermet, E. (2001) *Wage Formation in Europe*, Brussels: ETUI.

Morton, A.D. (2001) 'The Sociology of Theorising and Neo-Gramscian Perspectives: The Problems of "School" Formation in IPE', in A. Bieler and A.D. Morton (eds) *Social Forces in the Making of the New Europe: The Restructuring of European Social Relations in the Global Political Economy*, London: Palgrave. pp. 25–43.

Morton, A.D. (2003a) 'Historicizing Gramsci: Situating Ideas in and Beyond their Context', *Review of International Political Economy*, 10/1: 118–46.

Morton, A.D. (2003b) 'The Social Function of Carlos Fuentes: A Critical Intellectual or in the "Shadow of the State"?', *Bulletin of Latin American Research*, 22/1: 27–51.

Morton, A.D. (2006) 'The Grimly Comic Riddle of Hegemony in IPE: Where Is Class Struggle?', *Politics*, 26/1: 62–72.

Moses, J.W. (1995) 'Devalued Priorities: The Politics of Nordic Exchange Rate Regimes Compared', unpublished Ph.D. thesis, University of California, Los Angeles.

Mouriaux, R. (1996) 'Les grèves française de l'automne 1995: défense des acquis ou mouvement social?', *Modern and Contemporary France*, 4/3: 299–306.

Mulhearn, C. (2004) 'Beyond "Euroland": British Trade Unions, the Single Currency and European Integration', *Industrial Relations Journal*, 35/4: 296–310.

Munck, R. (ed.) (2004) *Labour and Globalisation: Results and Prospects*, Liverpool: Liverpool University Press.

Neufeld, M.A. (1995) *The Restructuring of International Relations Theory*, Cambridge: Cambridge University Press.

Notermans, T. (1993) 'The Abdication from National Policy Autonomy: Why the Macroeconomic Policy Regime Has Become so Unfavorable to Labour', *Politics & Society*, 21/2: 133–67.

Nugent, N. (1992) 'The Deepening and Widening of the EC: Recent Evolution, Maastricht and Beyond', *Journal of Common Market Studies*, 30/3: 311–29.

O'Brien, R. (2000a) 'Workers and World Order: The Tentative Transformation of the International Union Movement', *Review of International Studies*, 26/4: 533–55.

O'Brien, R. (2000b) 'Labour and IPE', in R. Polan (ed.) *Global Political Economy: Contemporary Theories*, London: Routledge. pp. 89–99.

O'Brien, R., A.M. Goetz, J.A. Scholte et al. (2000) *Contesting Global Governance Multilateral Economic Institutions and Global Social Movements*, Cambridge: Cambridge University Press.

Olsen, G. (1991) 'Labour Mobilization and the Strength of Capital: The Rise and Stall of Economic Democracy in Sweden', *Studies in Political Economy*, 34: 109–45.

Olsen, G. (1996) 'Re-Modeling Sweden: The Rise and Demise of the Compromise in a Global Economy', *Social Problem*, 43/1: 1–20.

Overbeek, H. (1990) *Global Capitalism and National Decline: The Thatcher Decade in Perspective*, London: Unwin Hyman.

Overbeek, H. (1999) 'Globalization and Britain's Decline', in R. English and M. Kenny (eds) *Rethinking British Decline*, London: Palgrave. pp. 231–56.

Panitch, L. (2001) 'Reflections on Strategy for Labour', in L. Panitch and C. Leys with G. Albo and D. Coates (eds) *The Socialist Register 2001: Working Classes, Global Realities*, London: Merlin Press. pp. 367–92.

Pelinka, A. (1999) 'The (In) compatibility of Corporatism and Federalism: Austrian Social Partnership and the EU', *West European Politics*, 22/2: 116–29.

Picciotto, S. (1991) 'The Internationalisation of the State', *Capital & Class*, 43: 43–63.

van der Pijl, K. (1984) *The Making of an Atlantic Ruling Class*, London: Verso.

van der Pijl, K. (1998) *Transnational Classes and International Relations*, London: Routledge.

Pontusson, J. (1995) 'Sweden: After the Golden Age', in P. Anderson and P. Camiller (eds) *Mapping the West European Left*, London/New York: Verso. pp. 23–54.

Premfors, R. (1991) 'The "Swedish Model" and Public Sector Reform', *West European Politics*, 14/3: 83–95.

Rhodes, M. (1998) 'Globalization, Labour Markets and Welfare States: A Future of "Competitive Corporatism"?', in M. Rhodes and Y. Mény (eds) *The Future of European Welfare: A New Social Contract?*, London: Palgrave. pp. 178–203.

Rhodes, M. (2000) 'Restructuring the British Welfare State: Between Domestic Constraints and Global Imperatives', in F.W. Scharpf and V.A. Schmidt (eds) *Welfare and Work in the Open Economy, Volume II: Diverse Responses to Common Challenges*, Oxford: Oxford University Press. pp. 19–68.

Rhodes, M. and B. van Apeldoorn (1998) 'Capital Unbound? The Transformation of European Corporate Governance', *Journal of European Public Policy*, 5/3: 406–27.

Robinson, W.I. (2001) 'Social Theory and Globalization: The Rise of a Transnational State', *Theory and Society: Renewal and Critique in Social Theory*, 30/2: 157–200.

Robinson, W.I. (2004) *A Theory of Global Capitalism: Production, Class, and State in a Transnational World*, Baltimore/London: John Hopkins University Press.

Robinson, W.I. and J. Harris (2000) 'Towards a Global Ruling Class? Globalization and the Transnational Capitalist Class', *Science & Society*, 64/1: 11–54.

Rosamond, B. (1993) 'National Labour Organizations and European Integration: British Trade Unions and "1992"', *Political Studies*, 41/3: 420–34.

Rosamond, B. (1998) 'The Integration of Labour? British Trade Union Attitudes to European Integration', in D. Barker and D. Seawright (eds) *Britain For and Against Europe: British Politics and the Question of European Integration*, Oxford: Clarendon Press. pp. 130–47.

Rosamond, B. (2002) 'Imagining the European Economy: "Competitiveness" and the Social Construction of "Europe" as an Economic Space', *New Political Economy*, 7/2: 157–77.

Ross, G. (1998) 'European Integration and Globalization', in R. Axtmann (ed.) *Globalization and Europe: Theoretical and Empirical Investigations*, London/Washington: Pinter. pp. 164–83.

Ross, G. and A. Martin (1999) 'European Unions Face the Millennium', in A. Martin and G. Ross (eds) *The Brave New World of European Labor: European Trade Unions at the Millennium*, New York/Oxford: Berghahn Books. pp. 1–25.

Ruggie, J.G. (1982) 'International Regimes, Transactions, and Change: Embedded Liberalism in the Postwar Economic Order', *International Organization*, 36/2: 379–415.

Ruigrok, W. and R. van Tulder (1995) *The Logic of International Restructuring*, London: Routledge.

Rupert, M. (2000) *Ideologies of Globalization: Contending Visions of a New World Order*, London: Routledge.

Ryner, M. (1994) 'Assessing SAP's Economic Policy in the 1980s: The "Third Way", the Swedish Model and the Transition from Fordism to Post-Fordism', *Economic and Industrial Democracy*, 15: 385–428.

Ryner, M. (2002) *Capitalist Restructuring, Globalisation and the Third Way: Lessons from the Swedish Model*, London/New York: Routledge.

Ryner, M. (2003) 'Disciplinary Neoliberalism, Regionalization, and the Social Market in German Restructuring', in A.W. Cafruny and M. Ryner (eds) *A Ruined Fortress? Neoliberal Hegemony and Transformation in Europe*, Lanham, MD: Rowman & Littlefield. pp. 201–27.

Ryner, M. and T. Schulten (2003) 'The Political Economy of Labour-Market Restructuring and Trade Union Responses in the Social-Democratic Heartland', in H. Overbeek (ed.) *The Political Economy of European Employment: European Integration and the Transnationalization of the (Un)employment Question*, London/New York: Routledge. pp. 176–98.

Sainsbury, D. (1991) 'Swedish Social Democracy in Transition: The Party's Record in the 1980s and the Challenge of the 1990s', *West European Politics*, 14/3: 31–57.

Sainsbury, D. (1993) 'The Swedish Social Democrats and the Legacy of Continuous Reform: Asset or Dilemma?', *West European Politics*, 16/1: 39–61.

Ste Croix, G.E.M. de (1981) *The Class Struggle in the Ancient Greek World from the Archaic Age to the Arab Conquests*, London: Duckworth.

Sandholtz, W. (1993) 'Choosing Union: Monetary Politics and Maastricht', *International Organization*, 47/1: 1–39.

Schmidt, V.A. (1997) 'Running on Empty: The End of Dirigisme in French Economic Leadership', *Modern & Contemporary France*, 5/2: 229–41.

Schmidt, V.A. (2002) *The Futures of European Capitalism*, Oxford: Oxford University Press.

Scholte, J.A. (2000a) *Globalization: A Critical Introduction*, Basingstoke: Palgrave.

Scholte, J.A. (2000b) '"In the Foothills": Relations between the IMF and Civil Society', in R. Higgott, G.R.D. Underhill and A. Bieler (eds) *Non-State Actors and Authority in the Global System*, London: Routledge. pp. 256–73.

Schulten, T. (1996) 'European Works Councils: Prospects for a New System of European Industrial Relations', *European Journal of Industrial Relations*, 2/3: 303–24.

Schulten, T. (1999) 'Europäisierung der Tarifpolitik – der Koordinierungsansatz des Europäischen Metallgewerkschaftsbundes (EMB)', in T. Schulten und R. Bispinck (eds) *Tarifpolitik unter dem EURO. Perspektiven einer europäischen Koordinierung: das Beispiel Metallindustrie*, Hamburg: VSA-Verlag. pp. 197–226.

Schulten, T. (2000) 'Zwischen nationalem Wettbewerbskorporatismus und symbolischenm Euro-Korporatismus – zur Einbindung der Gewerkschaften in die neoliberale Restrukturierung Europas', in H.-J. Bieling und J. Steinhilber (eds) *Die Konfiguration Europas: Dimensionen einer kritischen Integrationstheorie*, Münster: Westfälisches Dampfboot. pp. 222–42.

Schulten, T. (2001) 'The European Metalworkers' Federation's Approach to a European Coordination of Collective Bargaining – Experiences, Problems and Prospects', in T. Schulten and R. Bispinck (eds) *Collective Bargaining under the Euro: Experiences from the European Metal Industry*, Brussels: ETUI. pp. 303–32.

Schulten, T. (2002) 'Europeanisation of Collective Bargaining: An Overview on Trade Union Initiatives for a Transnational Coordination of Collective Bargaining Policy', WSI Discussion Paper 101. Düsseldorf: Wirtschafts- und Sozialwissenschaftliches Institut in der Hans-Böckler-Stiftung.

Schulten, T. (2004) *Solidarische Lohnpolitik in Europa: Zur Politischen Ökonomie der Geserkschaften*, Hamburg: VSA-Verlag.

Schultz, D.M. (1992) 'Austria in the International Arena: Neutrality, European Integration and Consociationalism', *West European Politics*, 15/1: 173–200.

Shields, S. (2003) 'The "Charge of the Right Brigade": Transnational Social Forces and the Neoliberal Configuration of Poland's Transition', *New Political Economy*, 8/2: 225–44.

Siegel, D. (1992) 'Die Bedeutung österreichischer multinationaler Konzerne für die Internationalisierung', in W. Clement (ed.) *Neue Entwicklungen – neue Formen – neue Herausforderungen. Internationalisierung Band VI*, Wien: Signum Verlag. pp. 165–89.

Silvia, S.J. (1999) 'Every Which Way But Loose: German Industrial Relations since 1980', in A. Martin and G. Ross (eds) *The Brave New World of European Labour: European Trade Unions at the Millennium*, New York/Oxford: Berghahn Books. pp. 75–124.

Sisson, K., J. Arrowsmith and P. Marginson (2003) 'All Benchmarkers Now? Benchmarking and the "Europeanisation" of Industrial Relations', *Industrial Relations Journal*, 34/1: 15–31.

Sisson, K., P. Marginson, J. Arrowsmith et al. (1999) *The Industrial Relations Implications of Economic and Monetary Union in the UK: A Study for the European Foundation for the Improvement of Living and Working Conditions*, Warwick: Industrial Relations Research Unit, Warwick Business School, University of Warwick.

Sklair, L. (2001a) *The Transnational Capitalist Class*, Oxford: Blackwell.

Sklair, L. (2001b) *Globalization: Capitalism and its Alternatives (Third Edition)*, Oxford: Oxford University Press.

Smith, H. (2002) 'The politics of "regulated liberalism": A Historical Materialist Approach to European Integration', in M. Rupert and H. Smith (eds) *Historical Materialism and Globalisation*, London: Routledge. pp. 257–83.

Smythe, E. (2000) 'State Authority and Investment Security: Non-State Actors and the Negotiation of the Multilateral Agreement on Investment at the OECD', in R. Higgott, G.R.D. Underhill and A. Bieler (eds) *Non-State Actors and Authority in the Global System*, London: Routledge. pp. 74–90.

Spindler, M. (2003) 'Toward the Competition Region: Global Business Actors and the Future of Regionalism', in A. Hülsemeyer (ed.) *Globalization in the Twenty-First Century: Convergence and Divergence?*, London: Palgrave. pp. 119–33.

Stopford, J. and S. Strange (1991) *Rival States, Rival Firms: Competition for World Market Shares*, Cambridge: Cambridge University Press.

Strange, S. (1994) *States and Markets (Second Edition)*, New York/London: Pinters Publishers.

Strange, S. (1996) *The Retreat of the State: The Diffusion of Power in the World Economy*, Cambridge: Cambridge University Press.

Strange, G. (1997) 'The British Labour Movement and Economic and Monetary Union in Europe', *Capital & Class*, 63: 13–24.

Strange, G. (2002a) 'British Trade Unions and European Union Integration in the 1990s: Politics versus Political Economy', *Political Studies*, 50/2: 332–53.

Strange, G. (2002b) 'Globalisation, Regionalism and Labour Interests in the New IPE', *New Political Economy*, 7/4: 343–65.

Streeck, W. (1997) 'German Capitalism: Does it Exist? Can it Survive?', in C. Crouch and W. Streeck (eds) *Political Economy of Modern Capitalism: Mapping Convergence and Diversity*, London: SAGE. pp. 33–54.

Streeck, W. and A. Hassel (2003) 'The Crumbling Pillars of Social Partnership', *West European Politics*, 26/4: 101–24.

Swedenborg, B. (1979) *The Multinational Operations of Swedish Firms: An Analysis of Determinants and Effects*, Stockholm: IUI.

Swenson, P. (1989) *Fair Shares: Unions Pay, and Politics in Sweden and West Germany*, London: Adamantine Press Ltd.

Swenson, P. (1991) 'Labor and the Limits of the Welfare State: The Politics of Intraclass Conflict and Cross-Class Alliances in Sweden and West Germany', *Comparative Politics*, 23/4: 379–99.

Tálos, E. (1996) 'Corporatism – The Austrian Model', in V. Lauber (ed.) *Contemporary Austrian Politics*, Boulder, CO/Oxford: Westview Press. pp. 103–23.

Tálos, E. (2001) 'Ende der Sozialpartnerschaft?', in F. Karlhofer, J. Melchior and H. Sickinger (eds) *Anlassfall Österreich: Die Europäische Union auf dem Weg zu einer Wertegemeinschaft*, Baden-Baden: Nomos. pp. 35–43.

Tálos, E. and B. Kittel (2001) *Gesetzgebung in Österreich: Netzwerke, Akteure und Interaktionen in politischen Entscheidungsprozessen*, Wien: WUV Universitätsverlag.

Tálos, E. and M. Fink (2003) 'Sozialpartnerschaft in Österreich: Das korporatistische Modell am Ende?', in S. Jochem and N.A. Siegel (eds) *Konzertierung, Verhandlungsdemokratie und Reformpolitik im Wohlfahrtsstaat*, Opladen: Leske + Budrich. pp. 194–231.

Tálos, E. and C. Stromberger (2004) 'Verhandlungsdemokratische Willensbildung und korporatistische Entscheidungsfindung am Ende? Einschneidende Veränderungen am Beispiel der Gestaltung des österreichischen Arbeitsrechtes', *Österreichische Zeitschrift für Politikwissenschaft*, 33/2: 157–74.

Taylor, G. and A. Mathers (2002a) 'The Politics of European Integration: A European Labour Movement in the Making?', *Capital & Class*, 78: 39–60.

Taylor, G. and A. Mathers (2002b) 'Social Partner or Social Movement? European Integration and Trade Union Renewal in Europe', *Labour Studies Journal*, 27/1: 93–108.

Taylor, G. and A. Mathers (2004) 'The European Trade Union Confederation at the Crossroads of Change? Traversing the Variable Geometry of European Trade Unionism', *European Journal of Industrial Relations*, 10/3: 267–85.

Thelen, K. (2000) 'Why German Employers Cannot Bring Themselves to Dismantle the German Model', in T. Iversen, J. Pontusson and D. Soskice (eds) *Unions, Employers, and Central Banks: Macroeconomic Coordination and Institutional Change in Social Market Economies*, Cambridge: Cambridge University Press. pp. 138–69.

Thompson, E.P. (1978) 'Eighteenth-Century English Society: Class Struggle Without Class?', *Social History*, 3/2: 133–65.

Tidow, S. (2003) 'The Emergence of European Employment Policy as a Transnational Political Arena', in H. Overbeek (ed.) *The Political Economy of European Employment*, London: Routledge. pp. 77–98.

Tormey, S. (2004) 'The 2003 European Social Forum: Where Next for the Anti-Capitalist Movement?', *Capital & Class*, 84: 149–57.

Traxler, F. (1995) 'From Demand-Side to Supply-Side Corporatism? Austria's Labour Relations and Public Policy', in C. Crouch and F. Traxler (eds) *Organized Industrial Relation in Europe: What Future?*, Aldershot: Ashgate. pp. 271–86.

Trouille, J.-M. and H. Uterwedde (2001) 'Franco-German Relations, Europe and Globalisation', *Modern & Contemporary France*, 9/3: 339–53.

Tsoukalis, L. (2000) 'Economic and Monetary Union: Political Conviction and Economic Uncertainty', in H. Wallace and W. Wallace (eds) *Policy-Making in the European Union (Fourth Edition)*, Oxford: Oxford University Press. pp. 149–78.

UN (1991) *World Investment Report 1991: The Triad in Foreign Direct Investment*, New York: United Nations.

UN (1992) *World Investment Report 1992: Transnational Corporations as Engines of Growth*, New York: United Nations.

UN (1994) *World Investment Report 1994: Transnational Corporations, Employment and the Workplace*, New York/Geneva: United Nations.

UN (1999) *World Investment Report 1999: Foreign Direct Investment and the Challenge of Development*, New York/Geneva: United Nations.

UN (2001) *World Investment Report 2001: Promoting Linkages*, New York/Geneva: United Nations.

UN (2004) *World Investment Report 2004: The Shift Towards Services*, New York/Geneva: United Nations.

Underhill, G.R.D. (1997a) 'Introduction', in G.R.D. Underhill (ed.) *The New World Order in International Finance*, Basingstoke: Palgrave. pp. 1–13.

Underhill, G.R.D. (1997b) 'The Making of the European Financial Area: Global Market Integration and the EU Single Market for Financial Services', in G.R.D. Underhill (ed.) *The New World Order in International Finance*, Basingstoke: Palgrave. pp. 101–23.

Unger, B. (1999) 'Österreichs Wirtschaftspolitik: vom Austro-Keynesianismus zum Austro-Neoliberalismus?', in F. Karlhofer and E. Tálos (eds) *Zukunft der Sozialpartnershaft: Veränderungsdynamik und Reformbedarf*, Wien: Signum Verlag. pp. 165–90.

Vacca, G. (1982), 'Intellectuals and the Marxist Theory of the State', in A. Showstack Sassoon (ed.) *Approaches to Gramsci*, London: Writers and Readers. pp. 37–69.

Verdun, A. (2000) *European Responses to Globalization and Financial Market Integration*, Houndmills: Palgrave.

Waddington, J. (2003) 'Annual Review Article 2002: Heightening Tension in Relations between Trade Unions and the Labour Government in 2002', *British Journal of Industrial Relations*, 41/2: 335–58.

Waltz, K.N. (1979) *Theory of International Politics*, Reading, MA: Addison-Wesley.

Waltz, K.N. (2000) 'Globalization and American Power', *The National Interest*, 59: 46–56.

Waterman, P. and J. Wills (eds) (2001) *Place, Space and the New Labour Internationalisms*, Oxford: Blackwell.

Waters, S. (2003) *Social Movements in France: Towards a New Citizenship*, London: Palgrave.

Watson, M. (2003) 'Ricardian Political Economy and the "Varieties of Capitalism" Approach: Specialization, Trade and Comparative Institutional Advantage', *Comparative European Politics*, 1/2: 227–40.

Watt, A. (2005) 'Can Reform of the Macroeconomic Dialogue Improve Macroeconomic Policy-Making in Europe?', in E. Hein, T. Niechoj, T. Schulten et al. (eds) *Macroeconomic Policy Coordination in Europe and the Role of the Trade Unions*, Brussels: ETUI. pp. 237–59.

Weber, T. (2001) 'The European Sectoral Social Dialogue', in H. Compston and J. Greenwood (eds) *Social Partnership in the European Union*, Basingstoke: Palgrave. pp. 129–53.

Weiss, L. (1998) *The Myth of the Powerless State: Governing the Economy in a Global Era*, Cambridge: Polity.

Whyman, P. and B. Burkitt (1993) 'The Role of the Swedish Employers in Restructuring Pay Bargaining and the Labour Process', *Work, Employment and Society*, 7/4: 603–14.

Wilks, S. (1996) 'Class Compromise and the International Economy: The Rise and Fall of Swedish Social Democracy', *Capital & Class*, 58: 89–111.

Williamson, J. (1990) *Latin American Adjustment: How Much Has Happened?*, Washington, DC: Institute for International Economics.

Wills, Jane (2004) 'Re-scaling Trade Union Organisation: Lessons from the European Front Line', in R. Munck (ed.) *Labour and Globalisation: Results and Prospects*, Liverpool: Liverpool University Press. pp. 85–104.

Wood, E.M. (1995) *Democracy Against Capitalism: Renewing Historical Materialism*, Cambridge: Cambridge University Press.

van der Wurff, R. (1993) 'Neo-Liberalism in Germany? The "Wende" in Perspective', in H. Overbeek (ed.) *Restructuring Hegemony in the Global Political Economy: The Rise of Transnational Neo-Liberalism in the 1980s*, London/New York: Routledge. pp. 162–87.

Zacher, M.W. and R.A. Matthew (1995) 'Liberal International Theory: Common Threads, Divergent Strands', in C.W. Kegley (ed.) *Controversies in International Relations Theory: Realism and the Neoliberal Challenge*, New York: St Martin's Press. pp. 107–50.

Zahlnhöfer, R. (1999) 'Institutions, the CDU and Policy Change: Explaining German Economic Policy in the 1980s', *German Politics*, 8/3: 141–60.

Ziltener, P. (2000) 'Die Veränderung von Staatlichkeit in Europa – regulations- und staatstheoretische Überlegungen', in H.-J. Bieling und J. Steinhilber (eds) *Die Konfiguration Europas: Dimensionen einer kritischen Integrationstheorie*, Münster: Westfälisches Dampfboot. pp. 73–101.